C. H. Mackintosh, Leonard Stewart Channell

History of Compton County and Sketches of the Eastern Townships

District of St. Francis and Sherbrooke County

C. H. Mackintosh, Leonard Stewart Channell

History of Compton County and Sketches of the Eastern Townships
District of St. Francis and Sherbrooke County

ISBN/EAN: 9783337095642

Printed in Europe, USA, Canada, Australia, Japan

Cover: Foto ©ninafisch / pixelio.de

More available books at **www.hansebooks.com**

HISTORY

OF

COMPTON COUNTY

AND

SKETCHES

OF THE

Eastern Townships, District of St. Francis, and Sherbrooke County.

SUPPLEMENTED WITH THE RECORDS OF FOUR HUNDRED FAMILIES,

TWO HUNDRED ILLUSTRATIONS OF BUILDINGS AND LEADING CITIZENS IN THE COUNTY.

Compiled by L. S. CHANNELL.

INCLUDING

BIOGRAPHY OF THE LATE HON. JOHN HENRY POPE,

By HON. C. H. MACKINTOSH,
Lieutenant-Governor North-West Territories.

PUBLISHER:
L. S. CHANNELL,
COOKSHIRE, QUE.
1896.

Entered, according to act of Parliament of Canada, in the year eighteen hundred and ninety-six, by
LEONARD S. CHANNELL,
in the office of the Minister of Agriculture.

Engraved and printed by DESBARATS & Co., Montreal, Que.

INTRODUCTION.

FEW persons, reading any ordinary history, appreciate the amount of research necessary to obtain ample and accurate information on the subjects treated. This labor is enhanced when the value of the history depends upon the minuteness with which the events narrated are recorded. The history of an age or a country may be written in a broad, general way, in which the leading events stand out in large perspective, while the minor details are omitted or only introduced in a cursory manner. But the value of the history of a country consists largely in the extent and minuteness of the details furnished, and to obtain and verify these involves a vast amount of painstaking investigation.

In the present instance the difficulty of obtaining complete records is increased by the fact that no published book exists which might serve as a starting point. The only works extant of any use in describing the Eastern Townships, are those of Joseph Bouchette, Surveyor-General of Lower Canada for thirty years, published in 1815 and 1831, and Mrs. Day's "History of the Eastern Townships," published in 1869. I have availed myself of only a few extracts from these, principally in the Township histories. Nearly all the information has been gathered from old settlers, old newspapers, government reports, municipal records, and written accounts left by some of the pioneers.

The aim has been not to write a romance, but simply to give the facts as they have been found, after months of research and study. Every item of interest that could be learned concerning the County of Compton has been traced out and, so far as verified, here recorded.

The utmost pains have been taken to verify and accurately present all statements, biographical and historical. A copy of every biography has been submitted to each family for correction, before being printed, and I believe they are in every case correct as to dates and particulars. In the biographies the date of birth of the sons precede that of the daughters.

It is not, however, merely as a register of family history or local events that the present work is undertaken, but in the hope that it may also have a possible future usefulness as a contribution to the sources from which the history of the Dominion must be drawn, whenever in the twentieth century an exhaustive history of Canada comes to be written by some future Parkman, the materials for it will come from such volumes as the present, preserving records of a fugitive character which would else have been lost.

In searching for information I have met with courtesy and assistance on every side. Where all have been so kind, to make individual acknowledgment in this place would be impossible; but special mention is due Mr. J. A. Chicoyne, M.L.A., of Sherbrooke; Mr. Wm. Sawyer, ex-M.L.A., of Sawyerville; Mr. E. S. Orr, of Cookshire, and the Secretary-Treasurers of the several municipalities.

L. S. CHANNELL.

COOKSHIRE, April 30, 1896.

HISTORY OF COMPTON COUNTY.

CHAPTER I.

THE EASTERN TOWNSHIPS.

Origin of Name—The Townships So-called—When First Settled—Their Advantages.

THAT portion of the Province of Quebec with which we deal in this chapter, and of which Compton County forms a part, is called "The Eastern Townships." Many reasons for this special designation have been assigned by different writers, but when and how the name was first given is clouded in obscurity. One writer says it had its origin in "the fact of its having been laid out in territorial subdivisions of townships, to the *east* of the seigniories, which had been granted to French subjects by their monarch, before Canada had been wrested by the British arms from the grasp of La Belle France," in 1759. These townships, however, are not only east, but also south of the seigniories, and are the only townships in Lower Canada. The term "Eastern," therefore, on this theory, does not seem specially appropriate as distinguishing them from seigniories lying around them in the same province.

Another version, in which we are inclined to place more faith, is that these townships, being in Eastern Canada, are so called by contrast with those in Western Canada or Ontario. At the close of the Revolutionary War, in 1782, many thousand United Empire Loyalists were offered lands in Canada by the British Government. The offer was eagerly accepted, and from twenty-five to thirty thousand settled in the townships of Ontario. At the same time a few hundred families came to the townships of Eastern Canada. Their relatives and friends in Ontario and those who remained in the United States, acquired the habit of distinguishing the different settlements by calling these the Eastern Townships. As to how the name was acquired may be a subject of discussion, but it has so attached itself to this district of Quebec, that it is as well known throughout the world as though it was a separate province.

All that portion of Quebec which lies south of the River St. Lawrence, and was unconceded at the time of the Conquest, is classed as the Eastern Townships. During the French occupation and for at least ten years subsequent thereto, it was a vast wilderness covered with forest and untrodden by any but the wild man. The British Government, in maintaining the French laws, did not adopt the French system of settlement. They preferred their own Colonial system, and this unconceded part of the Province was laid out in the same manner as the lands of Ontario (Upper Canada), in townships, after the model of the New England Colonies. The genius of the two nations, widely differing in so many respects, differed materially in their Colonial systems. The French idea was to transplant the old country into the new, to reproduce France, with all its gradations of society, its religion, its laws, and feudal tenure, and to centralize power in the hands of the Governor and of those delegated by the Sovereign to represent him in the New France of the New World. Part of the strength, and all the weakness of the French *régime* in Canada arose from this system. The central power could always command the services of the entire population, when needed for any enterprise of defence or attack,—but the people, tied down to a rigid system of central responsibility, could not expand as did the English colonists. In the French case, the government was powerful, the people weak; whereas the exact opposite was the result of the English system, the government, or governments (for there were many), being weak, and the people strong.

The nature of the country forming the Eastern Townships differs greatly from the French country. Instead of great plains, we find hills and fertile valleys, traversed by mountain ranges, and intersected by numberless rivers and water courses, taking their rise in picturesque lakes. Thus, in addition to its fertile character, the Eastern Townships is a country famous for its scenery, a country retaining its green hue until late in the autumn, a continuation northwards of that green-mountain country to which the State of Vermont owes its name. In point of beauty it is not surpassed by any part of the American Continent, if beauty consists in the combination of the picturesque with adaptability to the wants of life. Many districts may be more grand, but grandeur alone is merely one of the elements of perfect beauty.

We find by reports of a special committee, published in 1851, which had been appointed by the Provincial Parliament, to enquire into causes retarding the settlement of the Eastern Townships, that they consider these townships as composed within the counties known at that time as Sherbrooke, Stanstead, Shefford, Missisquoi, Drummond, and Megantic, making 4,886,400 square acres, with a population, in 1848, that did not exceed 69,168. At the present day, the Eastern Townships are generally understood as comprising the ten counties of Missisquoi, Brome, Shefford, Drummond, Richmond, Sherbrooke, Stanstead, Compton, Wolfe and Megantic. Some authorities also include Arthabaska.

Rev. Charles Stewart, D.D., afterwards Lord Bishop of Quebec, in a pamphlet written in 1815, and published in 1817, says: "The Eastern Townships is a general name frequently given to all the townships extending east from the River Richelieu, to the eastern boundary of the Province, which divides it from New Hampshire and Massachusetts, and of the latter Maine forms part. All this country is a forest, except where cleared by man. In the woods, rivers and swamps, there are bears, wolves, and foxes, otters, beavers, martins, and muskrats; some wildcats, some deer and moose; hares and squirrels of various sorts. There are also wild ducks, and partridges (the partridge is a specie of the grouse), and other wild animals of the feathered race. But birds do not abound; and game and furred animals are not plentiful. * * * In some of the townships large quantities of potatoes are raised, from which a pretty good whiskey is distilled. * * * Average yield, 250 to 300 bushels. Cider is made * * * and it is to be hoped that, in the course of a few years, it will be the common beverage in all this part of the country." If Bishop Stewart could have lived to the present day, when cider is tabooed far more than potato whiskey was in those days, while the latter is not known of, he would be hardly able to realize the change that has taken place. The Lord Bishop goes on to say: "Black lead ore has been found in Newport and Eaton. * * * There is not any road established by law from any of these townships, either to Montreal, Three Rivers or Quebec, except one laid out by the Grand Voyer, from Compton towards Three Rivers (in or about 1809), and that one has not been worked upon. The need of some amendment of legal jurisdiction is apparent. From Three Rivers to Hereford is about 150 miles, according to the routes now travelled. The consequence is, that suits for ten shillings and less, in the distant townships, have cost as much as $14 for the service of the summons, and the return of the same to the court of Three Rivers, independent of further proceedings."

In the annals of the Eastern Townships no record is found of Indian villages, and never were the first settlers harrassed by Indian tribes in search of scalps and plunder. With the close of the war between England and France, in 1759, the stopping of all these Indian barbarities was accomplished. Previous to that time the whole energy of both countries was brought to bear to educate their Indian allies to commit the most inhuman practices on their enemies. The Eastern Townships were the hunting grounds of several tribes belonging to the Algonquin nation. The Iroquois, in New York State, (enemies of the Abenaquis who were enlisted on the French side) were too near to allow Indian villages to be established with any degree of security, and the English colonists had not pushed their settlements anywhere near this territory at that time.

The Abenaquis Indians, previous to the coming of the French Jesuits among them, had their villages principally in the eastern part of Maine. The Jesuit priests, as fast as they made converts to the Christian religion, endeavored to separate them from their heathen brethren, and at the same time bring them closer to Quebec and Montreal, where they would be more under the influence of the French. The result was that mission villages were established at Canghnawaga, near Montreal, on the Chaudière River, and one on the St. Francis River, near its confluence with the St. Lawrence. These last were Abenaquis converts, and became known as the St. Francis Indians. These mission Indians, as well as being taught the principles of Christianity, were always at the command of the French General, and committed some of the most horrible massacres known of in Indian warfare. For barbarity they exceeded their heathen brethren. The French cannot be blamed more than the English, for the latter set on their Iroquois allies to emulate the outrages of their opponents. The thoroughfare between the mission village of the Abenaquis Indians was generally up the St. Francis River, as far as the present city of Sherbrooke, across to Lake Memphremagog, and down the Connecticut to the English settlements. The Indians of the mission village on the Chaudière River, also used the Connecticut River to reach the same settlements. Bouchette in his Typographical Dictionary, published in 1815, mentions that there is a sort of Indian path through the township of Auckland, from the Connecticut in the direction of the River Chaudière.

In 1790 a proclamation was issued by George the Third, King of England, establishing the first parliament in Canada. Antecedent to this time the whole of Upper and Lower Canada was dominated the Province of Quebec. Owing to difficulties in managing so large a territory, it was judged that it should be divided, which plan was sanctioned by the British Parliament. The Province of Lower Canada was divided into the districts of Montreal, Three Rivers, Quebec, and Gaspé. The land now known as the Eastern Townships was located in the three first named districts.

There can be no doubt that United Empire Loyalists took up their residence in our Townships before 1792, but the official records of such are missing. The first settlers are heard of on Missisquoi Bay and Lake Memphremagog. At the head of the Connecticut River in the township of Hereford, Colonel John Pope settled as early as 1792, and there is not much doubt but that settlers were there for several years previously. As early as 1752 townships were surveyed and stockades erected by the British at Coos, distant from Hereford about 20 miles, on the Connecticut River. It is true this was relinquished shortly after, but at the close of the war in 1759 settlers rapidly pushed their way up the Connecticut. Authentic and official information confines us to the early part of 1792, as the time when the first settlers came into this territory.

From the Land Register, of Quebec, which is nothing else than a registry of the Procès Verbaux of the awards and correspondence of the Committee whose duty it was to administer land, we learn that on the 26th February, 1792, the Surveyor-General, Samuel Holland, proposed to the Land Committee to employ a certain number of surveyors, whose names he gives. Among these are to be found that of Pennoyer, who is recommended by him for the District of St. Francis. From this we are led to believe that this territory was designated by this name years before the Inferior District of St. Francis was created in 1823. Further on we discover, "The 5th March, 1792, the Committee of Crown Lands commissioned Mr. Pennoyer to make the survey in the District of St. Francis, and gave orders for the immediate commencement of the work." We read on page 64 of the Land Register, under date 11th April, 1792, "on the petition of Wm. Matthews, Isaac Friot, and twenty others: That a warrant of survey issue for a township on the east of Lake Memphremagog, and that a grant pass to the subscribing petitioners for two hundred acres each, and that the question as to any further quantity stand over till return of survey."

In the year 1796 the first lands in Lower Canada were granted in free and common soccage. About 1820 the system of granting lands was through a township agent. He superintended the settlement of each township, and was obliged to reside in or near to said township. Every settler was compelled to clear a road to the width of 20 feet, in front of his lot. The agent received five acres out of every 100 granted, and was also allowed for postage, stationery, etc., 2s. 6d. At no preceding period did these townships show so rapid growth as between 1820 and 1828. In 1827 there were in Lower Canada about 25 township agents, and during that year the agencies were done away with, the government selling direct to purchasers.

In 1831 there was a population in the Province of 561,051. Of these seven-eights were Catholics; one twenty-first, Episcopalians; one twenty-first, Presbyterians; and one thirty-second, Dissenters. About 20,000 of the Catholics were Irish emigrants, whilst 470,917 were native Canadians.

In 1803 the courts of Montreal rendered a decision that no right of property in slaves could exist in Lower Canada, and the few slaves in this country were thus manumitted. The people in the Townships were too poor to own slaves in those days, and two only are known to have been in what is now Compton County. They belonged to Colonel John Pope, and remained with him until their death when they were sent back to the old plantation in Massachusetts for burial.

In the works of Jos. Bouchette, for many years Survey-General of Lower Canada, may be found a complete table of the post towns, and rates of postage for a single letter, in Halifax currency, as given by Deputy Postmaster-General, F. A. Stayner. In the year 1829, mails left Three Rivers every Tuesday at 10 p. m. To Sherbrooke from Halifax—885 miles—2s. 1d.; from Quebec—185 miles—9d.; from Three Rivers—95 miles—7d.; from Richmond—27 miles—4½d.

Extract of a despatch from Lord Aylmer, Governor-in-Chief of Lower Canada, to the Secretary of State, England, dated Quebec, 12th October, 1831 : " I have visited the Eastern Townships as far as the frontier of the State of Vermont, in the United States. It is extremely difficult to form an estimate of the numbers which the uncultivated parts of the Eastern Townships will bear; but I think I am within the mark in saying that 500,000 persons might be added to the existing population, with a certainty of raising sufficient agricultural produce for their own subsistence, and for the purposes of commerce necessary for their other wants. The country which goes under the name of The Townships, appears to me the most eligible for settlement of any I have yet visited."

Joseph Bouchette, in 1831, speaking of the Eastern Towuships, says : " In dismissing the consideration of this part of the country, we would remark the broad and conspicuous distinction existing between two classes of the people of the same province, in a small comparative extent of territory, as betwixt the inhabitants of the seigniorial settlements and those of the townships, differing as they do in their language, their religion, their habits, their systems of agriculture, the tenure of their lands, and partially in their laws. The prevalent language in the townships is English, the tenure of the lands free and common soccage, and the laws by which lands descend by inheritance are English. The French idiom is universal in the seiguiories, the tenure of the lands, feudal, and the law of descent by which property is governed, is prescribed by the custom of Paris."

An anonymous writer says: "The present population of these Townships is of very mixed character. Besides the original loyalist stock from over the border, the Mother Country has sent her children, English, Scotch and Irish, to take root in the soil. They, and their children, are the English-speaking Canadians of the Eastern Townships, but there has been also an immense influx of French Canadians from the overcrowded French parishes, who, next to the Indians, may lay claim to be children of the soil. The French Canadian people are employed in farming, and in the towns and villages often follow the professions, many of them becoming priests, notaries, lawyers and physicians. They are also largely engaged in trade, and they are invaluable as a labouring population from their handiness and docility. This mixed population lives harmoniously together, the French Canadians co-operating and harmonizing with their British-born brethren. Differences will be found in the habits of life and tone of thought of a people so diverse in race, in social habits, and in creed, but these differences do not lead to strife, they tend rather to soften the manners and it has been remarked by careful observers, not themselves Canadians, that the tone of society of these Townships shows traces of refinement due to a mixed population. The Eastern Townships members of Parliament have been generally not a little distinguished for their ability, their courtesy of manners and their power of adapting themselves to the varied circumstances of life, and this again has been ascribed as in some measure due to the mixed character of the society to be found in the Eastern Townships. Loyalty to their native country is a well-known characteristic of the people, and it is combined with loyalty to the Mother Country. This loyal feeling to Canada arises out of the circumstances of their settlement. The spirit of attachment to the paternal home is invariably found to be strongest amongst those who have known what it is to endure hardships. When this "hearth love" grows up in a country, which, by its beauty, its fertility, its advantages of every kind, gives scope for the attainment of material prosperity, the love of country amongst the descendants of the pioneers, becomes mingled with a wholesome pride that they are indebted for their prosperous condition, to the toils and dangers incurred by their fathers."

CHAPTER II.

DISTRICT OF ST. FRANCIS.

When Created Boundary Dates of Enquêtes, Courts, etc.—Names of Past and Present Court Officials—Its Educational Advantages.

IN 1823 the Inferior District of St. Francis was established, by an Act of the Provincial Legislature, chap. 77, of the 3rd year of George IV., with appeals to lie in either of the Judicial Districts of Three Rivers or Montreal. Bouchette says: "This district is in the form of a parallelogram, more than 50 miles in width from west to east, and upwards of 100 miles from north to south. Its superficial extent is supposed to cover 3,500 square miles. Situated in the District of Three Rivers, except four townships and part of a fifth in the District of Montreal. It extends from the southern bounds of Wickham, Simpson, Warwick and Arthabaska, to the southern boundary of the Province. Its western limits are Lake Memphremagog and a line traversing Bolton, between the 22nd and 23rd ranges, and extending along the eastern boundaries of Stukely, Ely and Acton. On the east it extends to the western bounds of the counties of Megantic and Beauce. Contains 38 townships and part of another. Population in 1831, 13,500." Or in other words composing the present counties of Stanstead, Compton, Sherbrooke, Richmond and Wolfe, together with four townships, afterwards added to the District of Arthabaska—Chester, Tingwick, Kingsey and Durham.

By an Act of the third year of William IV., (1833), this was called the District of St. Francis. After the formation of the County of Stanstead, in 1829, the remainder of the District formed the County of Sherbrooke. The District now consists of the counties of Stanstead, Compton, Sherbrooke, Richmond and Wolfe, and the city of Sherbrooke, which is the chef lieu. The Court House, jail, and public offices for the District are located at the city of Sherbrooke.

The Queen's Bench meets on the first of the months of April and October. The terms of the Superior Court are held from the 20th to the 26th of the months of February, May and October; and from the 21st to the 26th of December. Superior Enquêtes, from the 28th to the end of the months of January, February, March, April, May, June, September, October, November and December. The Circuit Court for the District of St. Francis is held from the 10th to the 15th of the month of February; from the 11th to the 16th of May; and from the 10th to the 16th of the months of October and December. Enquêtes, Sherbrooke, from the 21st to the 23rd of January; April 9th; June 25th and 26th; and from the 9th to the 11th November.

Records in the Prothonotaries office at Sherbrooke, do not indicate that any legal business was done in this District previous to 1828, although it had been created an Inferior District five years before, in 1823. Previous to this time all business was transacted at Three Rivers. This necessitated very heavy expenses on both sides, with the result that courts of justice were very seldom called on. The people took the law into their own hands, and settled their difficulties either by arbitration or in some other way, without having recourse to the courts. Instances are known where a suit for ten shillings, brought against a defendant in Compton County, cost as much as $14 for the service of the summons, and return of the same to the Court of Three Rivers, independent of further proceedings.

The Registry Office for all this territory was also located at Three Rivers, not being moved to Sherbrooke until 1830. The first deed registered was on July 6th of that year. In April, 1856, the Registry Office at Richmond was established, and in 1869 the Registry Office for the County of Compton was opened at Cookshire. The following is a list of those who have acted in the capacity of judges, prothonotaries, sheriffs and criers, since 1828. Judges—Hon's. J. Fletcher, R. H. Gardner, E. Short, J. S. Sanborn, Marcus Doherty, E. T. Brooks and Wm. White. Prothonotaries—C. Felton, W. Bell, Bell & Bowen, Bell & Short, Short & Morris, Short & Cabana, Cabana & Bowen. Sheriffs—C. Whitcher, G. T. Bowen, W. H. Webb, E. R. Johnson, J. L. Terrill and John McIntosh. Crier and Janitor—C. Hyndman. Crier—S. A. Stevens. Janitor—Joseph Griffith. The judicial officers at the present time are: Superior Court judge, Hon. Wm. White; Sheriff, John McIntosh; Prothonotaries, Cabana & Bowen; Deputy Prothonotaries, John Short and C. H. Hackett; High Constable, Hiram Moe; Crier, F. Camirand; District Magistrate, G. E. Rioux. Owing to illness Judge Rioux has not been able to fulfill and in hopes of his recovery an acting magistrate has been appointed his duties for sometime, from time to time. For several months this position has been ably filled by R. P. Vallée, of Quebec.

The District is in great part watered by the St. Francis River and numerous tributary streams. Some of the waters of the northern and eastern parts find their way to the St. Lawrence by lower confluents, while a few small streams pass into United States territory. There are many lakes, those of larger size being Memphremagog, Megantic, and Massawippi. The agricultural products are mostly confined to beef, mutton, cheese and butter. Horses and beef have not been so profitable for the past eight years, with the result that cheese and butter factories have been numerously erected throughout the District. Comparatively little grain is raised, and the cropping is principally for domestic consumption. Maple sugar is made by nearly all farmers, largely for export, bringing a price higher than granulated sugar can be purchased for. Fruits do well, and the cultivation of apples has extended rapidly, during the past few years. A practically unlimited amount of water power is a guarantee of the future prosperity of this district. The principal product, especially in Compton and Wolfe counties, is lumber. Saw mills are numerous on all rivers of any size.

The whole District of St. Francis is well supplied with railway communication, no less than four different roads centering at Sherbrooke, including the two great systems, Canadian Pacific and Grand Trunk. The Quebec Central and Boston & Maine are the other two. The Maine Central, with terminus at Lime Ridge, connects with the Q. C. R. at Dudswell Junction, and with the C. P. R. at Cookshire, and traversing Compton County gives good connection with all U. S. cities.

In mining there is no doubt a great future in store. Asbestos and slate quarries in Richmond, copper mines at Capelton, and lime works in Dudswell, are yet in the infancy of their development. A gold mine in Ditton was profitably worked by the late Hon. John Henry Pope for many years, while in Dudswell gold is found in several places in paying quantities.

The educational facilities throughout the District are good. Nearly all townships have academies or model schools, generally run on the separate school system, the Roman Catholics having School Boards and schools of their own. Lennoxville may be called the educational centre, for there is established Bishops College University, possessed of a Royal Charter for conferring degrees in arts, divinity, law, and medicine. The Arts, Divinity and Law Faculties of this university are carried on in the College buildings at Lennoxville, its Medical Faculty in Montreal. In connection with the College there is the College School, which has turned out many young men who have earned distinction in the various walks of Canadian life. The Institution, although under the government of the Church of England, admits persons of all religious denominations to its educational course. It exacts no tests, only requiring from such of the pupils as are members of the Church of England, regular attendance on the services of the Church.

In Sherbrooke excellent educational advantages are offered the Protestants, through their high schools, and young men and young ladies' academies. The colleges, convents, and high schools of the Roman Catholics for the District are located here. They offer every advantage to this constantly increasing part of our population, to secure an education equal to that supplied by the Protestant colleges.

At Stanstead Plain is located the Stanstead Wesleyan College, and in 1895 there was added thereto the Bugbee annex, which is used as a commercial college, offering all the advantages for a business education that may be found elsewhere. This college is affiliated with McGill, of Montreal, and although under the control of the Methodist Church, offers a high education to all, the rules being such that it is liberally patronized by every denomination. This college is open to both young ladies and young men, on equal terms. In 1894 a debt of some $18,000 was cleared off by contributions from friends throughout the country. At Stanstead Plain $10,000 of this was raised, the largest givers being those of other than the Methodist denomination. The prospects for this Institution are bright.

At Richmond is located the St. Francis College, one of the oldest educational institutions in the District. Its work has been good, and at the present time it is under excellent management, and in a prosperous condition.

The Compton Ladies' College is a prosperous institution, and further particulars of the same will be found in this book in the history of the Township of Compton.

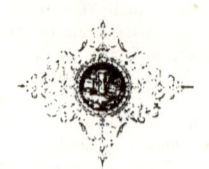

CHAPTER III.

EARLY HISTORY—1692-1791.

Indian Fight Between the Iroquois and Abenaquis Indians—Rogers Attack on the St. Francis Village—Arnold's Expedition to Quebec.

IN the foregoing chapters we have given a brief outline of the Eastern Townships, and the District of St. Francis. We now narrow our subject down to the county of Sherbrooke, as it was known from 1829 to 1853, and which comprised the present counties of Compton, Sherbrooke, Richmond, and Wolfe. Previous to 1791, when the first Parliament of Canada was elected, this territory was all dense woods, untrammelled by the foot of a white man. In that year the first steps for surveying the land were taken and the surveyors were closely followed by settlers.

The River St. Francis was the great thoroughfare for the Indians for years immemorial, and the territory now occupied by farms in state of high cultivation was then their hunting grounds. The St. Francis River owes its name to the tribe of Abenaquis Indians, known by the name of St. Francis, and whose descendants still live on the Indian reservation, near the conjunction of this river with the St. Lawrence, in Yamaska County.

The Jesuit priests who first came out from France in 1632, were fired with a holy desire to convert all of the Indians of America to the Christian faith. Whatever may have been said against them, their zeal in their work was certainly commendable. These Jesuit priests suffered the greatest hardships, torture and finally death, in their desire to convert the heathen Indians. The territory of which we write was the hunting ground of the Abenaquis Indians, who roamed through a greater part of Maine. The labor of the Jesuits was rewarded by converts, and as fast as they were made in the Indian tribes they were sent to villages near the French soldiers and French garrisons. Thus were the Indian villages established at Caughnawaga, near Montreal, on the Chaudière River, near Quebec, and on the St. Francis. These converted Abenaquis were known as the St. Francis Abenaquis, in distinction from their heathen brethren.

In the Indian Department at Ottawa may be found records of a story, handed down by the St. Francis tribe, dating as far back as 1692. The story goes as follows: In February of 1692, a company of Iroquois Indians from New York State, started on the war path, intending to attack the village of the St. Francis Indians, who were then their enemies. The Iroquois Indians were encouraged on in their attacks by the English and Dutch settlers, who had commenced to push out their settlements, located on the New England coast. The French Government protested against these encroachments, and labored to have the Abenaquis and other Indian tribes make war on and exterminate the English and Dutch settlers. In this the French Jesuit priests were of great assistance to their government, at times showing as great zeal in trying to promote strife as in converting the Indians. For this reason there were incessant hostilities going on between the Iroquois and Abenaquis. This Iroquois war party made their way to Lake Memphremagog, through that lake and down the Magog River, camping on the present site of Sherbrooke. At that time it was known by the Indians as Skaswantegou, meaning "River where we smoke," and evidently was a place for all parties to camp just before or after "carrying" around the rapids on the Magog River at this place. About the same time a party of Abenaquis Indians from the

St. Francis Village, were making their way up the St. Francis River. They also encamped at the same place, only lower down the river. Shortly after making camp the Abenaquis saw smoke arising on the Magog, and on investigation found it to be the camp of the Iroquois Indians. Both parties were of about the same number and strength, therefore being equally divided. As they were thirsting for scalps and a fight was inevitable, while the progress of both parties was stopped, a consultation was agreed upon. At this meeting of the leaders of the two war parties, it was agreed that the Iroquois and Abenaquis should each choose one of their best warriors, and superiority of either party should depend on the physical endurance of the warrior chosen. The terms of the contest were, that the two men should run around a pine tree on a small island in the St. Francis River, just below the present city of Sherbrooke.

In this singular contest referred to, the warrior who could endure the running for the longest length of time, was to kill his opponent, and have the scalp as his reward. The result to be accepted by both sides as final. The two war parties lined up on each side of the river to watch the battle between the strongest and best men of each tribe. The winning of this contest involved not only the result of the success of one party, but also, practically, the control of that part of the St. Francis River. At a given signal the men started on what meant death to one of them. For a while the running was easy, and not very exciting for either side, but as they round and round kept going, it could be seen there was a gradual decrease of speed on the part of both. The rough surface of the ground soon was the cause of falls, each one receiving grunts of satisfaction from the opposite side, who were becoming intensely interested. The men were making a grand struggle but nature must ultimately win. It was evident both were about evenly divided as to enduring qualities, and the result uncertain. The falls became more numerous, the breathing short and quick, while these two noble warriors, worthy representatives of their respective tribes, fought for life and fame. Finally the Iroquois falls, he does not rise, and the Abenaquis, with arm almost limp, cleaves his head with the tomahawk, the winner of the fray, but by no means with strength to spare. Thus the Abenaquis Indians win the St. Francis Valley as their own. This way of settling a battle, that had to be fought, showed wisdom and unanimity, that might be copied with profit by the civilized nations of the world.

There is now, at the same place, pine tree, alive and vigorous in growth, which is supposed to be the same one referred to here. The late Mr. Moe said that he could remember the tree eighty years ago, and it was then the same size as now. A limb of the tree was a few years ago sent to Laval University, at Quebec, and, on examination, one of the professors said it was quite possible that the tree may be three hundred years old, and standing at the time of the fight here referred to. The rock or island on which this pine acts as solitary sentinel, probably was much larger than at present, for the rock has fissures through it, and would indicate that as the years have passed away large pieces have broken off, and been carried away by the ice and high water, with which it has to battle each spring.

EXPEDITION OF ROGERS IN 1759.

The next important event that took place on the St. Francis River, was in 1759, when Rogers made an attack on the village of the St. Francis Indians, and retreated up that river, making his way to the Connecticut. Major Rogers was a daring, native American, who had figured with credit, in several attacks on the French and Indians, in the war which had then been going on for several years. He was under the command of General Amherst, stationed at Ticonderoga and Crown Point, on Lake Champlain, while his men were those used to Indian warfare, and able to endure the severest hardships. Francis Parkman, in the second volume of his book, "Montcalm and Wolfe," describing this attack, says :

"Major Robert Rogers, sent in September (1759) to punish the Abenakis of St. Francis, had addressed himself to the task with his usual vigor. These Indians had been settled for about three quarters of a century on the River St. Francis, a few miles above its junction with the St. Lawrence. They were nominal Christians, and had been under the control of their missionaries for three generations; but though zealous and sometimes fanatical in their devotion to the forms of Romanism, they remained thorough savages in dress, habits and character. They were the scourge of the New England borders, where they surprised and burned farmhouses and small hamlets, killed men, women and children without distinction, carried other prisoners to their village, subjected them to the torture of 'running the gauntlet,' and compelled them to witness dances of triumph around the scalps of parents, children, and friends.

"Amherst's instructions to Rogers contained the following : ' Remember the barbarities that have been committed by the enemy's Indian scoundrels. Take your revenge, but don't forget that, though those dastardly villains have promiscuously murdered women and children of all ages, it is my order that no women or children be killed or hurt.'

"Rogers and his men set out in whaleboats, and, eluding the French armed vessels, then in full activity, came, on the tenth day to Missisquoi Bay, at the north end of Lake Champlain. Here he hid his boats, leaving two friendly Indians to watch them from a distance, and inform him should the enemy discover them. He then began his march for St. Francis, when, on the evening of the second day, the two Indians overtook him with the startling news that a party of about four hundred French had found the boats, and that half of them were on his tracks in hot pursuit. It was certain that the alarm would soon be given, and other parties sent to cut him off. He took the bold resolution of outmarching his pursuers, pushing straight for St. Francis, striking it before succors could arrive, and then returning by Lake Memphremagog and the Connecticut. Accordingly he despatched Lieutenant McMullen by a circuitous route back to Crown Point, with a request to Amherst that provisions should be sent up the Connecticut to meet him on the way down. Then he set his course for the Indian town, and for nine days more toiled through the forest with desperate energy. Much of the way was through dense spruce swamps, with no dry resting place at night. At length the party reached the River St. Francis, fifteen miles above the town, and, hooking the arms together for mutual support, forded it with extreme difficulty. Towards evening, Rogers climbed a tree, and descried the town three miles distant. Accidents, fatigue, and illness had reduced his followers to a hundred and forty-two officers and men. He left them to rest for a time, and, taking with him Lieutenant Turner and Ensign Avery, went to reconnoitre the place; left his two companions, entered it disguised in an Indian dress, and saw the unconscious savages yelling and singing in the full enjoyment of a grand dance. At two o'clock in the morning he rejoined his party, and at three led them to the attack, formed them in a semicircle, and burst in upon the town half an hour before sunrise. Many of the warriors were absent, and the rest were asleep. Some were killed in their beds, and some shot down in trying to escape. "About seven o'clock in the morning," he says, "the affair was completely over, in which time we had killed at least two hundred Indians and taken twenty of their women and children prisoners, fifteen of whom I let go their own way, and five I brought with me, namely: two Indian boys and three Indian girls. I likewise retook five English captives.

"English scalps in hundreds were dangling from poles over the doors of the houses. The town was pillaged and burned, not excepting the church, where ornaments of some value were found. On the side of the rangers, Captain Ogden and six men were wounded, and a Mohegan Indian from Stockbridge was killed. Rogers was told by his prisoners that a party of three hundred French and Indians was encamped on the river below, and that another party of two hundred and fifteen was not far distant. They had been sent to cut off the retreat of the invaders, but were doubtful as to their designs till after the blow was struck. There was no time to lose. The rangers made all haste southward, up the St. Francis, subsisting on corn from the Indian town; till, near the eastern borders of Lake Memphremagog, the supply failed, and they separated into small parties, the better to sustain life by hunting. The enemy followed close, attacked Ensign Avery's party, and captured five of them; then fell upon a band of about twenty, under Lieutenants Dunbar and Turner, and killed or captured nearly all. The other bands eluded their pursuers, turned southeastward, reach the Connecticut, some here, some there, and, giddy with fatigue and hunger, toiled wearily down the wild and lonely stream to the appointed rendez-vous at the mouth of the Amonoosuc.

"This was the place to which Rogers had requested that provisions might be sent; and the hope of finding them there had been the breath of life to the famished wayfarers. To their horror, the place was a solitude. There were fires still burning, but those who made them were gone. Amherst had sent Lieutenant Stephen up the river from Charlestown with an abundant supply of food; but finding nobody at the Amonoosuc, he had waited there two days, and then returned, carrying the provisions back with him; for which outrageous conduct he was expelled from the service. 'It is hardly possible,' says Rogers, 'to describe our grief and consternation.' Some gave themselves up to despair. Few but their indomitable chief had strength to go farther. There was scarcely any game, and the barren wilderness yielded no sustenance but a few lily bulbs and the tubers of the climbing plant, called in New England the ground-nut. Leaving his party to these miserable resources, and promising to send them relief within ten days, Rogers made a raft of dry pine logs, and drifted on it down the stream, with Captain Ogden, a ranger, and one of the captive Indian boys. They were stopped on the second day by rapids, and gained the shore with difficulty. At the foot of the rapids, while Ogden and the ranger went in search of squirrels, Rogers set himself to making another raft; and, having no strength to use the axe, he burned down the trees, which he then divided into logs by the same process. Five days after leaving his party he reached the first English settlement, Charlestown, or 'Number Four,' and immediately sent a canoe with provisions to the relief of the sufferers, following, himself, with other canoes, two days later. Most of the men were saved, though some died miserably of famine and exhaustion. Of the few who had been captured, we are told by a French contemporary that they 'became victims of the fury of the Indian women,' from whose clutches the Canadians tried in vain to save them."

The subjoined account is taken from Mrs. Day's history of "The Eastern Townships," published in 1869. Francis Parkman notes having seen the same, and says: "If such an incident really took place, it is scarcely possible that Rogers would not have made some mention of it. On the other hand, it is equally incredible that the Indians would have invented the tale of their own defeat. All things considered, it is, probably, groundless." Notwithstanding this the story has sufficient evidence of truth to warrant reprinting.

"The late Jesse Pennoyer, Esq., of Compton, Government Land Surveyor, while on a professional tour of exploration and survey in the townships, was accompanied by Captain St. Francis, late chief of that tribe of Indians, and one of the few survivors of the pursuing party. This captain St. Francis gave Mr. Pennoyer the following relation of the affair, which was corroborated by a person named Bowen, son of one of Roger's men; and still further in its main features, by the descendants of a person named Barnes, one of the recovered captives mentioned:

"On the morning of the fifth of October, 1759, the assault took place; two hundred Indians of all ages and sexes were slain; some few taken prisoners, and a number of

English captives retaken; when Rogers, with his party, prisoners and rescued captives, made a hasty retreat up the St. Francis River. The chief of the tribe (father of the Captain St. Francis, above named), with a number of his warriors, had come in during the day, and immediately held a council of war, at which, it was decided that all present should start in pursuit the next morning; and that as many more of their warriors as they could call in should start, with canoes, on the second day. Accordingly, on the morning of the sixth, about fifty warriors, each armed with a gun, tomahawk and scalping knife, started up on the north shore of the river; and on the seventh, about forty-five more, armed like the others, set off in seven large canoes. These overtook the party that had started the day before, at the rapids, in the Township of Wendover, where the first detachment had awaited the arrival of the canoes; and at day-break, on the morning of the eighth, they all set off together. They came up with Rogers' men in Kingsey, and in the skirmish that ensued, the Indians lost several men, while only three or four of the other party were slightly wounded. As soon as the Indians discovered any of their enemies, they fired and often missed aim; in fact, their shots seldom took effect, and before they had time to reload they were shot down, or if the savage was separated from his fellows, his enemy quickly rushed up and dispatched him with the bayonet. The Indians sustained considerable loss, in this manner, throughout the day, though they succeeded in doing but little injury to their enemies. On the morning of the ninth, they held a council, at which it was proposed and urged by quite a number of their party to abandon the pursuit and return. Well would it have been for them had they done so; but the majority of them were for pushing forward to the 'Little Forks' (now Lennoxville) where they intended to give their enemies another battle. On the tenth, Rogers crossed, with his men, to the opposite shore of the river, near Brompton Falls, and while the Indians were making the *portage*, pushed on towards the 'Big Forks' (now Sherbrooke) and gained an elevated point. His experienced eye, at once, saw the strategic importance of the position thus gained, and he at once determined to avail himself of the advantage, to attempt the defeat of his enemies, and put an effectual end to further annoyance from them.

"The river, which here makes a short turn, on one side has a high bank, which was then thickly wooded; while the opposite point was low, and then covered with a thin growth of stunted bushes. From this height Rogers had a fair view of the river for a distance of two miles down. For the purpose of deceiving and misleading the enemy's scouts, he sent a small party of his men on to the 'Little Forks,' with instructions to build fires, in a manner similar to what had been done in their former camping grounds, and then return to join the main body at the heights beyond the mouth of the Magog.

"In the meantime the Indian scouts passed up the north shore till they saw the fires at the 'Little Forks,' and thinking that Rogers' party were encamping there, returned to the falls with the intelligence. Those who had completed the *portage* immediately set out in the canoes, leaving the others to follow up the north shore, expecting to find their enemies in camp at the 'Little Forks,' and hoping to surprise them and cut off their retreat. But their vigilant foe had not been idle. During this time he had posted his men in such a manner that, while they were out of sight themselves, they had full view of the approaching canoes a long way down the river, and, as they came near, could tell about the number of savages on board of each, by the number of paddles. He then arranged for the attack by appointing a certain number of men for each canoe, equal to the number of paddles in each; and detailing a man to fire at each Indian separately from the first to the last, gave strict orders to aim well and not to fire till the signal was given by himself. Everything was quiet until about one-half of the canoes had turned the point, when the signal was given, and the men fired with such sure precision and deadly effect that almost every savage in the canoes was either killed or mortally wounded. The Indians on the north shore had got a little in advance of the canoes by crossing the point, with the intent of fording the river, but on hearing the firing they hastened back to the point. By this time Rogers' men had reloaded, and, being still in ambush, again fired and killed several, while the others retreated up to the crossing, and forded the river. The English still kept on the heights, and a general and irregular skirmish followed; but as the savages were in the open woods on the intervale below the mouth of the Magog River, while the others were covered by the thick forest on the hill, the result was that most of the whole Indian force was either killed or badly wounded, while but few of their enemies were either killed or hurt.

"It being now near sunset, the English party crossed the Magog, and proceeded up to the 'Little Forks,' where they encamped for the night, and the next day Rogers addressed his men, thanking them for their bravery and obedience to his orders, and for their faithfulness and perseverance from the first of the difficult enterprise which had been undertaken and carried out, in order to pay their savage foes in their own coin, for their repeated cruelties to the colonists in former years.

"This they had now achieved by the almost entire annihilation of that tribe of their enemies.

"Then, ordering the remaining prisoners to be shot, he resigned his command, advising the men to divide themselves into small companies, each of which should take a somewhat different route to reach the appointed rendezvous on the Connecticut River. This method he deemed best, as affording to small parties a greater chance for game, on which all had now to depend for food. The advice was followed, some of the men going up the St. Francis to the mouth of the Eaton River, others taking the Massawippi or Coaticook."

ARNOLD'S EXPEDITION TO QUEBEC IN 1775.

The third event worthy of notice took place in the fall of 1775, and happened in part of what is now Compton County. This was the march through the wilderness and expedition to Quebec of Benedict Arnold. Whatever the verdict of people may have been on his betrayal of his trust a few years later, certainly no man ever showed more energy and determination to overcome difficulties than did Arnold on his trip to Quebec. In this narrative we have made copious extracts from the "Life of Benedict Arnold," by Isaac N. Arnold.

When Washington reached Cambridge and assumed command, on the third of July, 1775, he had already favorably considered the plan of attacking Quebec, and obtaining military possession of Canada. Schuyler had been selected to lead an army into Canada by way of the northern lakes. It was now proposed by Arnold that an expedition should march by way of the Kennebec River, through the wilderness over the mountains, in Maine, to Quebec, to capture the city by surprise and co-operate with Schuyler. The plan of reaching Quebec by this route is said to have been suggested by Arnold. After several conferences Washington heartily adopted the project.

Conscious of the difficulties to be encountered, Arnold selected the best material in his army for the expedition. The field officers were Lieutenant-Colonels Christopher Green, of Rhode Island, and Roger Enos, of Connecticut; Majors Return J. Meigs, of Connecticut, and Timothy Bigelow, of Massachusetts. Among the captains was the celebrated Daniel Morgan, the famous rifleman of Virginia. The detachment consisted in all of 1100 men, from the mountains of Virginia and Pennsylvania; hunters and Indian fighters, familiar with woodcraft, the rifle, the hunting-knife, and the birch-bark canoe; men who could endure hunger, exposure and fatigue; who knew how to find subsistence and shelter in the forests;

who could supply themselves with food from the deer, the bear, and other wild game, and from fish from the rivers. This little army started from Prospect Hill, near Cambridge, Mass., on the eleventh of September, 1775. They reached Fort Western, on the Kennebec River, opposite the present city of Augusta, Maine, on the twenty-third of September.

All the information Arnold could obtain of the route was what he could glean from the meagre journal of Montresor, who had passed from Canada to the Kennebec fifteen years before; some facts gathered from a party of St. Francis Indians, who had lately visited the camp of Washington; and a rude and imperfect map made by a surveyor of the Kennebec.

The route selected as the most feasible was to ascend the Kennebec to what was called the great carrying place between it and the Dead River; then turning west, surmount the carrying place; thence on over the extreme summit which divides the waters of New England from those of the St. Lawrence. Crossing this, they hoped and expected to strike the head-waters of the Chaudière, and from thence descend to the St. Lawrence and Quebec. With his very limited knowledge of the country and the route, the commander deemed it prudent to send forward a small exploring party in advance, who were expected to move with the utmost rapidity in bark canoes, to ascertain the obstacles and dangers, and explore and mark the best route. This party had instructions to go as far as Lake Megantic, or, as it was then called, Chaudière pond. The man selected to lead this advance party was Archibald Steele, a bold, active, hardy, and resolute young soldier.

An outline of the trip of this pioneer party may be of interest. Starting from Fort Western, on the twenty-third of September, in birch-bark canoes, the party passed on rapidly to Fort Halifax, and thence to Skowhegan Falls, four miles east of the village of Norridgewack. Here they met the first *portage*, or carrying place, around the rapids and by *blazing* the trees marked the route of those who were to follow.

They ascended the river rapidly, *blazing* the trees at every carrying place. Leaving the last habitation of the white man at Norridgewack, the party passed on into the wilderness. Having passed many falls, rapids and carrying places, on the twenty-ninth of September they arrived at the great carrying place, distant about sixty miles from Skowhegan. The distance across the *portage* to Dead River was twelve miles, but there were three or four ponds which could be used to lessen the land carriage. Steele's party, leaving the Kennebec, struck out towards Dead River, and at evening encamped on the margin of the first pond, sleeping, as usual when on shore, on branches of the fir, hemlock and other evergreens. The ground across this carrying place was rough, rocky and rugged, interspersed with bogs, in which the men often sunk to their knees. It was now decided by Steele to divide his little party, leaving the weakest and half the provisions, while he pressed forward with the strongest and most enduring of his men. Two days of very hard work brought him to the banks of Dead River.

Pressing on, each day meeting new difficulties, their provisions grew scant, and the party put themselves on short rations, and resolved to eat their pork raw, and to eat but twice each day, morning and evening.

October fourth brought the party to the deserted wigwam of Natanis, an Indian chief, then supposed to be in the pay of the English as a spy, but who with a part of his warriors was afterwards induced by Arnold to join the expedition, and who with his men faithfully accompanied him to Quebec. The country grew more and more rough and difficult as the party advanced, and having now reached nearly to the high lands dividing the waters which flow to the Atlantic from those which empty into the St. Lawrence, the weather became bitterly cold, and snow and ice added to their difficulties.

At length, on the seventh of October, the party of Steele, weary and worn, reached the end of their explorations—the head waters of the Chaudière. Gathering around the roots of a pine, which rose forty feet without a branch, Steele asked if any of the party could climb it. Robert Cunningham, an athletic young soldier, twenty-five years of age, instantly began the ascent, going up with the activity almost of a squirrel. From the top he could trace far away towards the north the meanderings of the river, until it expanded into Lake Megantic, fifteen miles distant. Elated with their success, the party turned their faces back towards their comrades, toiling far behind in the depths of the forests.

Far from their companions, and nearly famishing, where were they to obtain food to sustain life? They made all possible haste, looking constantly for game, and finding none until the ninth, when they fortunately shot a small duck, called a diver. At night when they gathered around their camp-fire, they anxiously discussed the question how this duck and their little pittance of remaining food could be most effectually used to prolong life. They decided to boil the duck in their camp kettle, each man putting in his last bit of pork, and each marking his own by running through it a small wooden skewer, marked with his own private mark. The broth so made was to be all the supper the poor fellows had, reserving the boiled pork for breakfast, and the duck to be divided and laid by. Rising early next morning, each man took his mouthful of pork, and breakfast was over. The duck was then separated into ten parts, the number of the party, and divided in the hunter's usual way—that is, one of the party turned his back, and then Steele asked of the man whose back was turned to the fragments, "Whose shall this be?" The man answered, naming the party.

On the seventeenth this pioneer party and the advance of the main body met, and they were welcomed as brave men welcome comrades who have escaped a fearful danger. More than three weeks had passed since they had left Fort Western.

The main body had followed as soon, after these scouts, as possible, moving in four divisions, one day's march apart, to avoid confusion in passing rapids and *portages*.

Arnold remained at Fort Western to see all embarked, and then in a fast birch-bark canoe, paddled by Indians, he pushed rapidly forward, and, passing each party, overtook Morgan and the riflemen at Norridgewack Falls. From this place the march was to be through a wild and uninhabited wilderness, without paths, and often without even an Indian trail. Across dismal swamps and deceptive bogs, up rocky precipices and almost inaccessible mountains, along streams full of rapids and falls, and along and over all these obstacles, the rude batteaux, the arms and ammunition with which to attack the strongest fortress in America, and all their provisions, supplies and clothing, to protect them from the rigor of a Canadian winter, now too rapidly approaching, were to be transported.

As the soldiers pushed their boats up Dead River, passing around a bend, a high mountain, covered with snow, rose before them. Encamping near the foot of this mountain, Arnold raised his flag; and the incident has been commemorated by giving the name of "Flagstaff" to a village near by, and the mountain has been named Mount Bigelow, after Major Bigelow, who is said to have climbed to the top, in the hopes of seeing Quebec.

On the twenty-fourth of October, it was supposed that they were within thirty miles of Lake Megantic, and that their provisions might, with great care, hold out for twelve or fifteen days. Another council was called, and it was decided to send back to the hospital the sick and feeble, and that only the strong and hardy should go forward.

Meanwhile Arnold himself was hurrying on with all possible despatch. The rain changed to snow, ice covered the water, and the men, wading and breaking through snow and sleet, at length reached the very summit which separated the waters of New England from those of Canada. Another *portage* of four miles brought them to a small stream, along which they passed to Lake Megantic, or Chaudière pond.

John Joseph Henry, one of the survivors of Arnold's campaign, has left a narrative of the trip. It seems remarkable that those men should have suffered for food in passing through a country which at the present day abounds with fish and deer. Henry mentions the appearance of moose, with antlers of enormous size. One pair, he thinks, stood eighteen feet high, while a pair that had been shed, and which they found, he could stand under. He says no deer were seen at that time. Henry, continuing, says: "Thus we proceeded, the pale and meager looks of my companions, tottering on their feeble limbs, * * * and coming to a sandy beach of the Chaudière (Lake Megantic), some men of our company were observed to dart from the file, and with their nails tear out of the sand roots which they deemed eatable, and eat them raw. Powerful men struggled, even with blows, for these roots, such was the extremity of their hunger." Old moose-hide breeches were boiled, and then broiled on the coals and eaten. Some tried to make soup out of their old deerskin moccasins, but, although the poor fellows boiled them long, they were leather still. Many died from fatigue and hunger, frequently in four or five minutes after giving up and sitting down. Henry says these hardships produced among the men a willingness to die.

Arnold pushed on far in advance of his men to secure them food. On the thirtieth October, at night, he reached the first house on the Chaudière River, eighty miles from Lake Megantic, and with the next morning's sun a supply of fresh provisions and flour had started and was hastening back, with all possible speed, yet none too soon to save the lives of his famishing soldiers.

Henry says they reached Height of Land on the twenty-eighth of October; the Chaudière, or present Arnold River, the twenty-ninth of October; and left Lake Megantic on the second of November. He says that chaudière, in French, means a caldron or boiler, and that in this case it is well termed.

It is evident from Arnold's and Henry's accounts that the army moved in sections in some cases several days apart. Arnold must have reached the present site of Lake Megantic Village on the twenty-seventh or twenty-eight of October, while his soldiers arrived in small companies day by day thereafter.

By the eighth of November nearly all of the detachment, except the rear division, had reached Arnold's camp at the French settlements, and by the thirteenth of December he had all of his men with him at Point Lévis, while across the River St. Lawrence towered the Citadel of Quebec. Here was he to meet defeat, and his hardships and trials on this remarkable march were to be for naught. Not until after 1850 were the places where these hardships took place, again visited by man.

To the present day occasional traces, on the Arnold River, may be seen of camps having been made by Arnold's men. Only a few years ago a French bayonet was found in this river, and later a bunch of bullets such as were used in the guns of that day. The leather case in which they had been enclosed had decayed and fallen away. In 1858 a musket was discovered. The stock had entirely decayed, and the mountings and barrel had fallen to the ground. This gives an idea of the lovely, inhospitable solitudes through which these men passed. During this period of more than eighty years, the pioneer had penetrated every bay and harbor of the great western lakes, and, crossing the Mississippi, and scaling the rocky mountains, he had erected his settler's cabin along the shores of the Pacific; but into these gloomy solitudes of Maine and Compton, during all this time, no wanderer had gone.

CHAPTER IV.

BUCKINGHAM COUNTY.

1791-1829.

ANTECEDENT to 1791, the whole of Upper and Lower Canada was denominated the Province of Quebec, and previous to 1791 no records of any settlement in the Eastern Townships are to be found. In 1783, there was a total population in Canada of 113,000, exclusive of 10,000 Loyalists, who had located in the upper portions of the Province. When the new law came into operation, Canada passed under the rule of the fourth government set over her during the thirty-one years succeeding the conquest. First, there was martial law, from 1760 to 1763; military sway, from the latter date to 1774; a species of civil rule, from 1774 to 1791; and, finally, a partially elective system to commence in 1792.

After dividing Canada into two provinces, and apportioning the laws and regulations which were to prevail in each, the new constitution provided that all public functionaries, beginning with the Governor-General, should be nominated by the Crown, and be removable at royal pleasure; and that the free exercise of the Catholic religion, with the conservation of its rights, should be guaranteed permanently. In each province there was to be instituted a Legislative Council and a Legislative Assembly.

The Province of Quebec was divided into three chief districts, known as Quebec, Montreal and Three Rivers. The districts were further subdivided into counties. The present County of Compton was situated in the County of Buckingham, District of Three Rivers, with the exception of part of the Township of Compton, which was located in Richelieu County, Montreal District, along with the present County of Stanstead. Buckingham County sent two representatives to the Legislative Assembly, being sub-divided, in 1829, into the six counties of Sherbrooke, Megantic, Lotbinière, Drummond, Nicolet and Yamaska.

The first settlements in Compton or Sherbrooke Counties date back to as early a date as any in the Eastern Townships. The settlers around Missisquoi Bay are supposed to have arrived there about 1792. In Hereford, at the head of the Connecticut River, we have records of Lemuel Pope having been born there in 1792; while it is very probable settlers were in that township, which had not then been surveyed, for several years previous.

As early as 1794, prospectors made their way through Clifton into Eaton, and located sections on which, in a year or two, they settled with their families. In the year 1796, six brothers, of the name of Hyatt, of Arlington, Vt., came to Canada and settled on part of the tract now known as the township of Ascot, which was organized and granted 5th March, 1803. The first settlers on the present site of Sherbrooke, as far as can be learned, were David Mol, Gilbert Hyatt, and Samuel Terrill. Mrs. Day says : " Others, still, even affix a later date than 1803; yet, these differences may be set aside by the fact that David Mol, who, at an early date, located just outside the limits of Sherbrooke, built the first frame barn that was put up in the settlement, on a board of which building the date 1800 was engraved ; showing the barn to have been built that year. Such being the case, a saw-mill must have been in operation previously." Settlements on Lake Memphremagog were made in 1792, and the first opening at Stanstead Plain in 1796.

During the ten years following the coming into effect of the law of 1791, the Eastern Townships made rapid advancement towards settlement. Under the supervision of Joseph Bouchette, Esq., Surveyor-General of Lower Canada, the townships were surveyed, named, and laid out for settlement. In Compton County, the townships of Compton, Eaton, Clifton, Hereford, Westbury, Newport, Auckland, Marston and Clinton were surveyed, while Bury, Lingwick, and Ditton were only surveyed in part. The townships of Emberton, Chesham, Winslow and Witton were only projected, and not surveyed until after 1831. There was a township projected, to be known as Drayton, lying to the east of Hereford and south of Auckland. By the settlement of the boundary between the United States and England, in 1842, this projected township was found to be nearly all in territory belonging to the United States, with the exception of a small piece in the north-west corner, which was added to Hereford. Another projected township on the boundary, wholly obliterated, was known as Croydon.

Joseph Bouchette, writing in 1831, says of the projected township of Drayton : " It is in the rear of Auckland and Emberton, bounded south by main branch of the River Connecticut. A tolerably large settlement has been formed on Indian Stream and River Connecticut by persons from the United States, who claimed to have commenced their settlement in 1792, under the auspices and by virtue of a proclamation of Sir Alured Clark, at that time Governor-in-Chief. The settlement consists of 20 families, who have made extensive improvements and are respectably settled. The land which these persons occupy forms one of the points in dispute between Her Majesty's Government and the United States. Population about 60. The principal settler is a Dr. Taylor, who occupies 1,000 acres, 100 of which are cleared. This gentleman has a good house and distillery. The township is watered by Indian Stream and Hall's Stream, also by Back Lake and other small lakes. There is a private school, with 12 to 15 scholars."

These townships, as fast as they were laid out, or projected, were named by the Government officials, the names being taken from men and places in England. For that reason, no local causes can be found for the different names. The present City and County of Sherbrooke derived its name, in 1818, from Sir John Sherbrooke, then Governor-General, who is said to have visited the village at that time. There is no authentic record of his ever having made the visit. Previous to that time it was known as the Lower Forks, and Lennoxville had the name of Upper Forks. This was due to the junction of the St. Francis River with the Magog and Massawippi rivers, at the respective places.

In those early days, the market of Compton County and other places near the St. Francis River was at Three Rivers. In the winter time, a good road was kept open on the ice, while in the summer the carrying of goods to Three Rivers and returning with supplies for the settlers, by means of boats on the St. Francis River, was a business by itself. The principal product sold by the settlers was pearl-ash, which brought about $12 per cwt. in Three Rivers or Montreal, and $5 at the pearl-ashery. It was made from hard wood ashes, elm being considered the most productive. The ashes were put into leaches holding about six bushels each, wet down with hot water, the lye running into a trough at the bottom. This was continued until the strength was all out of the ashes. The lye was then put through a process similar to sap in the making of maple-sugar : being boiled down to salts. The latter were dried down, or what was called scorched. When done, they were of a brown or snuff color. After this, they were put into an oven, something similar to those used in bakeries, and a fire kept going, while a man was continually stirring the salts until they became white, like chalk. When cool, they were ready to barrel up for market. The pearl-ash was used in place of soda or baking-powder. Potash was made by boiling the salts down till, when cool, they were like crystal.

In making the trips down the St. Francis River to Three Rivers, Brompton Falls was the worst place that the boatmen had to contend with. It was always necessary to "carry by" in both directions, while the stories of accidents and narrow escapes were numerous with those who used to go up and down the river. During the war of 1812–15 most of the supplies for the settlers in this region were obtained in this way, as for a certain period no communication was allowed with the neighboring States. It was during one of these trips that a most melancholy and afflictive accident occurred, in 1815, when two lives were lost at Brompton Falls. Three persons from Eaton, named respectively John French, John Hurd, and —— Lebourveau, were on an expedition down the St. Francis. At the falls the freight was removed, and the three men remained to pass down with the boat. Unfortunately, it struck a rock and capsized, when French sank at once; Hurd was seen to strike out for the shore, and, being an expert swimmer, hope was entertained by those on the bank that he might be saved, but from some cause he too sank and was drowned. Lebourveau at first sprang upon a rock, to which he continued clinging as he saw his companions drowning, but could neither save them—nor yet help himself, till a rope was thrown from the shore, which he fastened around his waist, when, plunging into the boiling current, he at first disappeared, but was finally drawn to land.

About 1815 efforts were started to have Buckingham County subdivided, so as to give representation to the English-speaking residents in the Townships. The French seigniories, near the St. Lawrence River, had a much larger population; and the result was that they always elected both representatives to the Legislative Assembly. The need of better accommodation for legal and judicial purposes was also felt by the settlers in these Townships, for the nearest court was at Three Rivers or Montreal. Down to 1830 all registration of deeds had to be done at Three Rivers.

In 1823 the Inferior District of St. Francis was created, with appeals to either Montreal or Three Rivers. The dividing of Buckingham County and representation in the Assembly, was not granted until 1829, when it was divided into the six counties of Yamaska, Lotbinière, Megantic, Nicolet, Drummond and Sherbrooke, and thus was Buckingham County legislated out of existence.

CHAPTER V.

SHERBROOKE COUNTY.

1829–1853.

BY ACT of Parliament, 9 George IV, Chap. 73, assented to 5th October, 1829, the County of Sherbrooke was created, being one of six counties into which Buckingham County had been subdivided. This Act says: "The County of Sherbrooke shall contain the townships of Garthby, Hatford, Whitton, Marston, Clinton, Woburn, Stanhope, Croyden, Chesham, Adstock, Lingwick, Weedon, Dudswell, Bury, Hampden, Ditton, Emberton, Drayton, Auckland, Newport, Westbury, Stoke, Ascot, Eaton, Hereford, Compton, Clifton, Windsor, Brompton, Shipton, Melbourne, and Oxford, together with all gores or augmentations of the said townships." Practically, these townships comprised the present counties of Richmond, Wolfe, Sherbrooke, and Compton. These townships were all in the District of Three Rivers, and with the exception of Croyden and Whitton, in the Inferior District of St. Francis.

The following is a statistical statement, for December, 1827, of the territory above described, and, in 1829, known as the County of Sherbrooke: Population, 5,471; churches—England, 2, parsonages, 2; Catholic, 1, presbytery, 1. Three villages. Total number of houses in towns and villages, 110; 1 court house, 1 gaol, 9 schools; mills—16 corn, 30 saw, 4 carding, 4 fulling; 2 distilleries, 2 tanneries, 11 potash factories, 11 pearl-ash factories, 2 shop-keepers, 5 taverns, 54 artisans. Territorial extent, 2,786 square miles; waste lands, 706 square miles; extreme length, 68 miles; breadth, 57 miles. Rank of county with others in Lower Canada: Population, 32nd; territorial extent, 14th; agricultural production, 17th.

The produce of Sherbrooke County in 1827, on an average for three years: Wheat, 80,871 bushels; oats, 62,910 bushels; barley, 3,619 bushels; peas, 18,280 bushels; rye, 19,043 bushels; buckwheat, 2,291 bushels; Indian corn, 13,260 bushels; mixed grain, 3,180 bushels; maple sugar, 709 cwts.; potatoes, 103,119 bushels; hay, 30,500 tons; flax, 381 cwts.; butter, 2,009 cwts.; horses, 3,161; oxen, 3,872; cows, 5,408; sheep, 11,836; swine, 4,995: cloth, 24,233 French ells; flannel and home spun, 20,100 French ells; linen, 35,400 French ells. Of the land there were 395 acres of loam; 10,180 acres under crop; 19,940 acres fallow and meadow; total in culture, 30,120 acres.

In those early days the Government tried to further the culture of hemp throughout the townships. The following letter speaks for itself:

"ASCOT, February 26, 1828.

"JOSEPH BOUCHETTE, Esq., Surveyor-General:

"SIR,—Agreeable to your request on the subject of the culture of hemp in the townships, I can safely say that if a ready market for it was established in the province, and within reach of the township settlements, I have no doubt it would be raised on an extensive scale, and become an object of profit both to the inhabitants of the country as well as to Great Britain. I have a knowledge of the late Mr. Pennoyer, of Compton, raising five to seven tons of hemp, and who had commenced a manufacturing mill for preparing hemp, but he failed by adopting a wrong method for its preparation for market. Several others did also cultivate hemp at that time; but, no market being found, the culture was in consequence discontinued. The townships generally are particularly calculated for the culture of hemp, and I trust the time may come when it will be cultivated on an enlarged scale. Many of the inhabitants of the townships make their own bed, cords, and ropes for their use.

I am your obedient, humble servant,

CHAS. F. H. GOODHUE."

The first elections for Sherbrooke County were held in 1829, and Messrs. Benj. Tremain and Samuel Brooks were elected. A full political history of the county, down to the present day, will be found elsewhere, under a separate chapter.

In 1830 the Registry Office was opened at Sherbrooke, previously to that time all work of this kind having to be done at Three Rivers. In 1833 the District of St. Francis was created, the name, Inferior, being dropped.

Under date of June, 1833, Samuel Brooks, Esq., of Lennoxville, gave the following information, in answer to questions submitted to him, and which was afterwards published by the British American Land Company: "We generally have snow sufficient for sleighing from 20th November to the 15th March. Good farm horses are worth from £7 10 s. to £15; oxen, the pair, same price; cows, from £2 10 s. to £6 5 s.; ploughs, £2 10 s. to £3 10 s.; ox carts, £7 10 s. to £10; waggons, £7 10 s. to £15. There are about 3,000 casks of pot and pearl ashes manufactured annually in the Townships. The price of butter is from 6d. to 9d.; cheese, from 4d. to 6d. Salmon are plenty in the season, say July, August, and September. Plenty of black-bass, trout, pike, pickerel, and maskinonge. Abundance of moose-deer, bears, rabbits, partridges, water fowl, &c. From Stanstead, to and from Montreal, freight usually is £5 per ton, each way; from Lennoxville or Sherbrooke to Three Rivers or Sorel, will average about £3 15 s. per ton, each way. There are in the County of Sherbrooke about seventy primary or elementary schools, and two high schools: one at Sherbrooke, the other at Shipton. The elementary schools are principally supported by legislative grants—£20 per annum to each,—and the high schools partly in the same manner."

THE BRITISH AMERICAN LAND COMPANY [*] has done much to settle and improve this part of the Eastern Townships, and for this reason we here give a synopsis of its origin and history to date. This Company has its head office in Sherbrooke, and owes its origin to the successful establishment of the Canada Land Company in Upper Canada.

In the Company's office in London, Eng., there is on record the report of a Provisional Committee, dated sixth February, 1832, recommending the immediate establishment of the British American Land Company. In this report it stated that in or about the year 1825 two independent committees, neither having any knowledge of the intentions of the other (one in Montreal, the other in London, Eng.), proposed the establishment of a company in Lower Canada, similar in character to the Canada Company, which had been successfully launched in Upper Canada. The Montreal Committee deputed the Hon. W. B. Felton (a member of the, then, Legislative Council) to visit London, and furnished him with letters of credence to gentlemen in London connected with the colony, in the hope of interesting some

---

[*] The following sketch is derived largely from information kindly furnished by Dr. R. W. Heneker, of Sherbrooke.

of them in the formation of a company. Mr. Felton found on his arrival a committee already in existence for this very purpose, and a coalition took place between the two bodies. This led to definite arrangements being made for the formation of a company on the basis of the Upper Canada Company. Negotiations were at once entered into with His Majesty's (King George IV.) Government, and proper arrangements made. Indeed, the whole business was proceeding satisfactorily in every way when the disastrous financial events of 1825 put a stop, for a time, to the carrying out of the scheme. Meanwhile the success of the operations of the Canada Company produced a favorable effect, and offered great inducements to the renewal of the scheme when the proper time should arrive. At length, in 1832, the matter was again taken up and a prospectus issued.

In this prospectus we find: "The objects of this company are to purchase or obtain grants and possession of lands from His Majesty's Government, corporate bodies or individuals in the Province of Lower Canada, ⁂ for the purpose of opening roads, building bridges, erecting mills, etc., and preparing lands for occupation, and disposing of such lands by sale, lease, or otherwise, to emigrants and others. The joint stock of the Company shall consist of £500,000, to be raised in 10,000 shares of £50 each. No individual to be allowed to subscribe for more than 100 shares nor less than five shares." This prospectus was signed by G. R. Robinson, chairman, and John Galt, honorary secretary.

It is necessary now to return to the proceedings in Canada. News had reached the Colony of the steps taken to form the Company, and on the 15th October, 1832, a meeting was held in Lennoxville favoring the scheme. Messrs. Shubael Pierce, J. C. Gillman, E. Bacon, John Lebourveau and Thomas Gordon, were appointed a Committee to communicate with the Company and assure them of the co-operation and support of the inhabitants of Sherbrooke County. At the same time petitions from the St. Francis District were presented to the Legislature in favor of the scheme.

In the minutes of the Court of Directors of the Company, June 12, 1833, mention is made that Mr. Samuel Brooks (father of Mr. Justice Brooks), who had been sent from the Eastern Townships of Lower Canada, appeared and gave general information as to the state of these townships.

On December 3, 1833, negociations had proceeded that far that the British American Land Company, in England, issued a pamphlet for the purpose of interesting emigrants. We take the following extracts from same:

"His Majesty's Government having agreed to sell to the B. A. L. Company the Crown Reserves and other Crown Lands in the southern counties of Stanstead, Shefford and Sherbrooke, in the Eastern Townships of Lower Canada, the Company is in progress of making arrangements for commencing the sale and settlement of the same in the ensuing spring.

"1st.—Crown Reserves and surveyed Crown lands. About 251,000 acres, situated in the counties of Shefford, Stanstead and Sherbrooke. These lands are situated for the most part in detached lots of farms of 200 acres each, scattered throughout the settled parts of the country, and from their contiguity to mills, shops, schools and churches, are exceedingly eligible for settlement. In many of the townships several of these lots lie together, so that settlers and emigrants may purchase larger farms from 400 and upwards of a thousand acres in extent.

"2nd.—The St. Francis Territory, containing about 596,000 acres, in the County of Sherbrooke. This large tract of land is comprised in the townships of Garthby, Stratford, Whitton, Weedon, Lingwick, Adstock, Bury, Hampden, Marston, Dilton, Chesham, Emberton and Hereford, and is situated between the upper waters of the St. Francis and Lake Megantic.

"By the agreement between His Majesty's Government and the Company, upwards of £50,000 of the purchase money to be paid by the latter are to be expended on public works and improvements in that part of the Province in which the lands sold to them are situated. The public works and improvements are high roads, bridges, canals, market houses, school houses, churches, and parsonage houses, and any other works undertaken and calculated for the common use and benefit of His Majesty's subjects."

In addition to the purchase from the Government, the Company subsequently acquired a very large quantity of lands at Government Auction sales, and from private individuals as well as the town property of Sherbrooke, bringing up the total quantity to 1,094,272 acres, and including with wild lands, many improved farms and town properties. The management consisted of a Court of Directors in London, Eng., who appointed Commissioners in Canada.

The first of these Commissioners were the Hon. Peter McGill, and the Hon. Geo. Moffatt, merchants, of Montreal, who acted jointly. Their appointment is dated 10th July, 1834. They were, both of them, gentlemen of the highest character, well-known and respected both in Canada and in England. Subsequently, in February, 1835, Mr. Arthur C. Webster was appointed by the two Commissioners to act as their attorney for the administration of the property. The power of attorney instituting Mr. Webster is witnessed by "A. T. Galt" (the future statesman), who was at the time a clerk in the office of the Company.

During Mr. Webster's time the business of settlement was carried on with great vigour. Immigrants in great numbers settled in Bury, and the Highland settlements in Lingwick were established. The Improvement Fund was expended in the opening of roads, the building of bridges, the erection of churches, all under the direct authority and sanction of the Governor-General of British North America. Lands were cleared and houses built for settlers, and even provisions furnished to incoming settlers, enabling them to live until they became accustomed to the new ways required to make a living in a new country, and the outlay of the Company was most lavish.

The income of the Company bore no proportion to the outlay, and the claims of the Government for principal and interest on the unpaid portion of the property could not be met. The rebellion of 1837-8 also told against the Company, so that at last they were compelled to enter into negociations with Lord Sydenham, and in 1841 abandoned the whole of the great block of the St. Francis Territory, comprising the unsurveyed purchase. It was a severe blow to the prosperity of the Company, but it could not be helped. After the cession of the St. Francis Territory, the Canadian Government gave away free tracts to settlers, drawing them from the British American Land Company's lands, after sales had been made, and in many cases houses built, lands cleared, and provisions given to these men. Not only was the loss great, but the Company became unpopular, and were charged with monopoly, and wrong doing, for not following the Government example in giving away their property.

The agreement with Lord Sydenham is dated July 5th, 1841, the Company's Commissioner at the time being John Fraser, who succeeded Mr. Webster in 1837. During Mr. Fraser's management the Company did not prosper. The years of rebellion were disadvantageous to immigration, and political strife raged throughout the country. Mr. Fraser was succeeded in office by Mr. (afterwards Sir) A. T. Galt, one of the greatest statesmen which Canada has produced. His commission is dated April 18, 1844, and from the date of his appointment signs of revival in the affairs of the Company were apparent. Mr. Galt may be said to have been the main instrument in the building of the railway from Montreal to Portland, now the Grand Trunk. Soon after the completion of the railway Mr. Galt found that his time was so much taken up with public affairs and large private business that he retired from the Company in 1855, when the present Commissioner, R. W. Heneker, was appointed, and has continued since to perform the duties of the office for the space of 41 years. Mr. Heneker is a man of wide experience, exceptional executive ability, and high education. He is sought after throughout the Province for positions of honor and trust.

It has been above stated that the Company's property comprised at one time 1,094,272 acres. In 1841 they renounced 511,447 acres, leaving as a remainder 582,825 acres. The present holding, as per the Company's Balance Sheet, December 31st, 1895, is 119,499 acres, showing that they have so far disposed of 463,326 acres to settlers and others.

This brief narrative would not be complete without a reference to what has been done in developing the town plot of Sherbrooke. When this property was first acquired there were one or two very small industries already established, and it was the policy of the Company to develop the great water power of the River Magog, and render it available for a high class of manufactures. They furnished for all the early industries buildings and power on terms of lease for 15 years, but all their efforts to attract capitalists on an extensive scale were unavailing until the present Commissioner, in 1866, secured a free gift of land and power on the part of the Company, when there was established the woolen mills of the Paton Manufacturing Company. The promoters were Mr. Geo. Stephen, of Montreal (now Lord Mount Stephen), the Hon. John Henry Pope, M.P., of Cookshire, and Lieutenant-Colonel Benj. Pomroy, of Compton. They were ably assisted by the Commissioner, Mr. Heneker. The services of the late Mr. Andrew Paton as manager were secured, and the new mills went into operation in 1867. Later, in 1871, it was greatly enlarged. The mills were still further enlarged later by the erection of a worsted mill, and now employ over 700 hands.

Besides the above, sales of land and water power have been made to some six or eight other companies, while shops and mills have been built and leased for other manufacturing purposes.

The Company, having been in existence for over 60 years, is gradually winding up its business, which, however, cannot be done suddenly. Its early history was no doubt very unprofitable, but of late years some return has been received on its capital; the sanguine anticipations of its founders have, however, never been realized.

During the Papineau troubles of 1837-38, the County of Sherbrooke remained loyal to the Government and furnished volunteers.

On August 9, 1842, the treaty between Her Majesty's Government and the United States, was signed at Washington. This settled the boundary between the two countries, which had been in dispute for years. The terms of the treaty as referring to that part of the Southern boundary of the present County of Compton, were as follows: "From the Metjarmette Portage, thence down along the said highlands which divide the waters that empty themselves into the River St. Lawrence from those which fall into the Atlantic Ocean, to the head of Hall's Stream; thence down the middle of said stream, till the line thus run intersects the old line of boundary, surveyed and marked by Valentine and Collins, previously to the year 1774, as the 45th degree of north latitude." By this treaty Sherbrooke County lost the townships of Drayton and Croydon.

In 1840, at the union of Upper and Lower Canada, the town of Sherbrooke was created an electoral district, with same boundaries as the present electoral county of Sherbrooke.

In 1853 it was decided that the County of Sherbrooke should have better representation in Parliament, and out of it was created the counties of Compton, Richmond and Wolfe. The town of Sherbrooke, including Ascot and Orford, was part of Compton County for all purposes except electoral. The division stood thus until 1871 when the County of Sherbrooke was again established.

For municipal purposes only the Township of Compton was added to Sherbrooke. Their first county council meeting was held June 14, 1871, present: J. G. Robertson, mayor of Sherbrooke; Robinson Oughtred, mayor of Ascot; and Hiram Moe, mayor of Orford.

HISTORY OF COMPTON COUNTY.

Compton Township was first represented at the March meeting, in 1872, by A. W. Kendrick, Esq.; J. G. Robertson, Esq., was chosen warden, and J. R. Woodward, secretary-treasurer.

Sherbrooke was changed from a village to a town in 1852, the first sitting of the council being held on August 14. The members of the Council present at that meeting were: Geo. F. Bowen, mayor, J. G. Robertson, John Griffith, Leonidas Goodall, Adam Lomas, Oliver Camiran, and Albert P. Ball. The present secretary-treasurer, Wm. Griffith, was then chosen and has held the position since that time. Sherbrooke received its charter as a city 24th December, 1875.

CHAPTER VI.

COMPTON COUNTY.

1853 – 1896.

COMPTON County derived its name from the township of Compton. When the Townships were first surveyed they were all named by British officials, then in this country, after men and places in England.

By Act of Parliament, 16 Victoria, cap. 152, art. 41, assented to 14th June, 1853, the county of Compton was created, having previously formed part of Sherbrooke county. By this Act we find: "The county of Compton shall be bounded on the east by the county of Beauce, on the southeast by the limits of the Province, on the northwest by the counties of Wolfe and Sherbrooke and the town of Sherbrooke, and on the southwest by the western and southern limits of the township of Compton, and the western limits of the township of Hereford; the said County so bounded comprising the townships of Compton, Westbury, Eaton, Clifton, Hereford, Bury, Newport, Auckland, Lingwick, Hampden, Ditton, Winslow, Whitton, Marston, Chesham, and part of the township of Clinton." In this county, until 1871, was included the electoral division of the town of Sherbrooke, for municipal purposes. Cookshire is the *chef-lieu*. Compton county always offered exceptional advantages for farming, and has been built up by its agricultural products. Here may be found some of the finest farms in Canada, and as progressive farmers as can be found on the American continent. Here also has been raised thoroughbred stock of such quality and breeding as to command the highest prices, for shipment to all parts of the world.

The increase in population has been rapid, still of a safe nature, showing gradual growth. In 1871 the population was 13,665; in 1881, 19,581; and in 1891, 22,779.

The early settlers of Compton county all came from the United States, and it was not until about 1835 that immigration from other places became noticeable. At the time of the organization of the British American Land Company, in 1833, no settlements in the County had been made east of Eaton, and in fact no bridge crossed the Eaton River, giving access to the eastern part of the County until one was built at Cookshire by this Company in 1836. In that year they commenced to bring in settlers from England and other parts. Their first venture was not a success.

In 1836 the British American Land Company built up a village known as Victoria, situated about one and a half miles west from Scotstown, on the Salmon River. Nearly one hundred families were brought over by the Company, and located, partly near this village, and others through the township of Bury. There were between one hundred and two hundred inhabitants in the village, which consisted of over thirty houses, a saw mill, a large building used as a church, school house, and office of the Company's agent, Mr. Hardwood, also two or three stores. The houses were built of logs, sheathed with fine and good sawed boards for flooring, gable ends, partitions, and shingled. The Company paid the passage over of these settlers, and supplied them with provisions the first year. The flour was brought down by boat from Upper Canada to Port St. Francis, and carted from there to Victoria by teams from the old French settlements. Besides good wheat flour, these first settlers had also pork, sugar, tea, rice; in fact, they "lived on the fat of the land." There was located at Victoria as well as sung by a local bard at the time, a "Dr. Hardon, gentleman, to keep them all alive." The settlers were also provided by the Company with clothing, kitchen utensils, axes and grub hoes, and a man was sent to show them how to use the grub hoes, build cabins, fell trees, and pile and burn them.

Some of those early immigrants would not and did not work, but others fell in quickly with their changed surroundings and made good farmers. Provisions were so plentiful that dough made from the flour given them was used to plaster their houses, instead of clay.

Fair crops were raised by some the first season about Victoria, but they soon saw that the soil was poor. At the close of the first year's work it was rumored that the Company intended to make all pay for the provisions advanced, as well as the passage over, and a good price for their farms. On this becoming known there was a general exodus from the place; and the village of Victoria, that had seemed so promising and prosperous, was deserted by all but five or six families, and in a short time no one was left but one Dutchman by the name of Christopher Rochart and his family. About a year after Rochart and his eldest son were drowned in the Salmon River, being carried over the falls. The grave can still be seen on the bank, overgrown with bushes and a second growth, while a cedar stake stands at the head.

Some of the Scotch immigrants later on were tempted to settle in Victoria, but when they saw the poor soil and heard the Company's terms, after a few weeks residence the ill-fated village was the second time deserted. The money here expended was a total loss. Some years after the bricks in the high chimney of the old church were carried to Gould and used in building the Presbyterian church and manse at that place. It is also said that when the Scotch settlers wanted nails they would go to Victoria, burn down one of the houses, and, after cooling off, pick the nails out of the ashes.

The place where the once brisk village of Victoria stood is again a forest, and but few traces can be seen of its ever having been settled, or that there stood the first village erected in Compton county, east of Cookshire.

The British American Land Company, profiting by experience, did not again attempt immigration on so large or expensive a scale. The first Scotch immigrants were eight families who came from the Island of Lewis, in 1838, and settled in Lingwick. The next Scotch settlers came in 1841, and for fifteen or twenty years after, these were increased by accessions from Scotland, until to-day there are upwards of four hundred and fifty families, distributed over the townships of Lingwick, Winslow, Hampden, Marston, and Bury.

Mr. T. Boutillier, Inspector of Agencies, in his report to the Legislative Assembly, in 1855, speaking of Compton, said: "The settlements have made rapid progress in Winslow; more than fifty families have come to reside since last year. The progress of agriculture and commerce, however, was but slow until the British American Land Company was formed, about twenty years ago. * * * With the exception of the places over which the operations of the Company had some influence, the Eastern Townships, with but few exceptions, remained in a stationary condition."

On the twenty-fifth of August, 1869, the Registry Office for Compton county was established at Cookshire. Hereford and West Clifton were detached October thirty-first, 1888, and added to the Coaticook Registry Office.

Through the good report of the late Rev. Thomas W. Constable, Methodist minister at Sawyerville, from 1858 to 1860, the present Registrar of the County, Mr. E. S. Orr, was influenced to leave his native county, Argenteuil, and settle in Sawyerville. He came to Sawyerville in October, 1859, and spent several days visiting Cookshire, Eaton and East

Clifton. He was convinced that the land was of good quality, and noticed, particularly, the large tracts fit for settlement, but which were covered with timber. In May, 1860, he rented the store in Sawyerville, where the post office is now kept, afterwards purchased and still owned by him. Mr. Orr was so well pleased with the outlook that he used his efforts to have others come from Argenteuil county and settle here. In that county there was a section known as the North Gore, now Lakefield, where the land was rather rough, being a thin covering over laurentian rocks. The younger part of the community were restless and dissatisfied with their surroundings. Some of them had gone to Ontario, and the Western States (we had then no Canadian Northwest). Mr. Orr says: "I thought it would be well to try to induce them to come here. I felt sure it would be to their advantage, and they were well suited to become settlers in this county." A circular letter was addressed to them, and in response, in the fall of the year, Messrs. Edward Graham, John Lee, and Thomas Johnston, came to investigate. To the land now forming the High Forest settlement they were attracted, and made arrangements to settle. They were followed at intervals by many others. They were mostly, if not entirely, people of religious principle and good morals. Some of them had some means to begin with, while others had but little. They have helped to improve the County, some settlements having been made by them almost entirely. Some have died, others have gone away, but the majority are yet here, many of them well-to-do, and some of them comparatively wealthy. Mr. Orr says: "None of them ever reproached me for inducing them to come."

The following are the names of some of the families who settled in the County, coming from Argenteuil, in addition to those mentioned: Alexander Johnson, who lived several years near Sawyerville, and left some years ago for the West; the late James Hamilton, with his wife, and their sons, John, Matthew, Joseph and William, and three or four daughters; Matthew and Joseph Boyd, with their father Valentine; Matthew and James Christie, with their father, William John; William Gordon and wife; William Hammond and wife; Robert, Samuel, and John Kerr, and Robert Kerr, senior, and wife; James and Richard Elliott and their wives; William and James Miller, with their families; some families of the name of Seale; some Westgates, Wilsons, and Bryants; Jesse Renny and his aged mother; Richard Graham and family; Mark Berry and wife, both deceased—they had a large family; John Burns and wife, with a numerous family; Edward Parker, a widower, with several sons and daughters; the late Wm. Smith, J. P., of Sawyerville, and wife, and their venerable sister, now about ninety years of age, blind from her childhood; Richard Dawson and wife; some families of the name of Wood. The Island Brook settlement contains several of the families here mentioned. George M. Orr, a brother of Mr. E. S. Orr, came to Cookshire and traded for some time. Later he moved to Calgary, N. W. T., and is at present mayor of that place. The movement to this County from Argenteuil has, perhaps, not yet ceased. Within a few years Messrs. Burwash, King, and McAllister have moved from Dalesville to Newport.

At about this same time Mr. Joseph Lowry, of Leeds, Que., was a delegate to a Methodist District Meeting, held at Cookshire. He was so impressed with the advantages offered for settlement that on his return there was about as large and, perhaps, as important an immigration from St. Sylvestre, Megantic county, and other places in that vicinity. Some of the names, now familiar, of those settlers, are the Mackays, Macraes, Coopers, Flaws, Edwards, McVetys, etc.

There was another class of immigrants came into the County about 1861. They were known as "Skedaddlers." This word is given in the Standard Dictionary as slang, meaning to flee, to run away in haste, etc. It is of American origin, and, though once very familiar in this county, is now nearly forgotten. During the rebellion between the Northern and Southern States, a considerable number of people from Maine and other Eastern States, being Democrats, and not in sympathy with the Republican party, which was carrying on the war, removed to the Eastern Townships. Compton county, lying on the frontier, received a good many of them. They thereby escaped the compulsory draft. It was, no doubt, with sad hearts, and at considerable sacrifice of comfort, that they took their way to a strange country. Among them were many respectable people, possessed of some means. They brought their "States money" with them and had to part with it, at the rate of $3 for $2, to procure the necessaries of life. Some were poor and had to cast about for means of support. Many of them had been "shingle weavers," and took to shingle making. Split shingles are now a very scarce article; then they were plenty enough, of various qualities, good, bad, and indifferent, as the skill of the makers varied. When the war closed most of the "Skedaddlers" returned to where they came from, some of them between sunset and sunrise, leaving accounts scattered about as a slight memento of their visit to Canadian soil. A few of those who came to the County during the war purchased property and remained here, making good citizens.

Previous to 1870, the proportion of French-Canadians to English-speaking residents, in Compton county, was small. About that time colonization societies were formed through the Province, assisted by the Government, for the purpose of influencing French-Canadians who had gone to the United States to return and settle in their native country. Three of these societies obtained land in this county, and from that time the growth of French-Canadians has been gradual. The principal townships benefitted by this immigration, were: Auckland, Ditton, Emberton, Chesham, Clinton, South Marston, and part of Hereford. Lake Megantic Village, North Winslow, and North Whitton, have also been settled by this nationality. The population of the two latter municipalities is more of an overflow from the old French parishes on the Chaudière. The increase of French-Canadians has been such that they now number nearly half the population.

In Compton county there are still left many thousand acres of land available for settlement, and in many parts good land. The hundreds of acres that are being cleared annually by the lumber companies can be purchased at a very low price. Compton county does not, by any means, offer good farms to all, for at least one quarter of its land is not adapted to agricultural pursuits. Notwithstanding this a large portion is capable of being farmed at a profit equal to any in the eastern part of the American continent.

Lumbering and farming are the principal occupations in the County. In 1891, there were fifty-five saw mills. They had a fixed capital in land of $263,020; in buildings, $84,320; in machinery and tools, $168,130; working capital, $381,076. These fifty-five mills employed five hundred and thirty-nine hands, and paid out in wages during the year, $92,371.

The total number of industrial establishments in Compton county is two hundred and thirty-two. Fixed capital in land, $360,570; in buildings, $245,307; in machinery and tools, $338,753; working capital, $889,123. These two hundred and thirty-two establishments employ nine hundred and thirty-six men, forty women, eighty-nine boys, and thirteen girls. Total amount paid in wages during the year 1890, $254,965; total value of raw material, $568,108; total value of articles produced, $1,197,165.

Until 1891 Compton county was always supplied in the way of local newspapers from Sherbrooke. On December 31, 1875, a paper was started at Cookshire, known as the *Canadian Independent, and Home Journal.* A. N. Donahue was the editor and proprietor. For two or three weeks only was it issued, when the office was closed up owing to lack of funds. On February 25, 1891, the first issue of the *Compton County Chronicle* was printed.

HISTORY OF COMPTON COUNTY.

The office was opened in Mrs. Willard's block, corner of Railroad and Pleasant streets. A first-class plant for doing printing of all kinds was installed, and from the first the paper was a success. The promoter, editor and publisher, was Mr. L. S. Channell. During the summer and fall of 1892, Mr. Channell erected an office and private dwelling on Main street, and, in December of 1892, the *Chronicle* was issued from its new quarters. On January 1, 1896, Mr. Channell sold a half interest in the paper to Mr. L. E. Charbonnel, advocate, of Sherbrooke, when a partnership was formed under the name of the Chronicle Printing Company. The paper is now issued by this company, under the management of Mr. Charbonnel. It has met with general acceptance from the public, and may now fairly be regarded as one of the permanent institutions of the County.

An incident in the history of Compton county, that took place in 1889, is known as the Donald Morrison affair. He was a young man, Scotch by birth, who had gone West and earned some money. He purchased a farm near Lake Megantic, and returning afterwards attempted to carry it on. In this he was unsuccessful, and finally lost all of his property. This made him reckless, to such an extent that he became insane over this special farm. A Frenchman shortly after occupied the place, and while his wife was winding the clock, one night, a rifle was fired near the window, the bullet passing close to her head and smashing the face of the clock. The barns were afterwards burned, and soon after the house, the occupants barely escaping with their lives. On this a warrant was issued for the arrest of Morrison, but no one could be found to serve it. Finally a dissolute fellow, by the name of Warren, from the United States, made threats of what he would do. He took the warrant, and, learning that Morrison was in Lake Megantic, after bracing himself with strong liquor, went out to meet him. This Warren was armed, as well as Morrison. As the latter paid no attention to him, Warren started to draw his revolver, when Morrison shot him dead, afterwards walking quietly out of the village. Large sums were offered for his capture, and heavy penalties proclaimed against all who should harbor him. Notwithstanding this, months elapsed before he was arrested. The clannish Highlanders could not be frightened into refusing him aid. The Government was, finally, obliged to send large numbers of Provincial officers into this section, and for weeks they patrolled the roads of the Scotch settlements in vain. Donald knew the country perfectly well, and as more than half was woods, the officers could do nothing. They finally succeeded in wounding him, one night, when he was escaping from his father's house, and thus was he captured, after an expense of thousands of dollars. He stood his trial at Sherbrooke, was sentenced for a long term of years, but did not live long, dying of consumption about five years after his committal. His body was brought back to his home for burial.

Previous to the establishing of a branch of the People's Bank of Halifax, at Lake Megantic, in December, 1893, all the banking business of the county of Compton was done principally at Sherbrooke. And when in March, 1895, another branch of the same bank was established at Cookshire, it enabled them to do the banking business for more than half of Compton county. The general wish of the majority of the people was that they might have a branch of the Eastern Townships Bank, which many of the old settlers had been largely instrumental in starting. This was, however, refused and gave a chance for an outside bank to get established and work up a lucrative business.

The People's Bank of Halifax, N. S., was incorporated in 1864, with a capital of $200,000. In 1866 it was increased to $280,000; in 1867 to $340,000; in 1868 to $400,000; in 1873 to $500,000; in 1874 to $600,000; and in 1892 to $700,000, the present capital. The January report for 1896 gives the reserve as $175,000; total assets, $3,054,000; deposits, $1,600,000; total liabilities, $2,140,000. Surplus over all liabilities, $968,000. The officers are: Patrick

HISTORY OF COMPTON COUNTY.

O'Mulliu, president; James Fraser, vice-president; John Knight, cashier; D. R. Clarke, accountant. Head office, Halifax, N. S. They have agencies at the following places: Edmundston, N. B., Woodstock, N. B., Shediac, N. B., Fraserville, P. Q., Halifax (north-end), Canso, N. S., Lunenburg, N. S., Wolfville, N. S., Windsor, N. S., North Sydney, C. B., Port Hood, C. B., Levis, P. Q., Lake Megantic, P. Q., Cookshire, P. Q., and Quebec City.

The agencies in Compton county are under the charge of Mr. W. H. Gossip, agent at Cookshire, with Mr. R. A. E. Aitken acting agent at Lake Megantic.

The Eastern Townships Bank received its charter from the Parliament of Lower Canada, in 1855, with an authorized capital of $400,000. They commenced business at Sherbrooke in August, 1859, with a capital paid up of $136,000. To the late Col. Benj. Pomroy, who was the first president, is due the credit for establishing this bank, ably assisted by the late Hon. John Henry Pope and other men of prominence in Compton county. The bank at present has a paid up capital of $1,500,000, with a reserve fund of $720,000, and deposits over $3,000,000. For many years the bank has paid semi-annually a dividend of three and a half per cent. The officers at present are: R. W. Heneker, president; Hon. M. H. Cochrane, vice-president; Wm. Farwell, general manager; directors: T. J. Tuck, N. W. Thomas, Israel Wood, J. N. Galer, Thomas Hart, Gardner Stevens, and John G. Foster. The bank now has branches at Stanstead, Waterloo, Coaticook, Cowansville, Richmond, Granby, Bedford, Huntingdon, Magog, St. Hyacinthe, and is about opening one in Montreal. M. S. Edgell is local manager at Sherbrooke.

The following statistics of Compton county are taken from the census returns of 1890-91: Compton county contains 883,400 acres and 1,380 square miles; total population, 22,779; families, 4,309; dwellings occupied, 4,095; average size of families, 5.2; male population, 12,039; females, 10,740; married—males, 3,940; females, 3,936; widowed—males, 290; females, 489; children and unmarried—males, 7,809; females, 6,315; French Canadians, 10,335; other nationalities, 12,444.

Religions: Roman Catholics, 11,150; Church of England, 3,232; Presbyterians, 3,561; Methodists, 2,711; Bible Christians, 11; Brethren, 3; Lutherans, 85; Baptists, 410; Free Will Baptists, 229; Congregationalists, 424; Adventists, 473; Universalists, 311; Protestants, 10; Salvation Army, 5; Jews, 14; other denominations, 13; not specified, 137.

Places of birth: Quebec, 19,070; Ontario, 112; Nova Scotia, 28; New Brunswick, 19; Manitoba, 2; British Columbia, 2; Prince Edward Island, 2; Northwest Territories, 2; England and Wales, 761; Scotland, 1,077; Ireland, 339; United States, 1,124; Scandinavia, 97; France, 74.

In the County there are 22 blind people, 7 males and 15 females; also 20 who are deaf and dumb, 11 males and 9 females; of unsound mind, 34.

For the year preceding that in which the census was taken there were 306 deaths in the County. Of these 10 were Baptists, 177 Roman Catholics, 27 Church of England, 34 Methodists, 36 Presbyterians, and 22 not specified. Their occupations were: farmers, 171; commercial, 5; domestic, 6; industrial, 15; professional, 3; laborers, 60; not classed, 46.

Educational status: can read and write—males, 7,254; females, 6,696; can only read—males, 653; females, 688; cannot read or write—males, 4,132; females, 3,356.

Number of churches and boarding schools: total churches, 55—Baptist, 1; Catholic, 14; Congregational, 2; Church of England, 14; Methodist, 15; Presbyterian, 7; other churches, 2; boarding schools for young ladies, 2; inmates, 22.

Occupiers of lands, and lands occupied: total occupiers, 3,899—owners, 3,639; tenants, 254; employés, 6. Total acres occupied, 456,776; acres improved, 200,245; under crops, 120,092 acres; in pasture, 78,554 acres; woodland and forest, 257,531 acres; gardens and orchards, 1,599 acres.

CHAPTER VII.

POLITICAL HISTORY.

1792–1896.

THE political history of those townships which now constitute the county of Compton in reality dates back only to 1829. In 1792 the first session of the first Parliament of Lower Canada was opened by Lieut. Governor Clarke. J. A. Panet was chosen Speaker. The house consisted of 39 knights, 8 citizens and 3 burgesses. The feeling against the Jews was so strong in those days that in 1808 Ezekiel Hart, Esq., was expelled from the House of Assembly for professing the Jewish religion. The whole of the present county of Compton was situated in the county of Buckingham, district of Three Rivers, with the exception of a small part of the township of Compton which was in Richelieu county, district of Montreal. Buckingham county extended as far as the St. Lawrence River. The population of the French-speaking people, near the St. Lawrence, was far in excess of all those in the Townships, even down to 1829. The result was that all candidates were chosen from that section. The English-speaking people had to make long journeys if they wished to vote, and being largely in the minority took no interest whatever in the result. The Rev. Charles Stewart, D. D., afterwards Lord Bishop of Quebec, writing in 1815, in a pamphlet issued in 1817, says: "The people of these townships can scarcely be said to be represented in the House of Assembly. The counties to which they belong are so large, and the places of election are, in general, so distant from them, that for the most part they do not take the pains of giving their votes in the election of a representative. * * * The better way of removing this difficulty would be the formation of new counties." To give better representation Lower Canada was further divided into forty counties, by act of 9, George IV, chap. 73, passed in March, 1829. By this act, Buckingham county was subdivided into the counties of Yamaska, Nicolet, Drummond, Lotbinière, Sherbrooke and Megantic.

Sherbrooke comprised the present counties of Compton, Richmond, Wolfe and Sherbrooke, and in 1827 had a population of 5,471 souls. Two members were allowed this constituency, and all votes were cast at the villages of Sherbrooke and Richmond. The basis of representation, in 1829, was two members for 4,000 and upwards; above 1,000 and under 4,000, one; under 1,000, to vote in nearest county.

On the 19th October, 1829, writs were issued for elections to be held in the counties of Drummond, Missiskoui, Sherbrooke, Stanstead and Shefford. These counties sent representatives, for the first time, at this election. The writs were returned by the Clerk of the Crown in Chancery, 7th December, 1829. The members elected were as follows: Sherbrooke—Charles Whitcher, returning officer—Benj. Tremain and Samuel Brooks. Stanstead—Wm. Ritchie, returning officer—Marcus Child and Ebenezer Peck. Shefford—Abijah Willard, returning officer—Lyman Knowlton. Missiskoui—Philip N. Moore, returning officer—Richard V. V. Freileigh and Ralph Taylor. Drummond—John L. Ployart, returning officer—Frederick George Heriot, C. B. These gentlemen were sworn in and took their seats at the third session of the thirteenth Provincial Parliament, held from 22nd January to 26th March, 1830. The writs for general elections for the fourteenth Provincial Parliament were issued 13th September, 1830, and returned on the 23rd November. The representatives elected for the county of Sherbrooke were Charles Frederick Henry Goodhue and Samuel Brooks. At the meeting of the House of Assembly, second session, held at Quebec, 15th November, 1831, the Speaker informed the House that since the last session Samuel Brooks, Esq., had vacated his seat as member for the county of Sherbrooke. The act of vacation was as follows: "On the 18th of July, 1831, before Wm. Ritchie, N. P., residing in Georgeville, L. C., county of Stanstead, appeared Samuel Brooks, of the township of Ascot, one of the members for the Province of Lower Canada, and declared himself as desirous of availing himself of 'an act to allow members of the House of Assembly to vacate their seats in certain cases, and for other purposes.' Wherefore Samuel Brooks, for certain good causes, hereby vacates his seat. Signed in presence of Robert Vincent and John Grannis, witnesses." A writ was issued accordingly on 23 August, 1831, and Bartholomew Conrad Augustus Gugy, Esq., elected in his place for Sherbrooke. Writs for general elections were issued 11 October, 1834, and returned 7 January, 1835. Messrs. B. C. A. Gugy and Col. John Moore were returned for the county of Sherbrooke.

This election through the Province strengthened the hands of those who supported the opposition to the Lieut-Governor, and which led up to the Papineau rebellion of 1837-38. Through the Townships the majority appears to have been on the side of the Governor. On the 10th February, 1838, in the first year of the reign of Queen Victoria, at Montreal, the first meeting of the Special Council of the Province of Lower Canada was held. It was under the presidency of Lieut-General Sir John Colborne, G.C.B., Administrator of the Government. It was enacted at this meeting that from the proclamation of this act in Lower Canada until 1st November, 1840, the Legislative Council or Legislative Assembly shall not be "called together without serious detriment to the interests of said Province." Hon. Edward Hale, of Sherbrooke, was appointed a member of the Special Council in 1839, and first took his seat on 11th November of the same year.

In 1841 a union of Upper and Lower Canada was effected, and on a redistribution of seats the townships of Ascot and Orford, with the village of Sherbrooke, were set off from the balance of Sherbrooke county, under the electoral name of Sherbrooke Town. Sherbrooke county comprised the present counties of Compton, Richmond and Wolfe.

For the town of Sherbrooke Hon. Edward Hale represented the constituency during the two Parliaments from 1841 to 1848, when he was followed by Col. B. C. A. Gugy. This gentleman was succeeded at the general election of 1851 by Edward Short, who served through one Parliament and was then elevated to the Bench. Mr. (later Hon. Sir) A. T. Galt was then elected by acclamation, and was re-elected at each general election thenceforward to and including 1867. He was unopposed on each of these occasions except in 1861, when he came before his constituents as a Minister of the Crown, in the Cartier-Macdonald Cabinet. His opponent at that time was W. L. Felton, advocate, of Sherbrooke, who had formerly represented Richmond and Wolfe. Mr. Galt retired from the representation of Sherbrooke in 1872, and Edward T. Brooks, son of Mr. Samuel Brooks, formerly member for Sherbrooke county, was elected without opposition, and in 1874 and 1878 he received repetitions of this compliment from the electors. Previous to 1871 the town of Sherbrooke had remained part of Compton county for all purposes, except electoral. In that year the county of Sherbrooke was established, which included the townships of Ascot, Orford and the village of Lennoxville, and, for municipal and registration purposes only, the township of Compton and the village of Waterville. Mr. Brooks was elevated to the Bench in 1882, and succeeded by Rob't N. Hall, a prominent lawyer of Sherbrooke. Mr. Hall was appointed a judge of the Court of Appeals in 1891, and succeeded by the present member, Hon. W. B. Ives, Q. C., who was called to the Privy Council in 1891 and was afterwards Minister of Trade and Commerce in the Cabinet of Sir Mackenzie Bowell.

The representation of Sherbrooke in the Quebec Legislative Assembly has not been favored with much variety. Hon. J. G. Robertson, the present post-master at Sherbrooke, represented the constituency from 1867 to 1892, when he was defeated by the present member, L. E. Pannetou, advocate. Mr. Robertson was Treasurer of the province for a number of years. He was opposed in 1867 by R. W. Heneker, and in 1879 by Æneas McMaster.

The county of Sherbrooke, in 1841, comprised the present counties of Compton, Richmond and Wolfe. At the general elections, held 14th June, 1841, Col. John Moore was elected. At the general elections, held 28 November, 1844, Col. Moore was succeeded by Mr. Samuel Brooks, who was the first member elected for Sherbrooke, in 1829, having resigned in 1848. Mr. Brooks was re-elected 25th February, 1841, but by his death in the following year his seat became vacant. Political feeling then ran very high, in consequence of the recent passage of the "Rebellion Losses Bill," and a formidable agitation for annexation to the United States disturbed the current of politics in this part of the Province. The advocates of that scheme tendered the nomination for the vacant seat in Parliament to A. T. Galt, then a young and promising man, employed in Sherbrooke, in the interest of the British American Land Company. Mr. Galt was elected by acclamation, but resigned his seat soon after for private reasons, whereupon the annexationists brought out John Sewall Sanborn, then a young advocate of Sherbrooke. It was at this time that the late Hon. John Henry Pope first took an interest in politics. The petitions and speeches being made throughout the County warmed up his U. E. Loyalist blood to such an extent that he entered the arena with a determination to defeat Mr. Sanborn. The Conservative candidate chosen as his opponent was C. B. Cleveland, a tanner of Richmond, and father of the present member, Mr. C. C. Cleveland. The contest was a fierce one. Mr. Sanborn, having the support of the majority of the influential men of the day, was successful and sat out the balance of that Parliament. On December 16th, 1851, another general election occurred, and Mr. Sanborn was again a candidate. This time his opponent was Mr. J. H. Pope, whom he defeated.

Hon. John Sewell Sanborn, A. M., Q. C., LL. D., was born in Gilmanton, N. H., 1st January, 1819. Graduated from Dartmouth College in 1842, and received the degree of A. M. three years later. The same degree was conferred upon him by Bishop's College, Lennoxville, P. Q., in 1855. From the latter institution he also received, in 1873, the honorary degree of D. C. L., and a year later the honorary degree of LL. D., from Dartmouth College.

On leaving college, Mr. Sanborn came directly to Canada, and became principal of the Sherbrooke Academy, a position which he held for three years, during which he commenced the study of law with Mr. Justice Short, finishing his legal studies with Messrs. A. and W. Robertson, of Montreal. He was admitted to practice in January, 1847. In 1858 he was associated in partnership with his brother-in-law, E. T. Brooks, which continued until his appointment as a judge for St. Francis district in 1873.

Mr. Sanborn was in Parliament from 1850 until 1857. He did not again offer himself for re-election. In 1863, upon the death of the late Honorable Hollis Smith, Mr. Sanborn was elected by acclamation to represent the division of Wellington, in the Legislative Council, for the remainder of the electoral term, and re-elected by acclamation to the same office for the next eight years. While this term was passing, the Act of Confederation was passed, and he was called by Her Majesty to the Senate of the Dominion in 1867, as one of the original members of that body, and he continued in this position until 1873, when he was appointed to the Bench.

His appointment to the office of judge of the Superior Court, on the demise of Judge Short, was made by his political opponent, Sir John A. Macdonald. When he had discharged his duties for little more than a year, the Liberals being in power, and a vacancy occurring on the Queen's Bench, he was transferred to that court. Three years later, on 17th July, 1877, his death occurred. He was buried in Mount Royal cemetery, Montreal.

In youth he became a "teetotaller," stuck to his pledge all his life, and was at one time president of the Temperance and Prohibitory League of this Province.

Judge Sanborn was twice married; first, in 1847, to Eleanor Hall Brooks, daughter of Samuel Brooks, Esq., of Sherbrooke—a lady of great excellence of character, who died in 1853, leaving three children; and the second time, in 1856, to N. Judson Hazeltine, of Bradford, Mass., a woman of many noble qualities, who died in December, 1874, leaving one child. Of the three children by the first wife two are living. Elizabeth Maria is the wife of Thomas J. Tuck, druggist, of Sherbrooke; Ellen Brooks is the wife of Henry D. Lawrence, advocate, Sherbrooke; Samuel Brooks Sanborn, advocate, died in the fall of 1884. The child by the second wife, Mary Abigail, is unmarried, and resides at Sherbrooke with her sister, Mrs. Lawrence.

The *Sherbrooke Gazette* well said of Judge Sanborn :

"As a private citizen, a lawyer, legislator, and judge, his example is worthy of imitation, and the world will be all the better, the more closely his example in private and public life is followed."

In 1853, by Act of Parliament, several new counties were created. In the change the county of Sherbrooke went out of existence, being sub-divided into the present counties of Compton, Richmond and Wolfe. At the general elections in 1854, Richmond and Wolfe were included in the electoral division of the town of Sherbrooke, not choosing a member of their own until the general elections of 1857-58, when Wm. H. Webb was returned. The first general election for Compton county, held August 5, 1854, was one of the hardest contested ever held in the County. Judge Sanborn, the former representative of Sherbrooke county, again offered himself as the candidate, and was opposed by Mr. John Henry Pope, whom he defeated by only eight votes. At the general elections for the sixth Parliament, Mr. Pope for the third time offered himself for election, and was returned by acclamation 24th December, 1857, and held the seat by acclamation until Confederation. He was returned by acclamation in 1867, 1871, and 1872. On one of these dates Mr. Henry Layfield, of Gould, was nominated in opposition to Mr. Pope. He was not strong physically, and while addressing the electors fainted. His friends intervened and Mr. Layfield resigned the same day. Mr. Pope entered the Cabinet of Sir John Macdonald, as Minister of Agriculture, 25th October, 1871, and remained in the Cabinet up to the time of his death, with the exception of five years, from 1873 to 1878, when the Conservatives were on the opposition benches. On the 25th September, 1885, the representative for Compton accepted the portfolio of Railways and Canals, which he held up to his death, April 1, 1889.

Rufus Henry Pope, the present member, succeeded his father, being elected in the fall of 1889, at a bye-election. He was again returned at the general elections of 1891, and accepted the nomination of his party for the general elections held during 1896, being again elected.

The elections held in Compton County for a member of Parliament, since Confederation, have given the following results:—In 1867, 1871 and 1872, Hon. John Henry Pope, by acclamation; first election, 1874—candidates, Hon. John Henry Pope and Hugh Egbert Cairns, of Clifton; Pope received over 800 majority; election of 1878—candidates, Hon. J. H. Pope and Hugh Leonard, of Winslow; Pope received about 800 majority; election of 1882—candidates, Hon. J. H. Pope and H. E. Cairns, poll stood : Pope 1,612, Cairns 823, majority for Pope, 789; election of 1887—candidates, Hon. J. H. Pope and T. B. Monroe, of Bury, majority for Pope about 800 ; bye-election of 1889—candidates, R. H. Pope and T. B. Monroe, majority for Pope over 800 ; election of 1891—candidates, R. H. Pope and Seth P. Leet, of Montreal ; majority for Pope 1066, and Leet lost his deposit of $200, not having received the minimum proportion of votes required by law.

The elections for a member of the Legislative Assembly at Quebec, since Confederation, have resulted as follows:—1867, candidates, James Ross, of Gould, and Alden W. Kendrick, of Compton, majority for Ross, 194; 1871—candidates, James Ross and W. M. Sawyer, of Sawyerville, majority for Sawyer, 276; 1875—Wm. Sawyer, by acclamation; 1878—candidates, Wm. Sawyer and James Doak, of Compton, majority for Sawyer, 453; 1881—candidates, Wm. Sawyer and Æneas MacMaster, of Scotstown, majority for Sawyer, 507; 1886—candidates, John McIntosh, of Compton, and Hugh Leonard, of Winslow, majority for McIntosh, 720; 1890—candidates, John McIntosh and Geo. Layfield, of Gould, majority for McIntosh, 770; 1892—McIntosh returned by acclamation. In 1892 Hon. John McIntosh took a seat in the DeBoucherville Cabinet. In 1894 he resigned to accept the position of Sheriff of St. Francis District. At the bye-election of 1894 the candidates were Charles McClary, of St. Edwidge, and J. B. M. St. Laurent, of Compton; majority for McClary, 688.

Rufus Henry Pope, M. P., was born in Cookshire, Que., September 13, 1857. His father was the late Hon. John Henry Pope, whose portrait and biography are to be found in this volume. His parents were descended from old and distinguished families of U. E. Loyalist stock, and show the earliest records of any settlement in Compton county, having located in Hereford previous to 1793. Our subject was educated at Cookshire Academy, Sherbrooke High School, and under a private tutor. He also studied law at McGill, but his tastes were in the line of agriculture, and he took possession of the fine estate, comprising about 1,400 acres, known as "East View Stock Farm," previously owned and occupied by his father. He proved himself a born agriculturist, and applied his energies to the importation of thoroughbred stock, making a specialty of the Polled Angus or Aberdeen Cattle, and has the credit of introducing this breed into America. Compton county is celebrated for high-class farming, and Mr. Pope has ranked foremost among those who have been instrumental in raising the standard of agricultural science.

On the death of his father, April 1, 1889, Mr. Pope was chosen, as their candidate, by the Liberal-Conservatives of Compton county. Much against his personal wishes and business interests he accepted the nomination for the unexpired term. He was returned with a handsome majority over Mr. T. B. Munro, of Bury. At the general elections, in March, 1891, Mr. Pope was again the candidate. His opponent was Mr. Seth P. Leet, a lawyer from Montreal, who was defeated by 1,066 majority, losing his deposit of $200. The Liberal-Conservative party, in convention assembled, have

RUFUS H. POPE, M. P.

again chosen Mr. Pope as the candidate for general elections of 1896. Although he expressed an earnest wish to retire, the party would not hear of it. He is one of the most popular members at Ottawa; his independent, genial, outspoken manner, makes friends on all sides, and gives him unusual strength with the Government.

Outside of farming, Mr. Pope has done more for the employment of labor than any other man in Compton county. His wealth has always been invested in local enterprises, assisting his fellow men and building up the country. He was one of the promotors of the Hereford Railway; is the active partner of the Cookshire Mill Company, managing director of the Royal Paper Mills Company, and a director of the Paton Woolen Mills Company, Sherbrooke, Dominion Line Company, Scotstown Lumber Company, Canada Provident Assurance Company, and several other minor concerns. He has always been very liberal, assisting those in trouble in an unostentatious manner. Anything that will help mankind, his town or county, he is always ready to assist with money and his own labor.

He was married at Lennoxville, Que., September 18, 1877, to Lucy, daughter of Major C. Noble, of Cookshire. Issue, six children: Lottie Adelle, born August 4. 1879; Beatrice Ethel, born April 10, 1881; Desmond Ives, born February 4, 1883; John Henry, born November 16, 1884; Gladys Clara, born January 7, 1887; Cecil Colin, born December 11, 1888. With views of Cookshire, may be found a photo-engraving of the handsome residence of Mr. Pope, erected in 1880, known as "East View." It is at the top of the hill overlooking Cookshire, with an extensive view for miles both up and down the Eaton river. It is one of the most attractive homes in the Eastern Townships.

Charles McClary, M. L. A., farmer, whose portrait is here reproduced, was born in Stanstead, March 3, 1833. At Compton, March 28, 1855, he married Jane A. (born August 12, 1832), daughter of the late Andrew McClary. Issue, one son, John Andrew, born June 10, 1868; married Luvia L. Woodward, of Hatley; 1 child, residence Compton. The father of our subject came from Epsom, N. H., in 1801, when nine years of age. He married Betsey Cass, of Stanstead, whose parents were also from Epsom. Charles McClary, when 15 years of age, with his parents moved to Barnston, where they lived and died. At the age of 22 he moved on to the farm where he now resides.

He was the first settler in the present municipality of St. Edwidge de Clifton. There was then no road within six miles. The next settlers were men who worked for Mr. McClary and took up adjoining land. By hard work he has cleared a good farm and erected thereon large and attractive buildings. He is a man of strong character, and very popular with all classes. He has held the office of councillor for 28 years, mayor for 26 years, and warden of the County for two terms. On

CHARLES McCLARY, M. L. A.

the resignation of Hon. John MacIntosh as member of Legislative Assembly for the County, after several hours' voting, Mr. McClary was unanimously chosen on September 20, 1894, by the Liberal-Conservative party in convention, as their candidate. He was elected on October 19, 1894, over Mr. J. B. M. St. Laurent, of Compton, with a majority of 688.

For representation in the Dominion Senate, Compton county is in the district known as Wellington. Hon. Mathew H. Cochrane, of Compton, was called to the Senate to represent Wellington, on October 17, 1872. In politics he is Conservative. Senator Cochrane is a native of this county, having been born at Compton, November 11, 1824. His father, James Cochrane, was from the north of Ireland, and for many years was merchant, farmer and cattle-breeder in this province. Matthew lived on the farm until eighteen years old, when he went to Boston, Mass., and engaged in the shoe business, returning to Canada in 1854, and engaging in the same business in Montreal. At first he was in company with Samuel G. Smith, the firm being Smith & Cochrane. Mr. Smith died in 1868. In 1873 Charles Cassils, a native of Dumbartonshire, Scotland, became a partner of Mr. Cochrane in the business. The firm of Cochrane, Cassils & Co. employs about three hundred men and women, and does business to the extent of from $450,000 to $500,000 a year.

In 1864 Mr. Cochrane purchased a large farm at Compton, adjoining the one on which he was brought up, and commenced farming and cattle-raising. His place, known as "Hillhurst," now contains about one thousand acres, largely rolling land, and almost in one block, with brooks and springs furnishing an abundance of good water.

When Mr. Cochrane commenced his improvements at Compton, but little had been done in the way of progress among the stock farmers of this province; and his enterprise in this direction marks an epoch in this part of Canada. As a pioneer in this line, Mr. Cochrane began with a determination to have the best specimens of Short Horns that money could purchase from the best cattle-breeders of the Old World. His first notable purchase was in 1867, when he imported the famous cow Rosedale. At the same time he also imported a choice cargo of Cotswold, Southdown, Leicester and Lincoln sheep, Suffolk horses and Berkshire pigs. * * * Rosedale's first calf, after coming into Mr. Cochrane's hands, a heifer, was sold, when a year old, to an Illinois stock-breeder for $3,500, and re-sold by the latter, three months later, to Col. King, of Minnesota, for $5,500. The next year Mr. Cochrane paid one thousand guineas for Duchess 97th, by the 3rd Duke of Wharfdale, of the noted Wetherby herd—the first heifer of her family which had been brought from England since the great American purchase of 1853. The price which he paid for her is said to be the highest at that time ever paid for a female Short Horn. At the same time, among other cattle, Mr. Cochrane also bought, for two hundred and fifty guineas, a fine Booth animal of striking beauty.

To outdo himself and every other cattle-breeder in America, in 1870 Mr. Cochrane brought into Canada no less than forty heads of Short Horns, the aggregate cost of them, including a hunting mare, and a lot of Cotswold sheep and Berkshire pigs, amounting to about $60,000. The extent of his investments, in 1870, had a great influence on the English Short Horn market.

Mr. Cochrane has from year to year made valuable importations of live stock, having become known as one of the largest breeders in Canada, if not in America. Of late years he has devoted more time to horses, and has some valuable Hackneys. In addition to his extensive farm at Hillhurst, which is under the charge of his son, James A. Cochrane, he has a large ranch in the Canadian northwest.

The representative in the Dominion Cabinet of the Protestant minority of Quebec Province is Hon. W. B. Ives, Q. C., of Sherbrooke, minister of Trade and Commerce. He is also a native of this county, having been born in Compton, November 17, 1841. His parents, Eli and Artemissa (Bullock) Ives, were of English descent, and came to this country from Connecticut, U. S., with the U. E. Loyalists. Mr. Ives began his education in a common school, near his birth-place, and afterwards attended the Compton Academy for some four or five years. He subsequently continued his studies privately, and later on prosecuted the study of law, and was admitted to the Bar in 1867. From 1867 to 1878, he practiced in Sherbrooke, and was, during that time, created a Q. C. He has had the honor to be mayor of Sherbrooke and also member for Richmond and Wolfe, redeeming the County from the Liberals against Henry Aylmer. In 1882, he was re-elected by acclamation, and in 1887, he had a successful contest with J. N. Greenshields, of Montreal, and in 1891 was elected for Sherbrooke. In 1879 Mr. Ives became interested in manufacturing. Among other enterprises he is interested in the Paton Mills of Sherbrooke, president of the Salmon River Pulp Company, at Scotstown, and equal partner with Mr. R. H. Pope, M. P., in the Scotstown Lumber Company, Cookshire Mill Company, and Royal Paper Mills Company, of East Angus, director Dominion Line Company, and interested in the Sherbrooke Gas and Water Company. Mr. Ives built the Hereford Railway, now operated by the Maine Central Railway. In business he has been signally successful, and it is considered a guarantee of success to have his name connected with any business enterprise. He was married, November 17, 1869, to Elizabeth, daughter of the late Hon. John Henry Pope. Mr. Ives entered Sir John Thompson's Cabinet in December, 1892, as President of the Council. On reconstruction, after Sir John Thompson's death, in 1895, by Sir Mackenzie Bowell, Mr. Ives took the portfolio of Trade and Commerce, and was called to the same office by Sir Charles Tupper, when Premier Bowell resigned in April, 1896.

CHAPTER VIII.

MUNICIPAL HISTORY.

Early Records—Council Proceedings—Members County Council.

TO the township of Newport, in Compton county, is probably due the credit of doing the first municipal business in the Eastern Townships. The first settlers were a law-abiding people, and as there was no law for carrying on town business, they met together and organized under their own rules, on the same lines as the law provided in the United States. Their first meeting was held September 28, 1799, and continued quarterly until 1814, when the organization became disbanded. A moderator or chairman, and a clerk were chosen each year by election. All the settlers would sign the different acts agreed upon. Further particulars of these proceedings are to be found in the history of the township of Newport.

The first municipal laws in the Province of Quebec went into effect in 1841. The Province of Ontario, then known as Upper Canada, had a municipal law for several years previous, which had materially assisted in the development of that province. In Lower Canada, before the establishment of district councils in 1841, all roads were laid out under the supervision of the Surveyor General or Grand Voyer. Of municipal business there was none.

Under date of Kingston, U. C., August 6, 1841, the Hon. Edward Hale issued notices to all of the townships in the District of St. Francis, to elect one councillor to represent them in the District Council, to meet at Sherbrooke.

Under date of 8th September, 1841, the first meeting of the Council of the district of Sherbrooke, was held in Sherbrooke. The following are those who were returned as eligible to sit in the Council: G. D. Innes, Brompton; Eros Lebourveau, Eaton; John McConnell, Hatley; Shadrac Norton, Barnston; Thos. Tait, Melbourne; Thos. Davis, Dudswell; Patrick Ivers, Lingwick; Philip Rogers, Stanstead; Benjamin Pomroy, Compton; Samuel Brooks, Sherbrooke; Tyler Stafford, Ascot; Chester B. Cleveland, Shipton; Elisha Pope, Hereford; John Gilman, Stanstead; Thomas Brown, Bury. Those townships in the district of St. Francis not here mentioned were joined to some of the other townships, in order to make up the required number of population to send a representative. The Hon. Edward Hale had been appointed warden by the Lieutenant-Governor, and held that position during the existence of the District Council. Mr. Jos. S. Walton, editor of the *Sherbrooke Gazette*, was accepted by the Lieutenant-Governor as clerk. At the first meeting all necessary rules and regulations governing the Council, were accepted. By reading the minutes of the different sessions, which were held quarterly and lasted for several days at a time, it is evident the principal business transacted was the laying out of roads and building bridges. Their power, however, reached nearly as far as the Provincial Legislature of the present day, for they had full charge of the schools, and the right to lay an assessment on "buildings, personal property, etc." As far as can be learned, the Sherbrooke District Council fulfilled their duties in a manner satisfactory to the inhabitants.

In 1847 a change was made in the law, setting off the county of Stanstead into a separate municipality, and erecting the municipality of Sherbrooke out of the county of Sherbrooke, which then included the present counties of Compton, Richmond, Wolfe and Sherbrooke. In 1845 the law had been changed, creating local municipal councils, of seven members each, this being virtually the same as our present law with regard to municipal and county councils. The first meeting of the municipality of Sherbrooke was held at the Court House, in Sherbrooke, on Tuesday, October 12, 1847. Present, as members of the Council, from townships of Orford, Hollis Smith and John Griffith; Ascot, Wm. L. Felton and Charles Brooks; Brompton, Samuel Pierce and William Webb; Compton, Avery O. Kellum and Wm. Fling; Shipton, James Smith and James Bontelle; Melbourne, Adolphus Aylmer and David G. Sloane; Eaton, Newport, Ditton and Clinton, H. N. Hill and John Henry Pope; Dudswell, Windsor, Weedon and Stoke, James Munkittrick; Bury, Westbury and Lingwick, Hammond McClintock and James Ross; Hereford, Clifton and Auckland, Joseph Weston. Mr. Hollis Smith was chosen mayor, and Mr. J. G. Robertson, secretary-treasurer. The necessary "standing rules" were adopted. The mayors of the municipality of Sherbrooke were: 1847 to September, 1851, Hollis Smith; 1851 to September, 1852, A. G. Woodward; 1853 to end of the council of Sherbrooke in 1855, Charles Brooks. Mr. J. G. Robertson (after Confederation treasurer of the Province for several years) held the office of secretary-treasurer during the existence of the Council.

Again the law was changed, and in 1855 there came into force the "Lower Canada Municipal and Road Act," passed that same year. With few changes this law is still in force. In 1853 the county of Sherbrooke had been subdivided into the counties of Compton, Richmond, Wolfe and Sherbrooke. The new law above mentioned had been created to facilitate the transaction of municipal business in the different counties throughout the Province, which had been legislated into existence. Previous to 1855 the local municipal councils had very little power, and in many cases were not kept alive until after the passing of this Act. This is evidenced by there being no existing records of many townships previous to 1855. The county of Sherbrooke was included in the new county of Compton for municipal purposes.

"Agreeably to the provisions of the Lower Canada Municipal and Road Act of 1855, a meeting of the mayors of the several local councils in the county of Compton, was held at the Academy in Cookshire, in the township of Eaton, on Wednesday, September 5, 1855. There were present the following mayors: B. Pomroy, Compton; Charles Brooks, Ascot; A. P. Ball, town of Sherbrooke; Geo. Bonallie, Orford; C. A. Bailey, Eaton; A. Learned, Newport; L. Pope, jr., Bury; James Ross, Lingwick; Colin Noble, Winslow; D. H. Pope, Clifton; Levi R. Dean, Hereford." Mr. Charles Brooks was chosen as warden and Mr. S. A. Hurd as secretary-treasurer. The first by-law passed was one fixing Cookshire as the place for the future meetings of the Council. Up to December, 1856, all reference to money in Council proceedings was in pounds, shillings and pence. The first reckoning in dollars and cents is found on the aforesaid date. The value of rateable property in the county of Compton, according to the assessment rolls of 1856, was as follows: Ascot, $406,606; Westbury, $24,421; town of Sherbrooke, $564.900; Winslow, $25,080; Eaton, $300,205; Orford, $104,937; Lingwick, $99,238; Hereford, $90,763; Clifton, $92,192; Bury, $123,652; Compton, $416,946; Newport, $78,569; Auckland, $14,400; Ditton, $7,700; Clinton, $7,800; total amount, $2,357,410. In 1860 the total assessment had increased to $2,934,134.

In 1859 the county building, located in Cookshire, was purchased from the school commissioners of Eaton, having been used previous to that time as an academy.

From 1855 up to about 1880, many records are found of petitions having been sent to Parliament, praying for changes in laws, or protesting against proposed acts. Those motions on the part of the councillors show that they took a lively interest in the public affairs of the country.

The following resolutions, touching the rights of the Protestant minority at Confederation, show that Compton county, at least, was alive to their interests. On June 13, 1866, it was "moved by Councillor Chaddock, seconded by Councillor Lebourveau, and resolved: "That the warden and secretary-treasurer petition Parliament at its present session, to the effect that previous to Confederation of the British North American provinces, the rights of the Protestant minority in Lower Canada, as respects municipal and school matters, be guarded and protected in such a manner that hereafter, should Confederation take place, the majority may not have the power to interfere with the action of the Protestant minority on those points." At the forty-fifth quarterly session, September 12, 1866, "Councillor L. Pope moved the following resolutions, seconded by Councillor Lebourveau : 'That the warden and secretary-treasurer shall, on behalf of this council, petition the Imperial Parliament to the effect that the rights of the English-speaking Protestant community in Lower Canada be protected by the introduction into the constitution of Lower Canada of clauses therein similar to those introduced into the last session of the House of Assembly, but withdrawn, referring to educational matters. And that the Protestants in Lower Canada be allowed the management of their own schools and of contributing their money to the support of Protestant schools only, if they see fit, and that a committee consisting of the warden, secretary-treasurer and Councillor Robertson, prepare such petition." Carried unanimously.

On March 13, 1867, "The warden read and presented a copy of a despatch from the Secretary of State for the Colonies, acknowledging the receipt of a petition through the Hon. A. T. Galt, addressed to Her Majesty the Queen, and forwarded to him by the Governor-General's secretary, for the information of the council and municipal officers of the county of Compton." This petition stated that the Secretary of State for the Colonies would see that the subject of education for the minority should be thoroughly discussed with the representatives of British North America.

At a regular meeting of the council held on September 9, 1868, steps were taken to have a registry office established at Cookshire, which was done in the summer of 1869. Previous to this it was necessary to go to Sherbrooke for registration purposes.

In 1870 the townships of Compton, Orford, Ascot and town of Sherbrooke were separated from Compton county, and formed into the municipality of the county of Sherbrooke, for municipal purposes. This was partly brought about by the intense feeling caused by passing by-law No. 37.

On July 5, 1877, Sir John A. Macdonald visited Bury. At that time he was leader of the opposition, and had just enunciated his national policy, which was successful at the polls in 1878, and which has carried the Liberal-Conservatives to victory at every election since that date. Hon. John Henry Pope was one of his strongest supporters. On the above date a special meeting of the County Council was held, and an address, from which the following extracts are taken, adopted and presented to Sir John A. Macdonald at Bury : "It affords us the highest gratification to have this opportunity of expressing our entire confidence in you as the acknowledged chieftain of that great political party. * * * Through your ability, with the assistance of that great statesman, the late lamented Sir George E. Cartier, whose high-toned character calmed the conflicting elements of the various minds of a mixed population, has the great work of Confederation been accomplished. * * * We have every confidence in you as the leader of the present opposition * * * * and sympathize with you in your efforts, particularly the interest you have taken to obtain protection for our various industries and commercial enterprises, and we consider protection of so much importance to the welfare of this Dominion that unless it is obtained the result must inevitably cripple our industries, cramp our energies, and bring financial ruin upon our commercial interests. The retirement of your government from office has been a national calamity, and we look forward to a speedy return.

C. A. BAILEY,
Secretary-Treasurer.

THOS. BENNETT,
Warden.

J. W. Rogers.   G. M. Stearns.
V F Hodge.   R. Le Cowan.   A. Ross, Sec'y-Treas.   C. Martin.   R Campeau
J D. Morrison.   P. Rosa.   E. Roberge.   C. N. Cass.

MEMBERS COMPTON COUNTY COUNCIL for 1895.

In 1878 the members of the County Council, by a large majority, were strong supporters of the Conservative party. They took a lively interest in politics, as evidenced by the following resolution, passed March 13, 1878, with only one dissenting: "Moved by Councillor Paquette, seconded by Councillor McDonald, and resolved: 'That we, the warden and county councillors of the county of Compton, in council assembled, regret to see the unjustifiable course taken by the Lieutenant-Governor, in regard to the late crisis in the Quebec Legislature, and do condemn his actions, believing them to be, if not unconstitutional, subversive of the rights of a free people, such as we, British colonists, claim to be. That we

HISTORY OF COMPTON COUNTY.

unanimously and heartily endorse the course taken by our representative in the Legislature during the late crisis and wish to extend to him our continued confidence and esteem.' "

From 1855 down to the present day, the wardens of Compton county have been men of exceptional ability. As the parliamentary representatives from Compton county have always been men who took leading parts in the governments of the country, so the wardens have been men above the average in ability. The following is a complete list, with years they were in office: 1855-63, Charles Brooks; 1864-66, A. W. Kendrick; 1867-70, Benj. Pomroy; 1871-72, L. Pope; 1873-76, Moses Lebourveau; 1877-79, Thos. Bennett; 1880-81, Moses Lebourveau; 1882 until his death, October 14, 1885, Lewis McIver. The Council passed

H. A. CAIRNS. J. P. Wilson. K. W. McLeod. Allan McLeod. Hugh Leonard. J. Hunt.
E. Grenier. Wm. Lefebvre. A. S. Farnsworth, *Warden.* Jos. Agagnier. P. L. N. Prevost.

MEMBERS COMPTON COUNTY COUNCIL for 1895.

resolutions of sympathy and attended the funeral in a body. December 9, 1885-86, Charles McClary; 1887, A. Ross; 1888, W. H. Learned; 1889, C. H. Parker; 1890, A. Grenier; 1891 until his resignation in September, 1892, W. H. Learned; balance of year 1892, Jos. Agagnier; 1893, Hugh Leonard; 1894, Nap. Lemieux; 1895, A. S. Farnsworth. There have been only three secretary-treasurers during all these forty years. Mr. S. A. Hurd was appointed at the first meeting in 1855. He resigned March 9, 1864, when Mr. C. A. Bailey was appointed and held the office for twenty-six years. His resignation being submitted, the present secretary-treasurer, Mr. Alexander Ross, was appointed September 30, 1890.

HISTORY OF COMPTON COUNTY.

During the year 1895, the Council for the county of Compton, was composed of twenty-one members. On January 1, 1896, the municipality of Clifton, familiarly known as West Clifton, was divided, by act of the Provincial Legislature, passed in 1895, into St. Edwidge de Clifton and Clifton, Martinville and the English-speaking portion retaining the name of Clifton. Engravings of all the members of the County Council for 1895 will be found on adjoining pages, including the secretary-treasurer, A. Ross, Esq. Following will be found a short sketch of each councillor:

Artemus Stevens Farnsworth, warden of Compton county and mayor of the township of Newport, was born in Eaton, December 3, 1855. He is one of the successful farmers of the County, his farm being located between Clauders and Sawyerville. He has been councillor for the past eight years, and mayor for three years. Married in Newport, October 9, 1884, to Luvia A. Bowker. Issue, four children.

Volney French Hodge, mayor of the township of Eaton, was born in Eaton, November 18, 1850. Farmer by occupation. He has held the office of councillor for three years. Married at Sawyerville, May 21, 1873, to Mary Edith Clough. Issue, one daughter.

Hugh Leonard, mayor of South Winslow, was born in Bury, November 29, 1847. Has held the office of mayor for twenty-one years and warden in 1893. He is a justice of the peace, and a large mill owner and trader. Has never married.

George McClellan Stearns, mayor of Lake Megantic, was born at Stanstead Plain, April 16, 1864. Came to Lake Megantic in 1889, and at present holds the position of manager of pulp mills, belonging to the Montague Paper Company. Has held the office of mayor for two years. Married at Burlington, Vt., January 16, 1890, to Katharine Johnson. Issue, one daughter.

Allan MacLeod, mayor of Marston, was born in North Ely, Que., September 1, 1843. Came to Lingwick in 1846, and moved onto his present farm in 1854. Was secretary-treasurer of Marston for thirteen years, and mayor the past ten years. Married at Lake Megantic, December 29, 1869, to Anna MacDonald. Issue, six children.

James Frederic Wilson, mayor of Westbury, was born in Compton, March 14, 1858; moved to East Angus in 1884. He is a member of the firm of Planche, Wilson & Co., general merchants. Married at Haskell Hill, near Lennoxville, February 18, 1880, to Mary M. Johnston. Issue, four children.

James Hunt, mayor of Bury, was born in England, June 22, 1835. Came to Bury in 1836. Is a prosperous carriage-maker and trader. Has been a member of the Council, its mayor, and a justice of the peace for a number of years. Married in Bury, December 20, 1859, to Jane Stokes. Issue, three children.

Pierre Louis Napoleon Prévost, mayor of Ditton and Clinton, was born in Quebec city, May 11, 1856. He came to Ditton in 1876, where he has followed farming principally. Has been school commissioner several years, and a municipal councillor since 1878. For several years Mr. Prévost was one of the associate editors of *Le Pionnier*, of Sherbrooke. He married Céline Morel de la Durantaye, at La Patrie, September 4, 1877. Issue, nine children.

Elzear Roberge, mayor of Chesham, was born at St. Norbert d'Arthabaska, June 25, 1864. Came to Chesham in 1875, where he has followed farming and kept a general store at Notre-Dame-des-Bois. He held the office of secretary-treasurer for seven years. Was married at Chesham, July 6, 1886, to Marie A. D. Laplante. Issue, one son.

Kenneth W. MacLeod, mayor of Whitton, was born in Winslow, May 4, 1857. He has held the offices of school commissioner seven years, councillor six years, and mayor two years. Is one of the successful farmers of Whitton. First marriage April 10, 1885, to Catharine MacIver, who died in 1891, leaving four children. Second marriage August 30, 1893, to Mrs. Annie MacLeay. Issue, one child.

Carlos N. Cass, mayor of Clifton, was born in Stanstead, January 20, 1838. Came to Martinville in 1846, and is now a successful mill owner and lumber dealer. Has been councillor of his town for a number of years. Mr. Cass has been married twice. First to Sarah Clark; second marriage to Lora A. Pierce. Issue, four children.

Charles Martin, mayor of Emberton, was born in North Ham, Que., May 13, 1855. Came to Emberton in March, 1876, where he has been a successful farmer. Married Marie Bissonette, January 12, 1873. Issue six children.

Remi Campeau, mayor of North Winslow, was born at St. Romain, September 12, 1859. He has always lived in his native place and is one of the leading farmers. He married Phebroma Gagné. Issue, four children.

Pierre Rosa, mayor of North Whitton, was born in St. Anselme, Que. He came to Ste. Cecile in 1876. A farmer by occupation. Was married at St. Sébastien, Que., to Marie Maheux. Issue, three children.

Alfred Lefebvre, mayor of Hereford, was born in Yamaska county, September 17, 1837. Came to Paquetteville in 1861. Occupation, farmer and carpenter. Has been a councillor of Hereford for over ten years. Was married January 7, 1859, to Herminie Maloin. Issue, three children.

Hollis Alpheus Cairns, mayor of East Clifton, was born in Eaton, January 1, 1853. Has held the office of mayor since 1884, and postmaster for over twenty years. A successful farmer. Married 9th July, 1884, in Compton, to Sarah A. Harkness. Issue, two children.

Joseph Agagnier, mayor of Auckland, was born at Laprairie, Que., March 31, 1842. Came to St. Malo in 1868, and is now a leading farmer and mill owner. Has held the office of councillor since 1870 and of mayor since 1875. Married in Chateauguay county, September 9, 1867, to Françoise Gagnier. Issue, three children.

Joseph Edmond Grenier, mayor of South Marston, was born in Montreal, in 1850. He purchased a farm and moved to Piopolis in 1872, where he was married in 1876. Issue, thirteen children.

Randal Young Cowan, mayor of Lingwick, was born in the same township, February 10, 1842, where he has always lived. Has been councillor and school commissioner for a number of years, and is a prominent member of the R. T. of T. Mr. Cowan was one of the first children born in Lingwick. He married Sarah Young, of Lingwick, on April 28, 1869, Issue, six children.

John D. Morrison, mayor of Hampden, was born at South Dell, Ness, Scotland, October 1, 1852. Came to Compton county with his parents in 1856. At present he is postmaster at Millen, also mill owner and lumber dealer. Mr. Morrison married Effie Campbell. Issue, five children.

John Willard Rogers, mayor of Sawyerville, was born in Eaton, January 3, 1844. Moved onto his present farm in 1879. Was a councillor in Eaton for nine years, and mayor of Sawyerville for several years. Married at Huntingville, Que., January 21, 1879, to Mrs. Hibbard. Issue, one daughter.

Alexander Ross, secretary-treasurer for the county of Compton, was born in Lingwick, August 1, 1850. Was secretary-treasurer of the school commissioners from the time he was sixteen years of age until he was twenty-one. A member of the board for twelve years, and chairman most of that time. He was a councillor for seventeen years, mayor of Lingwick for fifteen years, and warden of the County in 1887. He was in trade in Lingwick and Scotstown until 1889, and first mail clerk on the old International railway. Mr. Ross moved to Cookshire in September, 1890, when he was appointed secretary-treasurer of the County. In January, 1891, he received the appointment as first collector of customs for the port of Cookshire. On July 13, 1892, he was married to Ada Planche.

CHAPTER IX.

THE MILITIA.

Early History—Organization First Troops—Hereford Railway Riot—Present Officers.

THE military history of Compton county dates back to about the time the first settlers came into the Eastern Townships. Many of those hardy pioneers had taken part in the Revolutionary war between England and her colonies, now forming the United States. Their sympathies, however, were in accord with England's form of government, and losing all, they were obliged to make homes elsewhere than in those states which had been granted their independence. The many thousands thus situated wended their way, principally to the townships in Ontario, but there were also several hundred families who came to the Eastern Townships. A military spirit came with these men, and quite naturally they and their descendants have always been found ready to defend the country of their choice. The first records of any military force in the County date back to the time of the second war between England and the United States in 1812-15. At that time there was in Eaton an organized company, under the command of Colonel John Pope, the great-grand-father of R. H. Pope, Esq., M. P. This company was ordered to report at St. Johns, Que., but when they reached Compton village, on their march to St. Johns, the order was countermanded and they returned to their homes. It is said the order was given more to test their allegiance than for any other purpose. In 1823 Capt. John Pope, father of Hon. John Henry Pope, raised a troop of cavalry, and July 4 was the day appointed for organization. The first authentic and published records are found in Jos. Bouchette's works on Canada, who was, for upward of thirty years, surveyor-general for Lower Canada. The Government in 1830 called upon the county of Sherbrooke, which then included, Compton, Richmond and Wolfe, to form "one battalion of infantry and two troops of volunteer cavalry." The act under which these were formed, called for "every able-bodied male inhabitant of the Province, above eighteen and under sixty years," as liable to serve as militiamen, unless exempted by law. Exemptions, however, were very numerous, being extended to the "clergy, civil and military officers of His Majesty's Government, physicians and surgeons, notaries, land surveyors, ferrymen, millers, all teachers of colleges, academies and schools." (See Bouchette's works.) This law applied to the sedentary militia, and as a reserve is still in force. The sedentary militia, however, is a dead letter at the present day, having become so by neglect on the part of the Government, which have not appointed the officers, as they have passed away. This was not the original intention of the militia law of 1855, but rather that the sedentary militia should be always ready as a reserve. Back in the days when this militia was the only protection the County had, they would meet once a year at their military head-quarters. Cookshire was always a military centre, and here would congregate the many men for their annual one day's drill. Everyone in those days was expected to partake of a little whiskey for their stomach's sake, and at these annual meetings as they gathered around the hotellier, the renowned saying, "If this be war let there never be peace," was often heard. Mr. Charles Lebourveau, in his short history of Eaton, published in 1894, mentions that during the Papineau rebellion he, in company with nine others, was stationed at Sherbrooke for two weeks. And a guard was kept there during the winter, ten men being relieved every fourteen days. The Court House was used as a barrack.

On August 16, 1855, the present law authorizing "Active or Volunteer Militia Force," was issued as general order No. 1.

Militia general orders, under date of Toronto, February 7, 1856, authorized the formation of the following:

"Military District Number Four, Lower Canada: One troop of volunteer militia cavalry, at Cookshire, to be styled the Cookshire Troop of Volunteer Militia Cavalry, the following officers are appointed to this troop, viz.: To be captain, John Henry Pope, esquire; to be lieutenant, James H. Cook, gentleman; to be cornet, William Cumming, gentleman; to be sergeant instructor, Geo. P. Ward; to be bugler, Erastus Caswell."

This was the first troop organized in Sherbrooke or Compton county under this new act.

On March 20, 1856, a company was organized at Sherbrooke, Que., to be known as No. 1 Rifle Company, with officers as follows: captain, W. E. Ibbotson; lieutenant, ——— Hopkinson; ensign, W. A. Morehouse.

For the first ten or twelve years it was difficult to keep the Cookshire troop of cavalry in existence, and, in fact, it did become extinct, at two different times, in all but name. John Henry Pope (afterwards the Hon. J. H. Pope) retired with rank of major, February 1, 1859. On July 18, 1862, the first reorganization took place, when the following officers were gazetted: captain, James H. Cook; lieutenant, Geo. P. Ward; cornet, Craig Pope.

At the time of the Fenian scare on the border, in 1866, the troop was again re-organized and to this day has been kept under orders and ready for all emergencies. At this time the following officers were gazetted: captain, Wm. Winder; lieutenant, J. H. Taylor; cornet, C. W. B. French. The troop was immediately ordered to Stanstead Plain, to repel the gathering of Fenians, and were on active service from the 10th to the 19th of June, of that year.

Again in the year 1870, with Lieutenant J. H. Taylor as captain; lieutenant, C. W. B. French; and cornet, Henry Claddock, the Cookshire troop was on active service, from April 10 to 30, and from May 24 till June 7, at Frelighsburg, Que. They assisted in repelling the second attempt of the Fenians, and arrived within a few hours after the fight at Eccles Hill, having been several miles away at the time.

The first infantry company in Compton county was organized March 9, 1866, at Bury. This was brought about through the instrumentality of Captain F. M. Pope, who was at the time attending the military school in Montreal. Those in authority were aware of the intended Fenian raids and commenced to prepare accordingly. Captain Pope, who was then only a young man, by request left the school and started at once for his home, where, in a few months, he organized no less than four companies of infantry.

On October 11, 1867, a battalion was organized from the following independent companies, to be known as the 58th Battalion of Infantry, with headquarters at Robinson :—To be lieutenant-colonel acting until further orders—James H. Cook, Esquire ; to be majors acting until further orders—Colin Noble, Esquire, and N. O. Kellum, Esquire ; to be adjutant and battalion drill instructor (temporary)—Captain F. M. Pope, M. S., from No. 1 Company.

List of original corps of which battalion was formed :—No. 1 Company, Bury, organized March 9, 1866, captain—F. M. Pope, lieutenant———, ensign—Edmond Lockett; No. 2 Company, Gould, organized November 16, 1866, captain—J. W. Vaughn, lieutenant—A. McKennon, ensign—Alex. Ross; No. 3 Company, Winslow, organized November 16, 1866, captain—W. McDonald, lieutenant—J. T. McIver, ensign—Donald Beaton ; No. 4 Company,

Marbleton, organized November 16, 1866, captain—H. J. Wayland, lieutenant—W. W. Wayland, ensign—H. Lothrop; No. 5 Company, Lake Megantic, organized March 22, 1867, captain—J. D. Ramage, lieutenant—J. B. McDonald, ensign—R. McLeod; No. 6 Company, Compton, organized March 22, 1867, captain—C. D. Rice, lieutenant—W. B. Ives, ensign—W. A. Snow; No. 7 Company, Coaticook, organized June 8, 1866, captain—A. Shurtliff, lieutenant—D. P. Baldwin, ensign—D. T. Baldwin; No. 8 Company, Stanstead, organized June 8, 1866, captain—Jas. K. Gilman, lieutenant—A. Drew, ensign—J. S. Terrill; No. 9 Company, Winslow, organized May 29, 1868, captain—D. McIver, lieutenant—M. Leonard, ensign—M. McAuley; No. 10 Company, Eaton, organized May 29, 1868, captain—H. Bailey, lieutenant—Allen T. Hodge, ensign—Alonzo Sanborn. The last two companies were organized and added to the battalion after it had been formed.

On November 3, 1877, the 5th Provisional Regiment of Cavalry was organized by the consolidation of the following independent troops of cavalry, which had been organized as follows:—Cookshire No. 1 Troop, organized February 7, 1857, captain—C. W. B. French, lieutenant—Oliver A. Taylor, cornet—Henry Chaddock; Sherbrooke No. 2 Troop, organized November 13, 1860, captain—Lieutenant John Drummond, late Sherbrooke Cavalry, lieutenant—Wright Chamberlain, cornet—Simon Augustus Stevens; Stanstead No. 3 Troop, organized February 23, 1872, captain—Israel Wood, lieutenant—David A. Mansur, cornet—John W. Molton; Compton No. 4 Troop, organized February 23, 1872, captain—Frederick Smith Stimson, lieutenant—Walter George Murray, cornet—Edward William Jennings.

On November 14, 1879, the Sutton Troop of Cavalry, which was organized April 26, 1872, with the following officers, was attached to the 5th regiment, and was known as No. 5 Troop:—captain—S. N. Boright, lieutenant—Joseph P. Billings; cornet—James C. Gleason. The major commanding the regiment was: major and brevet—Lt. Col. John Henry Taylor, from the Cookshire Troop of Cavalry. The regiment wore the Hussar uniform.

In the fall of 1888, during the building of the Hereford Railway, two of the contractors absconded, one owing about one thousand Italians for their labor. These men, ignorant of the language and laws of the country, threatened to destroy the property of the railway company, and do other damage. They went so far that the warden of the County, W. H. Learned, Esq., and two justices of the peace, deemed it advisable to call out the militia to protect life and property. The following report made by the commanding officer, Lt. Col. F. M. Pope, covers fully the work of the militia:

"BURY, October 15, 1888.

"SIR,—I have the honor to report to you, for the information of the Adjutant-General of Militia, that on the twenty-fifth day of September last, at 6 P. M., I received a requisition from the warden and two justices of the peace of the county of Compton, requesting me to call out the militia in aid of the civil power. The information I received was to the effect that eight hundred Italians who had been employed upon what is known as the Hereford Railway, had been defrauded of their pay by the absence of the contractors, which had so enraged the Italians that they had taken possession of the railway, and that the lives and property of the people in the vicinity were in danger. I therefore ordered out companies Nos. 1, 2, 3, 4, 5, 9 and 10 of the 58th Battalion, which were concentrated at Cookshire on the following evening, being altogether about 200 men (the railway company having placed at my disposal an engine and some box cars). The next morning, upon the arrival of ammunition from Montreal, I despatched the cavalry to Sawyerville, a village about six miles from Cookshire, where trouble was anticipated, with orders to reconnoiter and report to me at the railway about two miles this side of the said village. I then proceeded with the infantry on board the train to Sawyerville, having taken all necessary precaution against accidents from rails being taken up, etc. Upon arrival, I found a hundred Italians who were in a very excited state, flourishing clubs and revolvers. Work was at once resumed by the men who had been driven off by the Italians the day before. The day passed off without any collision taking place.

"Not being able to billet more than one-half of the force at Sawyerville, I occupied it with the Troop of Cavalry and two companies of Infantry, returning with the balance to Cookshire for the night with the exception of a guard composed of one company which I placed to guard a valuable trussel bridge which the railway company were afraid would be blown up as the Italians had dynamite in their possession.

"During the evening alarming reports from Hereford reached me, and Mr. Ives, the managing-director of the company, requested that at least seventy-five men should be sent there at once. I then ordered out the captains of No. 6, Hatley, No. 7, Coaticook, and No. 8, Stanstead, to call out the men and proceed across country to the end of the road. The next morning, making an early start, brought up the men from Cookshire by train. The company having informed me that they feared that three store houses situated from eight to ten miles above Sawyerville with about $500 worth of property would be destroyed, I dispatched eighty men and four officers, under the command of Col. Taylor, to occupy and protect the said store-houses. The troop of cavalry I employed to patrol the roads leading to Sawyerville and to keep up communication between the different points guarded. Having been informed that the Italians were gathering in large numbers, up the line, with the intention of attacking the men who were laying iron, I proceeded with the balance of my force (consisting of about eighty men) to that point, where I found about three hundred Italians gathered. They were all armed with clubs and other weapons, and were very excited, and swore they would sooner die than allow the work to proceed. I took possession of a knoll about fifty paces from them and formed my men into a square, which gave me a very strong position. The magistrate then read the riot act, and as one of the Italian leaders could read English I had him read and interpret, the same to them. I then explained to them their position, threatening if they did not disperse within ten minutes I would fire upon them. They waited until the last minute, when they broke up and dispersed. I was subsequently informed that it was their intention to mix up with the troops and, being five or six to one, to grab the men's rifles, and as some of them had revolvers they thought, at close quarters, to get the better of the troops. But as they were made to keep at a distance, a collision was again averted. I had then sixteen miles of the Cookshire end of the road under military protection. As the Deputy Adjutant-General arrived during the night and was made acquainted with the position of affairs, he decided to proceed to Hereford and take command of that end of the line, taking with him the cavalry, one officer and fifteen men of the Infantry in wagons. Nothing of note took place at this end of the line until October 3 when I received notice in writing from the magistrate and wardens that the difficulties were arranged and that the militia were no longer required. I would add that the troops under my command behaved in a most exemplary way. I did not have to punish a man for misbehavior, nor was there a complaint from the inhabitants where they were quartered during the whole time.

I have the honor to be your obedient servant,

F. M. POPE, Lieutenant-Colonel,
Commander 58th Battalion.

To the Deputy Adjutant-General,
Commander M. D. No. 5, Montreal, P. Q.

List of officers who were out during the Hereford Railway Riots, and took part in the suppression of same:

Staff—Lieutenant-Colonel F. M. Pope, in command; Lieutenant-Colonel J. H. Taylor, Major M. B. McAuley, Adjutant E. S. Baker, Surgeon F. J. Austen, M. D., Surgeon Eli Ives, M. D., Quarter Master R. Wright; No. 1 Troop, 5th Regiment Cavalry—Captain J. F. Learned, Lieutenant G. W. L. French; No. 1 Company, 58th Battalion—Captain A. L. McIver, Lieutenant H. R. Bishop; No. 2—Captain A. Ross; No. 3—Captain J. F. McIver, Lieutenant G. L. McLeod; No. 4—Captain W. W. Weyland, Lieutenant C. Lothrop; No. 5—Captain Donald Beaton; Lieutenant J. B. McDonald; 2d Lieutenant M. Mackenzie; No. 6—Captain G. P. Hitchcock, Lieutenant George C. Billington, 2d Lieutenant H. M. Percy; No. 7—Captain R. G. Trenholm, Lieutenant C. W. Edwards; No. 8—Captain John Clark; No. 9—Captain James Kelly, Lieutenant B. McAuley; No. 10—Lieutenant C. W. Reade, acting captain.

The officers of the 58th Battalion of Infantry, on January 1, 1896, were as follows:

Lieutenant Colonel—Malcolm B. McAuley; Major—Edward S. Baker; Captains—No. 1 Company, Alexander Lewis McIver; No. 2, P. J. Gillies; No. 3, J. T. McIver; No. 4, R. W. Weyland; No. 5, Donald Beaton; No. 6, Gilbert P. H. Hitchcock; No. 7, Robert George Trenholm; No. 8, Hugh T. Elder; No. 9, ———; No. 10, Samuel H. Botterill; Lieutenants—No. 1 Company, ———; No. 2, John Macdonald; No. 3, ———; No. 4, Benj. A. Gilbert; No. 5, M. A. McLeod; No. 6, George C. Billington; No. 7, ———; No. 8, William P. Jenkins; No. 9, James Kelly; No. 10, ———; 2d Lieutenants—No. 1 Company, Osborne L. Pope; No. 2, ———; No. 3, Duncan L. McLeod and Henry W. Albro; No. 4, Levi Gilbert; No. 5, M. McKenzie; No. 6, Walter H. Murray; No. 7, ———; No. 8, James Park Breevoort; No. 9, Gilanders McIver; No. 10, Chas. N. Reade; Paymaster—Edmund Lockett, honorary major; Quartermaster—Robert Wright; Surgeon—R. H. Phillimore, M. D.; Company headquarters—No. 1 Company, Bury (Robinsons); No. 2, Scotstown; No. 3, Marsborough; No. 4, Marbleton; No. 5, Milan; No. 6, Massawippi; No. 7, Coaticook; No. 8, Beebe Plain; No. 9, Winslow; No. 10, Cookshire.

The 5th Provisional Regiment of Cavalry was uniformed and adopted the name of 5th Dragoons in June, 1893. The officers on January 1, 1896, were as follows:

Headquarters—Cookshire, P. Q.; Lieutenant Colonel—John Henry Taylor; Major—John F. Learned; Captains—A Troop, Cookshire, H. S. Farnsworth; B Troop, Sherbrooke, G. L. McNicoll; C Troop, Stanstead, John Clark; D Troop, Compton, Albert Lee Pomroy; E Troop, Sutton, Josiah S. Billings; Lieutenants—A Troop, ———; B Troop, Rupert F. Morkill; C Troop, George B. Hall; D Troop, ———; E Troop, Edwin B. Greely; 2d Lieutenants—A Troop, Alex. R. Pennoyer and George W. French; B Troop, Frank J. Barton; C Troop, Ben. B. Morrill; D Troop, F. W. Thompson; E Troop, Wm. C. Strong; Paymaster—Herbert A. Taylor; Quartermaster—Horace H. Pope; Surgeon—Alexander Dewar, M. D.; Veterinary Surgeon—Erastus P. Ball, V. S.

CHAPTER X.

RAILWAYS OF COMPTON COUNTY.

Grand Trunk—Canadian Pacific—Maine Central—Quebec Central.

THE first railway built in Compton county was a link of the old St. Lawrence and Atlantic Railway, which afterwards became part of the Grand Trunk Railway. This traverses through the township of Compton, from north to south, separating it into nearly equal proportions. The inception of this line was due to J. Pennoyer and Colonel John Moore, who first indoctrinated Sir A. T. Galt—who was at that time commissioner of the British American Land Company—with the importance to Canada of connecting the Atlantic sea-board with the St. Lawrence. The active and powerful mind of Mr. Galt gave effect to the suggestion of his subordinates, and after great difficulties the line was completed in 1852.

The Quebec Central Railway, giving a short line connection between Sherbrooke and Quebec, was built in 1875. To the Hon. J. G. Robertson is due the honor of the building of this road, which is now one of the best paying railway investments in America. In 1895, when a great depression was felt all over the country, the Quebec Central Railway was the only road in the United States or Canada that paid a dividend on its capital. This road passes through the township of Westbury, with one station at East Angus.

The two principal railways of the County are the Canadian Pacific and Maine Central. The former purchased the old International and the latter leased the Hereford Railway. As both of these roads were in their inception and completion due to the residents of Compton county, their history in full is here given.

INTERNATIONAL RAILWAY.

To the late Hon. John Henry Pope is due the credit for constructing the old International Railway, and its use as a connecting link of the Canadian Pacific Railway short line to Halifax, N. S. For many years before the charter was secured, Mr. Pope's energies and influence were directed toward building this road. And after it was completed it was his own private funds which, at different times, paid the expenses of the road and kept it open for traffic.

By Act 33, Victoria, assented to May 12, 1870, the following persons were incorporated as the St. Francis and Megantic International Railway Company: Benjamin Pomroy, Charles Brooks, Richard William Heneker, William Farwell, the younger; Lemuel Pope, Cyrus A. Bailey, Colin Noble, Edward Towle Brooks, William Farwell and Stephen Edgell, Esquires. "The said company and their agents and servants may lay out, construct and finish a double or single track, iron railway, from Sherbrooke to the Province line at a point near Lake Megantic, there to connect with a line of railway in the State of Maine, about to be constructed, and which will connect with the European and North American Railway, or a branch thereof, so as to form a continuous railway from the Grand Trunk

to the city of St. John, N. B. The capital stock of the said company shall not exceed, in the whole, the sum of $1,500,000, to be divided into thirty thousand shares, of $50 each."
The provisional directors were: John Henry Pope, M. P., Hon. John Sewall Sanborn, Hon. Sir Alexander Tilloch Galt, James Ross, M. P. P., Charles Brooks, Richard W. Heneker, Thomas S. Morey, Benjamin Pomroy, Cyrus A. Bailey, Lemuel Pope, Colin Noble and Lewis McIver, Esquires.

The annual general meetings were held on first Monday in September, of each year. At that time no bonuses were granted by the governments of the day to aid in building railways. For this reason those promoting the enterprise were obliged to use every effort possible to secure funds sufficient to go ahead with the work. In 1870 the town of Sherbrooke, and townships of Ascot, Orford and Compton, were included in Compton county for municipal purposes. As the proposed railway would pass through eight municipalities in the County, it was advocated that the County Council take a certain number of shares, in order to help along the work. The action of the Council raised a great deal of opposition, especially from those townships which would not receive the least benefit and still be obliged to pay their share of the liability. And down to the present day this bitter feeling against the well-known by-law, No. 37 remains in some cases almost unabated. During the rest of the political life of the late Hon. John Henry Pope, his opponents used this as their only weapon against him, while some attempt at the present day to use it as an argument against his son, R. H. Pope, M. P.

The action of the County Council over the question of subscribing for stock, having occupied so much of the mind of the public, during the past twenty-five years, the following particulars, in regard to the same, have been taken from the journal of the County Council proceedings.

On May 25, 1870, at a special session of the County Council, the secretary-treasurer, C. A. Bailey, Esq., presented petitions from Sherbrooke, Ascot, Eaton and Bury, asking that a special session of the County Council be held for the purpose of considering the propriety of extending aid to the "St. Francis and Megantic International Railway." "The Council took up the matter and after hearing addresses from the Hon. J. S. Sanborn, J. H. Pope, M. P., and others, it was deemed advisable; and by-law No. 35 read three times and passed, that the county of Compton subscribe for stock to the amount of $225,540. The votes of the qualified municipal electors in each local municipality were cast on the 21st and 22nd days of June, 1870. On June 30, another special meeting of the Council was held, when a report of the result of the votes cast for and against by-law No. 35, was laid before the Council. "The municipalities of Eaton, Bury, Newport, Lingwick, South Winslow and Whitton, 6--Yea. Auckland, Clifton, Orford, Westbury, North Winslow, Compton and Ascot, 7—Nay. No returns received from Sherbrooke or Hereford." There being a majority of votes against the by-law, the Council took no further action.

At the sixtieth quarterly session of the County Council, held September 14, 1870, petitions from the inhabitants of Sherbrooke and Westbury, and resolutions from the local councils of Bury and Newport, were presented, praying the Council to pass a by-law similar to No. 35, for the purpose of extending aid to the "St. Francis and Megantic International Railway." These petitions were referred to a committee composed of Messrs. L. Pope, H. Moe and John Keenan. After due consideration Messrs. Pope and Keenan brought in a report in favor of granting aid to the railway, Councillor Moe dissenting. On the report being put to a vote with the warden, B. Pomroy, Esq., in the chair, it was accepted on the following division : Councillors Brooks (Ascot), Sawyer (Eaton), Pope (Bury), McLeod (Whitton), Planche (Newport), Keenan (Lingwick), 6—Yea. Councillors Robertson (Sherbrooke), Moe (Orford), Claxton (Westbury), Hibbard (Hereford), 4—Nay. Councillors Haseltine (Clifton), Noble (South Winslow), Marceau (North Winslow), and Beloin (Auckland), were absent. It was ordered that the by-law No. 37 should be presented to the qualified electors of the local municipalities on the 18th and 19th of October, 1870, for their decision. An adjourned session of the Council was held on October 28, when the returns from the local municipalities on by-law 37, were received, resulting as follows: Municipalities of Whitton, Newport, South Winslow, Lingwick, Westbury, Bury, Eaton and town of Sherbrooke, 8—Yea. Municipalities of North Winslow, Auckland, Clifton, Compton and Ascot, 5.—Nay. No returns had been received from Hereford and Orford, but the mayors of these municipalities verbally said the vote had been nay. The by-law had carried by only one municipality.

On June 14, 1871, a resolution was passed authorizing the issuance of county bonds to the amount of $225,540, as authorised under by-law No. 37, payable in twenty-five years, with interest at six per cent. For several years the County was constantly harassed with law suits over the legality of this by-law, in which it won all, settling for ever the question of its legality. The feeling was so strong over this that in 1871 the municipalities of town of Sherbrooke, and townships of Ascot, Orford and Compton, withdrew from Compton county for municipal purposes, and formed a new municipality, known as the county of Sherbrooke.

Work was commenced on the railway in the winter of 1871-72. On July 15, 1875, the line was completed and opened for traffic between Sherbrooke and Bury. The following address was presented by the County Council to the Hon. John Henry Pope and Directors of the "St. Francis and Megantic International Railway," at the public opening of the railway on the above date:

"SIRS,—We have much pleasure in offering to you and those gentlemen who have so zealously laboured with you as directors, our congratulations upon the completion of the first section of this railway. The part that you gentlemen have taken in the promotion of this great enterprise, demands from us a recognition of the important services which you have rendered to this county. And sir, the confidence which we have reposed in you for many years, we feel has not been misplaced, and that in all your public career you have diligently and with the purest intention laboured for the interests of the country generally and this county in particular. * * * Associated as you are with gentlemen who share with you a deep interest in the promotion of this great undertaking, we have the fullest confidence that the work so far completed under your auspices, with many opposing elements, will be brought to a successful termination, and we beg to assure you that we shall ever remain your most sincere friends and supporters."

Signed on behalf of the Compton County Council.

C. A. BAILEY, M. LEBOURVEAU,
Secretary-Treasurer. *Warden.*

By Act 40, Victoria, assented to 28th April, 1877, the name of the St. Francis and Megantic International Railway, was altered to "The International Railway Company." The limitation of the issue of bonds was also changed to "$30,000 per mile, not to bear interest exceeding seven per cent."

In March, 1879, the railway was completed as far as Lake Megantic, at which date the following gentlemen were on the directorate: Hon. J. H. Pope, president; E. T. Brooks, vice-president; R. W. Heneker, T. S. Morey, M. H. Cochrane; C. C. Colby; L. McIver, L. Pope, Chas. Brooks, and C. Noble; J. Davidson, secretary.

On June 9, 1886, a special committee composed of councillors Charles McClary, W. H. Learned, J. A. Chicoyne, J. H. Morin, A. Ross and H. A. Cairns, made a report to the County Council, on an examination made into the affairs of the International Railway, in which the County held a large number of shares. A perusal of this report shows that up to September, 1885, $1,227,841.19 had been expended on the permanent way, an average of $14,973.67 per mile. "The road, although worked with extreme economy and showing a profit on its working, has never been able, out of net income, to pay the full interest on its bonded debt.

On September 8, 1886, a communication was read from W. B. Ives, Esq., authorized by Sir George Stephen, offering to purchase the stock in the International Railway, owned by the County, at fifty cents in the dollar, or a sum total of $112,500. After strong appeals made in favor of accepting the offer, by representatives from the County Council of Sherbrooke and city of Sherbrooke, a resolution was passed disposing of the shares for this amount. The money from the sale was used in purchasing the County bonds, at a premium of sixteen per cent.

On November 2, 1886, the International Railway Company, was acquired by the Atlantic and Northwest Railway Company, which in turn was leased to the Canadian Pacific Railway Company in perpetuity. At the time of the acquisition of the line by the Atlantic and Northwest Railway Company, the following gentlemen composed the directorate:

W. C. Van Horne, president; T. G. Shaughnessy, vice-president; Sir Donald A. Smith, K. C. M. G.; Sir Geo. Stephen, Bart; J. J. C. Abbott, R. B. Angus, E. B. Osler, Wm. Whyte, Sandford Fleming, and J. Davidson, secretary; D. E. McFee, general manager.

This road now forms a link of the Canadian Pacific Railway short line between Montreal and Halifax, with a large passenger and freight traffic.

HEREFORD RAILWAY.

For several years prior to work being commenced by the Hereford Railway Company, Mr. Wm. Sawyer, ex-M. L. A., and others, spent money and time in trying to have a road built from Cookshire through to the boundary line in Hereford. A few years before, A. M. Shanley, civil engineer, attempted to survey a route, passing through Paquetteville. He was not successful, and was obliged to give it up. At the time this was kept very quiet, in order that the prospects for building the railway might not be injured, for the promoters were men who were determined to succeed. If the road could not go one way they were determined some feasible route should be found; and the excellent railway that connects Cookshire, Sawyerville, and other places in Compton county with all the leading cities in the United States, speaks louder than words as to the foresight of those men.

In 1887, by Act 50-51, Victoria, chap. 93, the "Hereford Branch Railway" was incorporated. The petitioners and provisional directors were: John McIntosh, of Compton, merchant; Wm. Sawyer, merchant; Cyrus A. Bailey, farmer; Rufus H. Pope, farmer; Alden Learned, inn-keeper, all of Eaton; F. Paquette, of Hereford, merchant, and George Van Dyke, of McIndoe's Falls, N. H., lumberman. Mr. C. A. Bailey was appointed secretary-treasurer of the Company. The line authorized to be constructed is described in the Act as a railway to connect the Atlantic and Northwest Railway, now Canadian Pacific Railway, with the Boston, Concord and Montreal Railway, or any extension thereof, or with any other railway extending from some point in the United States northwards, and touching the boundary line of Canada on the northerly boundary of either the States of New Hampshire or Vermont, at a point within five miles from Hall's Stream. The capital stock of the Company was fixed at

$300,000. This Act was amended by 51 Victoria, chap. 81, and the name of the Company was changed to the "Hereford Railway Company." The capital stock was increased to $500,000 (and by subsequent Act, 53 Victoria, chap. 72, the stock was raised to $800,000), and bonding power was given for a sum not exceeding $15,000 per mile, including the mileage of an extension to the Quebec Central Railway. By this same Act power was also given to the Company to purchase or lease the Quebec Central Railway, and the railway of the Dominion Line Company, or either of them.

The necessary stock to secure incorporation was subscribed for in small amounts, principally by farmers, mill men and merchants along the route of the proposed railway. As the preliminary steps had now been taken, it was necessary to any further progress that men with large capital should become interested. Largely through the efforts of Mr. W. B. Ives (now Hon.), of Sherbrooke, the following men formed a syndicate to build and carry on the Hereford railway: Hon. Frank Jones, Portsmouth, N. H.; Charles Sinclair, Geo. Armstrong, J. P. Cook, of Boston; Hon. Irving W. Drew, Geo. Van Dyke, of Lancaster; W. B. Ives, Sherbrooke; R. H. Pope, Cookshire; Wm. Sawyer, Sawyerville; and E. C. Swett, Woonsocket, R. I. During the early part of 1888, Messrs. Pope, Sawyer and Armstrong sold out their interest to other members of the syndicate. At this time those who had locally subscribed for stock released their share to the above gentlemen, giving as a bonus what had been paid on the stock, a very small amount in the whole, not averaging $25 for each stock holder.

The first work on the railway was commenced December 26, 1887. During that winter from one hundred to three hundred men were employed chopping out a right of way, and piling up the cord word, for about twenty-five miles, between Cookshire and the boundary line in Hereford. Early in the spring the contract for building the whole line was let by the Company to Messrs. Shirley, Corbett and Brennan. During the summer the work was pushed rapidly ahead, from one thousand to twelve hundred men being employed. Of these, eight hundred or nine hundred were foreigners, largely composed of Italians. There were a few Swedes and Greeks.

Mr. David Williams was chief engineer and superintendent of construction. Mr. W. H. Learned, on whom fell all the responsibility of the work, acted as purchasing agent and paymaster, and later was general agent for the road until it was leased by the Maine Central Railway. Mr. W. B. Ives was treasurer of the Company and had the work generally under his supervision.

On September 20, 1888, the members of the firm who had the contract for construction, Messrs. Shirley, Corbett and Brennan, absconded with $25,500, leaving more than this amount due the laborers, farmers and merchants along the line. It took about two days for the laboring men to realize that they had lost all their wages, and then a tumult arose.

Those hot tempered men from sunny Italy, strangers in this country, who knew nothing of the laws, and could not understand the language of the people, worked themselves up into a terrible state of excitement. They finally went so far as to commence destroying property, throwing away quantities of small tools and pulling up a piece of the track. Their actions and threats became so alarming that the people called on the warden of the County, (who at that time was Mr. W. H. Learned) for protection. He, also fearing that the frenzy of the men might lead to their committing serious depredations, in conjunction with two Justices of the Peace, asked for military protection from the commanding officer of the District, Lieutenant-Colonel F. M. Pope, of Bury. Colonel Pope immediately ordered out Companies No. 1, 2, 3, 4, 5, 9 and 10 of the 58th Battalion, in all about two hundred men, who were concentrated at Cookshire the following afternoon, together with the Cookshire troop of cavalry. The following day Companies No. 6, 7 and 8 were ordered out, to report at Hereford. These men patrolled the whole line until October 3, when the excitement had so subsided that all danger was thought to be passed, and the men were ordered to their homes. The report of the commanding officer, Lieutenant-Colonel F. M. Pope, to the Adjutant General, giving full particulars of the work of the men under his charge, will be found in full in the military history of the County. There is no doubt that by the timely arrival of the volunteer militia, damage to property and perhaps loss of life, was avoided. This whole expense, amounting to about $4,600, was paid by the Hereford Railway Company.

The Company at once re-hired as many of the men as they could, which was most of them, and pushed the work forward to completion as rapidly as possible. It was a very disagreeable fall and rained nearly every day, which added expense and retarded the work. However, notwithstanding all these drawbacks, on January 6, 1889, the last rails were laid and the line completed between Cookshire and the boundary line. Here they connected with the Upper Coos Railway, which also gave connection to all points in the Eastern States.

The first shipment of freight was made by the Cookshire Mill Company, of several car-loads of lumber, on January 17, 1889. During the summer of 1889 thirteen miles of railway were built, from Cookshire to Dudswell Junction on the Quebec Central Railway, and the spur to Lime Ridge, belonging to the Dominion Lime Company, also purchased and the track put in good condition.

In the fall of 1889 the telegraph line was completed and passenger trains commenced running regular trips. Until leased to the Maine Central Railway the Upper Coos Railway ran their trains over the road and transacted the business for the Hereford Railway Company.

On completion of the road a large sum was due in subsidies from the Quebec Provincial Government. They, however, withheld the same and paid all claims presented against the estate of the absconding contractors, Messrs. Shirley, Corbett and Brennan. The result was that a sum of $45,000 was deducted from the subsidies, as having been paid to the creditors. The Company attempted to recover the amount from the Government, but the courts ruled against them. Notwithstanding all these heavy losses the construction of the railway proved to be a financial success.

The road was leased to the Maine Central Railway, by lease executed in Canada on the July 22, 1890, and in Portland on August 28, in the same year. The general terms of the lease are that it is made for nine hundred and ninety-nine years. The lessee, the Maine Central Railway, guarantees the payment of four per cent. on the stock of $800,000, also upon the bonds, amounting to $800,000. In other words, they pay an annual rental of $64,500, the $500 being allowed for expenses of keeping up the corporation.

The officers of the Hereford Railway Company, at the present time, are as follows: President, Hon. Frank Jones; secretary-treasurer, H. B. Brown, Q. C., Sherbrooke; directors, Hon. W. B. Ives, Hon. I. W. Drew, C. A. Sinclair and George Van Dyke.

CHAPTER XI.

TOWNSHIP OF EATON.

Including History Town of Cookshire and Village of Sawyerville.

This tract of land is bounded north by Westbury, east by Newport, south by Clifton, and west by Ascot. It contains 64,685 acres and 3 rods in superficies. The land is uniform and generally of good quality. It is watered by the Eaton river and small tributary streams. The Eaton river is formed by two streams which water the townships of Ditton, Newport and Auckland, and meet in Eaton, just above Cookshire; it then winds in a northerly course into Westbury, where it falls into the St. Francis river.

This tract was constituted a township named Eaton, December 4, 1800, and was in part granted to Josiah Sawyer and his associates, viz.: Israel Bailey, Orsemus Bailey, Amos Hawley, Ward Bailey (the younger), John Perry, John Cook, Royal Learned, Samuel Hugh, John French, Levi French, Luther French, Timothy Bailey, Abner Osgoode, Waltham Baldwin, Benjamin Bishop, Jesse Cooper. Abner Powers, Samuel Beech, Jabez Baldwin, John Gordon, Charles Cutler, Royal Cutler, James Lucas, Philip Gordon, William McAllister, Abel Bennet, George Kimpel, Calvin Rice, Charles Lathrop, Apthorp Caswell and Peter Green Sawyer.

Captain Josiah Sawyer, from whom the village of Sawyerville takes its name, was in all likelihood the first settler in Eaton. We find in a book kept for public meetings in the township of Newport from 1793 to 1814, that the said Sawyer and Edmund Heard, "in the year 1793, set out from Missiskoui Bay, on Lake Champlain, with provisions, tools, etc., through the woods, ninety miles from any inhabitants to the westward, and after traveling and exploring the woods thirty-one days, arrived on a hill now called Pleasant Hill, in Newport, where he and Sawyer began to make improvements, distant twenty-five miles from any inhabitants to the south and seventy miles from the French settlements to the north." Sawyer did not remain at Pleasant Hill for any length of time, but took steps to secure the grant of the township of Eaton, and moved to Sawyerville. "In the year 1794 Sawyer moved his family in," the said Heard not bringing in his family until 1795.

In 1797 Messrs. Samuel Hugh, Israel Bailey and Abner Powers moved into Eaton. John French and his son, and Rufus Laberee, also came to Eaton the same year. Hugh settled west of Sawyerville, but after a few years went west. Israel Bailey remained in Sawyerville the first winter, but in 1798 settled at Cookshire on the farm now owned by Col. J. H. Taylor. Abner Powers, after spending the first winter at Sawyerville, soon after settled on the farm in Cookshire now owned by R. H. Pope, M.P.; this farm he exchanged with John Pope for the Ezra Frizzle place at Sand Hill. John French also settled at Cookshire on what is now known as the Hurd place. Rufus Laberee settled between Birchton and Eaton Corner, on the farm now owned by Joseph Taylor. These men were soon followed by John Cook (after whom Cookshire is named), Jesse Cooper, Levi French, Luther French, Abner Osgoode, Orsemus Bailey, Ward Bailey and Ebenezer Learned.

These early settlers met with and overcame all the hardships which we may now hear the Scotch settlers of Lingwick tell about. Their first homes were log houses, with no conveniences, generally one room, one window, and in many cases no floor. The bed or beds, tables, chairs, etc., were all of home manufacture. Coupled with this was a scanty larder. Distant from all mills, they were obliged to almost wholly depend on game and wild roots for a supply of food.

In those days there were a few panthers; wolves were numerous; but the most destructive were the bears. Mrs. Day says: " Often large domestic animals, and sometimes colts in the pasture, were killed by the bears; and breaking into enclosures, they would carry off their living, struggling victims, clasped tightly in their arms as they walked away erect. Some years since, a monster of this species came out of his hiding place in the wilderness, near the township of Eaton, and for a length of time evaded all efforts to kill or take him while he carried on his work of destruction. Traps were set for him and guns fired at him in vain, as he was cunning enough to avoid the one, and his skin seemed impervious to the other. His death, which was finally effected, was a matter of public rejoicing, as his depredations had not been confined to one locality. Several balls were lodged in him before he finally yielded, and on examination of the skin, the tanner found others imbedded in it, over which the wounds had healed, showing that they must have been made some time previously."

The Government offered a large bounty on bears and wolves, which was the means in a few years' time of exterminating these destructive animals. Wolves are now never seen in these townships, but bears are occasionally found around the mountains where the lumberman has not yet been heard. The early settlers were nearly all good hunters, while some made hunting and trapping a business. Mr. Rufus Laberee was noted as being an expert at this.

The first *procès-verbal* of a road,* in Eaton, was made by a surveyor named Whitcher, from Three Rivers, brother of the late Charles Whitcher, of Sherbrooke. This was in 1812, being a continuation of the Craig Road (as it was then called), from the north line of Dudswell to Canaan, Vt., passing through Cookshire, Eaton Corner, Sawyerville, Clifton and Hereford. He laid out a road to Luther French's mills, just above the junction of the North river with the Eaton river, and commenced the Lennoxville road. He also laid out what was termed a bridle path, being the present Main street of Cookshire, from Learned's hotel to the river, with the right to use gates. The family of John French was the only one living east of the river at that time.

Up to the time of the building of the Grand Trunk Railway all marketing was done either by boat or team to Three Rivers or Montreal. The Eaton and St. Francis rivers gave the settlers good transportation for those days. The teaming was generally done by the way of Stanstead, Georgeville, across Lake Memphremagog, through Bolton, and on. The boats were sent down the St. Francis river to its junction with the St. Lawrence, and there produce was transferred to larger boats for Montreal, Quebec, Three Rivers and other places. The principal article exported in those days was pearl-ash, made from hardwood ashes. This sold for about $12 per one hundred pounds. Flour and other necessaries were brought back in exchange. These journeys by boat were always dangerous, and necessitated hard labor at places like Brompton Falls, where everything had to be carried around on land in both directions. It was at this place that a most lamentable accident took place whereby two Eaton men, named John French and John Hurd, were drowned.

Up to the year 1816 new settlers were continually arriving. In 1815 Bouchette says

---

* Some of this information has been gleaned from a " History of Eaton," written in 1891, by Mr. C. S. Lebourveau.

there was a population of six hundred. The late Alden Learned, of Learned Plain, has left a written account of those early days, and he says: "The 6th of June, 1816, it commenced to snow, with the wind from the north-west, and it snowed for three days, the weather as cold as winter. The leaves were all killed and nearly all the birds died. On account of the cold summer and hard frosts for two or three years in succession, provisions of all kinds were very high, flour selling from $15 to $18 per barrel. Many of the farms were left vacant, and half of the settlers left the country." It appears to have been very trying times in those days, for even those who remained were on the point of leaving when things changed for the better. Mr. Learned, continuing, says: "The spring of 1820 was very early, wheat being sown in some places the 10th of April, and planting all done by May 1." He thought it to be the warmest summer of his experience, and all crops grew wonderfully and ripened early.

The soil of Eaton was very productive in the early days, and crops gave large returns. Potatoes especially were prolific, yielding from three hundred to four hundred bushels to the acre. A very popular drink in those days was potato whiskey, which was nearly as free as water and looked upon as a nourishing drink. Two stills are known to have existed in the town, one at Eaton Corner and the other at Sand Hill. All kinds of fruits were plentiful, and not until about 1830 did the native apple begin to die out. The farmers then raised their own flax and the wives and daughters made their own linen, which was used in place of cotton.

In 1831 the township of Eaton was divided into two parishes for church purposes, by a line through the sixth range. The northern half was called St. Peter's, the southern part St. Paul's. In the same year Bouchette gives the population as eight hundred and five. This shows a gain of only two hundred and five in fifteen years. This was owing probably to the failure of crops between 1816 and 1820, when there was such an exodus. In 1831 there was one school with an average attendance of fifty; also two or three private schools; about nine thousand acres cleared; two Protestant churches, six saw mills, one tannery, one distillery, and two taverns.

At the time of the formation of the British American Land Company, in 1833, they acquired large tracts of land in Eaton, which they have since disposed of to a large extent. They erected the first bridge at Cookshire in 1834. There had been a bridge previous to this time at a point below Lake's mills, known as French's mill. The bridge and mills had been carried away about a year previously. This was caused by trying to divide the course of the river and to give to another mill a high fall of water, near French's mill. They built a canal, erected a mill, etc., and everything appeared to be working well. About this time there was a freshet, and the water gradually increased the width and depth of the canal, until it made that the main course of the river. It washed away the new mill, and made a cut of about fifty feet deep and over two hundred feet wide. The old mill and bridge were left high and dry, with no chance of turning the river into its old channel. The best water power in the township of Eaton was thus ruined. The bed of the river, where it used to run, can now easily be traced. The abutments of the old bridge are still to be seen.

Schools in the township of Eaton date back as far as 1810; however, the first school records are dated April 23, 1842, and the school district then comprised the united townships of Eaton, Newport, Ditton and Clinton. At this meeting there were present: Lockhart Hall, chairman; Ezra Taylor, Luke Hurd, Eros Lebourveau, and Benj. Lebourveau. On January 16, 1843, the following presented themselves for examination and were accepted as teachers: Luvina Sawyer, Emily R. French, Adeline Cummings, Maria Alger, and Ruth Alger. The following are the names of some of those who have been chairmen of the School Board: Lockhart R. Hall, Jos. B. Smith, S. A. Hurd, Hiram French, Luke Chaddock, T. W. Hurd, H. H. Hill, Jonathan Jordan, A. W. Pope, Eros Lebourveau, John L. French, John McNicol, Joseph Laberee, R. H. Wilford, Calvin Jordan, Henry Alger, A. J. Lindsay, L. A. Osgood, C. R. Lindsay, J. R. Cunningham, and Benj. Farnsworth. The secretary-treasurers have been: John Lebourveau, 1842-46; Moses Lebourveau, 1847-56; Hiram French, 1856-70; E. A. Sawyer, 1870-71; E. S. Baker, 1871-93; H. H. Winslow, 1893-95.

There are at present eighteen elementary schools in the township, with an academy at Cookshire, and a model school at Sawyerville. The town of Cookshire is still part of the town for school purposes, but steps have been taken for a separation for school as well as municipal purposes. Sawyerville is no longer a part of Eaton school district, having been set off about 1892. Further particulars, in regard to schools in Cookshire, are to found with the history of that town. The Board of School Commissioners for 1895 was composed as follows: Benj. Farnsworth, chairman; Willis Jordan, Austin Williams, Wm. Barrie, and John Picard; secretary-treasurer, W. S. Ward.

The municipal history of Eaton dates back to 1841, when district councils were first formed. From then down to 1855 very little interest was taken in municipal affairs, but on the coming into force of the new Municipal and Road Act of 1855, more particulars are obtainable. On September 3, 1855, the first meeting of the Council, under the new law, was held. At that meeting were present: C. A. Bailey, William Sawyer, Wm. Hodge, William Learned, Tyler W. Hurd, and Caleb Jordon. At the next meeting we find Jonathan Jordon as, also, one of the councillors. Rules for governing the Council were passed at the first meeting, also Mr. C. A. Bailey chosen as mayor and Mr. John L. French as secretary-treasurer. The past mayors have been: C. A. Bailey, Wm. Learned, Moses Lebourveau, Wm. Sawyer, W. H. Learned, and Ezra Frizzle. During the term of office of W. H. Learned, the town of Cookshire was incorporated as a separate municipality, when he and Councillor W. W. Bailey resigned their membership in the Eaton Council. The valuation of taxable property in the township is $499,045. The Council for 1895 was composed as follows: Mayor, V. F. Hodge; and councillors, Eugene Smith, Thomas Johnston, E. D. Alger, Silas Jenkins, H. S. Farnsworth, and R. Bridgette; secretary-treasurer, W. S. Ward.

In churches the township is well supplied. We give the history of each denomination as complete as possible.

The Church of England in Eaton. In the year 1810 or 1812 the first mission was established in Eaton, the minister appointed being the Rev. Jonathan Taylor. It has been generally understood that he was a Congregationalist, but by the following old records signed by himself, it will be noticed he signs himself Presbyterian minister. "John Stratton was buried December 15, 1815. Buried by me, minister of the first Presbyterian congregation of Eaton." The first baptism on record is: "The 7th day of June, 1816. William Augustus, born 1807, October 7; Mary Sturtevant, born September 22, 1809, and Elizabeth Shows, born March 22, 1810, children of Daniel Loveland and his wife Susana; baptized by me, Jonathan Taylor, minister of the first Presbyterian church, Eaton." He took up his residence in Cookshire, living in the first frame house in the township, situated where Learned's Hotel now stands. In 1816 Bishop Stewart visited the Eastern Townships, and through his influence Mr. Taylor was brought into the communion of the Church of England. When Mr. Taylor first came to Eaton, he was minister and school teacher, his time being divided between the two. He had a salary of $200, paid in meat, stock and grain. Rev. Mr. Taylor, when he joined the Church of England, received a salary of £100 ($500), paid by the Society for the Propagation of the Gospel. His congregation, composed of all denominations, followed him into the

HISTORY OF COMPTON COUNTY.

Church of England. In 1817 (some accounts say 1819), a wooden church was built in Cookshire. This was the fourth church built in the Eastern Townships, and until the building of St. Peter's church, Sherbrooke, in 1823, the nearest church building was forty miles distant. In 1826 another church was built at Eaton Corner, and Rev. Mr. Taylor was to divide his time between the two. The latter, however, was burnt in 1828 and never rebuilt, his whole time being given to Cookshire.

The first marriage on record reads: "In the year of Our Lord, 1828, on the 8th of September, Wadley Leavet, farmer, and Mary Percival, of St. Paul's parish, Eaton, spinster, were united in marriage by bans. Married by me, minister of the Episcopal church, Rev. Jonathan Taylor." Previous to this time the people generally went to New Hampshire, a few to Stanstead, to get married, and it is probable this is the first marriage Mr. Taylor had authority to perform. Later on in the register, records are found dated back as far as 1816. These were those married in the States, who thus had their marriage made legal here, according to an act of the Legislature.

In the memoirs of Bishop Mountain occasional mention is made of Eaton. Bishop (then Archdeacon) Mountain visited the Eastern Townships in 1820, and attempted to reach Eaton, but failed owing to lack of conveyance. His Lordship, however, visited Eaton in 1829. Mr. Slack, a half-pay officer of the navy, residing in Eaton, aided Mr. Taylor in doing good church work. In 1835 Bishop Mountain passed through Eaton to Bury, which was then newly settled by English immigrants from Norfolk. The Bishop directed Mr. Taylor to give one Sunday in the month to the settlers of Bury.

In 1844 Rev. Jonathan Taylor's health declined so much that a curate was appointed. Rev. Wm. Jones came in the early summer and stayed until the spring of 1845. One marriage at which he officiated was that of the late Hon. John Henry Pope to Persis Maria Bailey. Mr. Taylor's health continued to decline so that it was frequently necessary to employ a lay reader to conduct the services. In 1849 the Rev. John Dalziel was permanently appointed to succeed him in the mission he had so long held. In May, 1852, Mr. Taylor died, aged sixty-nine years—a man beloved by old and young, whose life had been devoted to the cause of Christ, the Church in which he labored being always held secondary to the good he could do.

In 1850 the farm house belonging to Horace French was purchased for a parsonage. In 1854 a piece of ground to make an addition to the old cemetery was given by Mr. Heber Taylor, and consecrated some years later. In 1894, after the new cemetery had been opened, this strip was purchased by the town of Cookshire for $500, with the intention of turning the whole of the old cemetery into a park.

Rev. John Dalziel remained in Eaton until 1864, when he was succeeded on December 25 of that year by the Rev. Edward Cullen Parkin. In 1867 the wooden church, being very old, was torn down and a new stone church begun, being opened for public worship on September 25, 1869. The opening sermon was preached by Bishop Williams, of Quebec. Owing to a debt on the building it was not consecrated until October 17, 1881. The first marriage in this church was that of Hon. W. B. Ives, to Elizabeth, only daughter of Hon. John Henry Pope.

On October 18, 1881, the church at Sand Hill was opened for divine service. In the latter part of the year 1881 Mr. Parkin resigned, being appointed to the mission of Nicolet. In February, 1882, the Rev. Dr. Roe, professor of Divinity of Bishops College, Lennoxville, took up the work until the appointment of Mr. Arthur H. Judge, in July. In September Mr. Judge was ordained deacon and appointed to the incumbency of Cookshire; being ordained to the priesthood in St. Peter's church, Cookshire, December 9, 1883. During the incumbency of Mr. Judge, the parish made great progress. The old rectory was sold, and a new one built close to the church. Mr. Judge carried on missionary work outside the bounds of his own parish. In addition to his regular parish work he ministered to a colony of English and Swedes in Ditton, and a small church was partly built there, but the country being found unsuitable for them, they all left for other parts and the work necessarily discontinued. Mr. Judge started services in Randboro and a handsome little church was built there, and the foundation of a new mission, that of Newport, with two churches, at Randboro and Island Brook, was laid. Mr. Judge and Mr. Bernard held services at Scotstown ; a congregation was formed and a church was built.

The Bishops College missions of Sand Hill and Johnville were attached to the parish of Eaton ; and the rector, with his assistant, Mr. Thos. Lloyd, had the pastoral charge of the townships of Eaton and Newport, with five churches. In September, 1887, the Rev. Alex. Hume Robertson, of Bishops College, replaced Mr. Lloyd as assistant to Mr. Judge. On January 1, 1888, Mr. Judge left Cookshire for New York. The township of Newport was then detached from Eaton and formed into a new mission with Mr. Robertson as incumbent. On June 19, 1888, the Rev. W. G. Falconer succeeded Mr. Judge as rector of Eaton. Mr. Falconer resigned on account of ill health May 25, 1890.

On October 1, 1890, the Rev. Alex. H. Robertson became rector of Eaton. When the church at Eaton Corner was burnt, in 1828, services there were given up. After an interval of sixty-five years, Rev. Mr. Robertson, at the request of the church people in Eaton Corner, agreed to hold a service there on Sunday afternoons. A congregation was organized. In December, 1894, a building was purchased and fitted up as a mission chapel. It was dedicated on October 3, 1895, by the Right Rev. Bishop Dunn, under the name of St. Andrew's Chapel.

Upon the death of Hon. J. H. Pope, a legacy of $4,000 was left to the church, the interest of which is to augment the clergyman's stipend.

Rev. Alex. H. Robertson, the present incumbent, was born in Glasgow, Scotland. Came to Canada in 1864, and lived in Montreal, studied at McGill and took his divinity course at Bishops College, Lennoxville. He was ordained in 1887.

The Eaton Baptist Church was organized, December 15, 1822, with a membership of thirteen, viz.: William Alger, Rodolphus Harvey, Gordon Percival, Joanna Alger, Sally Heard, Edmund Alger, Simeon Alden, Nathaniel Currier, Hulda Alger, Mary Alden, Martha Currier, Mary Mallory and Betsey Morse. Of the above one is still living, Gordon Percival, who now is a resident of Spokane Falls, Wash., and is ninety-five years old. The right hand of fellowship was given by Elder John Ide, a missionary from the Massachusetts Missionary Society. In June, 1823, the membership had increased to twenty-five.

March 7, 1832, Amos Dodge was ordained and installed as pastor, which position he held until October, 1833, when the Rev. Edward Mitchell was installed as pastor. In November, 1841, the Rev. A. Gillies became the pastor and continued as such until 1878, when, on account of failing health, he was obliged to resign.

After the Rev. A. Gillies' resignation, the church had two pastors, viz.: Rev. A. Burwash and A. McNeil; also the help of the students, R. McKillop, W. J. McKay and Charles Gould. In March, 1890, the Rev. A. C. Baker became pastor, which position he still holds. During the seventy-three years since its organization, two hundred and sixty-four persons have been received into fellowship; of whom one hundred and eight are now living as residents, and non-resident members. The first church edifice was built by the united efforts of the Baptists and Free Baptists of Eaton and Newport, near the residence of the late Rev. A. Gillies, and was occupied by the Baptists and Free Baptists alternately. During this time the Rev. A. Gillies preached at the following out stations: Upper Newport, or what is now termed Maple Leaf; Martinville and Birchton. The Free Baptist church comprised Eaton and Newport, including what is now Bulwer. After a few years the Free Baptists became weak and were not able to keep up regular preaching, when that part known as Bulwer became identified in part with Moe's river. After this the Baptists occupied the church every Sabbath until the summer of 1889, when they thought it would be advisable to have the church in a more central place. Accordingly it was decided to remove the old church to Sawyerville, but upon more mature consideration they resolved to build anew, which they did, and the present Baptist church at Sawyerville is the outcome of that decision.

In the year 1891 or 1892 the Free Baptists invited the Rev. A. C. Baker to preach to them at Bulwer, which he did every alternate Sabbath in the afternoon, after about one year of labor. The then members of the Free Baptist church decided to fall into line with the regular Baptists, which they did, and were formally received; and the Rev. A. C. Baker became the pastor of this new church. The meetings were continued until the spring of 1895, when the church building was no more available for their use; they accordingly decided to build a church of their own. The Eaton (or, as it is now called, the Sawyerville) Baptist church offered to transfer their interest in the old church to the Bulwer church, who accepted the offer. The building was removed and is now completed; it was dedicated to the worship of God, December 1, 1895. The regular Baptists have two churches, where preaching is heard every Sabbath: Sawyerville, in the morning; Bulwer, in the evening; the Rev. A. C. Baker officiating as pastor for both churches.

Methodism in Eaton. The first preaching services of any kind held in Eaton were in 1805. The minister came in from Vermont through Hereford, and was a Congregationalist. In the course of his visit he informed the settlers that a Methodist minister would likely visit them in a few days, and promised that if they would not allow the Methodist to preach, he would guarantee them a missionary for six months. In due course of time the Methodist minister arrived, weary and worn with a long ride through a dense wilderness, guided by spotted trees. He was kindly received and hospitably entertained by a very respectable farmer named Colonel Williams, in Sawyerville. The minister was the Rev. Asa Kent, of the New England conference of the M. E. church. He was then a young man, but lived to old age, and from him, personally, Mr. Wm. Sawyer, ex-M. L. A., of Sawyerville, obtained the facts here narrated:

Colonel Williams informed Rev. Mr. Kent of the visit of the previous minister, and told him that the prospect of a missionary to preach to them was so great a boon that they had promised not to have him preach to them. This was a sore disappointment after having travelled so far to dispense the gospel of Christ without fee or reward. The young minister, however, accepted the result with as good grace as possible. After supper he commended the colonel and his family to God, earnestly imploring upon them all the divine protection.

On the following morning Colonel Williams met him with a smile, and said: "I have been reflecting on this matter much, through the night, and have come to the conclusion that we must not turn you away so coldly. *You must preach to us.*" It was then arranged that he should visit through the settlement and, on the following day, hold service in the house of Captain Sawyer, grandfather of Mr. Wm. Sawyer.

These arrangements having been made the young minister started at once on a house to house visitation. At Eaton Corner he met a good, pious man, a Baptist, by the name of Deacon Alger, who was said to be the only praying man in three townships. He had been absent when the promise was given not to allow the Methodist to preach, and was not bound by it. Mr. Alger strongly insisted on service being held in his house the next morning, which was cheerfully promised. Pursuing his course, Rev. Mr. Kent arrived about sun-down at a house where he had a letter to deliver, and hoped for an invitation to stay over night. He met a very cold reception, and no invitation to stay. Continuing on his way he followed a winding path into the forest, and night coming on he was in fear of being obliged to remain out without friend or shelter. But after some time his horse emerged into a small clearing, and in the distance he saw a glimmering light. Proceeding he found it came from a human habitation. He knocked for admission, the door opened, and he was bade welcome into a rude log cabin, small in size, destitute of windows or floor. It was occupied by a young couple who had immigrated from New York. For chairs, they had stools cut off from round logs. For a table, logs flattened and legs inserted in holes made with an auger. There was only one room. The bedstead was made of crotchet stakes driven into the ground, in which were laid round poles; and elm bark, strung across, supported the bed of straw, on top of which was a bed of feathers. The house was lighted by placing some grease in a saucer in which a cotton rag was inserted, the upper end being lighted. This is not an exceptional case of what the early settlers had to put up with. It is, in fact, a true recital of one of the hardships of hundreds of those who first came into the Eastern Townships.

This kind couple lived to a good old age and raised a large family. With a grateful heart the young man left them in the morning and returned to fill his appointment at Deacon Alger's. A large number of settlers had assembled and were standing in groups, or seated on logs, around the cabin, seemingly afraid to enter, though urged to do so. The more courageous ones ventured in when the singing commenced, and others during the opening prayer. By the close of the meeting there was a very good congregation. In the afternoon Rev. Mr. Kent preached at Captain Sawyer's, and left next morning for his own field of labor. He visited the settlements several times after, and preached to the great satisfaction of the people.

No more was heard of Methodism in Eaton for the space of eighteen years. The missionary stationed at Stanstead made one or two visits in 1822 and 1823. His name was Rev. Richard Pope. Years passed away, the settlements grew, and Baptists, Congregationalists and Episcopalians, all organized churches, but Methodism was not heard of, except in the distance, until 1836. In that year a minister of the Vermont conference located in Sawyerville. Active in the Master's service, he could not be idle, and he preached two years for the Baptists. Then he formed a society of Methodists. In 1837 or 1838 the Rev. J. Botterell was stationed on the St. Francis district. This field covered what are now Hatley, Coaticook, Compton, Lennoxville, Sherbrooke, Windsor, Melbourne, Danville, Ulverton, Sawyerville, Eaton, Cookshire, Island Brook, Robinson and Marbleton circuits. The Rev. E. S. Ingalls was associated with him. He took up a fortnightly appointment, week days, at Eaton Corner and Sawyerville, filled alternately by himself and Mr. Ingalls. In the summer of 1838 he held a quarterly meeting at Eaton Corner and baptized several persons, some of them by immersion in Eaton river. In conjunction with Rev. J. A. Swetland, the minister from Vermont, a society of about thirty persons was formed. It was hoped that an additional missionary would be appointed in the spring of 1839, but the missionary society had become embarrassed for want of funds, and instead of increasing their forces they dismissed them. Mr. Ingalls was removed and Mr. Botterell left alone with that vast field on his hands. The Vermont minister also returned to the States.

For seven years no sound of the gospel was heard from a Methodist unless it might have been from a passer-by. In 1846 Rev. John Douglas was sent to Sherbrooke. He made a monthly week-day appointment at Sawyerville. His health failing, he too was obliged to leave this appointment frequently unsupplied. Rev. Giffard Darey succeeded Mr. Douglas, and he too was in poor health.

In the spring of 1848 two men, one from Sawyerville and one from Dudswell, attended the May quarterly meeting at Sherbrooke. They urged that a supply should be furnished for Eaton and Dudswell. They were informed they could have one if a guarantee was forthcoming of incidental expenses, board, fuel, house-keeping, etc. The challenge was accepted, and Messrs. W. Sawyer and Albert Farnsworth guaranteed the full support of the promised minister. In September, 1848, a young man was sent to this appointment. For nine months Rev. J. Armstrong labored on this field with good success. His successor was Rev. A. McMullen, just from Ireland, who had lost his wife and seven children by that terrible ship fever which is commemorated by a large boulder erected near Victoria bridge, Point St. Charles, Montreal. In 1849 there was a membership of about one hundred and twenty on the Sawyerville circuit. The church at that place was built in 1850, and dedicated in December of the same year. In 1851 Rev. J. Armstrong was returned to Sawyerville, and in conjunction with Rev. A. McMullen the work made rapid advancement. Classes were formed in Clifton, Newport, Bury, Westbury and other places. In 1853 Rev. Robert Graham was sent to this circuit and remained for three years. His income from the circuit averaged about $250 a year. In 1856 Rev. Richard Wilson received the appointment, and at the same time Dudswell was set off as a separate mission. Rev. W. Constable arrived in 1858, and the present parsonage at Sawyerville was built in the fall of the same year. Mr. W. Sawyer donated five acres, on part of which it is built. A young man, the late Rev. Samuel Jackson, was associated with him in the work, and the following year Rev. John Johnston. Rev. Samuel Teeson held the same position with Mr. Constable in 1860. About 1861 Mr. E. S. Orr (at present registrar for the County) moved to Sawyerville from Argenteuil county. He was and still is a very efficient local preacher and assisted greatly in the work. At the conference in 1861 Rev. Robert Brown was sent here, and his assistant was Rev. Geo. Brown. During his time the church in Cookshire was built and Bury set off as a separate mission. Rev. Robert Brown died while on this circuit, and was succeeded by Rev. H. A. Spencer. Then came Rev. S. E. Maudsley. In 1865 Rev. George Washington was appointed to the circuit, and, during his incumbency, churches were built at East Clifton and Bulwer. A third one, at Island Brook, was in course of erection when he left. During this time Rev. Henry Maxwell was the junior preacher. He married Miss Sawyer, of Sawyerville, but she died about three years after. In 1868 Rev. E. E. Sweet was sent here, and during his time Cookshire was set off as a mission by itself. Rev. R. H. Smith was sent to Sawyerville in 1871, followed in 1873 by Rev. James Pearen, and in 1876 by Rev. W. J. Crothers. Revs. J. W. Clipsham, Robinson and Meyers, each followed for three years each. In 1888 Rev. Wm. Adams received the appointment, followed by Rev. C. S. Deeprose. The present pastor, at Sawyerville, is Rev. A. A. Radley, appointed in 1894.

The Eaton circuit was set off by itself in 1894, and a parsonage built at Birchton the same year. Rev. J. H. McConnell was appointed as minister. Services are held at Birchton, Bulmer and Eaton Corner.

The Methodist church, Cookshire, is forty-five by fifty-four feet, and a few years ago was finished throughout in hard wood. The audience room is the largest in the town, seating three hundred persons. The building was erected by Albert Hazeltine, in 1863, at contract price of $2,200. The project of building the church was started in March, 1860, by Rev. T. W. Constable. The first meeting to consider the matter was held in the house of H. H. French. There were present : Rev. T. W. Constable, C. A. Bailey, W. W. Weston, J. C. Cook,

John Statton, David Turner, Horace Sawyer, John Gamsby, Lucian Metcalf, Thomas Foster, George Anderson, William Sawyer and Edward Planche. Building committee: C. A. Bailey, H. H. French and Wilson Weston. Trustee board, appointed May 9, 1863: C. A. Bailey, H. H. French, G. M. Orr, Thos. Foster, Albert Farnsworth, Josiah Sawyer and Wm. Sawyer. The dedication was on Sunday, May 10, 1863. Ministers officiating: Rev. John Gemley, Edward Barrass, E. J. Sherrill and Robert Brown. The ministers residing here before the parsonage was acquired were Revs. Wm. Hicks, John Stewart and Samuel Cairns. The parsonage was acquired in 1869. Rev. Hiram Fowler was its first occupant. It has since been occupied by Revs. C. A. Jones, Nath. Smith, Jas. Peareu, Jas. Henderson, W. T. Smith, Edward Rason, W. W. Weese, M. Pratt, G. H. H. Davis, C. D. Baldwin and Rev. C. W. Finch, who was appointed to the circuit in 1895. A Sunday school was commenced about the time the church was opened, but ceased to exist for a short time in 1873. E. S. Orr became superintendent in that year, and still holds the office. East Angus is connected with Cookshire, and services are held every Sunday afternoon at that place.

The Congregational church, in Eaton was organized November 8, 1835, with a membership of nineteen. The Rev. A. J. Parker conducted the organization service. The first clerk and treasurer of the church was Mr. P. Hubbard. The first deacons were Mr. Joshua Floss and Mr. William Cummings.

The Rev. E. J. Sherrill was the first pastor, being ordained and installed June 13, 1838, by a council consisting of Reverends A. J. Parker, J. Robertson, O. Pearsons and R. F. Hall. The present church building was dedicated February 4, 1841, at which time the membership of the church had increased to one hundred and four. The Rev. Mr. Sherrill continued to minister to the church until 1875, when, in consequence of failing health, he was laid aside from active labor, and resigned the pastorate. He had been, for thirty-seven years, a faithful pastor, and under him the church was greatly prospered. His memory is "like ointment poured forth." Many of those who labored with him have, like himself, gone to their rest and reward. Many are in other fields of activity; while a few faithful ones are yet in Eaton, in life's calm evening, waiting the Master's call.

After Rev. Mr. Sherrill's removal, the pulpit was, for a time, supplied by students from the Congregational college, Montreal, among whom was Mr. W. H. Warriner, now Rev. Prof. Warriner, B. D., of Zion church, Montreal.

In 1878 Rev. W. W. Smith became pastor, continuing until 1881, when students again filled the pulpit for a time, among whom was Mr. Curry, now of the Cisamba Mission, West Central Africa. In 1884 Rev. George Skinner became pastor, continuing until 1889. For a number of years the church was without a settled pastor, the pulpit being occasionally filled by neighboring Congregational ministers. In 1894 the present pastor, Rev. R. Hay, late of Watford, Ont., was installed. The Sabbath school has been reorganized, an active Christian Endeavor society has been formed, and a Ladies' society called "The Helping Hand Society" is doing good work. A prayer meeting room has been added, and needed repairs are about to be made in the church building, for which funds are already in hand.

The Roman Catholic church in Eaton dates back to 1835. In 1823 John Brazel, with the first Catholic family, came into the township. In 1835 Catholic services were held for the first time, in Eaton, at the house of Thos. McLary, situated about one mile from Birchton, by Father McMahon, later on by Father Harkin, both from Sherbrooke, and also by Father Daly, the first resident priest at Compton.

In 1853 mass was said for the first time at Eaton Corner, in the house of Elie Laroche.

The same year a piece of land was given by Thos. McLary, and a new chapel was erected thereon at Eaton Corner. The building was afterwards used as a school house, and has now been turned into a blacksmith's shop. It is located two or three buildings north of the hotel. Father Dufresne, of Sherbrooke, celebrated the first mass in the new chapel.

In 1868 the Eaton Corner mission was moved to Cookshire, and the present church erected. It was first located on the Craig road, to the south of the town, facing the road leading to the river. In the same year Rev. T. E. Gendrean was appointed the first resident priest. In 1873 the following places were under the charge of Rev. Mr. Gendrean: Eaton, fifty-one families; Westbury, eleven families; Bury, thirty-one families; Newport, twenty-five families; Ditton, fifteen families; Auckland, twenty families; East Clifton, fourteen families; Chesham, two families; Lingwick, three families; and Emberton, one family.

In 1874 Rev. Mr. Blanchard, who is now located at Malone, N. Y., succeeded Rev. Mr. Gendrean, and he, in turn, was followed by Rev. Amédé Dufresne, who remained until 1883, and then removed to Sutton. In that year, Rev. T. H. Massé, now of Rock Forest, Que., was appointed to the Cookshire church. In 1887 there was purchased the fine lot of land, on Main street, and the church moved thereto, with arrangements underneath for a hall, and which is used as a school room. In 1894 Mr. Massé was succeeded by the present priest, Rev. Thos. Hannan.

The church has made gradual growth during all these years, and the building in Cookshire is now not large enough to accommodate the ever-increasing congregations.

In 1890 a Catholic church was built at Sawyerville, and mass celebrated for the first time in same by Rev. A. E. Martel, on September 28 of that year. The parish priest of Cookshire had charge of and attended Sawyerville until October 1, 1892. At that time the present incumbent, Rev. I. A. Lavallée, was appointed. He also has under his care the mission of Island Brook.

The first Presbyterian services held in Eaton were in 1885, when a young student from the Montreal Presbyterian college, named Langton, labored during the summer. He preached at North River, High Forest and East Clifton. He was followed the next year by Mr. Robertson. Mr. Langton returned the following year. Since then, Mr. Ferguson, of London, Ont., and Mr. Craig, from Quebec, have been on the field. In 1889 it was decided to build a church at Sawyerville. The building committee secured sufficient subscriptions to go ahead with the work, and the building was erected by the late A. S. Rand, of Randboro. The dedication services were held on November 25, 1890, and Rev. Donald Tait, of Quebec, preached the first sermon in the new building. Since then the appointment has been filled principally by students, Messrs. Logie, Polly, Tanner and Woodside. The membership is constantly increasing. The present pastor is Rev. Mr. Steele, who resides in Massawippi.

In the township of Eaton are to be found eight post offices. Cookshire and Sawyerville, being now two separate municipalities, are treated under their separate histories. The others are Eaton Corner, Birchton, Bulwer, Johnville, Sand Hill and Flanders.

Eaton Corner is located half way between Cookshire and Sawyerville, and is on the line of the Maine Central Railway. It is one of the oldest villages in the County, and, previous to the building of railways, was a centre for a large section of country. Twenty-five years ago this village showed prospects of growth, but the railway came just near enough to kill it, and still not near enough to do any good. Cookshire, Birchton and Sawyerville have taken the trade once done here. In 1857 the following are some of those who resided at Eaton Corner: Joseph Aubrey, carriage maker; C. M. Draper, M. D.; Joshua Foss, postmaster; S. A. Hurd, J. P. and secretary-treasurer; Eros Lebourveau, farmer; Moses Lebourveau, clerk; Thomas S. Morey, general merchant; James Osgood, harness maker; David H. Pope, hotel-keeper; A. H. Rodgers, M. D.; Green Sawyer, storekeeper; Rev. C. Sawyer, Baptist minister; Rev. E. J. Sherrill, Congregational minister; Charles Taylor, shoemaker; David Warby, chairmaker. Population in 1857, about two hundred. At the present time the population is not quite as large. There are two general stores, hotel, blacksmiths, carriage maker, harness shop, etc. Moses Lebourveau is postmaster. There is a daily mail. Postal revenue of 1895, $138.40. This post office is generally called Eaton, leaving off the word Corner.

Birchton is three miles south of Cookshire, on the Canadian Pacific Railway. Here are a general store, large cheese factory, steam saw mill, Union church, blacksmith, etc. Population, about one hundred and fifty. Postal revenue, 1895, $154.00.

Bulwer is three miles south of Birchton, on the Canadian Pacific Railway, and also the centre of a good farming community. Here are to be found a Methodist and Baptist churches, general store, blacksmith, etc. Population, about one hundred. Postal revenue, 1895, $93.00.

Johnville is a thriving little village, on the Canadian Pacific Railway, about half way between Cookshire and Lennoxville. Here are to be found saw and grist mills, general store, Methodist and Episcopal churches, separator for creamery at Cookshire, blacksmith shop, etc. It is the shipping point for Cleveland's saw mills and the village of Martinville. Population, two hundred and fifty. Postal revenue, 1895, $310.00.

Sand Hill is a farming community, eight miles from Cookshire, on the main road between Eaton and Lennoxville. Here is an Episcopal church, and separator for creamery. The land is good and the farmers are all well-to-do. Postal revenue, 1895, $21.00.

Flanders is four and a half miles south-east of Cookshire, and the centre of a farming community. It is a new post office opened within the past few years. Mail, tri-weekly. Postal revenue, 1895, $39.00.

The following statistics are given for the township of Eaton, including Cookshire and Sawyerville, by the census of 1891: Population, 3,078; families, 616; houses, 606; males, 1,604; females, 1,474; French Canadians, 714; others, 2,364. Religions—Roman Catholic, 778; Church of England, 817; Presbyterians, 118; Methodists, 768; Lutherans, 2; Baptists, 115; Free Will Baptists, 98; Congregationalists, 183; Adventists, 52; Universalists, 112; Jews, 4; other denominations, 5; not specified, 26.

The late Hiram French, farmer and insurance agent, whose portrait is inserted herewith, was born May 22, 1808, on the farm situated on the east side of Eaton river, in Cookshire, at present owned by Fred. Jackson. He died at Eaton Corner, on his own farm, September 6, 1892. John French, his grandfather, was born in Enfield, Conn., December, 1739. In the spring of 1796, his two eldest sons, Luther and Levi, came as far as Eaton Corner by a spotted line. They cleared a spot large enough to plant a peck of potatoes, on what is now known as the Alger sugar-place. In the fall they dug the potatoes and buried them ready for the next spring. This is thought by some to have been the first clearing or planting done in the township of Eaton. In 1798, Mr. John French and his two sons again came from the States, and made their way through Eaton Corner to where Cookshire now is. No reason is known why they gave up the clearing at Eaton Corner. They settled on the east side of Eaton river, and built a log house near the foot of the hill on the Bury road. In the fall of 1798, Mr. French moved in his family, consisting of his wife (Abigail Sage), four sons and three daughters. His son Levi, the father of Mr. Hiram French, was born in Enfield, Conn. He married, in 1805, Matilda Osgood. In the same year he built a house on the farm, previously mentioned as where our subject was born. Issue, eight children—five sons and three daughters—of whom only one survives, Luther French of Island Brook. Mr. Hiram French was married at Eaton Corner, on the farm where he afterwards lived and died, to Sarah Pond Williams, born October 8, 1811; died March 1, 1883. They at once moved into the township of Newport, and lived there seven years. In 1839 they returned to the old home of Mrs. French, on the meadow at Eaton Corner, where their son Levi now lives. Mr. French, in addition to being a prosperous farmer, was agent for the Stanstead & Sherbrooke Mutual Fire Insurance Company for over thirty years; deacon of the Eaton Congregational church thirty years, and member of the same for over fifty years. He held prominent offices in the town, and was secretary-treasurer of the school commissioners for twelve years.

Mr. French cast his first vote in 1829, when the first election in the Eastern Townships was held. At that time he had to go to Sherbrooke to vote, and he voted at every election down to the time of his death. By the foregoing marriage Mr. French had ten children, six of whom are now living: Hiram Elbridge, born March 2, 1833, died July 27, 1883; Levi William, born September 6, 1834, married Julia Ann Goodhue, March 29, 1859, four children, residence, home farm, Eaton; Cyrus Eames, born August 7, 1838, married Lois Hodge, September 10, 1863, residence, San Francisco, Cal.; Samuel Henry, born February 1, 1848, married Ellinor N. Ellis, July 3, 1869, four children, residence, Ashtabula, Ohio; Jonas Ludiah, born January 27, 1850, married Abigail S. M. French, January 2, 1889, two children, residence, Cookshire; Ellen M., born October 7, 1835, died April 14, 1860; Mary Key, born July 1, 1840, married Nathan W. Alger, November 9, 1860, seven children, residence, Albuquerque, New Mexico; Sarah Belle Caroline, born May 18, 1858, married Geo. S. Ramsay, December 27, 1883, two children, residence, Fresno, Cal. Mr. French was a man of high moral character, with considerable force and energy. His advice was often asked for, and he was held in high esteem by all.

LATE HIRAM FRENCH.

Samuel Alonzo Hodge, farmer, was born on the farm and in the same house where he now lives, August 17, 1846. His grandfather, David Hodge, was born in Burney, N. H., and married Catherine Sunbury, of Massachusetts. They moved into Eaton in 1800. He settled on lots six and seven in the seventh range, where he cleared one of the finest farms in town, and which is now occupied by his grandsons, Alonzo and Alton. When first coming to Eaton he worked for Orsamus Bailey, and felled the first tree on what is known as the Ward Bailey meadow, Cookshire. He was a good farmer, diligent, saving and successful, and considered one of the wealthiest men in town. He had ten children, of whom only one is living, Mrs. Scott Gamsby, Lennoxville. The father of our subject was Samuel Beech Hodge. He married Lois Hall, of New Ireland, Que, and lived on part of the home farm, which his son now owns. He died here April 28, 1886. Samuel Beech Hodge, like his father, was a successful farmer and a prominent man in the town, having held the office of councillor for many years. Mr. Alonzo Hodge, our subject, was married in Dudswell, June 4, 1885, to Nabbie Ann, daughter of Gershom Rolfe, of Dudswell. Herewith we give an engraving showing the farm, buildings and residence of Mr. Hodge, which is located about one and one-half miles from Cookshire, on the lower road to Eaton Corner. He may be seen standing on

FARM BUILDINGS S. ALONZO HODGE.

the driveway into the large barn, while his son is holding a young horse on the ground. The house is in the distance, just across the road. A very marked characteristic of this place, noticeable to all driving by, are two very large willow trees, of peculiar shape, with large branches extending over the road. They may be seen at the right of the picture, partially hid by a shed. It is said they have grown thus from two small walking-sticks that had been stuck in the ground. Mr. Hodge has only one child living, William B., born January 1, 1878.

James Alton Hodge, farmer, was born April 11, 1846, on the farm now owned and occupied by him. This is part of the farm cleared by his grandfather, David Hodge, who came in from the United States in 1800, of whom a more full account may be found in the history of Samuel

Alonzo Hodge, who occupies the adjoining place to Mr. Alton Hodge, the two farms having been originally in one and cleared by Mr. David Hodge. Two sons, Samuel Beech and James H., took the home farm and divided it between them. James H. was the father of our subject, and was born on this farm, where he lived until his death, September 5, 1892. He married Almeda Colby, of Eaton, who is still living with her son. James Alton Hodge, our subject, is a successful farmer, like his father and grandfather before him. He has a good farm, good buildings, and things generally around the place look prosperous. Accompanying this is a reproduction of a photograph of the residence of Mr. Hodge, which is located about two miles from Cookshire, on the lower road to Eaton Corner. In front of the house may be seen Mr. and Mrs. Hodge and

RESIDENCE OF J. ALTON HODGE.

their children. He has been one of the prominent men of the town and held several offices of trust. For fifteen years he has been valuator for the Township, was largely instrumental in establishing the St. Francis Live Stock Association at Cookshire, and for two years has been president of the same. He is also a deacon of the Congregational church at Eaton Corner. Mr. Hodge was married at Eaton Corner, March 21, 1867, to Jerusha A. Williams, of Cookshire, daughter of Ahira Williams, who died in Boston, Mass., in 1875. Issue, three children: Archie A., born May 20, 1875; Nellie M., born March 5, 1872; Edith G., born September 4, 1877.

VOLNEY FRENCH HODGE, farmer, was born on the farm where he now lives, November 18, 1850. This place is located about half a mile north of Eaton Corner, at the junction of the upper and lower roads from Cookshire to Eaton. Mr. Hodge is a grandson of David Hodge, whose history is specially mentioned in that of Samuel Alonzo Hodge. The father of our subject was David Edward Hodge, who settled on the farm first adjoining that of his brother James. He inherited the good business qualities of his father. He was born on the old homestead owned by Alonzo Hodge, and died where his son now lives, September 27, 1894, aged eighty-four years. He married Ann Gamsby, of Eaton, who died in 1883. Volney F. Hodge, our subject, has been a councillor of Eaton for three years and is serving his second year as mayor. His portrait will be found among the members of the Compton County Council. He was married at Sawyerville, May 21, 1873, to Mary Edith (born October 15, 1856), daughter of William Clough. Issue, one daughter, Cora Ann, born December 22, 1877. Miss Hodge shows exceptional talent as a musician.

RESIDENCE OF VOLNEY F. HODGE.

Accompanying this sketch is an engraving of the residence of Mr. Hodge, in front of which may be seen Mr. and Mrs. Hodge and Miss Hodge in the team. The other farm buildings are on the opposite side of the road.

GEORGE ALBERT HODGE, farmer, was born in the township of Eaton, where he has always lived, January 19, 1852. He is a son of Samuel Beech Hodge, who died April 27, 1886. Mr. Hodge is president of Compton County Agricultural Society, No. 1, also of the association P. of I. He was married at Cookshire, July 18, 1876, to Ada Maria, daughter of Jonathan French Taylor. Issue, seven children, five living: Alexander A., born June 19, 1877; Elwin B., born October 9, 1879; Clarence Herbert, born December 27, 1894; Winnifred Victoria, born June 20, 1887; Lucy Laura, born December 4, 1888.

HOLLIS MARBLE HODGE, farmer, was born in Cookshire, May 19, 1832. He is a son of the late Charles A. Hodge. Herewith we give an engraving of the home of Mr. Hodge, with himself and family in front. His farm is located about half a mile west of the Birchton post office, on the Lennoxville road, and is in a good state of cultivation, Mr. Hodge being a successful farmer. Our subject was married at Eaton Corner, January 29, 1870, to Maria C., daughter of the late Ephraim Barlow. Issue, four children: Marvin Barlow, born November 8, 1870, married Sophia T. Hyde, residence, Providence, R. I.; Charles Arthur, born May 21, 1884; Frederick Allen, born March 17, 1890; Effie Maria, born May 14, 1875.

CAPTAIN ALLEN T. HODGE, whose portrait accompanies this sketch, was born in Eaton, January 6, 1811. His father, Barzilla B. Hodge, was born in Stewartstown, N. H., January 13, 1809. On December 25, 1825, at Dorchester, N. H., he married Sarah C. Elliott. Issue, four children: Elizabeth Ann, born October 4, 1827, married Asa Knapp, of Brompton, Que., three children; Stephen, born November 2, 1830, married Maggie Lyons, one child, he lived in Eaton and worked at his trade (shoe-making) nearly up to the time of his death, February 27, 1891; Elliott B., born November 14, 1838, learned the photographing business and lived at Waterloo, Que., several years, then moved to Plymouth, N. H., married Marie A. Dolloff, of Dorchester, N. H., no children. In a few years he was appointed fish and game commissioner for the

RESIDENCE OF H. M. HODGE.

State, and by joint action of New Hampshire and Massachusetts was appointed superintendent of the fish hatcheries, which position he held up to the time of death, December 5, 1893, to the great credit of himself and the State as well. The fourth child is our subject, Allen Timothy. Mr. Hodge, after living in Dorchester a few years, removed his family to Colebrook, N. H., and, about 1836, from there to Eaton. He first settled near Johnville, but afterwards moved to a small farm, on the road leading from Chaddock's mill to Lennoxville. There, in a log house which he built, his two youngest children were born. He next leased a large farm from his cousin, Beech Hodge, for three years, and at the end of that time moved to a new house he had built at South Cookshire. A few years later he bought a meadow farm, formerly owned by Reuben Green, where he lived until his death, March 12, 1872, his wife having died March 4, 1872. Captain Hodge received his education at the Cookshire Academy. He learned the carpenter's trade of Lucien Metcalf, worked in Canada several years, and moved to Biddeford, Me., in 1862. Before leaving Cookshire he served in the cavalry two years. On October 29, 1863, he enlisted in the First Battalion Heavy

HISTORY OF COMPTON COUNTY.

CAPTAIN ALLEN T. HODGE.

Artillery, Massachusetts Volunteers, in company "C", and was honorably discharged at the close of the war. Returning to Eaton, he engaged in his trade and in the manufacturing of washing-machines. He assisted in recruiting No. 10 company, Fifty-eighth battalion, and was appointed lieutenant of the same. He served two years in that capacity, acting as captain, when called out during the Fenian raid. He received his military certificate September 27, 1870, and was commissioned captain of No. 10 company, May 4, 1871. Having decided to return to Massachusetts, he tendered his resignation and was permitted to retire, retaining rank. He settled in Lowell, where he now resides, engaged in the business of real estate and fire insurance. He is a prominent member of the G. A. R., and Knights of Honor, and has held leading offices in the same. Before returning to Eaton, after the close of the war, our subject was married, at Biddeford, Me., to Mary W. Boston. Issue,

LATE BENJAMIN R. LABEREE.

three children : Frank R., born July 27, 1866, married Sarah Scott, two children, residence, Atlanta, Ga. ; Burton A., born January 4, 1868, married Izettie L. Harden, one child, residence, Lowell, Mass. ; Fred. E., born April 1, 1877.

LATE BENJAMIN RICE LABEREE, in his lifetime a farmer, and whose portrait accompanies this sketch, was born January 25, 1834, at Jordan Hill, in Eaton, where he lived until his death, February 11, 1892, with the exception of two years in California. Mr. Laberee was a thorough and successful farmer, a man held in high esteem by all who knew him, and filled many offices of trust. He took a great interest in farming, and kept valuable horses and cattle. He was in demand throughout the Eastern Townships and neighboring places as a judge at agricultural exhibitions, his fair and just decisions being accepted by all. In anything that would assist the farmers, Mr. Laberee was always ready to give a helping hand. The Eastern Townships Agricultural Association, holding its annual exhibition at Sherbrooke, he took a great interest in, and ably assisted in starting it. He was one of the directors from its inception up to the time of his death. He was married at Melbourne Ridge, Que., September 26, 1860, to Mary Jane, daughter of Benj. S. Wakefield. Issue, three children : Oscar Green, born July 16, 1864, married Rose Clarke, residence, Ellensburgh, Wash.; Avery Wakefield, born May 19, 1878, residence, Waterville; Olivia Iola, born June 26, 1861, married Francis G. Gale, residence, Waterville. Mrs. Laberee survives her husband and resides with her daughter, Mrs. Gale, at Waterville. By turning to the engraving of the residence of Mr. F. G. Gale, Waterville, Mrs. Laberee may there be seen.

JOHN H. LABEREE.

JOHN HOLTON LABEREE, farmer, whose portrait we present herewith, was born at Sand Hill, July 4, 1848. He has always lived there, with the exception of two years in Cookshire. He has been warden of St. Luke's Episcopal church nine years. Has never married. He is a great-grandson of Rufus Laberee, one of the first settlers in Eaton. Rufus Laberee was born in Charleston, N. H., September 2, 1769, and came to Eaton with his wife, Olive Farwell, and six children, in the fall of 1798, when there were only four families in the town. They suffered all the hardships, trials, and privations of pioneer life. By his indomitable will, perseverance, and industry, he succeeded in making a good home for himself and family, and finally accumulated considerable property. Mr. Laberee was a man of more than ordinary ability, judgment and foresight. He was called to fill many responsible public positions, and his sterling qualities were appreciated by his townsmen. He died February 16, 1842, aged 78 years, and his wife died April 12, 1814, aged 45 years. They had ten children, who all settled in Eaton with the exception of Benjamin, who went to Ontario. Sophia married Capt. John Pope, being the mother of the late Hon. John Henry Pope, and grandmother of Rufus H. Pope, M. P. Henry remained on the home place, near Birchton, where his daughter, Mrs. Joseph Taylor, now lives. Rufus settled on Jordan Hill. The eldest of the four sons, John, the grandfather of our subject, married Nancy Pope, sister of Captain John Pope. They settled at Sand Hill, when there was not a clearing between Birchton and Lennoxville. He was born June 5, 1787, died in 1836. He lived to clear one of the best farms in Eaton, with fine location. He left two sons and one daughter. Alfred, the father of our subject, remained on the home farm, where he still resides, and is the only one living of the three. He married Mary Farnsworth, who died in middle life; later he married again. Mr. Alfred Laberee took a prominent part in the militia, and was appointed captain by Governor Sir Edmund Head.

HISTORY OF COMPTON COUNTY.

RESIDENCE OF RUFUS E. LABEREE.

RUFUS ERNEST LABEREE, farmer and postmaster, was born on the farm at Sand Hill where he now lives, December 4, 1860. A history of his grandfather and father will be found with that of his brother, John H. Laberee. Accompanying this is an engraving of his residence, with himself and family in front. He holds the appointment of post-master at Sand Hill. At East Angus he married Alberta Elvira, only daughter of Daniel B. Hall, of Linda. Issue, two children: Stanley O., born June 6, 1892; Milton D., born September 10, 1894.

JOSEPH L. TAYLOR, farmer, was born in Cookshire, November 25, 1829. He is a son of the late Ezra Taylor and nephew of the late Rev. Jonathan Taylor. The farm he occupies is the one originally settled on by the late Rufus Laberee, sr., in 1798. The house of which we give a photo-engraving herewith, was erected by Mr. Laberee in 1812. His son Henry occupied the place up to the time of his death in 1860, when it was acquired by Mr. Taylor and is now carried on by himself and his son, Edgar E. For several years Mr. Taylor taught school, afterwards becoming a farmer. He has held prominent public offices in town, such as councillor and school commissioner. He is Sunday-school superintendent at Birchton. On September 5, 1853, he married Theodotia, daughter of the late Henry Laberee. Issue, seven children: Edwin Augustus, born July 22, 1854, married Maggie Nuthrown, five children, residence, Bulwer; Orion Stewart, born January 30, 1857, married Katharine A. Vedder, of New York, two children, residence, Passadena, Cal.; Frederick Arthur, born March 23, 1859, married L. Gertrude McClary, of Compton, three children, residence, Birchton; Henry Joseph, born October 30, 1860, married Eva L. Todd, two children, residence, Birchton; Edgar Erwin, born January 7, 1873, married Etta F. Todd, one child, residence, Birchton; Harriet Theodotia, born October 30, 1866, married Henry A. Planche, six children, residence, Cookshire; Clara Persis, born December 31, 1864, married first the late S. W. Irwin, second marriage to Alton Brazzle, one child, residence, Sand Hill.

JAMES MAY, farmer, was born in Stanstead, March 6, 1825. When a young man he worked in

RESIDENCE OF J. L. TAYLOR.

RESIDENCE OF JAMES MAY.

a woollen factory in Stanstead for seven years, and for three years was in Butler's drug store at Derby Line, Vt. He came to Bulwer, his present home, May 1, 1856. His father, Hezekiah May, and mother, Sarah Hays, both came from Stratford, Vt., moving into Stanstead early in the present century. He was married in Eaton, December 10, 1856, to Amy, daughter of Renel Whitcomb. Issue, three children: Samuel J., born September 30, 1857, married Almina Coates, five children, residence, Bulwer; George J., born April 1, 1877; Sarah Julia, born April 9, 1861, married L. L. Manning, residence, Stanstead, Que. Presented herewith is an engraving of the home place, with Mr. May and his family in front. It is located about one mile north of Bulwer, on the road between that place and Birchton.

SAMUEL JAMES MAY, farmer, was born near Bulwer, his present home, September 30, 1857. He has always lived here with the exception of four years in Massachusetts as an engineer. He was married at Cookshire, May 4, 1880, to Almina Coates. Issue, six children, five living: Elmer Prosper, born May 27, 1881; James Walter, born September 9, 1884; Maud Emma, born December 20, 1882; Bertha Addie, born October 6, 1888; Ruth Whitcomb, born December 6, 1891.

EDSON CHARLES WARNER, farmer, was born at Sand Hill, November 21, 1859. He has always lived on the same farm, where he was born. He is a son of Charles Warner, who was born in Compton, July 10, 1826, and died at Sand Hill, August 1, 1886. Mother's name, Mary Bar-

RESIDENCE OF EDSON C. WARNER.

low, of Westbury. Mr. Edson C. Warner was married at Sand Hill, August 14, 1889, to Sarah (born January 10, 1858), daughter of Chester Warner, one of the first settlers at Sand Hill. He died in November, 1882. Issue, one son: Earl Cecil Rupert, born May 14, 1890. Mr. Warner has been a member of the Board of School Commissioners for the township of Eaton for several years. Reproduced herewith is a photograph of his residence, and in front he and his family may be seen.

WALTER NUTT, agent, was born in Hull, Yorkshire, England, December 28, 1860. In 1870 he emigrated to New York city, where he lived until 1879, when he came to Island Brook, moving from there to Eaton Corner in 1882. While in New York city was clerk in wholesale rubber goods firm, but on coming to Island Brook he became a farmer, and continued as such until 1889, when he went into trade at Eaton Corner. In January, 1896, he disposed of his store and accepted a position as agent. Mr. Nutt held the office of school commissioner in Eaton from 1888 to 1891. He is a past master of Friendship Lodge, A. F. & A. M. It was largely through his efforts that St. Andrew's Episcopal chapel was established at Eaton Corner, and he is one of the wardens. He was married at Cookshire, November 22, 1881, to Orra Harriet (born September 19, 1863), daughter of Ephraim Ward, of Eaton.

RESIDENCE OF WALTER NUTT.

Issue, three children : Walter Ward, born September 26, 1885 ; Orra Elizabeth, born July 5, 1887 ; Hassall Richard, born August 20, 1891. Accompanying this sketch is a photo-engraving of the residence of Mr. Nutt, in front of which he and his family may be seen.

SANFORD DINSMORE, farmer, was born at Colebrook, N. H., November 7, 1845. He came to Canada in 1864, and settled in Clifton. In September, 1870, Mr. Dinsmore moved to Bulwer, and settled on the farm where he now lives. Accompanying this sketch is reproduced a photograph of the farm house of Mr. Dinsmore, with himself and wife in front. The young lady, on horseback, is Miss Dora Dinsmore, the only child of our subject. Before coming to Canada, Mr. Dinsmore enlisted in the Ninth New Hampshire Regiment and served in the war of the Rebellion 1861–65. He was taken a prisoner at Fredericksburg, Va., but soon exchanged and transferred to the navy where he served one year in the United States frigate "Colorado." He was discharged from the navy June 16, 1864. In his adopted country, Mr. Dinsmore has held several offices of trust and is a P. P. of the P. of I. Association. Our subject was married at Eaton Corner, January 16, 1870, to Eliza L. (born August 7, 1849),

HISTORY OF COMPTON COUNTY.

RESIDENCE OF S. DINSMORE.

daughter of George D. Sunbury. Issue, one daughter: Dora Adaline, born September 23, 1876.

DAVID ALBERT FARNSWORTH, farmer, a resident of Flanders, was born in Cookshire, August 2, 1821. He has been one of the prominent men of the township, having filled numerous offices, and served as school commissioner. He has always lived in the township of Eaton. At Lennoxville, March 8, 1848, he married N. S., daughter of Gardner Stevens, who died in 1842. Issue, eleven children, nine living: Artemus S., born December 3, 1855, married Luvia A. Bowker, residence, Eaton, one child; Benjamin, born January 7, 1858, married Ella J. French, residence, Flanders, one child; Albert H., born December 1, 1866; Thomas O., born June 22, 1868; Phebe D., born October 23, 1850, married Alva Rankin, residence, Brompton, two children; Anna M., born April 22, 1852, married John M. Learned, residence, Learned Plain, five children; Catherine H., born November 13, 1859, married Rev. Barry Pierce, residence, Ontario, four children; Ormesinda C., born May 30, 1861, married H. R. Bowker, residence, Newport, Que.; one child; Dorothy M., born April 10, 1863, married Lyman Q. Bliss, residence, Compton. Reproduced herewith is an engraving of the residence of Benjamin Farnsworth, with his family in front. There may also be seen his father, our subject. Mr. Benjamin Farnsworth is a school commissioner for the township of Eaton, which also includes Cookshire.

OLIVIER DESRUISSEAUX, gentleman farmer, was born in Eaton, February 15, 1851. Most of his life

RESIDENCE OF BENJAMIN FARNSWORTH.

was spent in Sherbrooke, where he was very successful as a hotel-keeper. In 1893 he returned to Eaton and purchased a farm near Ascot Corner, where he now lives. Herewith will be found an engraving of Mr. Desruisseaux and his family, including an adopted daughter. His father, Léon Desruisseaux, was born March 16, 1820, and is now living at Sherbrooke. His mother's name was Domitile Martel, of Lake St. Francis. Mr. Desruisseaux, was married at Sherbrooke, May 5, 1874, to Marie Louise (born November 28, 1859), daughter of Joseph Champoux, of Arthabaska. Issue three children : George, born February 28, 1875 ; Henry, born October 10, 1877 ; Willie, born May 5, 1879. An adopted daughter, Eugenie Dubé,

OLIVIER DESRUISSEAUX AND FAMILY.

born February 4, 1880. He has always shown himself ready to assist all public enterprises. At present he is chief ranger of the Catholic Order of Foresters.

ANTHONY FREDERICK BOWEN, farmer, was born in Ascot, June 14, 1847. He moved on to his present farm near Learned Plain in 1878. His father, Israel Bowen, died at Island Brook, December 18, 1887. His mother, Mehitable Elliott, was born in Lennoxville, August 30, 1802, died at Island Brook in September, 1889. Herewith will be found an engraving of Mr. Bowen, his family and grandchildren. Our subject, before settling down to farming was a school teacher, and for a few years a photographer. He has held various municipal offices. Is V. C. R. in the I. O. F. ; S. C. in the R. T. of T. ; and held the office of secretary of the Patrons of Industry of Compton county in 1895. He was married in Newport, December 31, 1867, to Marion, daughter of Silas Harvey, who died at Island Brook, August 3,

A. F. BOWEN AND FAMILY.

1883. Issue, five children: Archibald R., born June 10, 1874; Ernest I. S., born October 20, 1881; Beatrice M., born November 24, 1869, married H. C. Bailey, June 18, 1890, residence, Eaton, three children, two living; (Reginald C., born November 6, 1891, Edna M., born September 2, 1895); Viviane A., born March 10, 1871; Mehitable E., born July 11, 1877.

BENJAMIN FRANKLIN BROWN, farmer, was born in Eaton, near Flanders Post Office, May 22, 1827. His father, Andrew Brown, was born in Framingham, Mass., June 22, 1801. In company with his father Ebenezer Brown, and another brother named Benjamin, they started for Canada in 1818. The father died at Concord, N. H., in March of that year, while they were on their way. The two boys continued the journey, and lived with their brother-in-law, Luther French, until they were of age. Andrew, the father of our subject, was married in Eaton, March 18, 1824, to Angeline Chaddock. In 1837 he purchased and moved on to the farm now owned by his son Benjamin, located about two miles east of Cookshire, on the Bury road. The engraving presented herewith shows that the old homestead has been kept in good repair. Mr. B. F. Brown stands in the foreground, being the only son out of six, who is now living. Those to the right are men employed on the farm. By the above marriage there were ten children, five now living: Wm. Andrew, born September 13, 1825, died in infancy; Benjamin Franklin, born May 22, 1827; Nancy K., born February 22, 1829, married, first, Thaddeus Chase, three children, second marriage

RESIDENCE OF BENJAMIN F. BROWN.

HISTORY OF COMPTON COUNTY.

RESIDENCE OF ALONZO TODD.

to Horace French, residence, Vermont; Fred. W., born January 1, 1831, died in Minnesota; Helen I., born July 17, 1832, married Ebenezer Learned, residence, Learned Plain; Achsah E., born December 27, 1834, married John French, residence, Eaton; John N., born January 31, 1837, died in Minnesota; James L., born June 21, 1839, married Sarah Pope, died in Minnesota; Maria Louisa, born September 27, 1841, married Perry Chase, residence in Vermont; Joseph W., born July 18, 1844, died in 1846. The father, Andrew Brown, died February 22, 1872. The mother died November 3, 1881. Mr. B. F. Brown went to Minnesota in 1855, where all of his other brothers had emigrated. After twenty years, most of the time in that state, our subject returned to the old homestead. While absent he was clerk of the school district for five years, and constable two years. He has never married.

ALONZO TODD, farmer, was born on the same farm where he now lives, at Birchton, December 2, 1832. He is a son of the late Elisha Todd, who came from New Hampshire, settled on this farm, where he died in December, 1861. Mr. Todd has been a successful farmer. He was married at Derby Line, Vt., January 29, 1862, to Susan Minerva, daughter of the late Giles Luther, of Eaton. Issue, five children, four living: Ernest, born September 4, 1869; Eva Lucinda, born August 8, 1862, married Henry J. Taylor, two children, residence, Birchton; Minnie Arabella, born January 15, 1864, married Albert Bridgette, one child, residence, Birchton; Mary Jane, born December 2,

RESIDENCE OF MR. BARLOW COATES.

RESIDENCE OF E. FRIZZLE.

1865, died June 7, 1875; Etta Fidelia, born August 24, 1871, married Edgar Taylor, one child, residence, Birchton. Mrs. Todd died March 21, 1895. An engraving is given here of the residence of Mr. Todd.

BARLOW COATES, farmer, was born in Eaton, September 13, 1853. Accompanying this sketch will be found a reproduction of a photograph of his home, located between Birchton and Sand Hill, on the Lennoxville road. Mr. Coates attended the best schools of Eaton, and has always lived in the township. He is a prosperous farmer, and held the office of councillor for six years. His parents were Prosper Harvey and Mary (Moulton) Coates. His father was born in Eaton, and died in 1866, aged thirty-nine years. Our subject was married at Huntingville, Que., December 3, 1874, to Miranda Malvina, born April 27, 1852, daughter of John Coates, of Eaton. Issue, two daughters: Persis Adeline, born January 6, 1882; Georgianna Elinor, born September 8, 1887. In the engraving may be seen Joseph McGowan, who was born in County Down, Ireland, March 30, 1874, and killed at Lowell, Mass., April 18, 1896.

EZRA FRIZZLE, farmer, was born in Eaton, August 15, 1847. Accompanying this sketch is an engraving of the residence of Mr. Frizzle, which is known as the old Eros LeBourveau farm. It is located about half a mile east of Sand Hill church, on the Height of Land, and is one of the best farms in Eaton. In front of the house is Mr. Frizzle and his family. He is one of the prominent men of the town, a successful farmer, and highly respected. He has held the office of councillor for twelve years. He was married in Eaton, October 16, 1879, to Abbie J., daughter of Wm. B. Brown. Issue, three children: Arthur W., born October 10, 1882; Roy E., born September 2, 1886; Laura A., born December 22, 1880.

MRS. ELLEN M. WARNER was born in Johnville, where she has always resided. She is a daughter of the late A. M. Smith. Mrs. Warner takes a great interest in the W. C. T. U., and is superintendent of the local flower mis-

RESIDENCE OF MRS. E. M. WARNER.

HISTORY OF COMPTON COUNTY.

RESIDENCE OF G. A. MANNING.

sion. Herewith is to be seen an engraving of her residence, with herself and children in front. She was married, in 1866, at Huntingville, Que., to Albert Warner, who died in 1890. Issue, two children: Ernest Ethan, born in 1878; Fannie Edna, born in 1884.

GEORGE A. MANNING, farmer, was born, November 2, 1863, at Johnville, where he has always lived. In 1862 his father, Isaac Manning, moved on to the farm which is the present Manning Homestead. At that time it was nearly all woods. When he died, July 19, 1885, at the age of sixty-nine years, he had a very pleasant home. Our subject was married at Martinville, June 8, 1887, to Luna A., daughter of Soll P. Merrill, of that place. She was born, October 25, 1864, in the State of New York. In 1868 her parents came to Canada and settled at Martinville, where her father still lives. Issue, one son: Clark M., born December 3, 1888. The photo of their residence, here reproduced, shows a cosy home, one mile from Johnville, on the Compton road. In front, may be seen Mr. and Mrs. Manning and their only child.

ROBERT BRIDGETTE, general merchant, and postmaster at Birchton, was born in St. Sylvestre, Que., February 10, 1846. He came to Eaton in 1878, and for several years followed farming previous to his going into trade at his present stand. The father of our subject, John Bridgette, died in Eaton in 1881. Mr. Bridgette is one of the councillors for the township of Eaton, having been re-elected by acclamation in January, 1896. At St. Sylvestre, Que., March 30, 1869,

RESIDENCE OF R. BRIDGETTE.

he married Susannah, daughter of James Moran. Issue, eight children, seven living: Arminc Allen, born November 2, 1871; Eliza Jane, born March 15, 1870; Susan Adelaide, born January 2, 1876; Eva Laura, born November 19, 1877; Edna Sarah, born January 12, 1880; Mary Amy Louisa, born August 28, 1883; Pearle May, born September 22, 1885. Accompanying this is an engraving of the residence of Mr. Bridgette, located just west of his store. In the upper corner will be found the portrait of his only son.

JOHN DEAN FRENCH, farmer, was born in the village of Dullingham, Cambridgeshire, Eng., September 18, 1824. He came to this country in 1843, and the same year settled on his present farm, located two and a half miles north of Cookshire. Accompanying this sketch will be found an engraving of the old homestead with Mr. French, and his son, Robert D. and family, in front. His occupation has always been farming, in which he has proved very successful. He was married at Cookshire, March 11, 1845, to Fanny, daughter of Wm. Mowle, who died in Cookshire in 1878. Issue, ten children, six living: William J., born August 16, 1847, married Mary Lough, residence, Glencoe, Ont.; Robert D., born April 4, 1860, married, first, Alice E. Cowling, of Bury, August 25, 1886, died November 14, 1891, two children (Dean A., born February 6, 1888; Fanny L., born August 2, 1889); second

RESIDENCE OF J. D. FRENCH.

marriage, to Ellen E. Farnsworth, of Cookshire, February 1, 1893, one child (James R., born November 22, 1893); Henry Archibald, born July 14, 1862; Alice H., born March 31, 1850, married William Newson, residence, Blenheim, Ont.; Emma S., born April 7, 1855, married Robert Cowling, residence, East Augus, six children; M. May, born June 24, 1870, married E. J. Planche, residence, Cookshire, two children; Ellener F. Wright, a grandchild, born January 2, 1868, always lived with her grand parents, her mother having died in December, 1868. She married Horace Farnsworth, residence, Cookshire, one child. The mother, Mrs. French, died October 23, 1888.

ABEL H. CHURCH, farmer and carpenter, was born near Quebec, March 17, 1861. He came to Johnville in 1870. His father, James Church, came into the County at the same time and is now living at Johnville. He was married at Lennoxville, September 27, 1877, to Rachel, daughter of Andrew Campbell, now living at Johnville. Issue, three children: Edmund Howard, born September 26, 1888; James Andrew, born April 29, 1893; Ella May, born June 16, 1895.

RUDOLPH T. WILLARD, mill owner, was born in Dudswell, Que., July 26, 1844. He is a son of the late John Willard. He came to Eaton in 1877, and settled on the place where he now resides. In 1875 he married Louisa, daughter of Antoine Martelle. Issue, four children: Henry Dexter, born May 31, 1880; Maria E., born August 17, 1877; Hannah S., born April 20, 1879; Minnie L., born August 6, 1882. A photo-engraving of the residence of Mr. Willard, which is located near Ascot Corner, is here given. In front he and his family are to be seen.

RESIDENCE OF R. T. WILLARD.

MATTHEW HAMILTON, farmer, a resident of Johnville, was born in Argenteuil county, Que., April 28, 1843. He came to East Clifton in 1865. His father, James Hamilton, is still living at Randboro, Que. Our subject was married at Compton, March 22, 1869, to Irene I. Pierce, widow of E. R. Mayo, by whom she had one daughter, Eva M., born February 1, 1864, married Egbert E. Cairns, residence, Massachusetts, two children. Mr. Hamilton has seven children: Hugh E., born October 20, 1871; Frank S. J., born September 13, 1873; Justin W., born June 22, 1877; Hattie M., born February 14, 1870; Lelia R., born March 1, 1875; Effie M., born May 7, 1880; Bertha I., born August 18, 1888. Mr. Hamilton is trustee and steward of the Methodist church, and superintendent of the Sabbath school.

OLIVER DESRUISSEAUX, farmer, was born in Eaton, August 15, 1852. When a young man he went to Connecticut, but returned and settled on his present farm in 1884. He has been councillor in the township of Eaton for three years. Was married at Huntingville, July 18, 1888, to Jennie, daughter of Samuel Paige, of Eaton. Issue, three children: Ray and Roy, twin boys, born October 23, 1889; Leon E. B., born October 31, 1895. Frederick Desruisseaux, brother of Oliver, was born in Eaton April 26, 1862, he also returned from Connecticut in 1884, and, in connection with his brother, purchased their present farm. He married Amy Paige, January 1, 1890, by whom he has one son: Oscar A., born April 18, 1895. A photo of Mr. Desruisseaux's house is given herewith.

RESIDENCE OF OLIVER DESRUISSEAUX.

HERMAN FASSET GATES, farmer and wool carder, a resident of South Cookshire, in the township of Eaton. He was born in Barnard, Vt., January 17, 1840, coming to Eaton, where he has always lived, in 1842. Mr. Gates is chief ranger of Court Island Brook, I.O.F. At Cookshire, on August 29, 1871, he married Lucy Ann, daughter of William Stevenson, of Learned Plain. She was born in Hereford, August 28, 1851. By this marriage there is one son, William H., born September 28, 1876.

THOMAS JOHNSTON, farmer, was born at Bourg Louis, Que., February 18, 1846. He came to Bulwer in March, 1867, and has lived there since. Previous to his going into farming he was in the railroad business. He is a son of Matthew Johnston, who is now living at St. Raymond, Que. Our subject has been a successful business man, and, for several years, one of the members of the Council for the township of Eaton, which office he still holds. We present herewith an engraving of the residence of Mr. Johnston, and in front of the house he may be seen with his family. At Manchester, N. H., April 20, 1871, he married Annie, daughter of Ruel Whitcomb, of Eaton. Mrs. Johnston's mother lives with them, and was ninety-one years of age in May, 1896; she remembers when there was but one house where the city of Sherbrooke is now. Issue, three children; Frank A., born September 27, 1875; H. Mary, born March 19, 1873, married Herbert Hodgman, one child, residence, Birchton; Elbridge M., born November 6, 1881, died May 30, 1884.

RESIDENCE OF THOMAS JOHNSTON.

ALVAN ALEXANDER BAILEY, youngest son of the late Cyrus A. Bailey, was born February 26, 1855, at Cookshire, and has farmed from youth up. He is a P. M., A. F. & A. M., and elected D. D. G. M., in 1896. Was quartermaster of the Fifth Dragoons (Canadian) for seven years; afterwards first lieutenant of No. 1 (Cookshire) troop, same regiment, for six years. He resigned his commission in 1890, retaining rank. He holds a first-class cavalry certificate. He was married in Sherbrooke, Que., December 28, 1882, to Cora J. B., daughter of Lieutenant-Colonel Thomas S. Barwis, now of Calgary, N.W.T., formerly of Arthabaskaville, Que. Lieut.-Col. Barwis once commanded the Fifty-fifth Megantic battalion; was appointed prothonotary for the district of Arthabaska in 1871, which position he held until a few years ago. Issue, eight children: Cyrus A., born March 30, 1892; T. S. Barwis, born April 15, 1894; Niva C. A., born December 9, 1883; Kathleen B. I., born September 1, 1885; Rahea W. E., born September 11, 1887; Creina M. G., born August 4, 1889; Thekla V. E., born March 30, 1892; Rizpah E. O., born December 24, 1895. Mr. Bailey moved on to his present farm, at Birchton, in 1893.

GILBERT A. TRENHOLME, M.D., C.M., was born in Drummond county, March 24, 1865. He is a son of Captain R. G. Trenholme, woollen manufacturer, Coaticook. We present herewith the portraits of Dr. and Mrs. Trenholme and their three children. He was married at Compton in September, 1890, to Myrtle Belle, daughter of the late Joel P. Thomas, farmer. Issue, three children: Marion, born in August, 1891; Gertrude, born in January, 1893; Robert, born in June, 1895. After finishing his studies at school, Dr. Trenholme was for three years in the audit office of the Canada Express Company, Montreal. Not being satisfied with the lot of an office clerk he decided to enter on the study of medicine. In September 1889, he passed the matriculation required by the Board of Physicians and Surgeons. During the summers, in order to pay his board and fees at college in the winter, he bought wool from the farmers throughout the counties of Stanstead and Compton, selling wherever he could secure a market. In this manner he worked his way through,

G. A. TRENHOLME, M.D., C.M., AND FAMILY.

graduating from the university of Bishops Medical College, at Montreal, in 1893. He settled at Eaton Corner in the fall of the same year, and soon had a large practice. In January, 1896, he decided to move to Coaticook, the home of his youth, where he is gradually securing his share of the practice. Dr. Trenholme is a nephew of N. W. Trenholme, D.D.L., Doctor of Law (McGill), B.C.L., Q.C., also of the late Edward H. Trenholme, M.D., C.M., Professor of Gynæcology, and one of the three who established Bishops Medical Faculty.

HENRY EDWARD CHAMBERS, farmer, is a son of Charles E. Chambers, who died in Eaton in 1866. His mother's name was Abagail Tarbell, she died in 1868. He was born in Eaton, August 18, 1834, and his farm is near Bulwer. On June 18, 1866, at Sawyerville, he married Matilda Rosanna, daughter of Charles Coates. He died in Eaton, June 20, 1878. Her mother's name was Mary Ann Bagley, and she died September 6, 1856. Issue, one child: Herbert Henry, born December 25, 1867, married in December, 1893, to Harriet Bulmer.

HISTORY OF COMPTON COUNTY.

AMOS WEBSTER WILLIAMS, agent and farmer, was born in Bulwer, June 19, 1841. He is P. C. R. of the I. O. F. Was married in Newport, June 20, 1865, to Fannie Gallop. Issue, four children: Allan E., born February 17, 1870, married Nettie J. Russel, residence, Colebrook, N. H.; Ermina M., born February 26, 1867, married Edgar A. Kingsley, one child, residence, Sawyerville; Esther L., born September 6, 1872, died January 19, 1894; Mary E., born May 28, 1874.

WELLINGTON LEONARD FISH, blacksmith, a resident of Johnville, was born in Hatley, December, 1850. He came to Johnville in 1873. In May, 1874, in Sherbrooke, he married Adelaide A. Fowler. Issue, two children: Hattie A., born in September, 1884; Arthur E., born in May, 1877.

JOHN MOORE LEARNED, farmer, was born at Learned Plain, within one mile of his present home, July 2, 1845. He moved onto lot three, range nine, township of Eaton, when twenty-two years of age. He holds the office of valuator for the township of Eaton, and is a prominent worker in temperance societies. His father, Alden Learned, was one of the first settlers in Newport, of whom more extensive mention is made elsewhere. Our subject was married in Eaton, December 31, 1874, to Anna M., daughter of D. A. Farnsworth, of Flanders. Issue, five children: Alden A., born April 2, 1876; Gardner E., born July 1, 1881; Phebe H., born February 19, 1878; Margaret E., born March 22, 1885; Catharine N., born July 18, 1888.

WILLIAM SPAULDING WARD, farmer, secretary-treasurer for the Municipal Council, and school commissioners, was born in Nottinghamshire, Eng., March 23, 1838. Came to Birchton in 1863, where he has since lived. He graduated from the Royal Military College, Sandhurst, Eng., and served as lieutenant in H. M., first battalion, twenty-second Regiment. Was married at Sawyerville, June 3, 1869, to Julia A. Hodge. Issue, one daughter: Arabella S., born November 14, 1877.

WELLINGTON ADMOND WARNER, farmer, was born at Sand Hill, where he now resides, October 24, 1856. His father, Chester Warner, was born in Compton in 1810 and died in 1882. His mother's name was Almeda L. Boyden, of Willoughby Lake, N. H. Our subject was married in Sherbrooke, June 8, 1880, to Beatrice E., daughter of R. L. Todd, of Island Brook. Issue, one child: Bernice Gertrude, born March 26, 1884.

HERBERT IRVINE TODD, farmer, a resident near Bulwer, was born in Eaton, where he has always lived, with the exception of five years in California. He holds the office of president of the P. of I. He was married at Bulwer, May 24, 1884, to Alberta Coates. Issue, two children, one living: Stearns M., born 26 March, 1885.

LATE WILLIAM NASON, farmer, was born in Holland, Vt., May 10, 1839, and died in Eaton, April 27, 1889. He came to this township in 1878. He was married in Holland, Vt., in 1860, to Malone Ward. Issue, six children: Luther, born March 31, 1862, married Mary Decato, residence, Barnston, Que.; Clark, born September 21, 1866; William H., born August 24, 1869, married Alma Moulton, two children, residence, Charleston, Vt.; Charles, born October 14, 1871; Gertrude, born September 23, 1878; Nellie, born July 17, 1881.

GEORGE EDGAR SMITH, farmer, born in Eaton, December 13, 1853, always lived here with exception of seven years in Minnesota. Mr. Smith is a steward and trustee of the Methodist church, Bulwer. Married at Learned Plain, April 6, 1881, to Elsie M. Learned. Issue, three children: Harold L., born January 6, 1885; Howard S., born December 15, 1887; Laurence L., born April 18, 1895.

SAMUEL LAKE, miller, of Lake's Mill, was born April 11, 1820, in Warham, Norfolk, Eng. Came to Eaton in 1837, and for over fifty years has run a grist mill here. Married Mary Sophia Hall. Issue, seven children, four living: George M., born November 13, 1849, died January 17, 1878, married Orpha Jordan, three children, residence, Eaton; Samuel F., born November 18, 1855, died February 19, 1896, married Augusta Bennett, one child, residence, Martinville; Alvin L., born July 5, 1859, married Emma LeBourvean, three children, residence, Eaton; Elizabeth M., born January 28, 1848, married Isaac Jordan, two children, residence, New Limerick, Me.; Mary S., born January 20, 1852, died March 14, 1892, married William Rogers, two children; Amanda M., born September 16, 1861, married R. E. Willard, residence, Dudswell; Lomenda, born June 21, 1864, married John Willard, three children, residence, Westbury.

IRA GALLUP, farmer, resident of Bulwer, was born in Melbourne, Que., December 17, 1837, and moved to Eaton in 1857, where he has always lived. At Ulverton, Que., August 17, 1863, he married Mary Cummings. She was born October 9, 1839, and died February 3, 1896. Issue, eight children, seven living: Herbert A., born July 28, 1872; Henry W., born May 8, 1877; Ernest H., born October 27, 1879; Attwood A., born April 22, 1883; Lucina M., born May 14, 1868, married Samuel Coates, residence, Bulwer, one child; Cordelia C., born September 11, 1869, married John Duffy, residence, Martinville, one child; Celia A. E. M., born June 5, 1881.

LAWSON DANFORTH, farmer, was born at Stanstead, on January 1, 1830. The same year his parents moved to Clifton and he remained there until 1877, when he came to Bulwer. His father, Hazen Danforth, died in Hatley in 1887. The subject of this sketch married Elvira, daughter of the late Joseph Bailey, of Compton, in Holland, Vt., February 28, 1876. Mrs. Danforth had one child by her first husband, deceased: Myron Mack, born April 6, 1853, married to Carrie Seymour, two children.

SIMON PETER CORK, farmer, was born in Staffordshire, Eng., February 3, 1835. His father, James Cork, died in Staffordshire in 1855. Mr. Cork came to Eaton and settled on his present farm, located at what is known as Wesleyville, in 1883. Since then he has prospered and has one of the best farms in that vicinity. Previous to his coming to this country he was a brick-maker by trade. December 31, 1853, at Staffordshire, he married Ann, daughter of Thomas Lawrence, of the same place. Issue, eleven children, ten living: Frederick, born April 2, 1855, married Maria Burgess, October 29, 1884, residence, Audley, Eng., six children; George, born June 4, 1859, married Mary A. Holland, June 14, 1886, residence, Wellington, B. C., three children; William, born November 30, 1863; Thomas, born October 10, 1868; Edmund, born June 11, 1869; James, born April 10, 1873; Oliver, born January 25, 1875; Martha, born October 19, 1865, married C. H. Hibbard, July 13, 1891, residence, Lowell, Mass.; Ann E., born February 21, 1871; Catherine E., born March 21, 1878.

GEORGE EDWARD KIRBY, farmer, living near Birchton, was born in Coventry, Warwickshire, Eng., and came to Canada in 1883. Previous to this time he was an engineer. Mr. Kirby was married in Montreal, in 1894, to Miss Amy Coles, of Lamington, Eng. Issue, one son: Guy Hurlston, born March 31, 1895.

WILLIAM LAFAYETTE TUBBS, farmer, resident near Johnville. Married, in 1850, to Cornelia Ellis. Issue, three children: Henry, born in June, 1864; William, born in August, 1871; Calvin, born in November, 1873.

WILLIAM H. SMITH, farmer, of Johnville, was born in Eaton August 6, 1856. Married at Cookshire, January 31, 1877, to Jane Kerr, of Island Brook. Issue, two children: Henry W., born April 25, 1878; Gertrude M., born August 6, 1882.

SAMUEL H. STONE, was born in Glover, Vt., February 3, 1844. Came to Johnville in 1877; at present is section foreman on Canadian Pacific Railway; previous occupation, carpenter. Holds office of president of P. of I. Married Emma L. Sanborn, who died August 17, 1891. Issue, six children, five living: Roy S, born March 25, 1879; John W., born April 17, 1881; Guy C., born November 11, 1888; Nellie B., born July 7, 1877; Eola O., born February 26, 1884.

PHILONAS K. MARTIN, farmer, living near Johnville, was born June 6, 1834. Lived in Clifton and Eaton. Previous occupation, trader. His father, Allen Martin, died in Barnston, Que., in October, 1893. Our subject was married, January 14, 1880, to Eliza J., daughter of James Wilson, of Lingwick. Issue, four children, three living: Albert J., born November 11, 1891; Mildred J. M., born October 18, 1880; Annie W. M., born July 22, 1883.

JAMES McVETTY, farmer, living half a mile from Cookshire, on Learned Plain road, was born in Megantic county, removing here in 1884. First marriage at St. Sylvestre, Que., to Mary Lowry. Second marriage at St. Sylvestre, on August 10, 1882, to Elizabeth Colvin. Mr. McVetty has three children living: James A., Elizabeth, and Emily. Elizabeth, married Alexander Miller, three children, residence, Island Brook.

EDWARD NEWTON LINDSAY, farmer, born at Bulwer, July 4, 1841, where he has always lived. Has held the office of councillor for nine years and valuator twelve years. Was married at Cookshire, October 21, 1862, to Ellen B. Garvin, deceased. Issue, five children, four living: Newton Edward, born November 5, 1882; Nellie Sanford, born May 25, 1867, married Bertrand A. Alger, residence, Eaton Corner; Anna Gertrude, born October 21, 1869, married Ernest E. Todd, residence, Birchton; Mabel Lillian, born September 9, 1879.

ISAAC COIT SMITH, farmer, born in Cookshire, January 12, 1820. He has always lived in the township of Eaton, with the exception of seven years in Minnesota. His father, Joseph B. Smith, was for a number of years deputy sheriff, and died in Johnville. Mr. Smith was married at Bulwer, January 12, 1848, to Julia Lindsay. Issue, four children, three living: George E., born December 13, 1853, married Elsie M. Learned, three children, residence, Eaton; Joseph C., born April 17, 1860, married Evelyn E. Learned, two children; Cecil Douglas, born June 16, 1889; Helen Learned, born February 14, 1893, residence, Eaton; Amanda E., born April 10, 1855, married Austin Williams, eight children, residence, Bulwer.

GEORGE OZRO BAILEY, farmer, was born at Moe's river, September 7, 1822. Mr. Bailey was married at N. Chelmsford, Mass., September 7, 1848, to Mary Ann, daughter of Isaac Wood. Issue, four children: George Harold, born October 17, 1855, married Adeline Butterfield, of Bristol, N. H., one child; Mary O., born July 26, 1852, married James Dawson, residence, W. Brattleboro, Vt., four children; Laura Etta, born December, 1853; Ada L., born September 7, ——, married Clark Harrington, residence, Knob View, Mo., six children.

HISTORY OF COMPTON COUNTY.

RESIDENCE OF JOHN SMITH.

JOHN SMITH, farmer, was born in Cookshire, April 5, 1827, his parents, shortly after, moving to Johnville, where he has since resided. He has held many of the public offices in town, among them being that of councillor, valuator, rural inspector and road inspector. He was married at East Hatley, Que., July 9, 1850, to Caroline, daughter of Pierre LaHaie, who died at Lennoxville in 1851. Issue, four children, three living: Eugene Pierre, born December 6, 1851, married October 10, 1880; Ida Alberta Maria Bagley, one child (Earle C. H., born December 26, 1887), residence, Johnville; Eustace L., married, first, Ada P. Colby, no children, second, Nellie M. Mitchell, two children (James R., born November 29, 1890, Mary M., born May 1, 1895); Reginald Alexis, born May 23, 1867, married, November 6, 1895, Flora D. Swan, of Birchton, residence, Johnville. We present herewith two engravings. In the one of the old home place, there may be seen Mr. and Mrs. Smith and their son Reginald. He is general merchant and postmaster at Johnville; the other is an engraving of the residence of Eugene P. Smith, and in front he and his family may be seen. For a number of years Mr. E. P. Smith was postmaster and general merchant at Johnville, afterward selling out to his brother and devoting his time to farming. He has held the offices of school commissioner, and is now one of the councillors of Eaton.

WARREN C. SMITH, carriage-maker, was born in Johnville, August 9, 1842, where he has always resided. He is a son of Abner M. Smith, who died March 21, 1894. He was married at Burlington, Vt., February 27, 1865.

RESIDENCE OF EUGENE P. SMITH.

to Hannah M., daughter of the late Ransome Ellis. Issue, one son, born in 1868, died in infancy. A photo-engraving of the residence of Mr. Smith accompanies this sketch.

EDSON ALBERT HASELTINE, farmer, resident near Sand Hill, was born in the same place on May 26, 1856. He has moved around some, having lived in Cookshire, Westbury, Scotstown, and Megantic, being occupied as scaler and lumber culler. His parents, Albert and Sarah (French) Haseltine, are both dead. At Sherbrooke, June 21, 1882, he married Clara Anna Hall, born in Maine, November 16, 1859. Issue, six children: Harold E., born August 10, 1886; Albert, born February 25, 1893; Rupert F., born February 25, 1895; Sarah B., born January 14, 1884; Myrtie P., born November 14, 1888; Ethel G., born February 16, 1891.

JOHN HAINES FRENCH, farmer, was born November 2, 1835, in the township of Eaton, where he has always lived, with the exception of two years in Newport, Que. At Sawyerville, Que., November 19, 1863, he was married to Achsah Brown. Issue, five children, four living: Frederick W., born November 26, 1866, married Fanny L. Gray, residence, Lawrence, Mass., one child; Melvin G., born July 25, 1868; Herbert O., born August 13, 1870; Helen M., born August 15, 1864.

RESIDENCE OF W. C. SMITH.

LATE WILLIAM WILLARD WHEELER, was born in Charlestown, N. H., November 7, 1807, died in Bulwer, April 3, 1881. He came to Compton county, with his father, Amos Wheeler, in 1811, and always lived in Eaton, where he followed farming. He was a deacon in the Freewill Baptist church. He was married in Bulwer, March 25, 1861, to Caroline Jordan. Issue, seven children: Ellsworth A., born March 18, 1879; Adelia L., born April 7, 1862, married Marshall Legget, residence, Auckland; Melvina L., born September 30, 1863; Lilly J., born November 26, 1865; Nettie E., born August 18, 1867; Mary M., born November 21, 1869; Minnie S., born April 13, 1872, married Wellington S. Brayel, residence, Allston, Mass.

GEORGE WASHINGTON SMITH, farmer, was born in Cookshire, August 23, 1824. He always lived in Eaton; at present in Johnville. He has held offices of councillor and school commissioner. First marriage, December 8, 1847, to Abigail Lindsay. Issue, Mary G., born June 22, 1849, married Robert Cairns, seven children; residence, Sawyerville. Second marriage, August 26, 1854, to Olive Jane Coates. Issue, two children: Hollis S., born July 16, 1856, married Jessie Manning, three children, residence, Johnville; Hibbard J., born September 11, 1862, married Minnie M. Sunbury, two children, residence, Johnville.

JEAN-BAPTISTE DELISLE, farmer, was born in Brandon, Vt., April 16, 1855. He came to Canada in 1857, and to Eaton in 1877. He married Rosa Caroline Clement, of Ascot, in Lennoxville, on May 2, 1881. Issue, eight children: Joseph J., born September 24, 1884; François H., born January 21, 1886; Damase P., born April 28, 1887; Arthur H., born October 27, 1892; Arthur Oliver, born February 17, 1895; Marie-Louise, born October 30, 1882; Marie A. Antoinette, born May 8, 1889; Marie F. Adonilda, born August 11, 1891.

JOHN GROVE SUNBURY, farmer, born in Eaton, February 12, 1822. After marriage he lived in Clifton for six years, then returned to Birchton. Was married in Eaton, October 31, 1848, to Mary Ann Parsons. Issue, ten children, eight living: Alonzo B., born August 23, 1856, married Christina Smith, one child, residence, Fairhaven, Minn.; Ozro W., born February 12, 1861, married Mary Bottger, two children, residence, San José, Cal.; George G., born July 9, 1863, married Mary Green, residence, Kimball, Minn.; Wilbert W., born August 28, 1866; Louisa M., born August 25, 1851, married Daniel Foss, one child, residence, Brighton, Me.; Mary A., born May 1, 1858, married Alphonso Hodge, two children, residence, Eaton Corner; Hattie E., born March 20, 1864; Alma Ida, born November 3, 1871.

GEORGE H. PARKER, farmer, resident near Johnville, was born in Ascot, October 13, 1856. His father, Daniel T., moved to Compton in 1858. Mr. Parker married Rue L., daughter of Benjamin C. Bailey, of West Clifton. Issue, two children: Bessie A., born March 24, 1890; Lizzie E., born March 11, 1894.

WILLIAM J. WHITEMAN, farmer and stone mason, living near Johnville, was born in Eaton, July 18, 1824. Married at Sherbrooke, October 16, 1862, to Elvira J. Smith. Issue, seven children, five living: William G., born October 22, 1863, married May M. Oxendozz; Belle R., born January 26, 1865, married Ed. Stevens; Alvin M., born August 19, 1869, married Effie Cairns, two children; Austin R., born January 22, 1871, married Emma Statton, one child; residence, Sawyerville; Eva M., married Herbert French, one child, residence, Warren, N. H.

LATE HENRY LEBOURVEAU, born in Eaton, October 2, 1837, died same township March 21, 1895. In his lifetime a farmer and postmaster. Was married in Eaton, February 15, 1859, to Phebe A. Currier. Issue, three children: Benjamin LeBourveau, born December 20, 1868, married Sarah H. Learned, December 18, 1895, residence, Flanders; Emma Persis, born March 30, 1862, married Alvin Lake, three children, residence, Eaton; Mary Ellen, born February 18, 1874, married Robert French, one child, residence, Newport.

EPHRAIM ABBOT WARD, farmer, was born in Eaton, December 26, 1822, and has always lived in Compton county. He was married at Cookshire, January 11, 1848, to Irene French, born July 23, 1826. Issue, eight children: Volney F., born September 17, 1848, married Salome Washburn, residence, Hopkinsonville, Ky., five children; George E., born June 18, 1850, married Susan Statton, residence, Whitefield, N. H., three children; Horace A., born October 26, 1855; Sarah J., born January 16, 1852, married Ira Parker, residence, Montreal, four children; Cora A., born August 12, 1857, married Charles F. Weston, residence, Denver, Col., seven children; Ellen M., born June 11, 1861, married Robert Chaddock, residence, Eaton, three children; Orra H., born September 19, 1863, married Walter Nutt, residence, Eaton, three children; Olive I., born January 19, 1869, married E. W. Phelps, residence, Cookshire.

BENJAMIN WILLIAM FRIZZLE, farmer, a resident of Bulwer, was born in Columbia, N. H., January 23, 1834. He came to Eaton with his parents, Orsamus and Drusilla (Hicks) Frizzle, in 1847. His father died July 27, 1894, aged eighty-seven years, his mother died October 24, 1886, aged seventy-three years. The subject of our sketch was married in Eaton, February 4, 1862, to Esther, daughter of Samuel Smith. Issue, two children: William Ira, born May 13, 1872; Cora Ada, born December 17, 1864, married Frank Winner, residence, Natick, Mass., two children, Ray F., born April 14, 1892; Earl W., born August 22, 1894.

WILLIAM OSCAR COLBY, of Johnville, was born at Bulwer, May 24, 1853. He has always lived in the township of Eaton, and for several years was a farmer, previous to his accepting a position as sectionman on the Canadian Pacific Railway. At Cookshire, October 20, 1874, he married Melissa Jane, daughter of Tyler Pope, Esq., who now lives in Lowell, Vt. Issue, seven children; George W., born December 31, 1879; Reginald J., born March 10, 1882; Archie C., born August 31, 1886; Philip D., born December 15, 1882; Myrtie C., born October 13, 1875; Grace L., born March 13, 1890.

WILLIAM FRENCH, farmer, a resident of Flanders, was born in Cornwall, Eng., in 1826. He came to this county in 1848, went to Massachusetts in 1849, came back to Eaton in 1861, and settled on the farm where he now resides. Previous to his settling here he was a cabinetmaker by trade. He has been road inspector and valuator and councillor for nine years. On January 2, 1857, in Massachusetts, he married Elizabeth McGee. Issue, eight children: James W., born April 20, 1862, married Bertha Scott, residence, Bloomfield, Vt.; William, born August 8, 1864, married Esther Burns, residence, Newport; Robert F., born December 4, 1866, married Mary LeBourveau, residence, Newport, one child; Henry, born November 3, 1873; Margery, born September 9, 1857, married W. Chamberlain, residence, Dixville two children; Mary, born May 23, 1860, married L. D. Chamberlain, residence, Dixville; Margaret L., born April 17, 1870, married Wm. T. Fuge, residence, Kansas City, Mo.; Lizzie W., born November 25, 1875.

EDGAR NORMAN CHADDOCK, farmer, was born October 26, 1858, at the present homestead. It is located about half a mile from Cookshire, on the Sawyerville road. He has always followed farming, and made a success of the same, never having left the home place. His father, Norman Chaddock, died here on December 27, 1879. At Cookshire, March 10, 1880, he married Jennie, daughter of the late John Clements (who died at Cookshire, January 25, 1888). Issue, three children: Guy, born August 20, 1884; Gladys J. C. E. E. C., born April 25, 1890, and a baby boy, born January 15, 1895.

ROBERT HENRY CHADDOCK, sr., farmer, living at Riverdale, Eaton. He was born in Eaton, July 24, 1827, and has always lived in the County. He has been a corporal and lieutenant in the Cookshire Troop of Cavalry. His father was the late Luke Chaddock, of Eaton. Mr. Chaddock was married at Eaton Corner, May 12, 1851, to Mary Ann, daughter of the late Luther E. Hall, of Eaton. Issue, eight children: Robert Henry, born February 29, 1852, married Nellie Ward, residence, Eaton, three children; James Craig, born April 23, 1854, married Liceua Hunt, residence, Milton, Mass.; Charles Edward, born August 27, 1862; Herbert Austin, born January 9, 1865; Abbie A., born March 21, 1858; Elva M., born April 19, 1860; Pertie E., born April 23, 1868, married Charles E. Hallett, residence, Milton, Mass.; Emma A., born July 2, 1872.

ROBERT HENRY CHADDOCK, farmer, living two miles east of Cookshire, on the Bury road, was born at Jordan Hill, township of Eaton, February 29, 1852. He has always lived in the Township and followed farming. Mr. Chaddock is V. C. R. Court Cariboo, No. 477, C. O. F. At Cookshire, February 23, 1886, he married Ellen M., born June 11, 1861, daughter of Ephraim A. Ward, Esq. Issue, three children: Luke W., born November 20, 1888; Wilber A., born April 27, 1891; Horace A., born March 22, 1895.

ANDREW HENRY IRWIN, farmer, came to Sand Hill in 1884, purchasing his present farm from estate late Chester Warner. He was born in Rodden, Que., September 21, 1851. His father, William Irwin, died at Sand Hill, November 28, 1877. First marriage at Sherbrooke, March 10, 1880, to Maria Ward, of Lennoxville, who died in 1887. Issue, two children: Charles Henry, born March 16, 1881; Frederick E., born December 26, 1882. Second marriage at Cookshire, September 16, 1891, to Celia Coates, of Birchton.

WILLIAM JOHN IRWIN, owner of the old Irwin farm at Sand Hill, was born at Rodden, Que., March 27, 1863. Came to Sand Hill with parents in 1876. At present Mr. Irwin is traveler for E. N. Heney & Co., Montreal; he was for four years turnkey in the Sherbrooke gaol; four years in charge of Sherbrooke library and reading-room, and several years traveler for H. C. Wilson & Sons, Sherbrooke. On August 25, 1886, at Sherbrooke, he married Florence L., daughter of Captain John Woodward, building and bridge inspector for the Canadian Pacific Railway. She died April 5, 1888.

EDWIN DIAH ALGER, farmer, son of Horace Alger (deceased 1886) and Jane Ross, of Vermont, his wife. He was born at Eaton Corner, May 10, 1851, in the house he now resides in. Mr. Alger went to California in 1878, where he remained nine years, when he returned to his paternal home and took to farming. He is a municipal councillor of his native township. His great-grandfather came from the state of Massachusetts in 1801, and settled at Eaton Corner, on a portion of which land the subject of this sketch now resides. His grandfather, Asa Alger, died within a few years, at Eaton Corner, at a ripe old age.

B. A. ALGER, farmer, a resident of Eaton Corner, was born at that place, May 16, 1858. He is a son of the late Henry Alger. On December 1, 1892, at Bulwer, Que., he married Nellie S., daughter of E. N. Lindsay, Esq. Mr. Alger has always followed farming on the old home place, which forms part of one of the first farms in Eaton.

TOWN OF COOKSHIRE.

This place derived its name from Captain John Cook, one of the first settlers, and was first called Cookshire by Colonel Taylor after Mr. Cook's death.

Previous to June, 1892, this formed part of the township of Eaton, but in that year it was incorporated as a town, with charter granted by the Provincial legislature. It is just two miles square, and has a population of one thousand.

According to the best data we can obtain, we are inclined to select the year 1897 as the time when the first opening was made at Cookshire in the great wilderness then stretching from Quebec to Lake Champlain in an almost unbroken surface. We find that what records the descendants of the early settlers do possess, do not strictly agree in all points. For instance, one account says that a Mr. John French and his two sons came

HISTORY OF COMPTON COUNTY.   105

into Eaton in 1797 and made the first settlement, while another informs us that in 1798 there were only four families in Eaton, viz.:—Josiah Sawyer at Sawyerville, a Mr. Powers at Cookshire, on the farm now occupied by R. H. Pope, Esq., M. P., a Mr. Bailey, near Eaton Corner, and a Mr. Hughes, three miles west of Sawyerville. If Mr. French and his sons had returned to the States temporarily for Mrs. French and his household effects and was absent from Eaton for this purpose during 1798, the seeming discrepancy might be thus explained, and we think this to be the probable reason, as we are also told that Mr. French's family followed him later. If this Mr. Powers was here with his family in 1798, it can be easily understood that he might have immigrated in 1797, and made the settlement of the town in that year, as some traditions have it.

Following soon after came John Cook, Jesse Cooper, Levi French, Luther French, Abner Osgood, Orsemus Bailey, Ward Bailey and Ebenezer Learned, and settled in and not far from the present limits of Cookshire.

The place made slow advancement up to the time of the building of the old International Railway, and twenty-five years ago the residents generally went to Eaton Corner to do their trading. Since then, however, quite a change has taken place, and people from Eaton Corner now come to Cookshire. The first hotel was erected in 1850. The first store was kept by John Farnsworth, and opened about 1830, at the top of the hill in the small old house at the fork of the road, owned by Mr. Alden Learned.

Mrs. Day, in her "History of the Eastern Townships," written in 1869, says:—"Cookshire is a diffuse village, or rather thickly-settled farming section, lying within the northeast quarter of the Township. In summer, the place has a delightfully cool and refreshing appearance, as from the rising grounds may be seen the white farm houses and their clusters of outbuildings in pleasing contrast with the beautiful green of the trees, pastures and fields ; and occasionally a glittering spire pointing heavenward, while in some directions a background is formed to the scene by prominent mountains. Of these, the Stoke Mountains are on the northwest ; the Megantic on the east ; the Hereford Hills on the south, while still further in the distance are the pale blue outlines of prominent peaks beyond the Provincial line."

The first municipal records are dated July 13, 1892, and the first members of the Council were : W. H. Learned, mayor, and councillors W. W. Bailey, Horace Sawyer, Geo. Flaws, H. A. Planche, L. J. D. Gauthier, and George Côté. Mr. Bailey followed Mr. Learned as mayor for two years. The Council for 1896 is as follows: W. H. Learned, mayor, and councillors W. W. Bailey, Horace Sawyer, Ayton Cromwell, T. A. Hurd, L. J. D. Gauthier, and George Côté. Mr. E. S. Baker has been secretary-treasurer of the town from the first.

There have been several improvements made in the place since its incorporation, among them being the expenditure by the Council of $30,000 for a system of water works and sewerage. The money was raised by bonds payable in twenty-five years. The valuation in 1896 for assessable property is $210,550; non-assessable, $28,050.

The first physician to locate in Cookshire was Dr. Rogers, in 1813. He built a home and occupied it where Mr. Frank Plaisance now lives. He practiced here for many years and then moved to Eaton Corner where he died. He was succeeded by a physician from Quebec, named Andrews, who moved away. After him came Dr. Carter. Dr. Hopkins came about 1862 and practiced until his death, leaving four sons doctors, Alfred, Herbert, Fred and Willie. The three first graduated as physicians and the last as a dentist. All practiced for a few years here but have since moved away, being succeeded in their practice in 1893 by R. H. Phillimore, M.D.

Dr. Alfred Orr, a Cookshire boy, graduated from McGill and practiced with success, but finally removed to Montreal. He sold out to Dr. Ford, and the latter to Dr. Alex. Dewar, a native of Winchester, Ont., in 1892.

The principal industries of Cookshire are the Cookshire Mill Company, Cookshire Flour Mill Company, Cookshire Machine Works Company (the latter are closed at present), stores and shops of all kinds. Here is the office of the *Compton County Chronicle*, and a branch of the People's Bank of Halifax.

Cookshire being the *chef-lieu* of the County, the court house, registry office and county buildings are here located. It is also the junction point of the Canadian Pacific and Maine Central railways, giving good freight and passenger connections to all points. The postal revenue for 1895 was $1,561.60.

RESIDENCE OF R. H. POPE, M. P.

There are three churches in the town: Church of England, Methodist and Roman Catholic. As the history of these churches is interwoven with that of Eaton, we have included all under the history of that township.

The first school in Cookshire was in 1810, and kept for a short time by a man named Prebble. From then to 1814 or 1815 there was no school, but in the latter year there was one started by the Rev. Johnathan Taylor, afterwards a Church of England clergyman. He was followed by Miss Laberee, and she in turn by Thos. K. Oughtred. He received a license from "The Royal Institution for the Advancement of Learning." "By virtue of the power and authority in us vested by His Excellency, the Governor in Chief of the Province of Lower Canada, we do hereby give you license and permission to act as, and be during pleasure the master and teacher of a certain school established in the district of St. Peters, parish of Eaton, with a salary of £20 cy. per annum, with full power and authority to teach the children in reading, writing and arithmetic. Signed in the name and on behalf of the institution, J. Quebec, principal." This document was dated 1823 and Mr. Oughtred had to pay £1 for it. His first term began in 1824, and he had to make reports to government at certain intervals. He was obliged by his agreement to teach gratis a certain number of scholars whose parents were too poor to pay the rate, and at one term he had as many as a half a dozen at least of these children. He also took a certain proportion of his salary in produce. He taught twelve years. In looking over copies of his school journal for the years 1824, 1826, 1834, we find many familiar names, such as Nancy Farnsworth, Henry (Hon. John) Pope, Cyrus Bailey, Rufus Pope, Johnathan French Taylor, John French, Moses Lebourveau, Charles Lebourveau, Charles Farnsworth, Frances Cummings, Isaac Smith, Albert Farnsworth, John McNicol, Persis Bailey (now Hon. Mrs. Pope), Richard Wilford, Albert Pope, Amanda Bailey, Luther French, Joseph Taylor, Aug. Taylor, Susan Oughtred (now Mrs. John Goodwin) John Bailey, Lucy Taylor, Jonas Osgood. Other teachers were Robinson Oughtred, Miss Emily French, Emily Cummings, Miss Susan Oughtred, Horace Metcalf, Miss Jane Wilford, Miss Sarah Hurd, Henry Hunting, Rodolphus Harvey, Miss Ella Parsons, Miss Maria Farnsworth, and W. B. Ives, (now Hon.), Miss Alice Taylor, Miss Aggie Wilford, Miss Stacey and Miss Miller. Miss Oughtred taught for twenty-six years at various periods.

In 1884 a move was made looking to the establishment of a model school. A committee consisting of W. H. Learned, W. W. Bailey and H. H. Sawyer was chosen to solicit subscriptions for the erection of a suitable building. They found this not to be practicable, and after duly considering the matter, they applied to the Board of School Commissioners to levy a tax upon the district. They consented, and twenty-five mills were laid, giving $2,300 for that object. The committee were also empowered by the commissioners to select a site for the building, buy and proceed with its erection, which they did at a cost of $3,500. At its completion many thought it too large for any school that would ever be taught in Cookshire, but in 1891 it had to be nearly doubled in size and is all occupied to-day. The school had the strong support of Hon. J. H. Pope, and at his death a legacy of $5,000 was left by him to be invested for its benefit. This has proved a very great help and insures its future success. The staff of teachers at present are Mr. Connolly, principal; Miss Ayerst, and Miss Stevens.

LATE CYRUS ALEXANDER BAILEY, farmer, was born in "The Old Home," of which we give an engraving herewith, on February 2, 1821. Mr. Bailey always lived in the same house and died there January 3, 1894. In the engraving Mrs. Bailey may be seen standing in the doorway, while those in front are Mr. F. E. Osgood (who now owns the home place), Mrs. Osgood and Misses M. A. and P. E. A. Bailey. Orsamus Bailey and his wife, Margaret Whitman (she came from Holland to America at the age of 16), came from Leamington, Vt., in 1797. They were among the first settlers that wintered in Eaton, traveling thirty miles into the woods with no other guide than a spotted line, and settling in Cookshire on the farm now occupied by Charles Frasier. Issue, nine children, and the four sons all settled on parts of the original Bailey property. Daniel married Betsey Sunbury, moving later to New Hampshire; Rufus married Mary Cook, died in Cookshire; Jared married Sophia Strobridge, died in Cookshire; Betsey married Hazzard Terrill, died in Sherbrooke; Mary married Amos Hall, of New Ireland, Que., died in Cookshire; Nancy married Ira Hall, died in New Ireland, Que.; Abigail married James Frasier and lived on the old home place with au unmarried sister, Almira, and all three died there. Ward Bailey, the second son and father of our subject, was born in Leamington, Vt., coming to Eaton with his parents when four years of age. He used to tell of often going to Sherbrooke when there were only three houses there. The nearest market for the settlers was Three Rivers. At that time the travel to market in winter was principally on the ice, and he often related narrow escapes from going under the ice. For many summers Mr. Bailey carried pearlash and produce of the townships in a boat down the St. Francis to Port St. Francis, returning loaded with necessaries for the settlers. He settled on part of the farm or land first taken up by his father in Cookshire, and lived there until his death, November 4, 1866. He married Sally Rogers in 1816, who died in the following year. For his second wife he married the widow French, née Amy Hall, in 1820, whose husband was drowned at the Brompton falls. She had three children: Abigail, married Tyler Hurd; Horace, now living in Scotstown, married Harriet Ward; John, married first Esther Barlow, second Esther Ward. By Ward Bailey's second marriage he had four children: Cyrus, William, Persis and Ann. William died when fifteen years of age. Persis married the late Hon. John Henry Pope; Ann married A. W. Pope, died in Cookshire; Cyrus, the subject of this sketch, received his education in the best schools of Eaton, and afterward at the school of Mr. T. Oughtred. He was married in Eaton, by Rev. E. J. Sherrill, on July 8, 1844, to Emily Ruhamah

RESIDENCE OF THE LATE C. A. BAILEY.

French, born October 30, 1820. Her father's name was Luther Sage French, born February 20, 1775, in Enfield, Conn., died in Eaton in 1859. Issue, eleven children: William W., born April 14, 1845, married Naomi N. Weston, seven children, residence, Cookshire; Maria A., born July 28, 1846, married C. W. B. French, three children, died February 2, 1880; Horace H., born December 7, 1847, married Martha E. Laberee, five children, residence, Ottawa; Ellen M., born August 24, 1849, married Richard M. Warren, four children, residence, Chester, Neb.; Charles C., born May 12, 1851, married Ella M. Pope, two children, residence, Cookshire; Arthur W., born May 15, 1853, died July 12, 1869; Alvan A., born February 26, 1855, married Cora J. B. Barwiss, eight children, residence, Birchton; Mary Abigail, born January 13, 1857; Emma M., born September 8, 1858, married Malcolm B. Macaulay, four children, residence, Scotstown; Persis Elvira Ann, born October 21, 1860; Laura A., born March 1, 1862, married Frederick E. Osgood, residence, Cookshire. Mr. C. A. Bailey, during his lifetime, was always active in business, foremost in public enterprises, and highly esteemed by his townsmen. He was mayor of Eaton for many years, and secretary-treasurer of Compton county for twenty-seven years, commissioner for Circuit Court from 1850 to the time of his death. Mr. Bailey spent much time in soliciting stock subscriptions for the Eastern Townships Bank, afterwards established at Sherbrooke. For many years he was a director of the Stanstead and Sherbrooke Mutual Fire Insurance Company, and at the time of his death held the office of vice-president. He helped, by his influence, to start the Eastern Townships Agricultural Exhibition at Sherbrooke, was also instrumental in constructing colonization roads in the townships of Ditton, Hampden, Chesham and Auckland. The construction of the old International and Hereford railways was largely assisted by Mr. Bailey, and he was secretary-treasurer of the latter road during its inception and building.

RESIDENCE OF WILLIAM W. BAILEY.

WILLIAM WARD BAILEY, manager for the Cookshire Mill Company, eldest son of the late Cyrus A. Bailey, was born in Cookshire, April 14, 1845. He attended school at the academy here, Sherbrooke academy, High school, Royalton, Vt., and for two years St. Francis college, Richmond. Mr. Bailey has spent his whole life in the business of lumbering and contracting. When a young man he went into lumbering at Island Brook. While there he was councillor of Newport for eight years, and mayor part of the time. Shortly after leaving Island Brook, he accepted a responsible position with the Cookshire Mill Company, and has since remained with them, at the present time having full charge of all their outside business. Mr. Bailey was a councillor in Eaton for many years, resigning when Cookshire was set off as a town, and chosen here by acclamation. He was mayor of the town in 1894 and 1895. He is a Mason and Forester, and been a justice of the peace for twenty-five years. Mr. Bailey has been a councillor for over twenty years, and during all that time has never had a contest at the polls. At Island Brook, November 1, 1871, he married Naomi N. Weston, daughter of James Weston. Issue nine children, seven living: Arthur H. W., born October 14, 1872; Rufus O., born December 19, 1877, died January 19, 1878; Clara M. M., born September 18, 1875; Georgianna R. G., born June 19, 1879; R. E. Evelyn, born October 28, 1881; Frederick H. W., born November 13, 1883; Lucy E. M, born May 28, 1885, died February 12, 1886; Lena B. M., born March 2, 1887; Gretchen L. L., born March 5, 1890. Accompanying this description will be found a picture of the residence of Mr. Bailey, located at the corner of Railroad and Pleasant streets, Cookshire, and in front part of which the family are grouped.

MR AND MRS. HORACE H. BAILEY.

HORACE HENRY BAILEY was born in Cookshire, Que., December 7, 1847. Received a common education at schools in Cookshire and Eaton. He enlisted in the Cookshire cavalry at the age of fourteen, was the first young man from Compton county to attend the Military school in Montreal, established by Militia General Order of February 10, 1865. He received a second-class certificate May 16, and first-class certificate June 12, same year. He raised and commanded the first company, consisting of fifty-eight officers and men, of volunteer militia in Eaton, in May and June, 1867. After he became of age he went to the Western States, remaining about three years, then returned to Cookshire and was engaged at construction work on the International railroad. On April 8, 1873, he received a request from the secretary of the navy at Washington, D.C., to proceed at once to Mare Island, Cal. Three days later he was married to Martha Eliza, daughter of Henry Edwin Laberee, of Eaton, and left immediately for the Pacific Coast, returning June 5, following. The following year he built and occupied the house between C. C. Bailey's and the Cookshire Mill Company's store, Cookshire. He was elected a councillor of Eaton in January, 1875, and served three years. In 1878 he went to the Madoc district in Ontario and erected mining machinery. Failing in his undertaking he went west of Lake Superior and did sub-contract work on the railroad. At the completion of work he went to Rat Portage, built the first stamp mill in the Lake of the Woods district. Later, in company with two others, procured timber limits and built a steam saw mill. During the

RESIDENCE OF CHARLES C. BAILEY.

trouble over the boundary between Ontario and Manitoba he took a very active part on the side of Manitoba. He was, on two different occasions, chosen by the Manitoba supporters in Rat Portage to wait upon the Manitoba government and lay before the ministers certain matters affecting their interests. During the first meeting, at the earnest solicitation of their premier, Hon. John Norquay, he was appointed and sworn in a justice of the peace for the province of Manitoba, under date July 27, 1883. In the fall of 1883 he returned to Cookshire with the intention of taking his family to the Northwest in the following year, to settle. In the meantime he was urged to accept a position of examiner of patents of invention in the civil service at Ottawa, and was appointed by order in council October 19, 1884. This office he now holds.

MRS. H. H. BAILEY was born at Eaton, April 6, 1853, married April 11, 1873. Issue six children, five living: Mary Emily, born in Eaton, April 30, 1874; Ethelyn Grace, born in Cookshire, November 26, 1875; Rufus Orsamus, born in Cookshire, February 16, 1879; Maria Augusta, born in Cookshire, September 16, 1884, died July 14, 1886; Lucy Lillian, born in Ottawa, May 22, 1888; Jessie Ellen, born in Ottawa, December 31, 1890. Photo-engravings of Mr. and Mrs. Bailey accompany this sketch.

CHARLES CLEVELAND BAILEY, watchmaker and jeweler, was born in Cookshire, May 12, 1851. He is a son of the late Cyrus A. Bailey, a prominent citizen of Cookshire, and well known throughout the Townships. Our subject lived in Cookshire until 1870, when he joined a company of volunteers and served one year in the first Red River expedition. From there he moved from place to place throughout the West, being three years in Kansas and Texas. Later he was in Qu'Appelle, N. W. T., from May, 1886, to June, 1888. In the latter year he returned to Cookshire, where he has since made his home. Mr. Bailey was appointed United States consular agent in May, 1889, which office he still holds. During the year 1895 he held the offices of treasurer A. F. & A. M.; N. G. of the I. O. O. F., and C. R. of the C. O. F. Mr. Bailey is one of the public-spirited men of Cookshire, always ready with his money and time to assist all local enterprises. At Cookshire, June 7, 1881, he married Ella Maria, daughter of Craig Pope, Esq. Issue, three children, two living: Edward Arthur, born July 10, 1882; Ethel Gertrude, born August 4, 1883; Carl Alexander, born February 2, 1886, died when three years of age. Accompanying this sketch is an engraving of the residence of Mr. Bailey, located at the corner of Railroad and Main streets. On the ground floor, facing Railroad street, is his jewelry shop and U. S. consul office.

A. H. W. BAILEY.

ARTHUR H. W. BAILEY, manager of the Cookshire Mill Company's dressing mill at Beecher Falls, Vt, is a son of William W. Bailey, of Cookshire, general manager of the same company. He was born October 14, 1872, at Island Brook. He was educated at the Cookshire Academy and Commercial School. Accompanying this sketch is the portrait of Mr. Bailey.

AMERICAN HOUSE, F. E. OSGOOD, Proprietor.

FREDERICK ELSWORTH OSGOOD, farmer and proprietor American House, was born in Cookshire, August 20, 1861. His father, Hollis Osgood, died in 1891; his mother, Sarah Garvin, is still living. He has always lived in and near Cookshire, residing on the home farm until 1888, when he purchased a half interest in the American House, and a short time after became sole proprietor, continuing the business at the present time. Mr. Osgood also deals extensively in horses, buying and selling at all times, and is considered one of the best judges of horses in this section. He was married at Cookshire, June 14, 1883, to Laura Alice, youngest daughter of the late C. A. Bailey. Issue, two children: both died in infancy. Accompanying this sketch is an engraving, direct from photograph, of the American House, Cookshire.

COOKSHIRE HOUSE, A. LEARNED, PROPRIETOR.

ALDEN LEARNED, proprietor of the Cookshire House, was born in Cookshire, October 15, 1842. He is a son of William Learned, and a grandson of Ebenezer Learned, one of the first settlers in Eaton, whose history may be found with that of John F. Learned and the home place. Alden Learned, our subject, in January, 1868, when twenty-five years of age, purchased his present hotel from Mr. H. H. French, now of Scotstown, who had erected the building in 1850. Previous to Mr. Learned's purchase the place had been carried on by Mr. H. H. French, Scott Gamsby, now of Lennoxville, and the late Jonas Osgood. In 1889 he thoroughly repaired the building at an expense of several thousand dollars, putting in steam heat throughout. Accompanying this is an engraving of the Cookshire House, in front of which may be seen Mr. and Mrs. Learned, Mrs. Moore and

Miss Learned. He is a public spirited man, who has conceived and carried through many beneficial measures, that have greatly assisted Cookshire. His judgment is much sought after, and his ever ready and practical help is often extended to those in trouble. He was one of the provisional directors of the Hereford Railway, and connected as stockholder and adviser with all local public enterprises. Mr. Learned was married at Cookshire, April 20, 1868, to Eliza, daughter of the late Rufus Pope, brother of Hon. John Henry Pope. He died in Cookshire in 1874. Issue, two daughters: Luvia, born April 17, 1868, married April 17, 1894, to W. R. Moore, book-keeper Connecticut River Lumber Company, one child, residence, West Stewartstown, N. H.; Georgie H., born November 27, 1877.

WILLIAM HENRY LEARNED, mayor of Cookshire and manager Cookshire Mill Company's store, was born in Cookshire, May 14, 1845. He is a son of the late William Learned.

RESIDENCE OF JOHN F. LEARNED.

Possessing good business abilities he has been active in both private and public affairs. For several years he was in trade at Lennoxville and later at Cookshire. He was cashier and purchasing agent during the building of the Hereford Railway. In 1882 he was first elected councillor for Eaton, and in 1883 chosen mayor, which office he held until the incorporation of Cookshire, when he was returned by acclamation and chosen mayor for two years, and again re-elected in February, 1896. He held the office of warden of the County in 1889. He labored hard in organizing the Compton County Liberal-Conservative Association, and held the office of secretary-treasurer until 1895, when he resigned. He has also been connected with all local enterprises, which he has assisted by money and labor. Mr. Learned was married at Lennoxville, July 4, 1876, to Miss A. E. Fisher. Issue, two children: William Edwin, born August 2, 1882; Helen Mabel, born August 31, 1879.

JOHN FRANCIS LEARNED, farmer, was born in Cookshire, November 17, 1857. He owns and occupies the farm originally cleared by the Learneds, one of whom was an associate in securing the grant for the township of Eaton. His great-grandfather, Abijah Learned, moved from Union, Conn., to Columbia, Coos county, N. H., in May, 1772. He was elected a member of the first New Hampshire Legislature, and while returning home from one of the sessions, died suddenly at Lancaster. Four sons of this Learned (sometimes called Larned), Abel, James, Royal and Ebenezer, came to Canada. Abel, eldest of the four, was taken prisoner during the revolutionary war and carried to Quebec. On the march he saw among his captors an Indian whom his mother had treated with kindness, and the Indian furnished him with food and helped him. He was about nineteen years of age at the time of capture, and confined at Quebec two years, suffering much for want of food and clothing, being exchanged at the close of the war. He came to Eaton about 1808, living here ten years, teaching school part of the time. He died at Ryegate, Vt., in 1836, having several times represented his town in the Legislature. James Learned was one of the first settlers on Lake Memphremagog, moving there with his family. He died April 4, 1799, leaving a widow (Theodata Smith, of Stratford, N. H.), and five children. Royal Learned was one of the associates to whom the Township was granted. He located on the west end of the present Learned farm, his house being built below the Exhibition grounds. Here he died in 1810, leaving a large family, all of whom have moved away. The youngest son, Ebenezer Learned, is said to have been the first white child born in Columbia, N. H., his date of birth being June 24, 1774. He was with his brother James at Lake Memphremagog, but came to Eaton in the spring of 1799, and commenced a clearing on land adjoining that of his brother Royal on the east. Here he built a log house where the present Learned homestead stands, and on October 1, 1799, married the widow of his brother James. He died June 3, 1842; she died in May, 1848. They had seven children. In those early days Mr. Learned passed through all the hardships suffered by other early settlers. The first grain he raised had to be carried on the back to Colebrooke, N. H., by a spotted line, to be ground. It is said Mr. Alden Learned, of Cookshire, resembles him in looks. He was a man commanding respect from all, of even temperament, and with good judgment, much sought after in arbitration. The sons, William and his bachelor brother, Israel, remained on the old farm and both died there. Another son, Alden, who was the first settler at Learned Plain, has left a short history of his life, in which he says: "I was born in 1803. The first I can remember, there were about fifteen acres cleared, a log house, with stone chimney, two fire-places and an oven. The house was divided into two rooms, with three six-paned windows. There was a framed barn, twenty-six by thirty, with stable, floor and bay, no floor in stable. The only buildings in sight were on lot twelve, occupied by Elias Gates. At that time my father owned a pair of steers, two cows and three or four sheep." That was the beginning of many of the best farms in the Eastern Townships. Herewith we present an engraving of the home place as it at present appears, with Mr. John F. Learned and family in front. Just beyond the house is located the extensive grounds of the St. Francis Live Stock Association, with a good half-mile track. Our subject is a son of William and Margaret (Keenan) Learned, and has always lived on the home place. His father died here May 7, 1874, aged sixty-two years, and his mother died March 1, 1894, aged seventy-two. He is one of the progressive farmers of this section, breeding high-class horses and cattle. He has been connected with the cavalry for the past fifteen years and now holds the rank of major of the Fifth Dragoons. He is a director of the Eastern Townships Agricultural Association, was one of the first directors of the St. Francis Live Stock Association, and is connected with other agricultural societies. Holds the office of S. W. in Friendship Lodge, No. 66, A. F. & A. M. Mr. Learned was married at Sherbrooke, June 15, 1881, to Emma A., daughter of the late Col. Jas. H. Cook, of Cookshire. Issue, three children: Edith Frederica, born May 21, 1886; Mildred Eliza, born July 5, 1888; Gladys Emma, born August 25, 1890.

GEORGE WELLINGTON COOK, farmer, was born on the farm where he now lives, March 1, 1852. His grandfather, Capt. John Cook, was one of the first settlers to come into Eaton, having married Esther Abbot before leaving the United States. He settled on lots 11 and 12 in the 9th range, and his house was on the opposite side of the road from

116   HISTORY OF COMPTON COUNTY.

that of our subject; shortly after, his log buildings were burned, when he erected a frame house on the same spot in about 1880. Captain John Cook died in 1820, having cleared up a large farm and accumulated considerable property. He was persevering and public spirited, and it was in honor of him that Cookshire received its name. He had seven children: James settled on the north side of the river, where his son John H. now lives; John Craig, who inherited many of the noble qualities of his father, took the home place, improving the farm and giving his assistance to all public enterprises. During his lifetime he filled many public offices, and at the time of his death, August 16, 1882, he was colonel of the sedentary militia. His son, George W. Cook, the subject of this sketch, has

RESIDENCE OF GEORGE W. COOK.

always lived on the home farm, having improved it and being considered one of the best farmers in this section. He was married at Sawyerville, June 9, 1879, to Eudora Isabella, daughter of Wm. Thomas, who died at Sawyerville in 1891. Issue, five children: E. Howard, born July 10, 1883; William C., born June 11, 1890; Bertha W., born December 10, 1885; E. Blanche, born May 30, 1887. The picture given herewith is of the homestead located just above the meadow, a few hundred feet south of the Eaton river. Those in the group are the families of Mr. Geo. W. Cook and his cousin Mr. John H. Cook, who are the only representatives left of the Cook name in the County.

CAPTAIN JOHN HENRY COOK, farmer, was born January 1, 1845, on the farm now occupied by him in Cookshire, and where he has always lived. Mr. Cook has been a councillor in the township of Eaton, school commissioner, warden of St. Peter's church, justice of the peace. Was the first secretary-treasurer of the St. Francis Live Stock Association. He was a member of the Cookshire Troop of Cavalry, from 1862 to 1870, then quartermaster of the Fifty-eight battalion, later adjutant, and retired in 1888, with rank of captain. He graduated in May, 1872, from the Montreal military school, receiving first-class certificate. As a member of the cavalry, he took part in the Fenian raid at Stanstead, in 1866, and at Frelighsburg in 1870. Mr. Cook was married in Sawyerville, December 30, 1869, to Maria, daughter of Cyrus Rice, Esq., who now resides with her. Issue, one daughter: Florence M., born July 18, 1871.

ERASTUS CASWELL, piano manufacturer, at present living in San Francisco, Cal., was born in Cookshire, July 22, 1833. He went to Tennessee in 1858, returning to Cookshire in 1861; afterwards he lived in Toronto and Indianapolis, Ind., going to California in 1874, where he has been successful. He was married at Ogdensburg, N. Y., May 14, 1864, to Charlotte Cordelia Gould, who died February 23, 1875. Issue, one daughter: Florence Estella, born December 16, 1865, married Alexander L. Murray, residence, Brockville, Ont., two children. Mr. Caswell's grandfather, Apthorp Caswell, was one of the first settlers and one of the associates who first took up land in Eaton, born April 12, 1770, died February 15, 1858, his wife, Amarilla

RESIDENCE OF J. L. FRENCH.

Holden, born January 18, 1773, died December 15, 1850. Issue, nine children: Erastus H. Caswell, the father of our subject, was born in Cookshire, March 18, 1803, died April 21, 1883, married Persis N. LeBourveau, born May 10, 1808, died July 25, 1833. Issue, two children: our subject and Persis A, born October 22, 1831, married John Goodwin, October 7, 1852, died June 29, 1853. Issue, one son: George A., present owner of the home place, residence, Carman, Man.

JONAS LUDIAH FRENCH, railway mail clerk, was born at Eaton, January 27, 1850. His parents were Hiram and Sarah (Williams) French, of Eaton Corner. Accompanying this sketch will be found an engraving of Mr. French and his family in front of their home in Cookshire. The house was built by Mr. French in 1894. He has been employed at various times as farmer, cheese-maker, and carpenter, previous to his entering the civil service. At present he is railway mail clerk, between Sherbrooke and Lake Megantic, on the Canadian Pacific Railway. He holds the office of treasurer in the C. O. F., and is a prominent member of the

Masonic lodge. Our subject was married at Cookshire, January 2, 1889, to Abigail S. M., daughter of John Ludiah French, who was born in Cookshire, January 29, 1816, and died here January 17, 1887. He was a prominent merchant of Cookshire for many years, and for some time secretary-treasurer of Eaton. Issue, two children: James Levi, born April 16, 1890; Esther Mary, born December 28, 1894.

JOHN WILKINSON, senior member of the firm of Wilkinson Bros., photographers, was born in Scotland, March 9, 1862. His father, Bathurst Edward Wilkinson, of Potterton, Yorkshire, Eng., late of the Fourth Dragoon Guards, served during the Crimean war; and also held the office of Chief County Magistrate of Leeds, Eng., for some time. John Wilkinson was educated at the Oxford military college, and came to Canada in June, 1884. He settled at Birchton and went to California in 1885, then back to the Old Country where he studied at the London Polytechnic School of Photography. Returning to Cookshire in 1891, he, in company with his brother Alfred, purchased the photograph business of H. H. Weeden, in the spring of 1892, which has since been successfully carried on. At Cookshire, October 1, 1885, he married Millicent, daughter of S. H. Botterill, who came to Cookshire in 1884, and died there in 1889. By this marriage there is one daughter: Eva Millicent, born August 5, 1886.

OPERATING ROOM, STUDIO OF WILKINSON BROS.

ALFRED WILKINSON, the junior member of the firm of Wilkinson Bros., was born at Antwerp, Belgium, December 14, 1867, and was educated at Wellington college, Berkshire, Eng. He went to California in 1888, coming to Cookshire in 1891, afterwards returning to California, he again settled here in 1893. He was married at San Francisco, Cal., April 4, 1893, to Ethel Bigland. The firm of Wilkinson Bros. took the photographs for the engravings used in the "History of Compton County," and the work here shown speaks for itself. We give herewith an engraving, showing inside view of their operating room at the studio, Cookshire.

ALEXANDER ROSS, collector of customs, was born in Lingwick, August 1, 1850. When sixteen years old he was appointed secretary-treasurer of the School Commissioners and held that position until he was twenty-one years of age. He was then elected a member of the board, holding office for twelve years. For seventeen years Mr. Ross was a member of the Council of Lingwick, for fifteen years mayor, and in 1887 warden of the County. He was in trade in Gould and Scotstown; first, with his father, the late James Ross, M.L.A., afterwards alone, and still later with his brother, until 1889, when they went out of business. Mr. Ross held the appointment of mail clerk for five years, and went with the first mail car ever run on the old International Railway. In September, 1890, he received the appointment of secretary-treasurer for Compton county, moving to Cookshire at the same time. On January 1, 1891, he was appointed Collector of Customs for the port of Cookshire, at that time first opened. Our subject has been married twice: first, January 9, 1878, to Maria J. Guy, who died at Lake Megantic, August 21, 1879; second marriage at Sherbrooke, July 13, 1892, to Ada Plauche, of Cookshire. Mr. Ross was an officer in the Fifty-eighth Compton Battalion of Infantry for about twenty-eight years. Was appointed ensign of No. 2 company when it was first organized in 1866; was later promoted to first lieutenant and then to captain of the company. Received brevet rank of major, July 3, 1884, and was promoted to senior major of the battalion July 11, 1890; retiring in 1894, retaining rank.

RESIDENCE OF SAMUEL COOPER.

SAMUEL COOPER, yard manager for the Royal Paper Mills Company, was born at St. Sylvestre, Que., December 26, 1857. He came to Compton county in May, 1871, living first at Eaton Corner, later his father, John Cooper, who is still living, moved to Sawyerville. Our subject was a clerk in several stores in Cookshire for a number of years. In 1894 he accepted a position with the Cookshire Mill Company, and when the new saw mill was completed at East Angus, by the Royal Paper Mills Company, Mr. Cooper was entrusted with the general oversight of the same. He is a P. M. of the A. F. & A. M., and secretary of the I. O. O. F. Was married at Sawyerville, June 28, 1887, to Margaret, daughter of Edward Montgomery, now of Boston, Mass., formerly major of the Fifty-fifth battalion. Issue, one son: Claude M., born May 8, 1891. The engraving herewith is of the house built and occupied by Mr. Cooper in Cookshire. Owing to the position he accepted in East Angus, he removed with his family to the latter place in January, 1896.

THOMAS MACRAE, general merchant, was born at St. Sylvestre, Que., in 1852. He married Mary A., daughter of Hugh

GENERAL STORE OF T. MACRAE & CO.

HISTORY OF COMPTON COUNTY.

Mackay, of Lower Forest, Eaton, in 1875, at Colebrook, N. H. Issue, four children, three living : Cyrus, born February 18, 1876; Lottie, born February 17, 1880; Gertie, born November 5, 1884. Mr. Macrae's father, the late William Macrae, moved to High Forest, East Clifton, with his family in 1869. Upon reaching manhood Mr. Thomas Macrae started for himself, first as a farmer. He afterwards took up the butchering business, which he successfully followed for some years. During this time he moved to Cookshire, and in company with his brother, the late Dr. Macrae, formed a partnership as T. Macrae & Co., going into trade as general merchants with stores both at Cookshire and Sawyerville. The store at Sawyerville was afterwards closed and the business carried on here by Mr. Thomas Macrae. In 1894 Dr. William Macrae retired from the firm. Our subject is one of the promoters of the Cookshire Flour Mill Company, and has always been ready to assist all local enterprises. He is a trustee and member of the Quarterly Board of the Methodist church, and is now chorister in same. For seven years he was W. M. of the Orange lodge at Sawyerville. He is a prominent member of the I. O. O. F., having held all leading offices, and is now Grand Chaplain of the Provincial Grand Lodge I. O. O. F. He takes a great interest in music and is an accomplished bass singer. We present herewith a reproduction of a photograph of the store of Mr. Macrae, located on Main street, just opposite the church of England. The Masonic lodge room

RESIDENCE OF COLIN NOBLE.

This building he purchased from Mr. W. H. Learned in 1894. is located on the second story.

COLIN NOBLE, retired merchant, was born in Inverness, Scotland, July 20, 1828. Married at Sherbrooke, in September, 1854, to Maria, daughter of the late Gaymer Hunt, of Bury. Issue, eight children, four now living: Lucy M., born July 15, 1855, married R. H. Pope, M.P., six children, residence, Cookshire ; Jennie, born September 3, 1856, deceased ; Frederick J., born May 6, 1858, deceased; Florence M., born April 10, 1861, deceased; Frederick A., born June 9, 1864, married Mary Adams, one child, residence Marbleton; Edward C., born March 1, 1867, deceased; Clara M., born December 18, 1868; M. Alberta, born April 16, 1874. Mr. Noble came to Canada with his father, Alexander Noble, in 1838. They settled near Sherbrooke, carrying on the farm known as "Meadowbank," then the property of Peter Patterson, of Quebec, now owned by Geo. F. Terrill. They remained there four years, removing to Gould in 1843. His father there carried on a farm and saw mill for nine years when he moved to Parkhill, Ont., where he died in 1875. When they moved to Gould in 1843 there were no roads beyond Bury, and they had to walk. The carts were afterwards taken around by Victoria, where there was a road when the river could be forded. In 1848 Mr. Noble and his brother John went to Massachusetts where they had a saw mill and furniture shop. In 1852 he returned and bought out the business of one Clintock, who had two years previously opened a store at Stornoway. The building was made of hewn logs. In those days there were no roads between Lingwick and Winslow, except in the winter. Mr. and Mrs. Noble in 1856 wished to make a visit to Lingwick in June, and they were obliged to carry the baby (now Mrs. Pope), nine miles, in their arms. Mr. Noble remained there until March, 1892, when he removed to Cookshire and purchased the brick residence which may be seen in the engraving presented herewith. In front are to be seen Mr. and Mrs. Noble and their two daughters. He was successful in business and owns considerable property in the eastern part of the County. He was the first mayor of Winslow and Whitton, and in the Council for many years, also connected with the Board of School Commissioners, a commissioner of the Court for thirty years, justice of the peace over thirty-five years, and postmaster at Stornoway for forty years; one of the two first majors of the Fifty-eighth battalion, from which he resigned, retaining rank, in 1867.

EDWARD STANDISH BAKER, major Fifty-eigth battalion, was born in Limerick, Ire., January 16, 1838. He came to Compton county in 1863, settling at Birchton. Later he moved to Cookshire, where he now resides. Mr. Baker was seven years in the Imperial army as a commissioned officer with the Seventy-seventh and Twenty-second regiments. He served on the following home and foreign stations : Manchester, Eng., Dublin, Ire., Isle of Wight, Malta, Australia, and India. When he first came to Birchton he started in as a farmer, but gave that up on coming to Cookshire. He held the office of secretary-treasurer for the township of Eaton and school commissioners for seventeen years. At present he is secretary-treasurer for the town of Cookshire, clerk of the Circuit Court and insurance agent. He married Amanda Coates, of Birchton, in 1867, who died in April, 1868. Issue, one daughter : Agnes Amanda, born April 18, 1868, married F. A. Hurd, residence, Cookshire. Second marriage was at Quebec, November 1, 1869, to Annie Chiverton, of Newport, Isle of Wight, who died January 2, 1891. Issue, four children : Charles S., born March 6, 1872 ; Florence E., born October 11, 1870 ; Leila E., born August 18, 1876 ; Kathleen A., born July 9, 1887.

RAYMUND HAWKESWOOD PHILLIMORE, M. D., C. M., born at Snenton, near Nottingham, Eng., was educated together with his two brothers, Reginald P. Phillimore, B.A., and W. P. W. Phillimore, M.A., B.C.L., at Queen's college, Oxford. His father, W. P. Phillimore, M. B., University college, London, after a course of study on the Continent, became resident physician to the Nottingham Union, and afterwards for many years medical superintendent to the county asylum of that town. He made several valuable contributions to medical literature, and was much esteemed among his professional brethren as a widely-informed man of erudite tastes. At the time of his death he was president of the Bromley House Library. His mother, daughter of Benjamin Watts, Esq., alderman of Bridgenorth, was a woman of versatile talents and a most prolific writer. Dr. Phillimore has inherited his parents' tastes, and for many years contributed leading articles, poems and short stories to well-known English journals. He is an excellent draughtsman and has had a good artistic training. He graduated at McGill University, in 1892, and is a member of the Zeta Psi fraternity. He at once settled in Cookshire, and has a large practice. He was captain in the Nottinghamshire Robin Hood Rifles, secured the markman's badge, and carried off several cups as trophies of his skill, and while at Oxford he was gazetted first lieutenant in the Oxford University Rifles. He now holds the office of surgeon to the Fifty-eighth batallion in the Canadian militia. He was for a time president of the St. Catherine's Debating Society at Oxford, being succeeded in this post of honor by Viscount Lymington, present Duke of Portsmouth. He married, September 11, 1894, Frances Gertrude, eldest daughter of Abraham Hopkins, M. D., B. A., Trinity college, Dublin, who, after touring abroad, finally settled in Cookshire. Dr. Phillimore has one son; Reginald DuGard Hopkins Phillimore, born October 29, 1895.

RESIDENCE OF R. H. PHILLIMORE, M.D., C.M.

JOHN J. McLEOD, general merchant, was born on the island of Lewis, North Scotland, December 25, 1865. He came to Scotstown with his parents in 1873, his father being one of the three first families to settle in Scotstown. In 1876 he moved to Milan, five years later to Lake Megantic, and May 1, 1893, he came to Cookshire. For seven years he worked on the railroad, but for the past ten years he has been in trade in the above three places. On his arrival in Cookshire he rented the store owned by Mrs. D. Willard, at the corner of Railroad and Pleasant streets, and two years later erected the neat and commodious store of which a good view is presented in the accompanying photograph. It is located on Main street, just below Learned's hotel. In front may be seen Mr. McLeod. At Sherbrooke, June 29, 1885, he married Ellen J., daughter of the late William Boyle, of Learued Plain, for years a member of the municipal council of Newport. No children. Just before leaving Milan Mr. McLeod was elected a member of the council of Whitton, and for two years was secretary-treasurer of the School Commissioners at Lake

Megantic. He is an active member of the C. O. F., and a P. C. R. of the same. Since coming to Cookshire he has been actively engaged in trade, in addition to his store, buying and shipping large quantities of railway ties and pulpwood. John McLeod, sr., returned to Stornoway, Scotland, in 1888, where he has since resided.

LATE TYLER WELLINGTON HURD was born in Newport, Que., August 11, 1806. He was a son of Edmund and Lucy (Bennett) Hurd, who came from Massachusetts in 1805. The Hurds originally came from Wiltshire, England. Our subject lived in Newport during his boyhood, but his life was mostly spent in Cookshire, where he died July 14, 1877. He married Abigail Sage French, who died August 4, 1891. She was a daughter of John French, who came from Connecticut and settled in Cookshire with his family, about 1796, being among the first to come into Eaton. The daughter, Abigail, wife of our subject, retained the home place, and for that reason it is known at the present day as the Hurd farm, being now owned by the son, Theodore A. Hurd. We give an engraving next page of the old home, in front of which, in the carriage, may be seen Mr. and Mrs. T. A. Hurd. This is one of the oldest buildings in Cookshire, having been built in 1805. It was used as a hotel for many years, and in the upper rooms were held regular communications of the first Masonic lodge in Compton county. The doors with peep holes are still to be seen. By the marriage of Tyler W. and Abigail Hurd there were nine children, three living: Theodore Augustus, born May 19, 1850, married first Anzerbella Alden, three children, one living. She died September 11, 1888. Second marriage to Eliza Coates, widow of Luke Pope, residence, Cookshire; Frederick Augustine, born May 1, 1857, married first Hattie Eva Davis, three children.

RESIDENCE AND STORE OF J. J. McLEOD.

She died in 1892. Second marriage to Agnes Amanda Baker; residence, Cookshire; occupation, manager of farm belonging to R. H. Pope, M. P.; Sarah Malvina, born March 25, 1836, married William Donald Frasier, residence, Cookshire.

ELIAS SAMUEL ORR, registrar for the county of Compton, was born of Irish parentage at Lachute, Que., July 11, 1829. In 1860 Mr. Orr came to Sawyerville, where he engaged in country store-keeping. In 1869 he received the appointment of registrar for the County, which office he still holds. Mr. Orr is a strong supporter of the Methodist Church, joining that denomination in 1839. In 1848 he was licensed as a local preacher, and has preached oftener at St. Andrews, Sawyerville and Cookshire than any other Methodist preacher. Mr. Orr has been interested in Sunday-school work for nearly sixty years, and at the present

RESIDENCE OF LATE TYLER W. HURD.

time is superintendent of the Methodist Sunday-school in Cookshire. He is also a strong advocate of prohibition, holding the office of chaplain in the R. T. of T. While at Sawyerville, Mr. Orr was a member of the Eaton municipal council for three years. On September 9, 1856, at Montreal, he married Miss Jane C. White, of that city. Issue, five children, two living: Alfred E. Orr, M.D., born June, 1861, married Florence E. Roe, January 28, 1896, residence, Montreal; Florence L. Orr, residence, Cookshire.

LATE WILLIAM MACRAE, L.D.S., was born at St. Sylvestre, Que., June 17, 1850, died at Cookshire, January 11, 1895. He was a son of William Macrae, who died in East Clifton, in 1886. Dr. Macrae first learned the trade of shoemaking, but not being satisfied with that, when twenty-three years of age, he commenced the study of dentistry. He graduated from Harvard College, Boston, Mass., in 1877, and received his licence to practice in Quebec the same year. He opened an office in 1877 at Eaton Corner, and two years later moved to Cookshire. He had great confidence in the growth of the place and purchased several acres of land, building thereon the residence now occupied by Mrs. Macrae. It proved a profitable venture, for he sold off the land in lots on which buildings have since been erected. Notwithstanding that for some years previous to his death he was in poor health, he was always in active business and ready to assist local enterprises. He was for three years school commissioner of the Cookshire academy, having been appointed by the Commissioners. He also was a trustee of the Union Ceme-

RESIDENCE OF MRS. WM. MACRAE.

tery Company, trustee and member of the quarterly board of the Methodist church, in which he took a great interest, vice-president local branch of the Equitable Savings, Loan and Building Association. He was largely instrumental in starting the Cookshire Flour Mill Company, and one of the heaviest stock-holders; one of the charter members of the I. O. O. F., and held all the principal offices in the same. He was very fond of music, and commenced its study when a young man. For several years he taught singing school, and was organist for some time in the Methodist church, both in Sawyerville and Cookshire. For fifteen years previous to his death he was choir-leader in the Methodist church here. He was ably assisted in this by his wife, who takes a great interest in music, and it is handed down to the daughters, Miss Mabel having been organist in the Methodist church for several years. Dr. Macrae was married at Sawyerville, January 10, 1878, to Christiana, daughter of John Cooper. Issue, three children: Mabel Gertrude, born January 21, 1880; Percy Douglas, born August 10, 1881, died December 23, 1882; Stella May, born November 20, 1883. Accompanying this is an engraving of the residence of Mrs. Macrae, located on Main street, in front of which she, her daughters, and others may be seen. In the upper corner is the photograph of Dr. Macrae.

MILL OF COOKSHIRE FLOUR MILL COMPANY.

COOKSHIRE FLOUR MILL COMPANY. The idea of erecting a roller process flour mill at Cookshire originated with the late Wm. Macrae, L.D.S., and Thomas Macrae, and they in company with the present manager, W. J. Edwards, carried out the plan. The mill was built in 1887, and machinery started in the building in December of the same year. The machinery was built by W. & J. G. Greey, Toronto, Ont., and the mill fully equipped with the roller process. At first it was carried on under the firm name of T. Macrae & Co. In October, 1888, Messrs. Dr. William Macrae, W. J. Edwards, Geo. Flaws, and Thos. Macrae formed a partnership known as the Cookshire Flour Mill Company. Owing to increase of business it was found necessary in 1891 to build an addition to the mill. This was done, and the new building gives them storing capacity for 13,000 bushels of grain. Owing to elevator arrangements they are able to unload a car of grain at a cost not exceeding seventy-five cents. They handle a large amount of grain from the surrounding country, and in addition purchase between fifty and sixty carloads of grain in Manitoba and western points each year. The business is under the management of Mr. W. J. Edwards, and has been successfully carried on from the first. They find a ready market locally and at stations on the Canadian Pacific and Maine Central railways. The brands of flour manufactured by them are: Harvest Queen, Strong Bakers, and

RESIDENCE OF H. H. POPE.

Eureka. In the fall of 1895 the Company leased the Cookshire bakery from Mr. James Planche and now carry on the same, under the charge of Mr. Geo. Flaws. Herewith is given an engraving of the mill, facing the railway tracks of the Canadian Pacific Railway and Maine Central Railway. The building is 30 x 70 feet, two and a half stories high, with engine room attached, 17 x 30 feet. The present members of the Cookshire Flour Mill Company are Mrs. Wm. Macrae, W. J. Edwards, T. Macrae, and G. Flaws.

HORACE HENRY POPE, butcher, was born in Cookshire, August 1, 1862. He is a son of Albert W. and Ann (Bailey) Pope. At Cookshire, August 18, 1882, he married Christina, daughter of the late Malcolm McCaskill, of Bury. No children. Mr. Pope has always resided in Cookshire, with the exception of two years at Lake Megantic, where he had charge of the Victoria Hotel, belonging to his father. During the building of the Hereford Railway he superintended the clearing of the right of way. For two years he was in the business of manufacturing furniture at Cookshire, from which he retired and purchased the butcher shop belonging to R. H. Pope & Co., in 1893, which he now carries on. He is quartermaster of the Fifth Dragoons, and has been for several years. In the fall of 1895 Mr. Pope purchased the old Hopkins' homestead, located at the corner of Railroad and Main streets; the photo-engraving here shown is of this place, where he now resides, and in front he and Mrs. Pope may be seen.

WILLARD S. RAND, dealer in fire-arms and ammunition, etc., was born in Newport, May 8, 1836.

RESIDENCE OF W. S. RAND.

His father, Artemus D. Rand, died in 1878. Mr. W. S. Rand moved to Cookshire several years ago, and has followed the trade of general mechanic, making a specialty of repairing firearms. He has one of the neatest residences in Cookshire, located at the lower end of Pleasant street. Accompanying this is a photo-engraving of the house and grounds, and in front may be seen Mr. Rand and family. He was married in Eaton, January 8, 1866, to Dorothy M., daughter of the late John Hall. Issue four children, three living: Ellen C., born February 4, 1867, died June 5, 1887; Elvira M., born June 27, 1869; John H., born January 6, 1873; Oscar W., born July 5, 1880. Miss Rand is an accomplished portrait artist, and owner of the Cookshire Portrait and Art Studio. She does fancy painting of all kinds, making a specialty of enlarging portraits. Her work goes to all parts of the country, and gives general satisfaction. She commenced her studies in Montreal in 1886, and graduated in Toronto in 1891. The eldest son, John H. Rand, does an extensive business in picture-framing, and is general agent for the Portrait and Art Studio carried on by his sister. Oscar W. Rand is one of the artists in the portrait gallery.

RESIDENCE OF F. R. WILFORD.

LIEUT.-COL. JOHN H. TAYLOR, farmer, was born in the house where he now lives, October 2, 1844, and has always lived in limits of the town. From 1876 to 1879 he was in trade in Cookshire in company with W. H. Learned, Esq., and shortly after purchased the home farm. His father, Jonathan French Taylor, is a son of Priest Taylor, who came from New Hampshire with the first settlers, and was the first stationed minister in this section. Mr. J. F. Taylor was born in the house, in Cookshire, now owned by Colin Noble, Esq. He lives with his son Lieut.-Col. Taylor. Our subject was the first president of the St. Francis Live Stock Association, for two years a director of the Eastern Townships Agricultural Association, and councillor for six years. He is now a director of the Stanstead and Sherbrooke Mutual Fire Insurance Company, and a prominent member of St. Peter's Episcopal church. He was married at Cookshire, March 29, 1871, to Mary H. Cook. Issue, one son: Herbert A., born April 18, 1872.

FREDERICK RICHARD WILFORD, civil engineer, was born in Cookshire, April 27, 1866. He is a son of R. H. Wilford, of Island Brook. He received his education at the Eaton Corner and Cookshire academies. In 1886 he was employed on the Cape Breton Railway, and in 1887 was appointed resident assistant engineer. He remained there until 1890. After being in private practice in Nova Scotia and Cookshire for one year, he accepted a position with the Canadian Pacific Railway. He was employed by them on railway construction in Ontario and Quebec until the spring of 1895. Since then he has been in private practice, principally employed by the Royal Paper Mills Company, at East Angus, superintending the construction of sidings, water works, etc. He was married at Lindsay, Ont., June 4, 1895, to Maud M., daughter of Lieut.-Col. Deacon. For many years Col. Deacon was mayor of Lindsay, he now holds the office of police magistrate for Victoria county. On preceding page is a photo-engraving of the old Wilford homestead in Cookshire, now occupied by Mr. F. R. Wilford.

FRANK L. PANDELETTE DE PLAISANCE, general agent, whose portrait is presented herewith, was born in Cookshire, July 29, 1867. His great-grandfather, with two brothers, left France in 1760, and settled in or near Quebec city. His father, Francis Xavier Pandelette de Plaisance, was born in 1826, and came from Lotbinière county to Cookshire July 10, 1850. He has since resided here, carrying on the business of wheelwright. He was married at Sawyerville, April 26, 1863, to Betsey Wright. She was born in Stanstead, April 17, 1835. Her parents were married in Ireland in 1829, starting for America the same day. They settled first at Georgeville, Que. By the marriage of F. X. Plaisance and Miss Wright there are five children: Walter Thomas, born May 24, 1865; Frank L. (our subject); Harry William, born April 19, 1869; George Edgar, born December 22, 1871; Persis Luvia, born July 13, 1875. In the fall of 1895, Mr. Frank Plaisance formed a partnership with Mr. J. H. Burton, of Cookshire, under the firm name of J. H. Burton & Co. They are agents for all kinds of agricultural implements, etc., besides doing a general commission business.

F. L. PANDELETTE DE PLAISANCE.

A. L. HUSBANDS, A.M., Canadian Society of Civil Engineers, was born in Nottingham, Eng., March 22, 1861. Was educated in private schools and obtained first class in South Kensington courses, afterwards being articled to engineer and surveyor, having extensive country practice. At expiration of articles he went to London, Eng., for a couple of years. In April, 1883, Mr. Husbands came to Cookshire with the intention of purchasing a farm. Before doing so, however, he changed his mind and opened up an office here as civil engineer. Mr. Husbands was on the survey of the Hereford Railway from Lime Ridge to the boundary line, and later had full charge of the erection of the large paper mills at East Angus. He designed and carried out the water-works at Knowlton and Beebe Plain, and engaged on work of a similar nature in other places both in the United States and Canada. In the summer of 1895 Mr. Husbands accepted a position on the engineering staff of the Boston & Maine Railway, with headquarters at St. Johnsbury, Vt., where he at present resides. Our subject was married at Cookshire, November 15, 1893, to Annie M., daughter of Edward J. Mowle, Esq. Issue, one daughter: Muriel Annie, born August 14, 1894. Accompanying this sketch will be found an engraving of the residence of Mr. Husbands, in Cookshire, with Mrs. Husbands and daughter in front.

COOKSHIRE COUNCIL, NO. 88, R. T. OF T., was organized November 15, 1893. The charter officers and members, eighteen in all, were: W. J. Gray, S.C.; J. A. M. Rankin, P.C.; Mrs. Wm. Macrae, V.C.; E. S. Orr, Chap.; Cyrus Macrae, R.S.; M. Hurd, Asst. R.S.; H. W. Parry, Treas.; Mrs. A. W. Pope, F.S; Lionel Pope, Herald; Miss N. Frasier, Dept. Her.; G. Flaws, jr.,

RESIDENCE OF A. L. HUSBANDS.

Sent.; J. Frasier, Guard; and Mrs. F. M. Frasier, Mrs. Ayton Cromwell, Miss L. Pope, A. Drennan, H. Frasier, and J. N. McLeod. The Council was organized and met until September, 1894, at the house of Mrs. F. M. Frasier, when they moved to the I. O. O. F. hall, Main street. Meetings are held every second Wednesday evening. Present officers: Cyrus Macrae, S.C.; J. A. M. Rankin, P.C.; Miss Lottie Planche, V.C.; W. J. Edwards, Chap.; Miss N. Frasier, R.S.; Miss P. E. A. Bailey, F.S.; Miss Mabel Macrae, Treas.; A. Drennan, Her.; Miss L. Macrae, Dept. Her.; Miss G. Planche, Guard; W. Warby, Sent. Total membership, thirty-five. The royal degree only is worked.

AYTON CROMWELL, carpenter and contractor, was born at St. Sylvestre, Que., September 17, 1860. He attended the high school in Leeds, coming to High Forest, Clifton, with

HISTORY OF COMPTON COUNTY.

RESIDENCE OF AYTON CROMWELL.

his parents in 1877. Mr. Cromwell went to Cookshire in 1882, where he has since resided. Previous to this time he was at work on the home farm. His father, Thomas Cromwell, and his mother (Elizabeth J. Kinnear), are both living, having moved from their farm to Sawyerville. Our subject was in charge of the large saw mill belonging to the Cookshire Mill Company, at Sawyerville, for five years, but for the past five years he has been principally engaged in contracting. In January, 1896, he was elected councillor for Cookshire, by acclamation. Mr. Cromwell was married at Eaton Corner, January 31, 1884, to Margaret M., daughter of Alexander Adams, who died in 1893, aged seventy-eight years. Issue, three children : Howard R., born November 18, 1889; Ellen E., born February 21, 1887; Edith M., born February 6, 1895.

LOUIS JOSEPH DAMASE GAUTHIER, tinsmith and hardware dealer, was born in St. Lin, L'Assomption county, Que., January 31, 1854. In 1872 he left St. Lin and went to Lowell, Mass., but after two years there he returned to Sherbrooke, and in March, 1875, came to Cookshire. Since 1872 he has followed the business of tinsmith, and, since coming to Cookshire, with success. At the time of the incorporation of Cookshire, Mr. Gauthier was chosen one of the councillors by acclamation, and in 1894 re-elected. He was instrumental in establishing the Cookshire Machine Works Company and held the office of president of the Company during its existence. At present he is one of the directors of

RESIDENCE AND STORE OF L. J. D. GAUTHIER.

the St. Francis Live Stock Association, chairman of the Catholic Board of School Commissioners, warden of the Catholic church, and D. H. C. R. of the Catholic Order of Foresters. Mr. Gauthier represented the C. O. F. of Cookshire at the Grand Lodge, held in Chicago in 1893, and also at the Provincial Grand Lodge, held at Montreal in 1895. He was married at Cookshire, January 21, 1884, to Eliza, daughter of François Delisle, of Bulwer. They have one adopted daughter, Marie Mathilda, born July 6, 1885. The store and house of Mr. Gauthier, of which we give a reproduction herewith, is built of brick, and one of the best business blocks in Cookshire. Mr. and Mrs. Gauthier may be seen standing in front.

R. A. DARKER.

ROBERT ALEXANDER DARKER, insurance agent, whose portrait accompanies this sketch, was born in Clousilla, Dublin county, Ireland, May 21, 1868. His father, Alfred Darker, was employed by the government as civil engineer, and died in Dublin in 1887. Mr. Darker came to Cookshire in August, 1888, and has since resided here, with the exception of fifteen months, when he was in charge of the Mount Tom lumber yard at Northampton, Mass. He has been employed most of the time by the Cookshire Mill Company. In 1894 Mr. Darker started an insurance agency at Cookshire, in which he has been very successful. At present he represents the following companies: North American Life; Travellers Accident; Manufacturers, for guarantee bonds; Travellers, for employers' liability; in fire he has the following: Ætna, Queen, Manchester, Lancashire, British America, Commercial Union, London & Lancashire, North British & Mercantile. Mr. Darker takes a deep interest in the Masonic and Odd Fellows lodges, holding the offices of G. M., A. F. & A. M., and R. S. N. G. of the I. O. O. F. He was married at Cookshire, December 27, 1893, to Agnes M., born May 15, 1869, daughter of Richard H. Wilford, of Island Brook, secretary-treasurer of the township of Newport.

COOKSHIRE MILL COMPANY, lumber manufacturers. This firm at present comprises the Hon. W. B. Ives, Q.C., M.P., and Rufus H. Pope, M.P. The latter manages the business. The Cookshire Mill Company was first organized in 1882, and comprised W. B. Ives, R. H. Pope, A. W. Pope and H. B. Brown. The interests of the two latter were soon purchased by Messrs. Ives and Pope. The saw mill at Cookshire was built by Henry Dawson in 1881, an Englishman, who purchased a large meadow farm about three miles south of Cookshire. The residents of Cookshire, by private subscription, had agreed to pay $500 bonus for a saw mill, and an additional $500 for a grist mill. The first $500 was paid over, but Mr. Dawson got into financial difficulties before the grist mill was added, and forced to sell his property.

The Cookshire Mill Company was then formed, more at request of the citizens who desired the mill should be kept in operation, than for any other reason. The new firm purchased the saw mill in 1882, and at once made extensive repairs, adding new machinery. The business was carried on at a profit, and a good market secured for the lumber in South America. The demand having exceeded the supply, the Company decided to erect a larger and more recent style mill at Sawyerville. This was built in 1889, having a capacity for sawing 100,000 feet every twelve hours. There was also in connection clapboard, lath, stave, and barrel machinery. The cost was $60,000. On September 7, 1895, this mill was burned, with insurance of $30,000. In its place was built a mill for sawing pulp-wood, for which the Company have a large demand, having just completed a contract for 2,000 car loads. Since the burning of the large mill at Sawyerville, many improvements have been made to the saw mill at Cookshire, which now has a capacity of 60,000 feet every twenty-four hours. This mill is kept running summer and winter; in the cold season logs being brought in by train. Lath and clapboards are also manufactured here, while an extensive new industry is the manufacture of packing-boxes. The largest part of the lumber is shipped to the South American market, and during the winter of 1895-96 between fifteen and twenty sailing vessels were wholly loaded at Portland, Me., with lumber from this Company. The annual export is about 50,000,000 feet with a gross value of $650,000. In addition to their own mill they also handle the cut of several others. Their lumber limits are extensive, warranting them a large supply of logs for years to come. They own 46,720 acres of wild land, all located within easy reach of the mill. In the saw mill there are employed eighty men; during the winter they have about five hundred men

STORE OF COOKSHIRE MILL COMPANY.

at work, and in the spring, on the drive, there are four hundred men employed. The head office and general management of the business is at Cookshire. There are also branch offices at 75 State street, Boston; 364 Commercial street, Portland, and 127 Water street, New York. Mr. Wm. W. Bailey has general management of the mills and making sales, while Mr. W. H. Learned has charge of the books and financial matters. In 1889, to handle the largely increasing business of the firm more conveniently, a large store was erected on Main street, Cookshire, with general offices in the second story. This is under the general supervision of Mr. W. H. Learned, with Mr. H. B. Spear as head clerk and buyer. They do the largest retail trade east of Sherbrooke, carrying a general line of goods, with average value of $17,000

SAW MILL BELONGING TO COOKSHIRE MILL COMPANY.

Annual sales are between $50,000 and $60,000. Accompanying this sketch are two large engravings, one is the saw mill and yard at Cookshire, the other is the store. In the second story of the latter are located the general offices of the Company, while the third floor is occupied as a hall by the I. O. O. F.

EQUITY LODGE No. 19, I. O. O. F. Bros. D. Williams, a member of Pioneer Lodge, Richmond; C. C. Bailey, of Unity Lodge, Sherbrooke, and W. J. Edwards, of St. John's Lodge, Whitefield, N.H., first conceived the idea of starting a lodge of Odd Fellows in Cookshire. After due consideration the following brethren, who had attained the third degree, made application to the Grand Lodge of Quebec for a warrant or charter, to institute a lodge: D. Williams, C. C. Bailey, W. J. Edwards, H. S. Mackay, W. Macrae,

Thos. Macrae, P. S. Flaws, J. Roydell, T. J. Edwards, J. A. Cooper, Wm. Smart, and Thos. Cromwell. The charter being granted, Grand Master J. J. Reed, assisted by a large delegation from Unity Lodge, Sherbrooke, instituted Equity Lodge No. 19, I. O. O. F., on January 1, 1889. That same evening the following officers were elected and installed: D. Williams, N.G.; C. C. Bailey, V.G.; W. J. Edwards, Rec. and Fin. Sec.; H. S. Mackay, Treas. The appointed officers were: Dr. Wm. Macrae, Chap.; J. A. Cooper, R.S.N.G.; Thos. Macrae, L.S.N.G.; Wm. Smart, Cond.; J. Boydell, Warden; T. J. Edwards, I.G.; Jas. A. Planche, O.G.; P. S. Flaws, R.S.V.G.; Thos. Cromwell, L.S.V.G.; W. J. Cairns, R.S.S.; L. R. Willard, L.S.S. At the time of instituting the lodge the store of the Cookshire Mill Company, on Main street, had just been completed, and a hall finished off in the third floor, which was leased by Equity Lodge for a term of years. Here they have always held their meetings. The following is a list with date of those who have held the office of Noble Grand: D. Williams, January to June, 1889; C. C. Bailey, July to December, 1889; P. S. Flaws, January to June, 1890; W. J. Edwards, July, 1890, to June, 1891; Thos. Macrae, July to December, 1891; T. J. Edwards, January to June, 1892; Walter Lindsay, July to December, 1892; Wm. Macrae, January to June, 1893; C. H. Edwards, July to December, 1893; S. Cooper, January to June, 1894; Thos. Macrae, July to December, 1894; C. C. Bailey, January to June, 1895; H. B. Speir, July to December, 1895. The following is a list of officers elected and installed in January, 1896: C. C. Bailey, N.G.; J. J. McLeod, V.G.; W. J. Edwards, Sec.; Jas. Cooper, Treas. Present membership is forty-three. Since organization the lodge has paid $756 in relief to its members. It is now in a flourishing condition. Meetings are held on Tuesday evening, fortnightly. On April 25, 1895, W. B. McCutcheon, Past Grand Master, accompanied by forty-three members of Princess Lodge No. 4, Daughters of Rebekah, of Sherbrooke, came to Cookshire to institute a lodge of Daughters of Rebekah. Twenty-one candidates were initiated and instructed in the work of Rebekah Degree. Bro. McCutcheon was ably assisted by P. G. M. Walley and Past Grands Thompson, Levinson and McCree, and "Vera" Lodge No. 8, Daughters of Rebekah, became a reality. The following officers were then elected and installed: Mrs. Wm. Macrae, N.G.; Miss P. E. A. Bailey, V.G.; Mrs. J. A. Cooper, R.S.; Mrs. S. Rand, F.S.; Mrs. C. H. Edwards, Treas. Too much praise cannot be bestowed upon the members of Princess Lodge No. 4 for the able manner in which they conducted the initiation ceremonies. Fourteen have been initiated since the institution of the lodge, making a total membership of thirty-five.

COURT CARIBOO, No. 477, C.O.F. This court of the Canadian Order of Foresters was instituted by Thomas Bown, D.D.H.C.R., on November 6, 1893. The first officers installed were: A. Ross, C.R.; J. O. P. Wootten, V.C.R.; H. L. Scott, R.S.; C. E. Weyland, F.S.; J. L. French, Treas.; E. Jackson, Chap.; H. S. Weston, S.W.; A. Lennox, J.W.; W. R. McClintock, S.B.; F. A. Bates, J.B.; A. Dewar, M.D., Physician; C. C. Bailey, P.C.R. The foregoing with the following comprised the charter members: A. Gamsby, J. A. Cooper, J. Ross, Wm. Ross, Wm. McClintock. On the next page we give an engraving of most of the present members of the lodge, with very appropriate surroundings. The name Cariboo and Foresters carries the mind toward the game here represented. This lodge, although young in years, has been very successful from the first, being now in a good financial position. The credit for its prosperity is due to Mr. A. Ross, who was C. R. for two years. The regular meetings are held in the I. O. O. F. hall, on the second and fourth Mondays in each month. Present membership in good standing is twenty-eight. The following officers were elected December 23, 1895, for the ensuing six months: R. H. Chaddock, C.R.; J. J. McLeod, V.C.R.;

J. O. P. Wootten, Chap.; A. Ross, R.S.; Geo. Flaws, F.S.; J. L. French, Treas.; A. Lennox, S.W.; Wm. Flaws, J.W.; W. Bagley, S.B.; Wm. McClintock, J.B.; A. Dewar, M.D., Physician; C. C. Bailey, P.C.R.

FRIENDSHIP LODGE No. 66, A. F. & A. M. The history of Masonry in Compton county dates back to the year 1813. In that year a lodge was formed in Cookshire, known as Friendship Lodge No. 18, which delivered up its charter in 1819. The meetings were held in the old Tyler Hurd house, situated on the side hill east of the Eaton river, in Cookshire, and at the present day the doors with loop holes in the upper rooms of the house still remain.

COURT CARIBOO, No. 477, C. O. F.

Some of the old books are now in the hands of the present lodge, from which are taken the following names as members of the old lodge: Abner Powers, Wm. Hudson, John LeBourveau, Luther French, Levi French, John Farnsworth, Amos Hawley, James Lowd, John French, jr., Nathan Graves, Josiah Hall, James Brown, David Metcalf, James Strobridge, Benjamin Osgood, Asaph Williams, Moses Rolfe, Manly Powers, Ezra Speer, Jeremiah Eames, 3rd; Joseph B. Smith, Samuel Farnsworth, Jonathan Taylor, Tillotson H. Hall, Longley Willard, jr.; Bradford Hammond, Hanniah Hall. A total of twenty-seven members. There is a photograph of a certificate of membership on the walls of the present lodge, the original of which is in the hands of Saginaw Valley Lodge, Saginaw, Mich., having been granted June 2, 1814, to Bro. Robert B. Hudson, and signed by Abner Powers, M.; William Hudson, S.W.; John LeBourveau, J.W.; John Farnsworth, Sec. On November 12, 1879, Friendship Lodge No. 64

(in January, 1884, changed to No. 66) was established and the dedicating of the present Masonic hall performed by M. W. Bro. J. H. Graham, G. M. of the G. L., A. F. & A. M., Province of Quebec, assisted by D. D. G. M. Dr. Keyes, Past D. D. G. M. James Addie, and others. The following officers were installed: V. W., W. H. Learned, W.M.; J. A. Donigan, S.W.; A. A. Bailey, J.W.; Jno. W. Rogers, Treas.; G. E. Garvin, Sec.; M. Knights, Chap.; C. F. Osgood, S.D.; Jno. L. Wilford, J.D.; Geo. N. Gamsby, I.G.; Geo French, Tyler. The above officers, excepting Geo. French, with the following, were the charter members: C. W. B. French, John Scott, and John G. Geddes. The majority of charter members of Friendship

John L. Wilford. W. H. Learned. S. Cooper. W. C. Wilford / L. C. Pope. A. A. Bailey. R. A. Barker. W. Nutt.

PAST-MASTERS OF FRIENDSHIP LODGE, No. 66, A. F. & A. M.

Lodge No. 66, as well as those of old Friendship Lodge were formerly members of Ascot Lodge, which was in existence from 1806 to 1822, and again revived in later years. With this description will be found an engraving of all of the past masters of Friendship Lodge No. 66, since its organization in 1879. The dates of their holding office as W. M. are as follows: V.W. W. H. Learned, November 12, 1879, to June, 1881; R.W. A. A. Bailey, 1881 to June 1883; W. L. C. Pope, to December 12, 1883, when he died while in office; R.W. A. A. Bailey, December, 1883, to June, 1884; R.W. John L. Wilford, 1884 to 1885; W. Wm. C. Wilford, 1885 to 1888; R.W. A. A. Bailey, 1888 to 1889; W. Samuel Cooper, 1889 to 1890; V.W. Walter Nutt, 1890 to 1891; W. Wm. C. Wilford, 1891 to 1892; R.W. A. A.

Bailey, 1892 to 1895. The following officers were elected June 5, 1895: Robert A. Darker, W.M.; J. F. Learned, S.W.; Dr. A. Dewar, J.W.; R.W. A. A. Bailey, Chap.; C. C. Bailey, Treas.; H. S. Farnsworth, Sec.; W. Wm. C. Wilford, Tyler; F. Urquhart, S.D.; H. L. Scott, J.D.; C. F. Osgood, I.G. Present membership is 127, being the third largest body of Masons in the province of Quebec. Two members of the lodge have held the office of D. D. G. M., Jno. L. Wilford in 1887, and A. A. Bailey the present year of 1896.

THE LATE LEMUEL POPE, SR., was born in Hereford, Que., in 1793, and died July 6, 1859. He was the son of Captain John and Fanny Pope, who came from Dorchester, Mass., and settled in Hereford some time previous to 1793. The exact date is not known, as there was some trouble between this son and his father's family, whereby he left home about 1780, and had no further communication with them. As Capt. John Pope was always very strong in his support of the British Government, and had a strong tendency toward English ways, it is generally supposed, and with good reason, that his leaving home was on this account, the American revolutionary war being fought at that time. His spirit of loyalty was strong down to the last, and he imbued all of his family with the same spirit. His death took place at Cookshire, at the residence of his grandson, the late Hon. John Henry Pope, on May 7, 1853, aged ninety years. His wife died February 12, 1843, aged eighty years. In 1796, Capt. John Pope, with his wife and ten children, moved into the township of Clifton, on the road between Hereford and Sawyerville. Shortly after the father moved to Cookshire and resided with his son, John Pope, the grandfather of R. H. Pope, M.P. Lemuel Pope, our subject, remained in Clifton and there raised a large family and cleared a good farm. He, for many years, owing to there being no lawyer in this section, did the legal work, having a natural bent in that direction. He was also identified with all matters of importance. When a young man he was thrown from a carriage, and received injuries from which he never recovered. For this reason he was not able to do heavy work, and for several years could not attend to business of any kind. From the effects of the injury, he died July 6, 1859. He was married twice. First, to Sarah Hughes, born August 6, 1814. Issue, four sons and one daughter: Lemuel, born September 24, 1815, died at Bury February 23, 1896; Elijah, born June 26, 1817; Samuel, born December 23, 1821; John A., born December 20, 1823; and Sarah, born April 10, 1832. His wife died in 1832. Elijah and Sarah (now Mrs. Lewis McIver) are living and reside at Robinson, Bury; and Samuel resides in Winchendon, Mass. Four years after the death of his first wife, Mr. Pope was again married to Hannah Prouty, of Carman, Vt. By this marriage he also had four sons and one daughter: George H., born August 15, 1837; Charles F., born February 5, 1841; Luke C., born February 23, 1845; Betsey H., born January 26, 1843, died March 18, 1847; William W., born January 4, 1849. George H., when twenty-one years of age, went to Ontario. He was married June 17, 1869, to Jane M. McMullen, and moved to Belleville, where he has been identified with large lumbering, commercial, railway and municipal interests. He formed one of a syndicate to introduce the export of beef cattle to Europe, and three years ago was appointed Dominion inspector of live stock at Montreal. Issue, one son: Edward L., residence, Belleville, Ont. When the rebellion broke out between the States of the North and South, in 1861, Charles F. enlisted in the Fourteenth Massachusetts Regiment and served until the end of the war. He married Sarah Reynolds; has one daughter, and resides in Fitzwilliam, N. H. The widow, with the pluck and energy that characterized her whole life, continued to work the farm with the aid of the two boys, Luke and William, assisted by Elijah Pope (who never married). She succeeded in keeping the home and rearing the two small boys until they were able to look out for themselves. Luke remained on the home place and married

MRS. LEMUEL POPE, SR., AND HER FOUR SONS.

Eliza Coates, September 1, 1869. In 1880 he moved with his mother to Sawyerville, and in 1881 to Cookshire. Luke C. died October 21, 1884. His widow afterwards married T. A. Hurd, and is now living in Cookshire. The mother, Mrs. Lemuel Pope, or more generally called Aunt Hannah, lived with Mrs. Hurd until her death, April 25, 1893, aged seventy-nine years. The youngest son, William W., studied law and moved to Belleville, Ont., where he commands a leading position as assistant to John Bell, solicitor of the Grand Trunk Railway Company. He was married October 20, 1875, to Myra White. They have one son: Wm. Macauley, born April 14, 1889. Accompanying this sketch is a photo-engraving of Lemuel Pope's second wife and her four sons, George, Charles, Luke and William.

CLYDE WOLSLEY FRENCH, manager Sawyer's saw mill, Sawyerville, was born in Eaton, March 4, 1861. He is a son of Luther French, who is now living at Island Brook. Accompanying this sketch is an engraving of the house owned by Mr. French, situated on Main street, Cookshire, where he lived for a number of years previous to his moving to Sawyerville in 1892. Our subject was first married to Hannah Hood, now deceased. Second marriage took place in Lingwick, February 10, 1892, to Annie J., daughter of the late Donald McFarlane. Issue, one son: Donald Alexander, born August 9, 1893.

LEONARD STEWART CHANNELL, compiler of this "History of Compton County," and whose portrait accompanies this sketch, was born at Stanstead Plain, Que., April 8, 1868. His parents are Charles E. and Emily (Benton) Channell. He is a descendent of early settlers at Stanstead and Georgeville, who came to the Eastern Townships about 1800. At fourteen years of age he

RESIDENCE OF C. W. FRENCH.

went to New York city, and there learned the rudiments of printing. After a year's absence he returned to Stanstead and continued his studies at the Stanstead Wesleyan College, graduating from the Commercial College, connected therewith, with honors. He then was employed in printing offices, on both daily and weekly papers, in New York, Boston, Stanstead, and Sherbrooke. In March, 1889, in company with W. L. Shurtleff, Esq., the Coaticook *Observer* was purchased. In December of the same year this partnership was dissolved by mutual consent, Mr. Shurtleff purchasing the entire plant. After communicating with the citizens of Cookshire, Mr. Channell came here in January, 1890, when twenty-one years of age, and commenced preparations for publishing the *Compton County Chronicle*. On February 25, of the same year the first issue of that paper was printed. In the spring of 1892 the business had outgrown the office room, and land was purchased for a new building centrally located on Main street, which was erected and occupied the same year. In the spring of 1895 he conceived the plan of compiling and publishing a "History of Compton County," the result of which this book speaks for itself. In January, 1896, a half interest in the *Chronicle* was sold to Mr. L. E. Charbonnel, advocate, of Sherbrooke, who, on April 1, 1896, assumed full management of the paper, leaving Mr. Channell free with his whole time for other work. He is secretary-treasurer of the Compton County Liberal-Conservative Association; for two years president of the Compton County Christian Endeavor Union; trustee and member Quarterly Board of the Methodist church; and connected as secretary-treasurer with several local organizations. On September 2, 1891, he was married at Barnston, Me., to Winnie I. M., only daughter of Charles S. Buckland, Esq. Issue, one daughter: Vera B., born September 3, 1894.

L. S. CHANNELL.

STEPHEN JONAS OSGOOD, postmaster and farmer, was born in Cookshire, January 20, 1849. His father, Jonas F. Osgood, was also born in Cookshire, being a descendant of the first settlers who came in from the United States. He died in Cookshire, February 15, 1895. Mr. Osgood was married January 19, 1871, at Cookshire, to Mary Jane, daughter of Jonathan French Taylor. Issue, five children, four living: Henry S., born March 29, 1873; Oren A., born August 26, 1874; Emma M., born December 11, 1872; Clara L., born December 3, 1886.

HERBERT CLARK, was born September 10, 1867, in Peckham, Surrey, Eng. In 1887 he came to Cookshire with the intention of learning how to farm. After a few years of farm life here and Brookbury, he clerked for T. B. Munro, Esq., of Bury, for awhile, and later returned to Cookshire, purchasing the stock in a fruit store. After a few months he sold out and accepted a position, in 1892, with the Cookshire Mill Company, and was gradually promoted until he held the responsible position of head clerk and buyer in their store. At Quebec, in the English cathedral, on July 14, 1891, he married Alice, only child of Adolphus Fisher, of Penge, Eng. Issue, one son: Herbert A., born May 29, 1893. In May, 1896, Mr. Clark left Cookshire for British Columbia with the intention of opening a business for himself.

ALEXANDER ROSS PENNOYER, medical student, was born in Sherbrooke, August 22, 1870. His parents moved to Gould in 1872. For a number of years he acted as private secretary for R. H. Pope, M.P., at Cookshire, leaving that position to commence his studies at McGill Medical College, Montreal, where he is at present. Mr. Pennoyer is secretary-treasurer of the St. Francis Live Stock Association, Compton County Agricultural Society No. 1, and the Cookshire Union Cemetery Company.

WILLIAM FREDERICK PENNOYER, farmer, was born in Waterville, May 31, 1856. His father, Charles Pennoyer, was for twenty-seven years general agent for the B. A. L. Co., and died at Cookshire in 1889. Our subject was connected with the S. R. Pulp Co., at Scotstown for several years, moving to Cookshire in 1893. He was married at Cookshire, April 10, 1879, to Harriet Persis French. Issue, seven children: Charles F., born October 24, 1879; Austin H, born July 26, 1881; Arthur J., born May 26, 1883; William F. E, born May 8, 1886; Oscar C., born November 11, 1888; Ethel M., born March 11, 1891; Cyrus A., born February 5, 1895.

CHARLES WILLIAM TAYLOR, lumber manufacturer and contractor; was born in Eaton, June 2, 1852. He has resided in Cookshire for the past sixteen years. He was married, here, July 1, 1881, to Annie A. Cook. Issue, six children.

ARCHIBALD LEFEBVRE, blacksmith, was born in St. Giles, Lotbinière county, Que, 1847. Came to Bury in 1869, moving to Cookshire in 1891. Was married at Canterbury, Que., March 22, 1877, to Martha, daughter of Robert Clark. Issue, six children: Margaret E., born 1878; John Wood, born 1879; V. Maude, born 1880; Muriel C., born 1886; Cecil Archibald, born 1888; Gladys Lena, born 1889.

JAMES A. COOPER, shoemaker, was born in St. Sylvestre, Que, February 13, 1858, and came to East Clifton with his parents in 1875, where his father, Samuel Cooper, died in 1891. By trade Mr. Cooper is a shoemaker, having resided in several of the villages on both sides of the line. Settled in Cookshire in 1890. He is treasurer of the I. O. O. F., Cookshire, as well as one of the trustees. July 25, 1892, he married Ida M., daughter of the late Dexter Willard, of Cookshire.

JOHN HAROLD PLANCHE, assistant mill manager at Cookshire for the Cookshire Mill Company, was born in Cookshire, July 26, 1865. He has been employed by the Cookshire Mill Company for the past seven years, previous to that, acting as store clerk. He holds the office of treasurer in the I. O. F.

GEORGE FLAWS, member of the Cookshire Flour Mill Company, and in charge of their bakery, was born in St. Sylvestre, Lotbinière county, Que., May 5, 1850. In 1875 he purchased a farm in Flanders, this county, where he lived until 1889, when he moved to Cookshire and entered as a partner of the above firm. Mr. Flaws was one of the first councillors of the town of Cookshire, and re-elected by acclamation in 1892. He is a prominent member of the A. F. & A. M., and financial secretary of the Canadian Order of Foresters. His father, James Flaws, was born in Scotland, in 1818, and was seven years with the Hudson Bay Company in the Northwest, settled in St. Sylvestre in 1847, and died in Flanders, 1885. Our subject was married in Quebec, March 26, 1873, to Sarah, youngest daughter of Alexander Fairfield, Esq., of Old Orchard Beach, Me. Issue, three children: William L., born March 13, 1874; Jeanette M., born September 28, 1876; George Orrin, born March 11, 1878.

JOSEPH I. MACKIE, notary public, revising officer of Compton county, deputy registrar, Cookshire, Que., was born December 20, 1844, in the parish of St. Pie, Bagot county, Que. After a thorough study of French and English in the leading educational institutions, he studied privately, successfully passing the examination before the Board of Notaries, September 16, 1868, and began to practice his profession that same year in Cookshire. He is one of the most able and highly esteemed men in the notarial profession in the Townships, and has a deservedly large and lucrative practice. He was married April 12, 1868, to Miss Clothilde Lantagne, of Stukely, Que.

JOHN WILLIAM ROBINSON, hotel clerk, was born in Rodden, Que., March 28, 1873, came to Maple Hill, Eaton, with his parents, who still live there, in 1884. In 1892 our subject moved to Cookshire, and has since filled the position of clerk at the American House.

NAPOLEON JOSEPH BIBEAU, lumber contractor, was born at Methot's Mills, Que., July 20, 1866. He came to Cookshire with his father, Elisse Bibeau, in 1876. Married in Cookshire, June 1, 1886, Philemonne Lepage, of Green Island, Que. Issue, four children: Henry P. J., born May 29, 1893; Marie C., born July 2, 1889; Vitaline M., born June 1, 1891; Marie A. L., born February 13, 1895.

MOSES T. O. DESROCHERS, marble and granite cutter, a resident of South Cookshire, was born in this town, September 29, 1854. Most of his life he has lived in Compton county. He is V. C. R. of the Catholic Order of Foresters, and a prominent member of the Canadian Order. Mr. DesRochers was first married in Cookshire, December 24, 1876, to Magaret McDermott, of Cookshire, who died in 1889. Issue, three children: Charles O., born December 29, 1877; Curtis L., born May 6, 1880; Leo M. F., born October 28, 1885. Second marriage took place at Cookshire, September 2, 1891, to Ella J. Rowell, of Johnville, Que. Issue, one son: Lockhart W., born May 1, 1893. On January 5, 1896, Mr. DesRochers was unfortunate in having his house and barns totally destroyed by fire.

VILLAGE OF SAWYERVILLE.

One of the first settlements made in Compton county was at Sawyerville by Captain Josiah Sawyer, after whom the place is named. Here were erected the first mills, and it has always been a natural centre for a large section of territory, covering the townships of Eaton, Newport and Clifton.

Captain Sawyer was the leader of the associates who received the first grant of land in Eaton. It is said that when he first came into the country in company with Edmund

Heard, he cleared a piece of land on the farm in Newport, now known as the Dudley Williams place, thinking it was in Eaton. Soon finding out his mistake he erected a log cabin at Sawyerville. Here it was that all first settlers made their headquarters, coming through the woods from Hereford as they did. William Sawyer, ex-M.L.A., a grandson of Captain Josiah Sawyer, now owns and lives on that land first cleared.

Sawyerville was set off from the township of Eaton as a separate municipality in 1892, and date of first council meeting is October 5, of the same year. The village contains 6,000 square acres, and has a valuation of $94,000. The first council was composed of John W. Rogers, mayor, and councillors Peter Coombs, Hollis Williams, Dr. McCurdy, Wm. Hodgen, Charles Harvey, and Herbert H. Hunt. The Council for 1895 comprised John W. Rogers, mayor, and councillors Charles H. Harvey, Richard Evans, Hollis B. Williams, Herbert H. Hunt, William Hodgen and Peter Coombs. W. T. Parker was the first secretary-treasurer and held the office until the first part of January, 1896, when Mr. H. J. Laberee was appointed in his place.

Sawyerville is separated for school as well as municipal purposes. A few years ago a fine, large brick model school was erected. The teachers at present are Miss E. J. Paintin, principal; Miss Lucy Annable, and Miss Mary McDonald. The school commissioners are H. E. Taylor, chairman; W. H. Osgood, R. C. Scott, E. A. Kingsley, and Hollis B. Williams. W. T. Parker was also secretary-treasurer for the Board, but was succeeded in January, 1896, by R. W. Montgomery.

In Sawyerville are located four churches: Methodist, Baptist, Presbyterian and Catholic. Their history is to be found with that of the township of Eaton.

The village is the centre for a large and good farming country. The surrounding land is productive and carried on by a class of farmers who, as a rule, know their business. In Sawyerville there are seven stores, a good hotel, two saw mills, a pulp-wood mill, large butter factory, grist mill, sash and door factory, three blacksmith shops, etc. In secret societies there are the I. O. F., R. T. of T., and a L. O. L. The revenue of the Sawyerville post office for 1895 was $715.50.

WILLIAM SAWYER, EX-M.L.A., saw and grist mill owner and lumber manufacturer, was born in Sawyerville, November 26, 1815. He has always resided here with the exception of seven years, from 1820 to 1827, when his parents lived in Stanstead. He is a grandson of Josiah Sawyer, after whom Sawyerville is named, and who was probably the first settler in Eaton. He first came in about 1792, and in 1796 brought in his family from the States. The father of our subject, John Sawyer, then a young boy, came in with his parents and lived to a ripe old age, when he died in Cookshire, in 1869. William Sawyer was married at Sawyerville, September 10, 1839, to Julia, daughter of the late J. B. Smith. No children. Mr. Sawyer has been one of the most progressive and enterprising citizens of Compton county. In 1871 he received the nomination of the Conservative party as their representative at Quebec, and was opposed by Mr. James Ross, the former member and an independent Conservative, whom he defeated by over three hundred majority. Mr. Sawyer continued to represent the County down to 1886, when he resigned, and Mr. John McIntosh, of Waterville, took his place. At Mr. Sawyer's second election he was returned by acclamation; third election, opposed by James Doak, Compton; fourth election, his opponent was Æneas Macmaster, of Scotstown. Both of these gentlemen were defeated by large majorities. He was a member of the Municipal Council of Eaton from 1855 to 1872, and for several years warden of the County. Mr. Sawyer has always been a strong supporter of the Methodist Church. His generous gifts to this denomination have materially aided in its

RESIDENCE OF WM. SAWYER, EX-M.L.A.

prosperity throughout this section, and his labor and money have been cheerfully given to the many Methodist churches that have been erected. For years, fighting opposition adversities, and discouragement, he labored to secure the building of a railway from Cookshire to the boundary line, through Hereford, and this he has lived to see accomplished in the present Maine Central Railway. He has carried on successfully large business interests, at Sawyerville. The present time, at an advanced age of nearly eighty-one years, he has good health and superintends personally all of his business, his faculties apparently being as keen as ever in the past. Accompanying this biographical sketch are two photo-engravings, one showing the grist and saw mills belonging to Mr. Sawyer, the other that of his private residence, where in front he and Mrs. Sawyer may be seen.

THE LATE REV. ARCHIBALD GILLIES, whose portrait is given on next page, was born in Argyleshire, Scot., July 15, 1812. His father, Duncan Gillies, and family, emigrated to Canada in 1818, settling in Dundee, Huntingdon, Que. Educational advantages were few in those days, but by perseverance and self-denial he attended the academy at Fort Covington, N. Y. While there he was converted, and September 11, 1831, baptized by Elder Safford. A few years later he entered the Baptist college, Montreal. During the summer vacation of 1841, he made a missionary tour through the Townships, reaching Eaton Corner one Friday evening in July. In his notes "for the children," he says:

GRIST AND SAW MILLS OF WM. SAWYER, EX-M.L.A.

"The next day I pushed on to the southern point of the East Clifton settlement, scattered an appointment for a meeting next morning in Mr. Wm. Stone's barn—On Sabbath morning found a large and attentive congregation—The same day, at five P.M., preached in the Congregationalist church at Eaton Corner. These were my first two sermons in Compton county. Text, Ps. 84, 11." After returning to college he accepted a call to the Eaton Baptist church, and left Montreal, December 29, 1841, crossed the St. Lawrence in a canoe, traveled by stage to Sherbrooke, thence by special conveyance to Eaton the evening of the 30th; stopping at Deacon Enos Alger's, where he found a comfortable home for nearly four years. His life-work began Sunday, the first day of 1842. The text 1 Cor. 2: 2, was most literally lived out during that long pastorate, closing nominally January, 1880, really, May 16, 1889, when he passed away. In February, 1842, he married Miss Hannah Stewart, of Fort Covington, a lady of most estimable Christian character, who died December 22 of the same year. February 27, 1842, he was ordained to the Gospel ministry. Briefly referring to his work, he says: "The first year of my pastorate was one of much anxiety and arduous work, a mixture of affliction, sorrow and mercies. The years that followed have been much of the same character." September 9, 1845, he was married by Elder Mitchell, to Miss Lucy Ives, of Magog, who died March 1, 1890, on her seventy-first birthday, having been through the long years a most devoted Christian wife and mother. Her father, Joel H. Ives, emigrated from Meriden, Conn., in 1798, remaining at Eaton Corner till 1848. The Gillies family removed to Grove Hill, Sawyerville. The children were: Lucy M., born 1846; Esther E., born 1848; Sarah J., born 1850; Mary L., born 1855, died January 26, 1861; Archie L., born 1858, married Miss Hattie M. Bryant, of Sherbrooke, November, 1890. They have two sons, and reside in Sherbrooke. Sarah J., married to Rev. A. C. Baker, of Brantford, Ont., died at Sarnia, Ont., July 13, 1888, leaving three sons and one daughter. Subsequently Rev. A. C. Baker, who became pastor of the Eaton Baptist church, married Lucy M. Esther E. resides with them at Grove Hill. During the early years of Mr. Gillies' pastorate many and long rides on horse-back, over rough roads, in all kinds of weather, were some of his hardships. Money was very scarce, and often it was difficult to raise even the subscription for weekly papers. At his fortieth anniversary he remarked that it was easier to raise five thousand dollars than twelve dollars forty years before. As a pastor he was prayerful, spiritual and sympathetic ; an able expounder of the Word, with which he had rare acquaintance. His preaching was with great earnestness, plainness and simplicity. The church he served so long is still reaping the fruits of his pure, devoted life. Though his last years, which were spent in the house that had been his home more than forty

LATE REV. ARCHIBALD GILLIES.

years, were years of much suffering and weakness, they were also years of cheerful, hopeful waiting, studying and meditating upon the Scriptures, spending the early morning hours in prayer for individuals, families, pastors and churches. A young pastor, in a loving tribute to his memory, says : " Father Gillies was strong and noble in possessing and developing humility, self-forgetfulness, patience, endurance, and a never-failing love and devotion to his brethren and to the cause."

LATE ROBERT CAIRNS, in his life-time general merchant, was born in Iberville, Que., April 4, 1844, and died at Sawyerville, September 20, 1892. We reproduce herewith a photograph of Mr. Cairns. Owing to its being a copy and enlargement from a group it is not as clear as could be desired. He came to Bulwer in 1870, where he held the office of postmaster, and carried on a general store. In October, 1876, Mr. Cairns moved to Sawyerville where he successfully carried on a general store, and for sixteen years previous to his death held the office of postmaster. He was a son of William Cairns, of Montreal, was always public-spirited, and took a great interest in Sawyerville, assisting in every way he could to further its progress. Mr. Cairns was married in Sawyerville, December 13, 1871, to Henrietta (born April 7, 1854), daughter of Wellington Osgood, who died in this village in 1878. Issue, four sons: Herbert N., born August 16, 1875, married Minnie Evans, residence, Sawyerville, succeeding his father as general merchant; Edward S., born May 29, 1878; Robert W., born July 3, 1882; William H., born January 19, 1892.

LATE ROBERT CAIRNS.

HERBERT CAIRNS, general merchant was born at Bulwer, August 16, 1873. On the next page will be found the residence of Mr. Cairns, who may be seen standing in front of the house with Mrs. Cairns. He is a son of Mr. Robert Cairns, for many years a successful general merchant at Sawyerville. His portrait and biography will be found on another page. Mr. Herbert Cairns is a graduate of the Stanstead Commercial college, and succeeded his father in 1893 as a general merchant and postmaster at Sawyerville. He is one of the most pushing business men in the County and has largely increased his business, occupying at present two different stores, with interest in one other. On April 11, 1892, at Sawyerville, he married Minnie, daughter of Richard Evans, a leading farmer, and member of the Village Council.

CHARLES HOLLIS HARVEY, contractor, was born in Newport, August 18, 1832, and has always lived in the County. Until a few years ago he successfully followed farming. He is a son of Galon Harvey, who was born in Newport and always lived there until his

RESIDENCE OF H. CAIRNS.

death in 1842. For many years our subject held the offices of secretary-treasurer for the Municipal Council and the School Commissioners of Newport, and was councillor for fifteen years. After moving into Eaton he held the office of councillor for six years, and since the incorporation of Sawyerville as a village he has been one of the councillors. Mr. Harvey has been married twice. First, in Eaton, in 1858, to Esther Julia Holmes, died in 1883. Issue, three children: Samuel Holmes, born September 24, 1859, married Laura B. Ives, of Huntingville, Que., residence, Lowell, Mass.; Arthur Warren, born August 27, 1865, married Lucia Cromwell, two children, residence, Sawyerville; Florence Lucretia, born March 4, 1872, married Robert A. McCullough, one child, residence, Sawyerville. His second marriage took place at Sawyerville, in 1884, to Elizabeth, daughter of William Cairns, of Montreal. She died in 1893. Accompanying this is an engraving of Mr. Harvey's residence at Sawyerville, with himself and others in front.

ARTHUR W. HARVEY, farmer and jobber, was born in Newport, August 27, 1865. His father is Charles H. Harvey, of Sawyerville, of whom a history will be found above. Our subject has lived in Sawyerville during the past few years, and at the present time is sanitary inspector. He holds the office of junior beadle in the I. O. O. F. Mr. Harvey was married in Sawyerville, December 22, 1887, to Lucia V. (born March 19, 1870, in Hereford), daughter of James Cromwell. Issue, three

RESIDENCE OF CHARLES H. HARVEY.

children: Galon Hazen, born June 11, 1890; Clifford Raymond, born November 17, 1891; Claude James, born May 25, 1894. We present herewith an engraving of the residence of Mr. Harvey, which is located on the Eaton road, just outside the village proper. In front may be seen Mr. and Mrs. Harvey and their children.

JOSEPH LABEREE, retired farmer, was born at Birchton, December 2, 1827. He has always lived in the County, moving to Sawyerville from Birchton in September, 1883. During his lifetime he has been a farmer, general merchant, and dealer in cattle, sheep and horses for export. He was school commissioner for a number of years, also assistant postmaster at Sawyerville. His father was Henry Laberee, a son of Rufus Laberee, the fifth family to come into Eaton, whose history may be found with that of John H. Laberee, of Sand Hill. Henry Laberee was born in Charleston, N. H., November 25, 1792, and died August 23, 1860. He married Harriet Chambers, of Eaton, February 26, 1816. She was born September 12, 1794, in Quebec city, and died October 28, 1872. They settled in the woods near Birchton and cleared a good farm, where the daughter, Mrs. Joseph Taylor, now lives. He was a successful farmer, having many of the sterling qualities of his father. He held several public positions and was one of the first councillors chosen in the township of Eaton. They had five children: Hannah, born September 12, 1821, married Charles C. Sawyer; Henry Edwin, born September 28, 1825, married Mary French, died in January 1863; Joseph, our subject; Araminta D., born August 7, 1830, married first, William Cummings, second, D. Metcalf, died August 31, 1881; Theodosia, born September 5, 1833, married J. L. Taylor. Joseph Laberee was married at Sherbrooke, on March 11, 1858, to Miss E. F., daughter of Rufus Laberee,

RESIDENCE OF A. W. HARVEY.

of Eaton. She was born August 23, 1832, and died April 15, 1895. Issue, two sons: J. Allison E., born April 7, 1859, married Carrie H. Root, of Olympia, Wash., their present residence, no children; Arthur A. G., born August 25, 1861, married Carrie V. Graham, residence, Sawyerville There was an adopted daughter, Minnie E. A. Luther, the child of Mrs. Laberee's sister, born March 15, 1868, married John Henry Osgood, no children, residence, Sawyerville. On next page is an engraving of the residence of Mr. Laberee at Sawyerville, in front of which he may be seen. Particulars in regard to the early settlement in Eaton of the Laberees are to be found in the biography of Mr. John H. Laberee.

ROBERT CAIRNS, farmer, was born in County Down, Ireland, November 26, 1833. On the following pages will be found engravings of the old home, situated near Sawyerville,

HISTORY OF COMPTON COUNTY.

RESIDENCE OF JOS. LABERER.

and of the family in a group. Mr. Cairns came to Sawyerville direct from Ireland, in June, 1843. Previous to his settling down as a farmer, he was in a carding mill, and afterwards general merchant at Sawyerville. His father, Hugh Cairns, died in East Clifton, December 1, 1883, aged ninety years. Our subject has always taken a deep interest in all temperance work, having held leading offices in the Sons of Temperance and R. T. of T. societies. Mr. Cairns has always been a strong supporter of the Methodist church, has been superintendent of the Sunday-school, recording steward and leader of the choir ever since the church at Sawyerville was built. His son, Hugh George, is a very promising young man in the Methodist ministry. Mr. Cairns was married at Johnville, February 10, 1870, to Mary Georgianna, daughter of George W. Smith, of Johnville. Mr. Smith has held the offices of councillor and school commissioner, in Eaton. Issue, twelve children, seven living: Hugh George, born November 8, 1870; Wm. Arthur, born April 7, 1874; John Anderson, born October 2, 1877; Robert Arnoldi, born July 8, 1884; Henry Judson, born September 15, 1891; Abigail Jane, born August 18, 1872; Evelyn Georgianna, born March 19, 1893.

J. WILLARD ROGERS, farmer and mayor of Sawyerville, was born in Eaton, January 3, 1844. He is a son of the late David Wells Rogers, who came into Eaton when fifteen years of age, his father having come from the United States into Hereford some years previously. Our subject always lived in Eaton, moving to his present farm in 1879, which is partly included within the limits of the village of Sawyer-

RESIDENCE OF ROBERT CAIRNS.

HISTORY OF COMPTON COUNTY.

ROBERT CAIRNS AND FAMILY.

ville. He was married at Huntingville, Que., January 21, 1879, to widow Esther M. Hibbard (born March 17, 1848), daughter of George I. Barlow, of Eaton, who died May 1, 1895, aged eighty-eight years. Issue, one daughter: Ethel A., born April 10, 1884. To be found on this page is an engraving of the residence of Mr. Rogers, located about half way between Sawyerville and Eaton Corner. He has been a successful farmer, and held several public offices to the entire satisfaction of his fellow citizens. For nine years he was a member of the Eaton council, and since the creation of Sawyerville into a village he has held the office of mayor. His portrait will be found among those of the County Council. He is one of the directors of the Sawyerville Creamery.

ELON R. FRENCH, foreman Cookshire Mill Company, at Sawyerville mill, was born in Eaton, September 6, 1863. On the next page we reproduce a photograph of Mr. French's residence in Sawyerville. He is a son of Mr. Luther French, of Island Brook. Mr. French was married November 26, 1889, to Miss Estella Lindsay. No children.

H. EDWIN TAYLOR, auctioneer and veterinary surgeon, was born in Eaton June 30, 1844. He is a son of the late Jas. Taylor, of Eaton. Mr. H. E. Taylor is one of the prominent men of Sawyerville, and has held several prominent offices. For several years he was chairman of the Board of School Commissioners, and has been one of the valuators since the setting off of Sawyerville as a village. He is

RESIDENCE OF J. W. ROGERS.

RESIDENCE OF ELON R. FRENCH.

a P. C. R. of the I. O. F. He has an extensive practice throughout the County as veterinary surgeon. As an auctioneer his services are in demand from all parts. He was married at Bury, January 13, 1869, to Mary A., daughter of the late Robert Rowe. Mr. Rowe was postmaster at Brookbury for over thirty years, and died May 3, 1895. Issue, nine children, seven living: Chas. Edwin, born September 21, 1877; Henry Kelsey, born December 30, 1881; Alice Mary, born March 13, 1872, married Charles Sawyer, two children, residence, Cookshire; Jessie May, born November 26, 1879; Pansy, born February 23, 1884; Grace Darling, born April 12, 1886; Gladys, born February 12, 1889. At the foot of this page is a photo-engraving of the residence of Mr. Taylor. His eldest son is attending the Toronto veterinary college.

WILLIS J. PHELPS, carpenter and undertaker, was born in Newport, September 9, 1836, and lived in that township until he moved to Sawyerville. He has in the past combined farming with his trade as carpenter. Mr. Phelps has held the office of school commissioner for several years, and is now one of the valuators of Sawyerville. He was married in Eaton, January 14, 1858, to Miriam B., daughter of Horatio Currier. Issue, four children, three living: Elbert W., born November 15, 1864, married Olive J. Ward, residence Learned Plain; Henry J., born January 21, 1870; Eva M., born December 25, 1874. On the next page is an engraving of the residence of Mr. Phelps.

RESIDENCE OF H. E. TAYLOR.

WILLIAM JAMES ALLEN EVANS, trader, was born in East Clifton, May 28, 1871, and moved to Sawyerville in 1883. He is a son of Richard Evans, one of the village councillors. The portrait at the foot of this page will be better recognized as that of J. A. Evans, the name by which he is more familiarly known. Our subject has been in trade in Sawyerville since 1893, dealing in tinware, stoves and agricultural implements. Mr. Evans was married at Sherbrooke, Que., July 3, 1895, to Maggie (born in 1871), daughter of James G. McLellan, formerly a farmer in Orford, but now living in Sherbrooke.

RESIDENCE OF WILLIS J. PHELPS.

HENRY THOMPSON, farmer, was born in Hemmingford, Que. He came to Sawyerville and purchased the farm where he now lives, in October, 1876. A photo-engraving of the residence is shown on the next page, where Mr. and Mrs. Thompson and their children may be seen. He was married at Sherrington, Que., in June, 1867, to Annie Dean. Issue, five children: Robert J., born March 10, 1868; Howard E., born May 24, 1870; Frederick W., born February 14, 1872; Joseph A., born August 3, 1874; Lilly G., born October 31, 1876.

CHARLES GEORGE BROUILLETTE, merchant tailor, was born June 22, 1866, in Stukely, Que. On the next page we present an excellent engraving of his store and residence, together with Mr. Brouillette and family. In 1891 our subject came to Sawyerville and established a tailor's shop, to which he has since added gent's furnishings. He is one of the pushing business men of Sawyerville, and assisted largely in forming the company and constructing the line of the Canadian Telephone Company, of which he was appointed manager. The father of Mr. Brouillette is still living in Stukely, holding offices of councillor and school commissioner. Mr. Brouillette was married at Magog, Que., January 14, 1890, to Olympe Varin, of Ely, Que. By this marriage are four children: Homère Hervé, born March 18, 1892; Marie A., born April 1, 1893; Ella B., born June 26, 1895.

COURT SAWYERVILLE, No. 590, I. O. F. This court was organized June 5, 1890, by John W. Stocks and Henry Williams, of Sherbrooke, assisted by James Montgomery, John Planche and Charles Loveland, of Court Cookshire, No. 176. Following are the names of the charter members and the officers elected, viz.: C.D.H.C.R., Henry E. Taylor; V.C R , Charles H. Loveland; R.S , Miron L Larabee; F.S , James Montgomery; Treas., Thomas J. Stevenson; S.W., John W. Jones; J.W., Thomas Johnston ; S.B., John Robinson ; J.B., John Reinhardt ; P.C.R , Richard Evans, and members, Bertram Sawyer, Norton Lindsay, Gilbert Hongh, Ames Williams, Edgar A. Kingsley, Victor Loveland (deceased), Horace Stevenson, Edward Dawson and F. A. Planche.

J. A. EVANS.

HISTORY OF COMPTON COUNTY.

RESIDENCE OF HENRY THOMPSON.

December 17, 1895, the following officers were elected, and now hold office (1896): C.D.H.C.R , James Montgomery; C.R., Hollis Cairns; V.C.R , Leonard Esam; F. S., Ephraim Evans; R. S., F. A. Planche; Treas., Charles H. Loveland; Chaplain, Charles French, S.W., William Riddell; J.W., Arthur Harvey; S.B., Alfred Kelley; J.B , William Graham ; P.C.R., Thomas McCurdy. At the institution of the court Henry E. Taylor was appointed C.D.H C R. He was succeeded in 1892 by Bro. Charles Loveland, who filled that office until 1895, when he was succeeded by Bro. James Montgomery, who holds the office at the present time. In January, 1892, Thomas McCurdy, M.D., was elected C.R , and held the office until December, 1895. The following members have been delegates to the different sessions of the High Court of the Province of Quebec, viz: Thomas McCurdy, James Montgomery, Rev. Herbert A Dickson. Of these two have held High Court offices. At a session of the High Court in Coaticook, in 1892, Rev. H. A. Dickson was chosen High Chaplain for the ensuing year, and in 1895, at a session of the High Court in Quebec, Bro.

James Montgomery was elected High Marshal for the Province of Quebec. Since the organization of the court, it has gone steadily on increasing, until at the present time there is a membership of forty-eight The court meets the third Wednesday of every month, in the Orange Hall, Sawyerville. On the next page is a photo-engraving of the officers and members, taken during the summer of 1895

LATE DAVID EDWARD METCALF, carpenter, was born in South Cookshire, February 5, 1837. He fol-

RESIDENCE AND STORE OF C. G. BROUILLETTE.

lowed farming at the same place until 1893, when he sold to Angus McLeod and moved to Waterville. In company with Mr. H. T. Sunbury, they carried on the hotel at that place until 1895, when he removed to Sawyerville. He held the office of councillor in Eaton for three years. First marriage was in Eaton, February 1, 1863, to Araminta D. Laberee, widow of Wm. A. Cummings. Issue, one daughter: Myrtie A., born December 27, 1869. Second marriage, in Eaton, February 28, 1882, to Alma M. Hodge. Issue, one son, Claude D., born July 15, 1888. Mr. Metcalf died at Sawyerville, February 24, 1896.

COURT SAWYERVILLE, No. 390, I. O. F.

WILLIAM BRYANT WILLIAMS, farmer, was born where he now lives, November 20, 1842. He has held the office of councillor, and is a trustee of the Baptist church. Mr. Williams' grandparents, Aseph and Jerusha Williams, came from Connecticut, among the first settlers. His father, Russell Williams, who died April 21, 1867, married Alice Hinkley, of Thetford, Vt. She died May 3, 1890 Nine of their children are still living. Our subject was first married May 30, 1878, to Mary L. Munn, who died January 9, 1893. Issue, one son: Archie B., born October 3, 1880. Second marriage, December 31, 1894, to Mary E. P. Sanborn, of Lowell, Mass.

ROBERT McCULLOUGH, blacksmith, was born November 16, 1866, coming to Clifton in 1885, and later moving to Sawyerville. Married at Sawyerville, October 25, 1893, to Florence, daughter of Charles Harvey. Issue, one child: Gleason Harvey, born September 9, 1895.

ROBERT HALLIDAY, farmer, a resident of Sawyerville since 1872, was born in West Clifton, October 27, 1843. At present he holds the office of councillor. In the past he has been councillor, school commissioner and valuator. Was married in Compton, October 7, 1873, to Henrietta Hitchcock. Issue, three children: John Leroy, born August 1, 1876; Ernest C., born August 11, 1878; George Courtland, born October 22, 1889.

EDGAR AUSTIN KINGSLEY, general merchant, came to Sawyerville in 1894. He was born at Bulwer, Que., February 24, 1861, where he always lived. By trade a carpenter, going into the mercantile business at Bulwer in 1889. Married at Bulwer, December 20, 1887, to Ermina M., daughter of Amos Williams. Issue, one son: Earl Gordon, born November 10, 1892. Henry Kingsley, the father of our subject, is still living at Bulwer.

HENRY JAMES LABEREE, jeweler and watchmaker, was born in Eaton, March 24, 1862. At the age of seventeen years he conducted the carding and clothier's business in Eaton. At the age of twenty-one formed partnership with H. A. Warby and erected a saw mill where the Symmes Hay Cap factory is now. In 1887, he went to Qu'Appelle, N.W.T., and was in the jewelry business there with C. C. Bailey; after a short time moved to Worcester, Mass., and in 1893 returned to Sawyerville. He holds the office of secretary-treasurer of the village of Sawyerville, and carries on a prosperous trade as jeweler. Mr. Laberee married Alice Hatton Thomas. Issue, one son: Harold, born October 27, 1890.

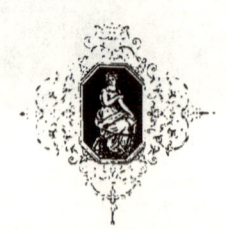

CHAPTER XII.

THE LATE HONORABLE JOHN HENRY POPE.

A LIFE EXAMPLE FOR THE YOUTH OF TO-DAY.

Written by the Honorable C. H. MACKINTOSH, Lieutenant-Governor of the Northwest Territories. *

The chronicles of the county of Compton would be incomplete indeed, without a concise biography of one whose masterful energies left their impress upon a majority of the public institutions of the Eastern Townships. The Hon. John Henry Pope was a distinctive personality, a lover of his native county, a benefactor of the community, a courageous, self-denying, zealous toiler in the cause of progress; not only a pioneer in the work of developing the material resources of his immediate neighborhood, but other momentous enterprises appertaining to the Dominion of Canada. To intelligently estimate the gradual expansion of a commonwealth, he who investigates must aim at being conversant with the character of those who made its laws, founded its institutions and fostered its industries. As with nations, so with communities, the component parts of which contribute towards perfecting the entire fabric. Hence, so long as intrepid courage, unflagging zeal, and untiring devotion to interests beneficial to mankind are appreciated, the names of great men will be honored by generations to come. The dull, cold ear of death may be insensible to praise or censure, flattery or candor, admiration or envy; still, the example of a life well lived, of duty performed, remains, stimulating those who come after to be faithful to every trust, and unflinching in their efforts for the betterment of the human race.

Friend and opponent alike, recognized in John Henry Pope a man above personal ambition; they saw in him no loiterer in the lap of luxury; no worshipper at the shrine of popular applause: on the contrary, a strong character, possessing the intellectual and physical fibre which is at all times the birthright of those whose individuality is stamped upon the history of their times.

The Honorable John Henry Pope was born in the township of Eaton (now Cookshire), on December 19, 1819, inheriting from his forefathers that spirit of self-reliance characteristic of his after life. His father, Colonel John Pope, was the son of a United Empire Loyalist, who, with others in the dark days, preferred the flag of Great Britain to that of the neighboring republic. The family originally removed, in 1800, from the vicinity of Boston, Mass., and the farm occupied in the Townships is embraced in the magnificent property now owned by Mr. Rufus Pope, M.P. At the time the Pope settlers came to Cookshire the district was known as the township of Eaton, and sixteen miles distant, where now stands the flourishing city of Sherbrooke, only one log house denoted the march of civilization. Wherever these U. E. Loyalists settled, well-to-do communities sprung into existence. Nova Scotia, New Brunswick

---

* NOTE.—The Honorable C H. Mackintosh was for many years one of the most active journalists and public speakers in the Dominion. In 1874 he accepted the editorship of the Ottawa *Citizen*, which he managed for nearly twenty years. In 1879, 1880, and 1881, he was elected mayor of the Capital, and sat from 1882 until 1893, with the exception of two years, as senior member for the city of Ottawa. In 1893 he was appointed lieutenant-governor of the Northwest Territories. Mr. Mackintosh was a close personal and parliamentary friend of Mr. Pope's, for many years, and frequently visited the Eastern Townships, particularly on the occasions of the annual meetings of the Conservatives of Compton. He therefore kindly consented to write a concise biography of the late Honorable John Henry Pope, for use in the "History of Compton County."—EDITOR

(and at that time Nova Scotia formed an integral part of New Brunswick), the Bay of Quinté district in Ontario, and what were known as the English or Eastern Townships, all owed much of their after-development and fame to the direct descendants of those chivalrous men, who devoted their fortunes and hazarded their lives, to maintain what they conceived to be the fundamental principles of British sovereignty. One in what was then looked upon as a misfortune, these vigorous offshoots of the parent stem united in enlarging and consolidating Imperial authority and Imperial interests, in the country they learned to love so fondly. Those who to-day enjoy every educational advantage, whose children are surrounded by splendidly equipped schools and colleges, find difficulty in realizing what a marvellous change has taken place within the last half of the present century. A common school training was, in the early days, all the majority of those who afterwards made their mark in public could possibly receive. The rudiments of education at the common school of Cookshire, were all that fortune vouchsafed Mr. Pope. The world's school of human nature, in which he was an apt and devoted student, was open to him; there he learned the lessons and matured the mental outfit that made him a leader of men and a giant amongst his contemporaries.

Never willingly idle, up with the sun, and toiling until it set, love for agriculture, stock-raising and grain-growing, justified the belief that his whole time and attention would be concentrated in cultivating the best farm, feeding the best stock, and importing the best cattle into the Eastern Townships. Not so: the markets of the world were open to him; he knew that sailing vessels and steamers plied the Atlantic; he had seen the cattle and timber trade at Quebec; and, gradually, working by day and driving by night, soon became a central figure, not alone locally, but in the Ancient Capital.

Mr. Pope was married on March 5, 1845, to Miss Bailey, daughter of Mr. Ward Bailey, of Cookshire, by whom he had three children: Lizzie, the wife of the Hon. W. B. Ives, M.P. for Sherbrooke, and, until the recent defeat of the Conservative party, Minister of Trade and Commerce, one of the foremost politicians in the Dominion—and Rufus H. Pope, the present able member for Compton in the House of Commons. The third child died when but an infant. It may be of interest in this connection, to mention that John Pope, grandfather of the subject of this memoir, died on May 7, 1853, aged ninety years; and Col. John Pope, his father, died on June 28, 1856, aged seventy years.

With many deserving enterprises of importance in the Eastern Townships, John Henry Pope was intimately associated. He was one of the original promoters of the Eastern Townships Bank, securing its first charter; was a member of its Board of Directors from its first organization up to the day of his death, and lived to see the institution which he was mainly instrumental in starting (commencing business in 1859 with the usual capital, $400,000), increased to a capital of $1,500,000, with a reserve fund of over $700,000, and to-day standing financially one of the first Canadian banks.

The International Railway, running from Sherbrooke to the province line, now a portion of the Canadian Pacific system, was another great enterprise in which he was deeply interested. It was originally projected by Mr. Pope with a view to opening up the Townships between Sherbrooke and the province line, giving them railway facilities, and carrying their products within commercial circles. It was also thought that, in time, it must form part of an air line from Montreal to the sea. The scheme was pushed by Mr. Pope with untiring energy and perseverance, against what seemed almost insurmountable obstacles. The county of Compton passed a by-law authorizing the County to take stock to the amount of $225.000. Submitted to the rate-payers, this by-law was defeated. Another one, known as by-law No. 37, to the same effect, was passed by the Council in 1870. This

THE LATE HONORABLE JOHN HENRY POPE.

was ratified by the rate-payers. Bonds were issued based upon the security guaranteed by this vote. Meanwhile, the validity of the by-law was contested; thus, for the time being, rendering the bonds unnegotiable. Mr. Pope pledged his property for the purchase of rails and supplies; the action taken by the opposition was decided adversely to them, and then carried to appeal, where defeat was again sustained. A contract was next entered into with Messrs. Brooks, Ryan & Co. for the completion of the building of the road. During its construction, Mr. Pope was repeatedly obliged to come forward and pledge his name and that of his friends to obtain money to go on with the work. Where other men would have succumbed, his indomitable pluck and energy achieved victory; the road was completed, opened for traffic, and now forms one of the most important links in the Canadian Pacific short line to the sea. The International Railway all but ruined Mr. Pope, both in health and purse. A friend of his, the Hon. W. Macdougall, hearing he was in London in 1874, called at his hotel near Euston station, where he found Mr. Pope very ill, but negotiating for money to complete the enterprise. He was suffering, but still hopeful, still cheerful. "Well," he said, "I've got a small room, and I burn a wax candle, but I'm quite contented. I'm pretty ill, but the doctor comes twice a day, and the people look after me here,—if money were as plentiful as physicians, I guess I'd pull through." He always looked upon the bright side of life, extracting amusement from the most sombre sources imaginable. Ultimately, the railway was completed. In the middle of his difficulties, a company of Americans commenced to build the Magawasippi Railway, but could not induce the township of Ascot to vote the necessary $50,000 bonus, or to subscribe sufficient stock. This road was important, in consequence of connecting the outer world with Sherbrooke. Mr. Pope was driving through Lennoxville one afternoon, when a gentleman, Lieutenant-Colonel Benj. Pomroy, accompanied by others, met him. "Well," said Mr. Pope, "how did you get along at Ascot?" "Badly," was the reply, "we can't raise more than $25,000." "Is that so?" he exclaimed, "well, I can fix that up. Go on with the road!" "What do you mean?" asked Pomroy. "What do I mean? just this, I'll subscribe the $25,000, and I mean what I say; go and build your road! and off he drove. Next day contracts were re-signed, and what is now a continuation of the Pasumpsic Railway became a reality within a few months.

Mr. Pope was intimately associated with the Paton Manufacturing Company of Sherbrooke, from its inception in 1866, being one of the original partners under the name of A. Paton & Co. He had always been a large stockholder, and taken a deep interest in its advancement, advocating extension of the mills in 1872, thus making them the largest in Canada at that time. In the depression of trade which marked the years 1873 to 1878, he never lost faith in the enterprise. In fact reverses seemed to develop his best qualities, and he was always found ready to back the management to the utmost of his ability. When the Paton Company was supposed to be on the decline, it was proposed to organize and incorporate a company of shareholders. Mr. Pope was applied to. He said: "Go and see our friend in Montreal" (the late Mr. A. Buntin), "and then I will speak." The Montreal gentleman replied: "No, get Mr. Pope, and I will take an equal amount to that subscribed by him." What was the consternation of the Montreal friend to learn that the member for Compton had subscribed $60,000! He was as good as his word, however, and promptly covered the sum. In 1874-77, the Company was again hard pressed during the crises of those years. Mr. Pope had faith; he put up another $60,000, and others contributed. To-day it is considered one of the best paying properties in the Dominion.

He was largely interested with the late Cyrus S. Clarke, of Portland, Me., in the Brompton Mills Lumber Company, and did a great deal towards the development of the lumber trade in that part of the country. During many years he drove day and night between the points of his operations—Brompton and the east part of Compton county; for two weeks he had been known to sleep in his sleigh at night rather than have his movements retarded—working all day, without even opportunity to change his apparel. On one occasion, during the spring, the roads broke up and the ice became fragile in the Felton river. Arriving there, he found teams and men, but was informed that it would be "impossible to cross." "Not cross!" he exclaimed; "why, that's what I came to do, and we've got to make a crossing." All night long he worked with his coat off, wielding an axe, felling the trees on each side The river not being very wide, these met and lapped midway, thus presenting insurmountable barriers to the floating ice; which, becoming stationary, froze into a solid body. All the men assisted, but their strength gave out. Mr. Pope continued, and at eight o'clock on the morning of the next day, every man and every team had crossed Felton river, greatly to the surprise of the neighborhood. The Scotch settlers, for years afterwards, when remarks detrimental to Mr. Pope were made, would say: "Mr. Pope can do anything; he can freeze the river!" Such qualities as these endeared him to the robust colleagues who toiled in the Eastern Townships. There were giants in the earth in those days; railways and modernized luxuries were read of, but not enjoyed to any extent, in that district. Life was a two-fisted struggle for the man who aimed at achieving success. Mr. Pope was a director of the Sherbrooke Water Power Company, the Sherbrooke Gas and Water Company, and honorary president and a large stockholder in the Eastern Townships Agricultural Association. The copper mines at Acton were also opened up and worked through his agency, as well as the gold mines of the township of Ditton. It is related that, hearing from an Indian that gold had been found in the township of Ditton, then twenty miles from civilization, he, in 1862, started with Mr. William Bailey and two neighbors, one named Weston, determined, if possible, to discover the truth of the report. They underwent many fatigues, searching during the day in vain. Mr. Bailey fished, and Mr. Pope explored. At last he returned with a comical smile on his face, remarking: "Look here, Bailey, you're having all the fun; I guess I'll fish," which he did, landing some very fine trout. At dusk, Luther Weston returned, exclaiming: "By George, I've found it!" displaying a small piece of gold, which he had carefully washed. They camped that night, and next day, instead of trout-fishing, gold-hunting was the excitement. The result was, Mr. Pope bought all the land within a given area, and had the property mined for years. He wore a massive gold chain, the product of the mine, and frequently remarked, with a sly twinkle in his eye: "I worked a good many years to get this chain—and got it at wholesale figures, too."

Possessing all the attributes of progressive manhood, John Henry Pope became a leader of men, not only on the farm, in lumbering camps, in railway enterprise, in financial operations, but in every avenue of life upon which he entered.

A well-known gentleman, Squire Laberee, had settled in the country years and years before. John Henry Pope's father, Colonel Pope, married Miss Sophia Laberee, a woman of great force of character, and all her qualities were inherited by the son. When danger threatened Canada, Mr. Pope organized the first cavalry company in Quebec province, becoming captain, and afterwards retiring with the rank of major. Naturally diffident as to titles or distinctive appellations, he was particularly averse to being addressed in accordance with military etiquette, and perhaps he was wise; at all events, common sense, and not false modesty, inspired these sentiments. It was his irrepressible pluck, his indomitable will and manly spirit, which contributed towards making him a central figure in every great undertaking throughout various portions of the province of Quebec; but more particularly in the Eastern Townships. He amassed wealth, but was exceedingly generous; every church, no matter of what denomination, received contributions, and large ones too, from the man who was himself toiling to complete immense works. French and English alike learned to admire and trust him, and this confidence was manifested by the political support recorded by all nationalities. To this day his name is revered by many of the Scotch settlers of Winslow and their descendants, for a hard and successful battle fought in their interests. It so happened that large tracts of land were cancelled by the Crown Lands Department at Quebec, for the time being the centre for political business. Mr. Pope, just elected to parliament, protested, but uselessly. Then he attended the sale, challenged anybody to purchase land upon which settlers were to be found, and ultimately forced the authorities to compromise by allowing every bona fide settler his lands. When he returned, the grateful Scotchmen turned out in force, and releasing the horses, amid wild enthusiasm drew his carriage three miles. In fact, in every walk of life, in everything to which he turned his attention, success was achieved by indomitable perseverance and unremitting industry.

One might be pardoned for entertaining a misgiving that the man who drove day and night to and from lumbering camps and mills, who explored a mineral district and built railways, who rejoiced in stock raising and had scarce a day of rest, must necessarily have neglected some portion of his vast responsibilities. Not so, however, for what he accomplished remains a monument of evidence to the contrary. While engaged in all other enterprises, he never lost interest in farming operations, prosecuting them with his customary energy, and importing large shipments of thoroughbred stock, with the creditable design of improving breeds of cattle in the Townships. His stock farm, "Eastview," at Cookshire, was, and is still, one of the finest model farms in Canada, and that this will continue is safe to predict, so long as the son, Mr. Rufus H Pope, M.P., directs operations upon the vast estate. He, too, possessing education, experience, courage and indomitable perseverance, is a living prototype of his father. Quick to perceive any advantage, to apply any labor-saving machinery, or adopt any device promotive of agricultural development, the successor of the lamented John Henry Pope commands respect and inspires confidence in all his undertakings.

We come now to another, and national phase in the career of one who rendered so much valuable service to the Dominion—that appertaining to his political life. Stormy days, those succeeding the operations of William Lyon Mackenzie, Cartier, Robert Baldwin, Louis H. Lafontaine, Wilfred Nelson, Louis Papineau, and their contemporaries. Dark days also, those who saw kindled the flame of sectional and racial passion throughout the old provinces, when a governor-general's life was threatened, and nation's deliberative assembly destroyed by fire, public libraries levelled with the ground, constitutional government brought into contempt, scoffed at and outraged. At this period, 1849, the undemonstrative John Henry Pope appeared, a lion in the political arena; the old United Empire Loyalist blood coursed hotly in his veins; the old United Empire Loyalist enthusiasm was aroused. Not only in Canada, but in portions of Great Britain, Lord Elgin was denounced for assenting to the Rebellion Losses Bill. Who, to-day, harbors even shadowy suspicion that that able statesman was inspired by ought save constitutional motives? Still, Mr. Gladstone denounced the bill as a "measure for rewarding rebels," and it should not be a matter for wonder that suggestions such as these added fuel to fire, and that the old "Family Compact" spoke disparagingly of Lord Elgin. Mr. Pope had, for some time, been a leading factor in municipal matters, had a seat in the Council (representing Eaton) at Sherbrooke, and strengthened himself by an organization of trusty friends and adherents prepared to follow him to the death. A marvellous organizer, he knew his men, and when selected, these proved he had not erred in judgment. He spurned annexation, based as it was upon absolutely disloyal designs, and said so. The rugged originality of John Henry Pope could not be more significantly illustrated than by a recitation of his course in connection with this wild movement. A majority of the monied men throughout the Townships, together with others who exercised considerable influence, were misled by the craze, probably in consequence of proximity to the American boundary. At that time, Mr. Pope thought more of improving his property than of engaging in windy controversies. It happened, however, that while shingling his house, just beyond the village of Cookshire, a gentleman called him down, presenting a paper for his signature. "What is it?" asked Mr. Pope. Upon reading, he discovered its purport, namely, annexation. "Here, take this back!" he exclaimed, "I'll not sign it, and you'll not get many signers around here!" and only one signature was secured in Cookshire.

Sir Alexander Tilloch Galt resigned his seat for the county of Sherbrooke, Mr. Pope at once advocated the nomination of Mr. Cleveland, of Richmond (father of Mr. C. C. Cleveland, ex-M.P. for Richmond and Wolfe), as a candidate. The late Judge J. S. Sanborn, suspected of annexation proclivities, and ultimately declaring his preference therefor, was also in the field. A bitter, uncompromising struggle followed, Sanborn being returned by a substantial majority. The Pope committee, however, in no way lost heart; day by day, and night by night, they toiled to perfect their system and to strengthen their ranks, and, on two occasions, the leader of this aggressive phalanx opposed Sanborn unsuccessfully, being only in a minority of eight on the second occasion. Ultimately Mr. Sanborn saw new light, and in 1857 renounced annexation, retiring in Mr. Pope's favor. That gentleman sat for Compton up to the day he passed away, on April 1, 1889.

It was during one of the early meetings of the Assembly, that the new member for Compton, being in Quebec, astonished a number of commercial and naval gentlemen by expressing an opinion that they were ignorant of the first principles of what he called the "application of leverage." The controversy arose out of the sea-faring men declaring that a sunken vessel near the harbor could not possibly be raised. "Very well," quietly remarked Mr. Pope, "you guarantee me so much money" (naming the amount), "and I'll guarantee to raise the boat." He made a contract, raised the vessel, got the money, and when telling this experience, usually added: "When a man feels that a thing can be done, he should be determined to do it." That was his creed throughout life. On the same principle, years and years after, he fought the Bell Telephone Company's contention with reference to certain patents.

It will be remembered that Parliament, prior to Confederation, met alternately at Quebec and Toronto. The member for Compton was known in Toronto as the "Log-roller," partially because of his being engaged in the lumber business, but, perhaps, candidly speaking, more because of his penchant for opposing legislation considered by him as jeopardizing Eastern Townships interests. Thus, when the late Hon. T. Lee Terrill, of Stanstead, applied for the incorporation of a Provincial bank, despite all the influences brought to bear, Mr. Pope condemned the enterprise and ultimately defeated the measure.

Few men have conferred more solid benefits upon their country, as legislators, than John Henry Pope. There was no ostentation, no display, no pride of office or assumption of intellectual brilliancy. Reticence was his strength. He seldom promised, but once promising, never failed to be true to an obligation. Entering the old Canada Assembly in 1857-58, one in an aggregate of one hundred and thirty members, Mr. Pope soon became an active spirit in the Conservative ranks. Kingston had sent Sir John A. Macdonald; Argenteuil, Bellingham, and afterwards J. J. C. Abbott; Brockville, George Sherwood; Carleton, W. F. Powell; Chateauguay, Henry Starnes; Cornwall, John S. McDonald; Dorchester, Hector L. Langevin; Drummond, Christopher Dunkin; East Durham, F. H. Burton; East Elgin,

Leonidas Burwell; Frontenac, Henry Smith; Glengarry, D. A. McDonald; Haldimand, William Lyon Mackenzie; Hamilton city, Isaac Buchanan; Hastings North, George Benjamin; Hastings South, Lewis Walbridge; Kent, Archibald McKellar; Lambton, Malcolm Cameron, and afterwards Hope F. Mackenzie; Leeds and Grenville, Ogle R. Gowan; Lincoln, W. F. Merritt, and afterwards J. C. Rykert; London, John Carling; Northumberland West, Sidney Smith; Ontario, Oliver Mowat; Ottawa city, R. W. Scott; Ottawa county (afterwards so ably represented by the late Alonzo Wright), D. E. Papineau; Oxford North, William Macdougall (succeeding George Brown); Perth, Thomas M. Daly; Quebec city, Charles Alleyn; Renfrew, J. L. Macdougall and afterwards W. Caley; St. Hyacinthe, L. V. Sicotte; Shefford, T. Drummond; Sherbrooke town, Alexander Tilloch Galt; Simcoe North, Angus Morrison; Toronto city, George Brown and J. Beverly Robinson; Verchères, George Cartier; Waterloo North, M. H. Foley; Welland, Gilbert McMicken; Wentworth North, William Notman—a galaxy of able men, from whose ranks Confederation—the union of all the provinces—virtually received its first inspiration. It was a great Parliament, for there began the struggle which resulted, years afterwards, in that union, declared to be a panacea for then existing and all possible future ills and bickerings, between Upper and Lower Canada. A born diplomat, John Henry Pope soon became the central figure of a group of notably bright and popular representatives. The times were exciting; the Hon. George Brown was a powerful factor in the body politic. His advocacy of representation by population, denunciation of Roman Catholic institutions, and agitation with reference to the rights of Upper Canada, having strengthened his cause, while seriously affecting the situation for his opponents. In 1863, surrounded by such men as William Macdougall, Oliver Mowat, Alexander Mackenzie, and scores of powerful debaters, his trenchant pen and eloquent tongue concentrated upon the enemies' batteries, it became evident that an era of chronic discord, sectional passion and agitation, threatened to produce a long and disastrous feud, inimical to Canada, and degrading to civilized and civilizing institutions. Governments did not last long; majorities were small; Sandfield Macdonald's administration came in and went out; the Conservatives followed in 1864, being defeated upon the Militia bill. Both parties were disconcerted. Outside the walls of Parliament, public sentiment was divided; an appeal to the excited populace seemed almost a mockery; statesmanship was at a discount, and the hour called for the man At that time Parliament met at Quebec, and the man the hour demanded was a guest at the St. Louis Hotel, Mr. John Henry Pope, who, consulting a few friends, sought an interview with the Hon. George Brown, discussed the subject of coalition, and ultimately a conference took place between John A. Macdonald and Mr. Brown. An agreement followed—a coalition government was formed, the programme being confederation of the Provinces of Upper and Lower Canada, Nova Scotia and New Brunswick, and it was hoped that this would be a final adjustment of all those vexed and vexing issues threatening severance of the ties hitherto existing between Upper and Lower Canada. On October 25, 1871, Mr. Pope was gazetted Minister of Agriculture, resigning office with his leader, the Right Honorable Sir John A. Macdonald, in November, 1873, returning to his department again in October, 1878, upon the defeat of the government of the Hon. Alexander Mackenzie. In his department Mr. Pope soon proved that early training and practical experience eminently fitted him for the position of Minister of Agriculture. He was a worker, throwing his whole energies into solving the diverse problems and complications daily arising. In the House of Commons he commanded the greatest possible respect and attention; he had made his place, and was not the mere accident of party exigence or cabal influence. Tall, commanding in appearance, with high forehead and pale, intellectual countenance; incisive, full of nervous vigor, he was, *par excellence*, the type of a class which builds, and after building, never pulls down, except to improve.

Tolerant towards his opponents; sometimes vehement, never hasty; possessing an extraordinary faculty for mastering details; never moved by gusty impulse, prudent, far-seeing, calm, determined, those who attacked him soon discovered an immense fund of reserve power, and those who encouraged and sustained him realized that their confidence was never misplaced.

One thing John Henry Pope had set his heart upon, namely, that the Dominion should have a Canadian Pacific railway,—a through route connecting the Atlantic and the Pacific. Years had elapsed since the subject first became a noticeable issue in public affairs; the preceding administration had made many efforts, but unsuccessfully. One man had confidence in it,—one man believed, one man was determined that the experiment should be tried. He was aware that Sir Charles Tupper was even then (1879) negotiating in England, and he (Mr. Pope) was acting minister in the department controlling railways. The writer well remembers calling at his office in the Department of Agriculture at that period, finding Mr. Pope contemplating a sheet of foolscap containing columns of figures, estimates and other data. "Come in; sit down," said Mr. Pope, "I'm going to build the Canadian Pacific Railway. Here are the figures and it can be done." Finally he informed him that he had decided upon resigning his portfolio, organizing a company, and constructing the railway. "However," he added, "come and see me again to-morrow and I'll tell you more about it." The writer kept the engagement. "Well, I'm not going out," quietly remarked Mr. Pope, with a smile containing a volume of suggestions, "but the railroad's going to be built. When I told Sir John of my intention, he asked me, 'Have you that much faith in the enterprise?' I replied, 'Yes.' 'Then,' said he, 'if you have, I'm with you. You, Tupper and I will have a talk and see what can be done either in England or in Canada or both combined.'"

So John Henry Pope remained in the administration, acting as Minister of Railways during Sir Charles Tupper's absence in England, where tentative negotiations with various parties concerning the Pacific road were pending. The year 1880 opened full of bright promises and cheerful prospects, and when Sir John Macdonald, Sir Charles Tupper, and the Hon. J. H. Pope engaged quarters at Batt'd Hotel in London, capitalists or their representatives were quite prepared to discuss the enterprise which had prompted this visit to England. Mr. Pope always favored the construction of the Pacific Railway by a company whose controlling interest should be in the hands of Canadians. He argued that these would more fully comprehend the position of affairs, command more local sympathy, and be more closely in touch with the great commercial houses of the Dominion. Mr. George Stephen, of Montreal, had already signified willingness to co-operate, and as he and Mr. R. B. Angus were both interested in the St. Paul, Minneapolis & Manitoba Railway, and had also been interested in the Pembina branch from Emerson to Winnipeg, the announcement that they were in England prepared to negotiate, caused quite a flutter amongst rival negotiators. Meetings, conferences, exchange of correspondence, sorely tried the patience of the Canadian ministers, more particularly as week followed week without definite results. Finally, Mr. John Puleston, M.P. (afterwards Sir John Puleston), arranged an interview with Sir John Macdonald and Sir Charles Tupper. This gentleman, though not a large capitalist, was allied with many home as well as foreign bankers, and anticipated being able to bring together a very powerful and wealthy combination. Only preliminary features of the proposed contract were talked over, Mr. Pope being absent. On his return, the Premier informed him that Mr. Puleston was prepared to take up the work on the terms to be agreed upon. "Very well, Sir John," was that gentleman's response, "I guess you havn't any further use for me; I'll get my grip and go back to Canada." Then the Premier and Sir Charles Tupper mollified their irate colleague, who at last said, "All right, I'll stay on one condition." "What is that?" asked Sir Charles Tupper. "Well, that Sir John sends for Mr. Puleston, and gives one week at the end of which he is to produce the names of the proposed organization, with their financial credit vouched for, or failing that,—to quit." This was done, but Mr. Pope used laughingly to say, "Except Baron Reinach, we never saw one of them again." Subsequently a contract was made with the Canadian capitalists.

In 1885 the Hon. John Henry Pope became Minister of Railways and Canals, succeeding Sir Charles Tupper, although on several occasions he desired to be free from the cares and anxieties of office. The Premier several times suggested his acceptance of Imperial honors, but he peremptorily refused to sanction it. He remained in the government, however, usually with the explanation, "Well, Sir John wishes me to stay, and his wishes are mine." Despite his admiration of, and personal regard for the Premier, he would not brook any interference in his department. On one occasion, and one only, had he and his leader any disagreement or misunderstanding, consequent upon Sir John Macdonald suggesting that certain orders given by the Minister of Railways should be countermanded. "All right, Sir John," exclaimed his colleague, "then you have no use for me; get some one else, for I'll never consent to it!" The great Chieftain not being used to even a semblance of insubordination, was naturally astonished. In a minute, however, he recovered, extending his hand with the remark, "I have use for you, my old friend, and as you are so determined, you must be right." Mr. Pope carried his point and remained at his post. That Sir John Macdonald harbored no ill-feeling, consequent upon this unpleasantness, was significantly proved some months after, when, discussing with the writer the subject of men in public life, the Prime Minister said: "John Henry Pope was the most prudent, clear-headed man in my government, and the shrewdest observer and manager of men I ever met on the American continent; had his education been perfected in early life, he would be Premier of the Dominion to-day." The writer ventured to suggest that these scholarly attainments "might have suppressed the development of that very originality by which he had achieved such success." "Perhaps so, perhaps so," quietly replied the Conservative chieftain, "nevertheless, he rendered great services to Canada." This was subsequent to poor John Henry Pope's death; less than two years after, loving hands, devoted followers, were placing memorial wreaths upon the bier of one whose chivalrous generalship had so often led them to victory.

Then came the Riel troubles of 1885-6, the member for Compton taking strong ground upon the advisability of maintaining law and order and respecting the constitution. In 1886, it became apparent that the Opposition in Quebec province was gaining strength from the results of the Riel agitation, while the extreme feeling in Ontario was moderating. At that time, not only a racial question with local coloring, disturbed the political atmosphere, but an imported question, "Home Rule for Ireland," had been forced to the surface. Discussing the prospect, Mr. Pope at once decided that the sooner a general election took place the better for his Conservative friends. Mercier was on the threshold of power, Mowat's government had just been sustained, and he logically reasoned that the Liberal party in Ontario had expended their strength, that Quebec Liberals would be powerful if Mr. Mercier came in, and that there was no other recourse except dissolution. Early in December he and Sir John Macdonald reviewed the situation, and in January, 1887, the House was dissolved; writs were issued, an election took place in February, and the Government of Sir John Macdonald was sustained. It is not to be imagined that even an iron constitution could remain intact after performing the work which not alone fell to the lot of Mr. Pope, but was absolutely covetted by him. His ceaseless energy was phenomenal; holidays were unknown to him; rest, in his estimation, was only another name for pampered luxury; in short, everything seemed like a waste of time, unless he was at his desk or on his farm, or discussing public affairs with the few men in whom he placed implicit confidence. Usually reticent, his whole heart was open where he trusted and had faith. No man was dearer to his friends, more loved, more admired, more eulogized; and these witnessed with ill-concealed anxiety symptoms of physical failure in one who had hitherto appeared invulnerable to fatigue. When at last, in the spring of 1889, he lay prostrate at his residence, on O'Connor street, still cheerful, hopeful, manly, it was felt the end fast approached. Throughout the earlier years of his struggles and vicissitudes, successes and triumphs, he had beside him a dear, devoted wife, who never failed him in the hour of need, and even now, although suffering from illness, she was unremitting in her attentions. Self-sacrificing in life, she was equally so now that the dread summons called the loved one hence. Finally, the spirit yielded, and all that was left of mortal, put on immortality. The loyal husband, the thoughtful and affectionate father, died as he had lived, calmly, unostentatiously; died with the hand of a loving wife clasped in his own, the voice of a daughter, to whom he was devoted, breathing tender solace in his ears; the manly utterances of a son in whom he placed implicit confidence, cheering his last moments—died, and the life went out of one of the noblest natures, one of the truest friends, and one of the most loyal men whose memory Canadians ever could or ever will be called upon to perpetuate. If proof were required, corroborative of the esteem in which John Henry Pope was held by those who knew him best, it was furnished when Sir John Macdonald, with bowed head and moistened eyes, gazed upon the cold, placid face of his dead friend and colleague; it was here in the sobs and stifled sighs of scores who looked upon the departed statesman for the last time. It was there in the cortege which accompanied his remains from his former residence at the Capital, to the railway station, and thence to the family burying-ground in Cookshire. It is to be found to-day in the voices of those within whose breasts still pulsates a kindly throb when the name of John Henry Pope is mentioned. Few knew the lamented gentleman as he appeared in the confidences of private life; few, save some who met him at the council board, realized the beautiful simplicity of his nature, coupled with giant intellectual faculties. Not mere flashy adornments, charming for the moment; but broad, practical, comprehensive views, manlike courage, untiring industry: in short, power drawn from the world's great school of practical experience, not from the artificial avenues of speculative theory or from half-digested opinions of closet students. Essentially a retiring man, preferring private life to the attractions of society, Mr. Pope held his position and commanded respect in every circle. He treated men as he found them, seldom making a mistake; a keen wit, a natural humorist, philanthropic to the deserving, the lamented gentleman was, from the day they first met, the friend of Sir John A. Macdonald, and whilst not unduly aggressive, forced those who questioned either his ability to grapple with intricate national questions, or the motive inspiring any action, to ultimately regard him as the safest and most progressive head which had presided over any department of administration since the Union. As Minister of Agriculture, and subsequently Minister of Railways, he worked in accord with Sir John Macdonald, who lost a devoted friend, an able counsellor, a sincere Canadian—whilst Canada was deprived of a man whose single purpose was to develop her immense resources, making her, as he firmly believed she should be, the greatest colony attached to the Empire, and eventually the greatest portion of the continent of North America. This was Canada's loss; how, then, estimate the loss of those who knew him personally, who enjoyed his confidence, who recognized that under that cold, impassive exterior, was stored a wealth of love and chivalry; all the elements of manliness; all the instincts of affection; all the attributes of patriotism? He has gone, but his example, his works, his achievements, still survive :

"And the tear that we shed, though in secret it rolls,
Shall long keep his memory green in our souls."

CHAPTER XIII.

TOWNSHIP OF COMPTON.

Including History of the Villages of Waterville and Compton.

This tract of land is bounded on the north by Ascot, east by Clifton, south by Barford and Barnston, and west by Hatley. It was erected into a township named Compton, and granted, August 31, 1802, to Jesse Pennoyer, Nathaniel Coffin, Joseph Kilborne and their associates, viz: John McCarthy, Ephraim Stone, Addie Vincent, Stephen Vincent, John Lockwood, Isaac Farwell, Oliver Barker, David Jewett, Samuel Woodard, Silas Woodard, Matthew Hall (the younger), Page Bull, Abner Eldridge, Samuel Hall, Nathan Lobdell, Ebenezer Smith, Tyler Spafford and Thomas Parker.

There are no mountainous elevations in Compton. It is a rich agricultural township, and has advanced ahead of other townships in the County in its material interests. The traveler is impressed with the air of thrift and comfort everywhere apparent. The land, which is mostly improved, lies rather high, and though originally to a great extent hard-timbered, is comparatively free from stones. There are no extensive swamps, and very little waste land. Dairying is the common industry, and cheese and butter are extensively made. It is specially noted throughout America for its high class of blooded stock, in both cattle and horses.

Its chief streams are the Coaticook, Salmon, and Moes rivers. The Coaticook has its source in two small ponds south of the province line, the outlets of which unite in Barford, and by other tributaries a considerable volume of water is accumulated. There are occasional rapids in its course through Barford and Coaticook, but as the river passes into Compton there is little descent, and it wends its way through the Township in a quiet manner. There are fine meadows along its banks, which are easily cultivated and very productive, but subject to sudden and destructive floods. Salmon river has its rise in Clifton and crosses the northeast corner. Moes river, which has its source in Hereford, runs from the southeast quite through the central part of the Township.

The associates and early settlers were from the United States, as were all the first pioneers in the Eastern Townships. Through Eaton, Westbury, Newport, and Clifton the first settlers came in by the way of the Connecticut river and Hereford. In Compton they came through by Stanstead, or down Lake Memphremagog. The people of the two sections have never mingled together to any great extent, and there appears to have gradually grown up a difference in habits and ways.

Bouchette says that in 1815 there was a population of 700 in Compton, and in 1830 this had grown to 1,202. At the latter date there was one church (Protestant), one school, two shop-keepers, two taverns, and seven saw mills. The first hotel (or tavern), as then called, erected, was at the corner of Main street, in Compton village, and the road leading to Johnville. The building is still standing and in good repair.

From 1820 to 1830, a number of persons came into the Eastern Townships and settled along the border. They left the United States for that country's good, but carried on quite a traffic here in counterfeit money. There were a few only came to Compton in comparison to some other places, but enough so that many tales are now told by the old settlers of how it was done. One of these is that a place was fixed up with all the appurtenances near Little Magog lake. The victim would be taken there, shown some counterfeit money, but always some excuse given why it was not in operation at the time. He would then be instructed in the mode of procedure for purchasing $2 for $1. This was generally done by his leaving the money at a certain place and coming back for the counterfeit. On his return he found either a bundle of blank paper or nothing at all. There was no use in making a fuss.

There are no authentic records as to the date of arrival of the first settlers in this township, but from what can be gleaned the year 1796 was probably the earliest date, and Jesse Pennoyer the first one. He settled just below the present village of Waterville.

The municipal records of Compton bear date August 23, 1841, working under the first municipal law of Lower Canada. A meeting of rate-payers was called on this date by Alexander Rea, Esq., authorized by Hon. Edward Hale, who had been appointed warden of the District. Elder John Gilson was elected by acclamation to represent the Township in the district of Sherbrooke. He declined to qualify, when another meeting of the inhabitant householders was called on Monday, September 6, 1841. Benjamin Pomroy was chosen by acclamation. At the first meeting in August, the following officers were also chosen: Clerk, John P. Bostwick; surveyor of highways, Joseph Smith; overseer of the poor, Dudley Spafford; collector, Matthew Bostwick; assessors, Lemuel Harvey, Benjamin Pomroy and Alden W. Kendrick; fence-viewers and inspectors of drains, William F. Parker, Lieut. R. N., John Haddock, yeoman, Warren Betts, Hiram Hitchcock and Alfred Parker; overseers of highways, Eli Ives, Andrew Pennoyer, Luke Wadleigh, Avery O. Kellam, Peter Bowen and Andrew Kerby; pound-keepers, Amos S. Merrill and Salvin Richardson.

A change in the law was made, and on July 14, 1845, a general meeting of the landholders and householders was held for the purpose of electing seven councillors for the township of Compton. It was presided over by Benjamin Pomroy, justice of the peace. The records say: "The meeting having been called to order by the said justice, it was by him proposed to adjourn to the Methodist chapel for the sake of convenience," and agreed accordingly. The councillors elected were: Arba Stimson, Noa Gliddon, Benj. Pomroy, Luke Wadleigh, Peter Bowen, Joseph Smith and Orange Young. Owing to some legal reason Benj. Pomroy could not act, and on July 19, A. O. Kellam was elected in his place. A. Stimson was chosen mayor, and John P. Bostwick, clerk. From 1848 to 1855 all records are missing.

The law under which our municipalities now work, with a few changes, came into force in 1855. At that time there was a cleaning up and starting anew in all townships. The old law had not proved satisfactory, and in many places it had been dropped, in so far as its being of any service. The reorganization in Compton township took place August 6, 1855. There were present: councillors Benj. Pomroy, Doak, Harvey, Henry, Hitchcock and Flanders. Selah J. Pomroy was chosen secretary-treasurer, and instructed to purchase necessary books for the town. At the same meeting a set of rules for the guidance of the Council was also adopted.

The mayors for the Township from 1855 to 1895 have been as follows: 1855-57, Benj. Pomroy; 1858-63, Jacob Gilson; 1864-67, Alden W. Kendrick; 1868-71, Benj. Pomroy; 1872-73, A. W. Kendrick; 1874, B. F. Harvey; 1875-76, J. D. Moore; 1877-78, B. F. Harvey; 1879-80, Q. Bliss; 1881-85, B. F. Harvey; 1886, S. J. Pomroy; 1887-89, C. H. Hackett; 1890-91, Jas. A. Cochrane; 1892, Geo. W. Merrill; 1893, H. D. Smith; 1894-95, Jas. A. Cochrane. The secretary-treasurers have been: 1855-62, S. J. Pomroy; 1862-74, R. S. Mayo; 1874-75, G. A. Kennedy; 1875-93, C. L. Farnsworth; April 4, 1893, to date, T. O. Ives.

HISTORY OF COMPTON COUNTY.

In 1876 Waterville was "set off" from the Township and created a separate municipality as a village. In 1893 the same was done with the village of Compton.

From 1873 to 1893 there were no liquor licenses granted in the Township. After the separation of Compton village a hotel license was granted, but in January, 1896, new councillors were elected and a prohibitory by-law has again been passed.

The Township now has a valuation of $562,480. In 1895 the number of provincial voters were 495. The Council in the same year was composed as follows: Jas. A. Cochrane, mayor; councillors, Geo. W. Merrill, John Manson, Zerah Whitcomb, Stephen A. Hyatt, Albert P. Farwell, and Wm. H. Boudreau; secretary-treasurer, T. O. Ives.

The first school commissioners of which we have any record were elected January 10, 1842, as follows: Rev. C. P. Reid, Luke Wadleigh, Wm. F. Parker, James Doak, and Eli Ives. Waterville and Compton villages are also separated for school purposes. In the Township there are now twenty-four elementary schools. The school commissioners are Jas. A. Cochrane, chairman, Thomas Ward, Wellington M. Hadlock, Wm. Pocock, and Edward Bellam.

In the township of Compton there are three post offices—Moes River, Hillhurst, and Compton Station.

Moes River is three miles east of Compton, the nearest railway station. It is situated on the river of the same name, and has a grist mill, steam saw mill, and sash and door factory. Here is located the glove and moccasin factory of D. J. Ayer & Son. There are also blacksmith shop, general store, Baptist and Universalist churches, etc. It is a busy little village with population of about two hundred. Daily mail. Postal revenue, 1895, $156.

Hillhurst, also known as Richby, is a station on the G. T. R., south of Compton. It is the centre of a farming community. About one mile distant is the extensive farm of Senator Cochrane, known as Hillhurst, and from which the post office derived its name. Here are to be found a grist mill, Union church, blacksmith shop, etc. Mail daily. Postal revenue, 1895, $208.90.

Compton Station is a small post office in the G. T. R. station, supplying a farming community to the West. Mail daily. Postal revenue, 1895, $96.50.

In the Township there are three churches—two at Moes River and one at Hillhurst.

Union church, Hillhurst.—The frame for this building was erected in April, 1845. The land on which it stands was given by Samuel Richardson, who with James Doak, John Elliott and James Carpenter, formed the building committee. The work progressed slowly and it was not until 1850 that the church was completed. Its cost was $2,500, the amount having all been raised in the immediate vicinity. The sale of pews at $25 each covered the final expense of finishing. It was dedicated in June, 1850, the services on that occasion having been conducted by Rev. Malcolm Macdonald, Methodist minister, then stationed at Compton village. It is a "Union" church, free to all denominations, with a proviso that no one denomination was to claim its use on two consecutive Sundays. For thirty years the services were conducted by Baptist, Methodist, and Universalist ministers; latterly by Presbyterians, while the Church of England has been represented at intervals throughout the entire period. It is a plain, square structure, with a seating capacity of 200.

Free Baptist church, Moes River.—The early records of this church have been lost, and all facts in connection therewith previous to 1867 have been gathered from memory. The Stanstead quarterly meeting was organized in 1828, and the following year mention is made of delegates from this church. As to whether it was organized previously there is nothing to show, but as far as can be learned it was about this time the first services were held. The services were conducted for many years by ministers from other places, who preached here as often as they could. Rev. Abiel Moulton seems to have been father to the cause, in the early days. Rev. Willard Bartlett, from Melbourne, followed him in the work, and he in turn was succeeded by Rev. Mr. Young, from Hatley. After the pastorate of the latter, for some time there was no minister, but services were continued by the laity, being occasionally visited by Elder William Simons. The following have been those in charge of this society down to 1867: Revs. Tyler, Norman Stevens, and Kendall. The latter was the first one to reside at Moes River. He was followed by the Revs. Moses Folsom, Charles Roberts, Proctor Moulton, Smith, and Birch. It was during the time of the latter that the present church was built. The meetings at first were held in private houses, and afterwards in the school house. The dedication services took place December 1, 1867. In 1873, Rev. W. H. Lyster took charge of the field, preaching also at Bulwer. In 1874, the parsonage was erected. In 1883, Rev. A. D. Jones accepted a call to this field, and after three years was followed by Elder Staples. In 1891, Rev. John Vance was settled here, followed in 1892 by Rev. James Billington, and he in turn succeeded in 1894 by Rev. R. Smith. The church is now supplied by Rev. W. P. Reekie.

Universalist church, Moes River.—Universalist services commenced in this place during 1888, and were maintained till the organization of the church with thirty members, on June 23, 1891. The previous pastors were Revs. J. W. McLaughlin and W. D. Potter. At time of organization the officers chosen were as follows: Pastor, Rev. W. D. Potter; trustees, D. J. Ayer, Alfred J. Waldron, and A. S. Crosby; wardens, Samuel Pierce and L. E. Doe; secretary, Mrs. A. M. Cowan; treasurer, L. E. Doe. The lot for the erection of a church was purchased in 1891, and the building erected and dedicated in August, 1893. Up to this time services had been held in the public hall. The church property, valued at $3,000, has been deeded to the Universalist Convention of Vermont and Quebec. At the time of dedication Rev. W. D. Potter was succeeded by Rev. F. G. Leonard, while he in turn was followed a year later by the present pastor, Rev. J. F. Willis. A Sunday school was organized in 1891 and has been carried on successfully. A Y. P. C. U. was organized in 1893, and since then conducts the service every alternate Sunday.

The following statistics for the Township, including Compton village, are taken from the Census of 1891: Population, 2,409; families, 486; houses, 460; males, 1,227; females, 1,182; French-Canadians, 644; others, 1,765; religious—Roman Catholic, 793; Church of England, 550; Presbyterians, 81; Methodists, 484; Brethren, 3; Baptists, 173; Free Will Baptists, 31; Congregationalists, 77; Adventists, 130; Universalists, 79; Salvation Army, 3; not specified, 5.

VILLAGE OF COMPTON.

This village was set off from the township of Compton, and erected into a separate municipality on June 12, 1893. It comprises 3,210 square acres. In 1894, the village had a population of 446, and a valuation of $142,180.

The first council meeting was held July 14, 1893. The election of councillors was held the same day, resulting as follows: Daniel Saultry, William Warren Paige, Beaman F. Hitchcock, Alexander Rea, Myron Blossom, Albert L. Pomroy, and Napoleon Drolet. A. L. Pomroy was chosen first mayor, and Mr. J. B. M. St. Laurent secretary-treasurer.

The Council for 1895 was composed as follows: Jos. A. Dufort, mayor; and councillors: A. L. Pomroy, H. D. Smith, M. P. Aldrich, Alexander Rea, Daniel Saultry, and W. W. Paige; secretary-treasurer, J. B. M. St. Laurent.

The Council, in 1894, granted a hotel liquor license, the first one for twenty years. By an election held in January, 1896, two new councillors were elected, and a prohibitory by-law since passed.

The village of Compton was erected into a separate school municipality, June 28, 1894. School commissioners elected were: Reginald A. D. King, M.D., chairman; Daniel Saultry, Benman F. Hitchcock, Myron P. Aldrich, and Jos. A. Dufort. The secretary-treasurer was J. B. M. St. Laurent, and he still holds the office. The present school commissioners are: A. L. Pomroy, chairman; B. F. Hitchcock, Osborne Batchelder, M. P. Aldrich, and Jos. A. Dufort. There is no dissenting board, the Catholic school being allowed $150 out of the general fund. There are two schools: Model and Catholic. The teachers in the model are: George A. Jordan, principal; and Miss Stenning, assistant. Miss D. Tetu is teacher of the Catholic school. The former has an average attendance of sixty-seven, and the latter thirty-seven.

Compton village is the centre of one of the best farming sections of Canada. No manufacturing is done here, but there are to be found stores and shops of all kinds.

In the fall of 1893 the Provincial Government established a model farm here. The village corporation purchased the B. F. Hitchcock farm of one hundred and fifty acres, one of the best in the country, and loaned it for the purpose of a model farm. However, in 1895, the Government, wishing to make improvements, decided to purchase the property from the village, which was done. It is managed by a board of trustees appointed by the Government. The resident manager is Mr. J. M. Lemoyne. Article 4 of the by-laws says: "Pupils shall have free board, lodging, light, heat and bedding." A regular course extends over two years.

In the village there are three churches—Anglican, Methodist, and Roman Catholic.

The first Anglican services in Compton were held between 1812 and 1815, by the Rev. Charles J. Stewart, afterwards Bishop of Quebec, when he was a missionary at Hatley. His successors, the Revs. Messrs. Johnson and Jackson officiated here at regular intervals. The sight of land where the present church stands, was given for this purpose, the deed bearing date July 18, 1815. Under the superintendence of Rev. Mr. Jackson, the first church was commenced, to complete which the S. P. G. F. P. granted £125. It was finished in 1826. The first resident clergyman was Rev. C. P. Reid, who commenced his labors at Compton in 1840. Previously Compton was connected with the Hatley parish. In 1845 the old church was taken down and moved to the village, near the corner of Main street, on the Hatley road. The object of this was that nearly all the church members lived near the new site, and found the old one too far away, being disagreeable in the winter to go such a distance. The old church on its new site was used until the completion of the present edifice.

Rev. C. P. Reid was followed in 1854 by Rev. Aaron A. Allen, who remained four years, and was succeeded by Rev. Wm. Richmond. In 1864 Rev. John Kemp came to Compton, and remained six years, when he was succeeded by Rev. Joseph Dinzey. In 1875 the present incumbent, Rev. Geo. H. Parker, became pastor of this church. Under his charge it has made good progress. Rev. Mr. Parker soon saw the necessity of a more commodious church building, and set about raising funds for the erection of one. The present fine structure is considered one of the best in the Quebec diocese. It is built of wood, beautifully finished on the inside, and erected at a cost of $5,000. It stands on the site of the first church, and on the land given in 1815. The architect was Mr. Donald Black, of Boston, Mass. It was completed and dedicated free of debt September 2, 1887, by Bishop Williams. The first parsonage was erected in 1861, being the building now owned by the Misses Holbrook. In 1875 this was sold and the present parsonage purchased.

Under the personal supervision of Rev. G. H. Parker there is also carried on here the

Compton Ladies' College, which is under the patronage of the Anglican church. The building is a substantial structure of brick, having a frontage of one hundred and sixty feet. The ground comprises six acres, partly laid out in flower beds, but the greater part used as play grounds, being arranged for lawn tennis, croquet, etc. The college was completed and first opened in 1874. For ten years it was carried on under charge and supervision of Rev. Mr. Dinzey. Proving a failure financially it was closed in 1884 for two years. In 1886 what is known as "The Corporation" was formed, when they re-opened the college, and it has since been successfully operated. The building accommodates forty-five boarders, and is generally well filled. "The Corporation" is composed of nine leading gentlemen of the Anglican church in the Quebec Diocese, who in turn select a managing board of five of their number. The present members of this board are Rev. Canon Foster, M.A.; Rev. Canon Thorneloe, M.A.; Rev. G. H. Parker; Hon. M. H. Cochrane; and Jas. A. Cochrane, Esq. Rev. G. H. Parker, as resident clergyman, has general oversight of the college. The present teachers are: Mrs. Brouse, Lady Principal; Miss Murphy; Miss Simpson; Miss Maud Johnson; and Professor Dorey. Lady Matron, Mrs. Bliss.

Methodist church, Compton.—The first records of this circuit are dated June 25, 1838, and are those of the old Sherbrooke circuit, which at that time comprised Hatley, Barnston, Compton, Ascot, Eaton, Dudswell, Orford, Brompton and Clifton. The minister at that time was the Rev. E. Botterell. He was followed in 1841 by Rev. John Tompkins, who resided here. It was during the time of Rev. Mr. Tompkins that the present Methodist church was deeded to that denomination. As to the exact date of its erection there is some difference of opinion, some claiming that it was built the same time as deeded, while others claim the erection to have taken place several years previously. The deed is from Jesse Bullock to Rev. John Tompkins and the following trustees: Benjamin Pomroy, Rev. John Glison, Alden W. Kendrick, Coit Stevens, Eli Ives, and Gladden Farwell, jr. Deed reads in favor of "that certain denomination of Christians called Wesleyan Methodists, of England, that were established February 20, 1784, under hand and seal of Rev. John Wesley." "And whereas the chapel or meeting-house now being on the hereby bargained and sold premises, was erected and builded by the means of voluntary contributions and donations, a further consideration is that the said chapel shall at all times be free to all persons on all funeral occasions and that without let or hindrance; and when not occupied by the said Wesleyan Methodists shall be free for all denominations of Christians for the worship of God, subject, nevertheless, in this instance last mentioned, to the control and consent of a standing committee of three, appointed by the trustees." Rev. E. S. Ingalls succeeded Mr. Tompkins in 1844; 1846, Benj. Short, and in 1848, Rev. Thomas Campbell. After this date records of births, deaths, and marriages are found for Compton, Hatley and Barnston. The following are the names of the ministers to date: M. Macdonald, Wm. Andrews, John B. Selley, Jos. Forsyth, S. G. Phillips, Benj. Cole, J. E. Sanderson, M. M. Johnson, J. E. Richardson, T. C. Brown. During the ministry of Mr. Brown, from 1873 to 1876, the church at Martinville was built, services having previously been held in the school house.

In 1876, T. W. Constable was appointed to this circuit; 1879, H. W. Knowles; 1881, W. K. Short; 1884, Geo. H. Porter; 1887, Sidney C. Kendall; 1890, James Lawson; 1893, T. S. Harris; 1895, Robert Smith. In 1883 the present fine parsonage was erected on a piece of land donated by the late Colonel Benjamin Pomroy. Previously there was a parsonage nearly opposite the church, which was sold. The Compton circuit also includes Martinville and Ives Hill. Present church membership, eighty-seven.

Roman Catholic church—Catholic services have been held here for over fifty years, and Rev. Father Daly was the first resident priest. This denomination now has a fine church and parsonage in Compton village. During 1895 the interior of the church was repaired and decorated at a heavy expense. The present pastor is Rev. J. E. Choquette, and he is very popular with all classes.

LATE COL. BENJ. POMROY.

THE LATE COLONEL BENJAMIN POMROY, whose portrait is here given, was born in Stanstead, Que., December 28, 1800, and died at Compton, April 2, 1875. The Pomroy families are of Norman-French extraction, coming to England in the days of William the Conqueror. Three brothers came to Massachusetts in the 17th century, and formed part of the old Plymouth colony of Puritan memory. Selah, the father of our subject, was a great grandson of Eldad Pomroy, one of the three brothers, and was born in Massachusetts, in 1775. In 1795, he married Hannah Thayer, of Massachusetts. Mr. Pomroy and his wife settled originally in Brookfield, Vt. They removed to Stanstead in 1798 and settled in the dense forest, half a mile east of Stanstead plain. Crystal Lake cemetery forms part of the original farm. He died December 23, 1856. Col. Benjamin Pomroy was the third and youngest son of Selah Pomroy. He received his preparatory training as clerk, with Ichabod Smith, at Stanstead, Que., began mercantile business at Sherbrooke, Que., in 1823. He returned to Stanstead in 1824, and married Lucy, daughter of Jedediah Lee. Issue, three children : Selah J., born January 1, 1825, married Victoria Adams, seven children, died November 21, 1891 ; Mary L., born August 16, 1827, married late A. P. Ball, Stanstead, eleven children, five living ; Erastus L., born June 3, 1837, died May 6, 1841. In 1854, Mr. Pomroy experienced a distressing bereavement by the accidental death of his wife. She was thrown from a carriage and killed while driving near Sherbrooke, the horse having been frightened by a passing train.

In 1830 he moved to Compton village, where he afterwards lived, accumulating considerable property and rising in the estimation of his fellow-citizens until his death. On this page will be found a biographical sketch of his son, Selah, and three grandsons, and on next page photo-engraving of the Pomroy residence at Compton. Col. Pomroy was, perhaps, as widely known as any man in the Eastern Townships; of an active temperament, and good business abilities, he took a leading part in public matters, not only in his own township, but throughout the country. He was one of the pioneers in the construction of the St. Lawrence and Atlantic Railway, now part of the Grand Trunk Railway. He was also one of the active promoters of the Massawippi Valley Railroad, from Lennoxville to Newport, and held the office of vice-president of same. He served during the Rebellion of 1837-38, as captain of the Queen's Mountain Rangers, and subsequently received the appointments of major of Militia and colonel of the Second Battalion of the county of Compton. He was a prominent mover in the establishment of the Eastern Townships Bank, and was elected its first president, which position he held until a short time before his death. He took an active interest in establishing the Paton Woollen Mills at Sherbrooke, and was a director and large stockholder. Col. Pomroy was, in fact, indefatigable in support of all practicable measures for improving the country and developing its resources. He was also a liberal contributor to institutions of learning and churches, his good deeds in this respect not being confined to any one denomination or wholly of a local character. His name is among the first in past history of the Eastern Townships to be honored and respected, and he lived a life worthy, as an example, to be looked up to and copied by all men.

THE LATE SELAH J. POMROY, in his lifetime farmer, was born in Stanstead, Que., January 1, 1825. His parents being Benj. and Lucy (Lee) Pomroy. When five years of age he came to Compton where he resided until his death, November 21, 1891. As a lad he was a clerk in the late A. Stimson's store, also clerk in the wholesale dry goods store of the late Walter Macfarlane, Montreal. Not liking the mercantile business he returned home. He always took an active and prominent part in the business of the town, first as Secretary-Treasurer, then following his father as Councillor and Mayor. In politics he was a Liberal-Conservative. As a progressive farmer he was among the first in the County, building the first silo, first modern barn; growing good crops, using modern machinery, keeping good cattle, but was more widely and generally known as a breeder of good horses, having several times introduced high-class stallions for the improvement of this kind of stock. He followed his father as a director of the Paton Woollen Mills. Mr. Pomroy was a generous and liberal supporter of the Wesleyan Methodist Church, giving freely of his means towards the construction of its churches, its educational institutions, and other objects connected therewith, not only at home but in other localities. He was strong in defence of temperance, and his good example contributed largely in the developement of the strong temperance sentiment in the community. He evinced the keenest interest in his town, and his admiration for Compton was always unbounded. He was eminently kind hearted and charitable, his gifts being unostentatiously bestowed. Mr. Pomroy was married June 30, 1857, to Victoria S., daughter of the late A. A. Adams, of Coaticook. Issue, seven children: Lizzie V., born May 15, 1858, married Eugene Cowles, two children, one living, residence, Compton; Mary A., born November 2, 1860; Benjamin A., born July 5, 1861, residence, St. Paul, Minn.; Albert L., born July 17, 1863, married Helen E. Davis, two children, residence, Compton; Aaron A., born July 13, 1865, married Winnifred Robinson, one child, residence, Compton; Lucy L., born November 7, 1870; Elsie B., born September 13, 1872. The two sons, Albert and Aaron, both live on parts of the old homestead, in Compton. The former has succeeded his grandfather and father as

Councillor and Mayor. A photo-engraving of the Pomroy homestead is presented herewith. In the upper corners may be seen miniatures of Mr. Selah Pomroy and his three sons. This place was sold to Mr. Robertson in the winter of 1895-96.

REGINALD A. D. KING, M.D., C.M., M.C.P. & S., was born in Bury, Que., December 25, 1845. His father was the late Rev. William King, rural dean, and at the time of his death was the oldest Church of England clergyman in the diocese of Quebec. From 1828 to 1836 he held the position of superintendent of schools in Newfoundland. Our subject, Dr. King, took his degrees at McGill Medical University in 1868. Practiced his profession at St. George

RESIDENCE OF LATE SELAH J. POMROY.

La Beauce for four years, removed to Compton in 1872, where he has since remained in actual practice as physician and surgeon, with the exception of one year. In 1885 he went to Florida and practiced medicine there under a special license for twelve months, making some investigations regarding climatic effects upon certain chronic diseases. He obtained second-class certificate from school of military instruction at Quebec, July, 1865, and first-class from same school in September, 1865; was drilled and did regular military duties in the Citadel at Quebec, under Lords Russell and Clinton, and attached to the P. C. O. Rifle Brigade during July, August and September of 1865. Served under Lord Wolesley, then Sir Garnet Wolesley, at the cadet camp, affiliated with the Montreal regulars, held at Laprairie, 1865. Served during the Fenian raid of 1866. Was principal medical officer to the brigade camp, military district, No. 7, at Levis, for a number of years. He served actively in the volunteer force until 1885, when he resigned on going to Florida. Dr. King has been interested in and connected with local mutual benefit societies, as well as the promotion of superior education, acting as commissioner to the Compton board, and chairman of the village commissioners. He is president of St. Francis District Medical Society. Read a paper on "Forestry" before the American Forestry Congress, when that body, in conjunction with the Royal Society, held their meetings in Montreal. Was elected a member of the Foreign Auxiliary Committee for Quebec, to the Pan-American Medical Congress, held in Washington 1892. Dr. King says: "A notable day in my early recollections was one passed roaming over and getting lost upon the decks of that unique ship, the Great Eastern. Another soon after, when I was projected by the crowd, in the narrow streets of Quebec, almost into the lap of the Prince of Wales, when His Royal Highness visited that city." He was married in the English cathedral, Quebec, in July, 1875, to Laura Alice (born January 12, 1858), daughter of the late Joel Shurtleff, of Compton. Issue, four children: Reginald Wm. Henry, born October 31, 1877; Ernest George Foster, born April 18, 1879; Philip Adolphus Hyde, born February 15, 1882; Grace Winnifred, born August 11, 1876. We present herewith an excellent view of the residence of Dr. King, at Compton, with himself and family on the lawn.

RESIDENCE OF R. A. D. KING, M.D., C.M., M.C.P. & S.

HERBERT DUDLEY SMITH, gentleman farmer, "Ingleside," Compton, was born in Montreal, May 31, 1867. His parents were Samuel G. and Mary Isabella (Macfarlane) Smith. His father was head partner of the firm of Smith & Cochrane, boot and shoe manufacturers, Montreal, one of the largest and most noted firms in the Dominion at that period. He died December 5, 1868, and his wife in 1872. The grandparents of our subject were Joseph and Alice (Gilman) Smith. Both came from Gilmantown, N. H., in 1808, and settled on what is now part of "Ingleside" farm, the property having never passed out of the hands of the family. They had eight children, six sons and two daughters: Gilman, Alfred, Frederick, Charles, Samuel Greeley, and George; Mary and Julia. When Mr. Joseph Smith settled in Compton his land was all a forest and the family suffered the hardships of pioneer life. He was successful, however, and cleared one of the farms for which Compton is noted as standing at the head in Canada. He erected the first board house in Compton township. Mr. H. D. Smith began his education at Bishops College, Lennoxville, where he remained six years, when he went to Scotland, and continued his studies in Lorette University, Musselburgh, near Edinburgh, taking a special course in modern languages and chemistry. From here, he removed to Geneva, Switzerland, to perfect his knowledge of the French and

German languages In August, 1887, he returned to Scotland to prepare for a tour around the world After visiting Italy, Egypt, India, Burmah, China and Japan, he landed on the Pacific Coast of America, visiting all the important western cities. He returned to Montreal in the winter of 1888. He now resolved to devote his life to scientific farming, on which subject he had gathered considerable information during his travels, especially in Scotland In farming he has always been specially interested, and pursued his studies in that line in all parts of the world. In June, 1889, he began farming operations on his late father's estate in Compton. It is known as "Ingleside" farm, and consists of nine hundred and twenty acres. The affairs of his farm are carried on after the most scientific methods. The

RESIDENCE OF H. D. SMITH.

Farmer's Advocate says of this farm: "On an elevation overlooking a fertile valley and a large tract of the surrounding country is erected a palatial residence, and close by are the comfortable cattle barns, and a grandly finished large horse stable splendidly fitted in the most convenient and approved style. For some years past the breeding of Hereford cattle has been a special feature on this farm, and a herd of unusual excellence has been established, without doubt the finest herd of this breed in Canada at the present time. In the horse stables we saw a fine pair of English thoroughbreds, and the hackney mare, Fairy. Improved Yorkshires and Tamworths are also included in the stock at Ingleside. A visit at the farm is indeed a rich treat to all true lovers of fine stock." In 1892 Mr. Smith was elected a member of the Municipal Council of Compton, and in the following year was made mayor. Owing to a portion of the municipality in which he resides being set off as a village corporation in the latter part of

1893, he resigned his seat in the old council, six months later was elected a member of the village Council and is now mayor. For the past three years he has been one of the directors of the Eastern Townships Agricultural Association. Was one of the first trustees of the Compton Model Farm, representing the village municipality, and is now one of the Government trustees of the same institution. On December 7, 1892, Mr. Smith was married in Montreal to Miss Mary Lake, daughter of D. T. Irish, Esq., of that city. Issue, one daughter: Hazel VanVliet, born December 27, 1893. Accompanying this biographical sketch are to be found two photo-engravings of views taken of "Ingleside." One shows the fine residence of Mr. Smith, the other the barns, and homes of employees on the farm. The whole is lighted throughout by electricity, from a private plant.

FARM BUILDINGS OF H. D SMITH.

GEORGE W. MERRILL, farmer, was born in Stanstead in 1827, and came to Compton with his parents in 1833. He at one time worked for Warren Page, stage proprietor at Compton for years. When a young man Mr. Merrill went to the White Mountains and was there driving large stages for twenty years, his time being divided between the Crawford and Profile houses. He made his home at Bethlehem, N. H., during that time. He then returned to Compton, and has since lived on the old farm. The place is located about half-way between Compton Station and Waterville. Mr. Merrill has been a councillor for nine years, and mayor of the town. He is a commissioner of the Court for trial of small cases. He has been successful in business, and is considered one of the "well-to-do" farmers of Compton. Has never married. In March, 1800, his grandfather, David Merrill, with his wife and twelve children, left Fishersfield, now Newbury, N. H., to find a home in Canada, his wife on horse-back, and he and the children with an ox-team. They were twenty-five or thirty days in getting through the woods to Duncansboro, now Newport, Vt. At Newport they put themselves and their team on board the scow, and proceeded down Lake Memphremagog, to the place where the Mountain House now stands, where they encamped for the night. They continued their course down the lake the next day, and disembarked on the eastern shore, some three miles below Georgeville. Here they pitched their tent, made a small clearing, and built a log house. They afterwards sold out in 1803, located on Lot 21, Range 3, Stanstead. This was the first settlement made between Georgeville and Fitch Bay. David Merrill died in December, 1831. His son, Amos S. Merrill, the father of George W., was born in New Hampshire, in 1798. Was married in 1823, to Lydia G., daughter of Deacon Reynolds, by whom there were four children: Amos A., Geo. W., Lydia G., and Alden K. Amos S., shortly after the death of his father, moved to Compton, in 1833, to make for him a home. During the Rebellion of 1837-38 he enlisted in the cavalry and acted as sergeant. For many years he carried on a blacksmith shop, and kept hotel in Compton village for twenty-five years. He built the hotel, now vacant, located near the three corners, in centre of the village. About 1865 he moved on to the farm now occupied by his son, George W., where he died in 1877. His wife died in 1891. The eldest son, Amos Adams Merrill, was born in Stanstead, May 19, 1825. He married May 23, 1850, Desiah R. Ellis (born September 15, 1830), a sister to Capt. J. M. Ellis, who served with credit in the Northern army in 1861-65, and is at present a contractor on the B. & M. R. R. By this marriage there are seven children: Georgianna M. B., born February 28, 1851, married Amos Pennoyer, in 1868, four children: Mary, Andrew, George and Altha; Lydia A., born July 31, 1852, married B. W. Ford, in 1871, four children: Emily, May, Albert, Willis; Florence J., born November 16, 1857, unmarried; George A., born June 6, 1861, married Mary Lanigan, in 1893, one child, Margaret, residence, Wyoming Territory; Amos M., born November 25, 1864, married Mattie A. Hartwell, in 1888, three children: Grace, Eva, Maud; Mary E., born September 10, 1867, married D. M. McLean, in 1888, two children: Kathleen, Clifford; Sarah A., born July 7, 1869, unmarried. Lydia G., only daughter of Amos S. Merrill, was born in Stanstead, in 1831. Married, in 1851, to Charles H. Adams, and at present resides in Marbleton, Que. They have two children: Sarah M., born in 1853, married in 1874, to Percival Rugg, two children: Hattie and Newtown, residence, Colorado; Mary L., born in 1869, married in 1893, to F. A. Noble, one child, Lucy P., residence, Marbleton. Alden K. Merrill, the youngest son, was born in Compton, in 1835, married in 1856, and died in 1858. He left one son, Arthur K., who lives in Compton, married in 1886, to E. Little, three children: Arthur, Alden, Elizabeth.

Parker F. Carr. Moodie S. Carr. Francis Carr. Guy Carr. Gilbert C. Carr.

HISTORY OF COMPTON COUNTY.

GUY CARR, Compton Station, was born on his present farm, August 24, 1861, where he has always lived. Mr. Carr is an enterprising farmer, being the proprietor of Maple Ridge Farm, which contains some four hundred acres, located in the Carr neighborhood, on the

RESIDENCE OF GUY CARR.

west side of the Conticook valley, one and one quarter miles south of Compton Station. He is a breeder of thoroughbred live stock, and has been awarded, in the United States and Canada, over one thousand prizes, in the last ten years. Upwards of eight hundred of these were first prizes. Our subject was the proprietor of the first registered herd of pure Canadian cattle in Canada, and was also the breeder and shipper of the first and only herd of that breed, in the United States to-day, among which is "Trixie," No. 923, who stands champion of the Southern States for butter fat, testing 9.6 butter fat, Babcock Test. Mr. Carr has held many prominent public offices and at the present time is a Commissioner of the Court; Fishery officer for the county of Compton, the waters of Massawippi Lake and its tributaries, being also vested by such office with the functions, ex-officio, of J. P.; valuator township of Compton; director of the Sheep Breeders' Association of Quebec, and of Compton County Agricultural Society No. 1; vice-president Compton Farmers' Club; secretary-treasurer Union Farmers' Club; S. W. and trustee I. O. F., No. 1473. Mr. Carr has never married. The grandfather of the above, Parker Carr, was born in Vermont, November 14, 1771, was married June 15, 1805, and moved into Compton at the same time. Francis Carr was born March 30, 1813, married March 14, 1840, to Susan H. Haines. Issue, eight children: Gilbert C., born August 1, 1846, now manager McCormack Manufacturing Company, for Michigan and north part of Ohio, residence, Jackson, Mich.; Parker F., born March 22, 1855, residence, Point View, Kan.; Moodie S., born August 28, 1857, died February 21, 1876; Guy Carr, the subject of our sketch; Marilla S., born March 9, 1841, married H. C. Cabana, residence, Sherbrooke; Amanda C., born April 15, 1845, married Malcolm McNaughton, residence, Huntingdon; Amelia S., born December 29, 1849, died June 1, 1853; Amelia S. J., born December 21, 1855, married C. J. Cushing, residence, Barnston. Francis Carr died March 11, 1894, and his wife April 28, 1894. Accompanying this sketch will be found an engraving of Francis Carr and his four sons, also of the old homestead, and the family monument in cemetery at Compton.

CARR FAMILY MON

THE LATE FREDERICK POCOCK, in his lifetime, farmer, was born June 4, 1831, at St. Sylvestre, Que., and died in Compton, September 13, 1885. He came here in 1863. On January 4, 1852, at St. Sylvestre, Que., he married Sarah (born February 1, 1832), daughter of the late John McKee. Issue, eleven children: Frederick J., born November 19, 1853; William S., born January 11, 1856, married, first, Louisa Church, three children: Ernest, Louisa and Sarah, second marriage to Isabella Church, two children: Gordon and Effie; Samuel, born October 11, 1859, married Addie E. Snow, three children: Leon, Eleanor and Mary; George, born January 23, 1862, married Ethel Corliss, two children: Ida and Harold; Abraham, born May 5, 1864; Stephen, born December 20, 1870; James H. H., born May 27, 1873; Charles

HISTORY OF COMPTON COUNTY.

RESIDENCE OF MRS. SARAH POCOCK.

E. A., born October 23, 1875; Jennie, born December 5, 1857; Isabella, born October 9, 1866; Annie E., born September 13, 1868. Herewith is shown a photo engraving of the home place, located near Hillhurst.

LIBERTY EATON DOE, farmer, was born in Newbury, Vt., January 5, 1820. His parents being Jacob and Lydia (Harding) Doe. He came into Compton on November 12, 1844, and lived at Waterville and Richby, before moving to his present farm, which is on the main road, about half way between Johnville and Compton. The engraving given below is from a photograph showing Mr. and Mrs. Doe, in front of their house. Previous to becoming a farmer Mr. Doe was a painter and furniture maker. He has held the office of councillor, and also minor town offices. He has been married twice, first to Betsey Fleming, second to Alwilda, daughter of Wm. Young, of Magog, Que. Mr. Doe has had no children.

LATE LYSANDER W. HOLBROOK, farmer, born in Waterford, Vt., December 29, 1805, died in Compton, July 1, 1879 He came to Compton in 1852. For several years held the office of councillor. At Waterford, Vt., January 24, 1833, he married Deborah Stevens, born November 13, 1805, died January 25, 1891. Issue, five children, three living: Lois, born December 12, 1833; Laura A., born April 12, 1835, married John O. Hale, residence, St. Johnsbury, Vt., six children; Victoria, born August 27, 1839. Mr. Holbrook was one of the first settlers locating where Martinville road now is, but then a wilderness.

WILLIAM D. BAILEY, farmer, son of Joseph Bailey, of St. Johnsbury, Vt., was born in Stanstead, February 10, 1821, in which year his parents moved into Compton County. He was married, in 1848, to Betsey, daughter of Ephraim Beede. Issue, seven children: Wellman J., born October 29, 1848; Henry W., born June 16, 1850; Liberty D., born February 18, 1853, married Charlotte Putney, residence, Shelbourne Falls, Mass., one child; Charles H., born May 28, 1855, married Eva Way, residence, Waterbury, Vt., two children; Loren B., born August 2, 1857, married Hattie E.

RESIDENCE OF L. E. DOE.

Parker; Walter S., born November 29, 1859; William M., born November 2, 1863, married Annie M. Robinson, residence, Compton, two children.

HORACE WESTON PARRY, of Compton model farm, was born in Torquay, Eng., December 7, 1872. Was educated at Seaford college, Sussex, Eng., later taking a special course in dairying at the Agricultural College in Tamworth, Eng. He came to Cookshire in 1890, and was employed on the farm of R. H. Pope, M.P., until April, 1895, when he accepted a position as head butter-maker at the model farm. He was very successful in securing first prizes on butter, fall 1895, at exhibitions in Sherbrooke, Montreal and Ottawa; also received first prize of thirty dollars offered by the Quebec Provincial Government for best essay on butter-making.

THADDEUS O. IVES, farmer, secretary-treasurer township of Compton, and postmaster, was born in Compton, August 16, 1844. His parents, Eli and Artemissia (Bullock) Ives, settled in Compton in 1832. The father died in 1863, and mother died in 1872. Mr. Ives has held the office of councillor and school commissioner for several years. He married Sarah L. Tiffany (born January 10, 1848), at Delaware, Ont., January 1, 1873. Issue, seven children, six living: Albert E., born January 31, 1883; Garnet T., born November 30, 1885; Gertrude A., born November 21, 1873; Edith L., born January 11, 1878; Genevieve, born October 14, 1880; Gladys, born June 4, 1890.

GEORGE BETTS, farmer, resident of Moes River since 1876, was born in England, August 13, 1834. Came to Compton county in 1836, and after living in the townships of Bury and Clifton, finally settled at Moes River. He is a Deacon of the F. W. B. church, was married in Compton, June 23, 1858, to Harriet, daughter of William Bellam, deceased. An adopted son: Norman, born in July, 1857, married Hattie Daley, of Pittsburg, N. H., one child.

JOSEPH BLOSSOM, farmer and breeder of Standard bred horses, was born in Compton, July 5, 1832, where he has resided up to date. Was married at Waterville, Que., January 23, 1862, to Mary E. (born July 9, 1842), daughter of Willis D. Lamkin. Issue, three children: Wilbert E., born October 8, 1874; Hattie E., born February 11, 1863, married George E. Harkness, two children; Lizzie M., born June 6, 1864, married C. H. Nutter, one child.

DANIEL SAULTERY, contractor and builder, was born in West Farnham, Que., February 2, 1837. Came to Compton in 1855. Has been councillor for several years, is now one of the Commissioners' Court, and a steward and trustee of the Methodist church. Was married in Compton, February 2, 1864, to Laura E. Webster, born March 8, 1840. Issue, three children: George A., born November 30, 1864, married Mary Coates, residence, Compton, one child; Nellie M., born May 23, 1868, married W. B. Ferrel, residence, Compton, one child; Minnie A., born December 26, 1871, married Archie Jamieson, deceased.

STEPHEN PARSONS, farmer, resident of Compton, was born in Bury, August 16, 1841, having always lived in the County. Married September 23, 1861, to Adelaide Sharmon, of Eaton. Issue, ten children: Wesley J., born July 29, 1865, married Melissa Crosby, two children; Albert G., born September 2, 1867, married Julia Demary; Ernest A., born May 27, 1870, married Effie Parsons; Percival A., born May 21, 1874; Charles T., born May 26, 1879; William C., born March 24, 1886; Walter S., born January 14, 1890; Ella H., born

October 28, 1863, married Geo. R. Crosby, three children; Edith M. E., born November 7, 1881; Cora M., born November 6, 1888.

PETER YOUNG, farmer, born in England, February 9, 1818. Came to Compton in 1853, where he has since resided. He has held the office of councillor for several years. Married in England, May 3, 1840, to Emma Parker. Issue, seven children: Fred., born February 22, 1844, married Emma Chesney, residence, Compton, five children; Arthur, born March 31, 1857, married Abbie Wilson, residence, Compton, three children; Priestly W., born January 1, 1863, married Hattie Hill, residence, Compton, one child; Adamenia, born January 31, 1846, married Henry Bernard, residence, Waterville, six children; Emma, born August 31, 1848, married Henry Draper, residence, Compton, three children; Annie, born April 18, 1860, married Osburn Hughes, residence, Compton, three children; Jane, born March 31, 1864, married Walter Brown, residence, Compton, two children.

ALFRED JOHN WALDRON, farmer, resident of Compton, was born in Clifton, November 16, 1855. He is a prominent member of the I. O. F. His grandfather came from Connecticut in 1798, and his father, Thomas Waldron, was born in 1818 and is living in Compton. Our subject married Elizabeth M., daughter of Samuel Pierce, of Compton, and widow of Daniel Alonzo Waldron, who died February 2, 1876, leaving two children: Homer D., born January 1, 1876; Bessie A., born November 6, 1873. Issue of above marriage, one son: Egbert A., born June 1, 1884.

J. WALTER M. VERNON, farmer and breeder of thoroughbred cattle, was born at Whitchurch, Shropshire, Eng., November 23, 1859. He received his education in Shrewsbury, Salop, Eng. Came to Waterville in 1882, moving to Compton Centre in 1894. He has held the office of Councillor, and is C. R. in the I. O. F. Was married, October 10, 1883, at Compton, to Ada A., daughter of the late Anson Bliss. Issue, three children: Clara, born October 9, 1884; Doris E., born May 21, 1886; M. C. Noeline, born July 18, 1888.

CHARLES L. FARNSWORTH, a resident of Compton, was born in Eaton, August 30, 1815. Mr. Farnsworth has always lived in the county, moving to Compton from Eaton. At the present time he is a Commissioner of the Superior Court. For a number of years he held the office of secretary-treasurer of the township of Compton, for the School Commissioners and Council. He married Adeline H. Haskell, at Lennoxville, October 22, 1835, who died October 6, 1843. Second marriage to Roxillania Ayer, June 9, 1844, who died June 12, 1893. Issue, four children, none of whom are now living.

WESLEY J. PARSONS, carpenter, resident of Moes River, was born in Bury, July 29, 1865. On August 13, 1888, he married Melissa B. Crosby. Issue, two children: Ethel A., born June 29, 1889; Gladys C., born May 25, 1894. Mr. Parsons is a deacon in the F. W. B. Church.

EDGAR CHASE, farmer, was born in the State of Vermont, August 18, 1837. His parents were Daniel and Isabel (Dickey) Chase, who were married in Vermont in April, 1830. The father died in Compton, April 5, 1874, aged seventy-two years, the mother died in Vermont, May 29, 1838, aged thirty-two years. The subject of our sketch came to Compton in 1853. February 14, 1861, he married Ellenor C. Batchelder. Issue, six children: Albert D., born July 25, 1865, died December 31, 1895, married Hattie F. Draper, three children; Walter E., born June 21, 1869; Charles E., born September 5, 1872; Henry G., born August 3, 1875; Isabel M., born June 6, 1862, married Albert G. Spafford, one child; Sarah E., born December 16, 1863. Mr. Chase has held the position of school commissioner for several years.

ROBERT ROBERTSON, farmer, born in Chateauguay, Que., January 7, 1857. Came to Compton as manager of Model Farm, in 1894, and fall of 1895 purchased the old Pomroy homestead, his present residence. Married October 28, 1886, to Sarah A. Logan (born November 2, 1865), of Chateauguay. Issue, three children: Robert J., born December 13, 1889; Winnifred S., born May 19, 1887; Maggie F., born March 6, 1893.

JOSEPH DeLANCY MARCOTTE, farmer, was born in Compton, November 15, 1855, and has always resided in the township. His father, Louis Marcotte, died in Compton, having lived in North Danville, Vt., before coming to Compton.

OZRO BAXTER McCLARY, farmer, was born in Compton, February 15, 1854. Hoved to Hatley in 1875, went to California in 1886, and returned to Compton in 1890. First marriage to Florence Wells. Second marriage to Lestina L. Hills. Issue, two children: Synthia H., born October 12, 1885; Miudia Leona, born February 23, 1894.

W. L. CARR was born at Compton, October 29, 1855, on the original Carr farm, still occupied by his father, Ira Carr, Esq. Educated at the Compton High School. Married Nettie J. Hartwell, of Compton. Issue, five children: Mary F., born February 4, 1884; Fred. E., born May 21, 1885; Jessie L., born June 10, 1889; Lucy M., born August 9, 1892; George I., born July 20, 1895.

EDGAR LANG, station agent and postmaster at Hillhurst, was born in Stewartstown, N. H., July 24, 1844. Came to Compton in 1854. Married at Coaticook, July 15, 1866, to Althea A. Pennoyer, born July 14, 1846. His father, Charles Lang, is still living at Canaan, Vt.

THE LATE STEPHEN BARTLETT, farmer, was born in Norwich, Vt., July 1, 1787, came to Compton in 1811, and settled on the farm now owned by the Quebec Government and carried on as a Model Farm. He was married in Compton, in 1812, to Lucy, daughter of Samuel Bliss. Issue, eleven children: Nelson, born February 9, 1814; George W., born July 26, 1831; William D., born February 12, 1837; Emma J., born October 7, 1815; Lucinda, born February 20, 1820; Martha A., born February 20, 1822; Celica B., born March 14, 1825; Sarah A., born March 17, 1829, married Warren J. Page, February 20, 1851, one child. Mr. Bartlett was a man of strong character and highly respected by his fellow citizens.

STEPHEN A. HYATT, a resident of Compton, was born in Ascot, January 16, 1842. He moved to Compton in 1857, where he has always lived. His occupation now is farming, but formerly he was a miller. At present he is a councillor. August 9, 1865, he married Amelia C. Sanders, of Compton, who was born December 16, 1844. Issue, seven children: John W., born January 11, 1868; Allan S., born January 16, 1873; Harry J., born September 21, 1878; Charlie G., born December 22, 1883; Ida M., born May 7, 1866; Minnie L., born August 13, 1869, married Richard D. Pallister, residence Moes River; Maud A., born November 5, 1887.

HISTORY OF COMPTON COUNTY.

LATE JAMES HARKNESS, farmer and wheelwright, born September 19, 1821, died in Compton, April 19, 1869. Married at Sherbrooke, October 7, 1859, to Mary J. Marlin, born March 16, 1831. Issue, four children: James J. G., born January 21, 1865; William J., born October 8, 1867; Margaret E., born July 19, 1860, married Edmund Stevenson, residence Braintree, Mass., three children; Sarah A., born August 17, 1861; married H. A. Cairns, residence East Clifton, two children. October 21, 1869, Mrs. Harkness was married the second time to Samuel Cairns, residence East Clifton. He died February 24, 1896, aged seventy-seven years. Issue, one son: Albert H. S., born February 9, 1880.

VILLAGE OF WATERVILLE.

Waterville[*] is on the river Coaticook, about three miles above its junction with the Massawippi, and is a station on the Grand Trunk Railway. The numerous springs and rills of its undulating surface, and the water power of the Coaticook about this spot gave rise, no doubt, to the appropriate name Waterville.

This place was previously called "Smith's Mills," from their owner Hon. Hollis Smith; before that "Ball's Mills," when owned by James Ball, and still earlier "Hollister's Mills," or "The Hollow," but first of all "Pennoyer's Falls," from the spot a little lower down the stream, on which Squire Pennoyer built the first grist mill on the Coaticook river about 1812.

Joel Tildon, about 1830, came from the southeast part of Compton and opened what was known as "Tildon's Tavern," at the corner of the old stage road between Stanstead and Sherbrooke, on the farm now owned by Walter Law. Before 1835 and long afterwards, and on the south side of the river, Washington Moore carried on a carding, cloth dressing and fulling business. On the north side Brooks & Smith had a large boarding house for their workmen, which later on became a hotel, kept successively by Capt. Alba Brown, Samuel Powers, Craig Flanders, O. Webster, and T. R. Paige. On the same side lived Doncaster, the miller, whose successors have been Canfield Hyatt, Charles Eastman, and the present miller, G. Libby. About the same time Reuben Bradley had a saw mill on the brook which bears his name.

The mills referred to as "Hollister's," then "Ball's," passed into the hands of Brooks & Smith, namely Hon. Hollis Smith and Samuel Brooks, M.P.P. These mills afterwards passed into the hands of Geo. Gale & Sons, and are now the property of C. J. Grant.

The first store in Waterville was located on the site of what is now Peterson's store, and was kept by a Mr. Kennedy. Senator Cochrane clerked here when a young man.

In 1857 Samuel Johnson built and occupied a tannery, and in 1871 sold it to Charles Brooks, and he to Hiram Moe, Sr. It afterwards became the property of Geo. Gale & Sons.

One of the oldest roads in this part of the country, was that which, coming from Sherbrooke, ran on to East Hatley and Stanstead, passing Tildon's tavern. The road which came from that main road through "The Hollow," and on to Compton Centre, left the stage road at a point a little north of Tildon's place, and ran in a south-easterly direction near the river, where Squire Pennoyer and his large family lived. The old bridge, known as the "Wyman bridge," crossed the Coaticook river a short distance higher up the stream than at present, and not far from the old grave-yard. The long-abandoned road to Sherbrooke may still be traced to the water's edge, and determines the site of the old bridge, a wooden one.

One of the most notable figures in the past history of Waterville, was Phillip Henry Gosse, the famous naturalist. He owned and lived on the farm now the property of Mr.

---
[*] We are indebted to Rev. E. A. W. King, for the loan of manuscript from which much of the information heregiven, was gleaned.

W. H. Wiggett, returning to England in 1839. He afterwards published some forty volumes of greater or less importance, and was elected a Fellow of the Royal Society in 1850.

The Waterville post-office was established on September 6, 1852. The persons in charge as post-masters have been, respectively: F. Webster, appointed in 1852; G. White, in 1854; Israel Wood, in 1855; B. A. Haskell, in 1856; Charles Brooks, in 1861; and L. W. Wyman, the present post-master, in 1867.

Waterville was separated from the township of Compton for municipal purposes in 1876. The election for councillors was held February 14 of that year, resulting in the election of

H. J. Pennoyer.   Jas McIntosh   Daniel Jones.
L. M. Johnson.   L. W. Wyman, Mayor.   Wm Wiggett

FIRST COUNCILLORS, VILLAGE OF WATERVILLE—1876

L. W. Wyman, Wm. Wiggett, H. J. Pennoyer, E. H. Langmade, James McIntosh, Daniel Jones and L. M. Johnson, and the first council meeting was held on the twenty-first of the same month. At this latter meeting L. W. Wyman was chosen mayor, and C. F. Wiggett, secretary-treasurer.

We here present an engraving of the first councillors, followed by a short biography of each.

LEVI WILLIAM WYMAN, mayor, was born in Waterville, September 5, 1832. His father before him was also born in Compton, his grandfather, Levi W. Wyman, being one of the first settlers in the township of Compton, coming in from the States by the way of Stanstead in 1803. Mr. Wyman received his education in the local schools. During his younger years he was farming. In 1861 he went into trade in Waterville, continuing the business until 1888. For four years previous to 1861 he was a clerk in stores at Sherbrooke and Stanstead. He was elected a member of the Board of School Commissioners for the township of Compton in 1866, and held that position until 1883, when Waterville was "set off" for school purposes; Mr. Wyman was chosen chairman of the new Board, which office he held until 1887. In 1867 he was appointed postmaster, and still holds this office. Mr. Wyman has been public spirited and assisted greatly in furthering a spirit of enterprise in the village. His labor and example has done much towards developing the strong temperance sentiment of the place. He is Past G. C. of the Royal Templars. He was warden of Sherbrooke county for one term, and has been a commissioner of the Superior Court for taking affidavits for ten years. At present he holds the office of secretary-treasurer of the Municipal Council and School Commissioners. Mr. Wyman was married at Hatley, Que., June 3, 1860, to Hannah (born May 25, 1839), daughter of Abraham Salls, of Stanstead. Issue, eight children: Lois S., born August 18, 1861; Nelly Gertrude, born August 9, 1863; Elizabeth Jane, born July 10, 1865; Maud May, born October 10, 1868; William L., born November 17, 1871; John W., born May 28, 1874; Clara Ethel, born August 20, 1877; Edith M., born October 3, 1879.

WILLIAM WIGGETT, retired farmer, was born in Norfolk County, Eng., in October, 1817. Came to Canada in June, 1836, and to Waterville in 1841. There he resided for forty-one years, following his trade as tailor and farming. He was School Commissioner and Councillor in the township of Compton for several years, and when the village of Waterville was incorporated he was elected one of the first councillors. His son, C. F. Wiggett, was the first secretary-treasurer. Mr. Wiggett has always been a liberal supporter of the Church of England. He was married in Hatley, in April, 1842, to Ann C. Moore. She was born in England in July, 1820. Issue, ten children, seven living: Edward C., born 1844, married C. A. Webster, five children, residence, Sherbrooke; William Henry, born September, 1846, married M. A. Fuller, three children, residence, Waterville; Charles Frederick, born November 6, 1851, married E. Burbeck, three children, residence, Lennoxville; Anthony John, born November, 1854, married E. E. Cuzner, four children, residence, Sherbrooke; Ellen Maria, born April, 1857, residence, Montreal; Emily A., born May, 1860, married M. J. McKerley, two children, residence, Montreal; Luvia L., born January, 1863, married J. Kitto, one child, residence, Montreal. Mr. Wigget is now living at Ayer's Flat, Que.

THE LATE JAMES McINTOSH, in his lifetime farmer, was born at Laprairie, Que., in 1843. He came to Waterville with his parents in 1859, where he resided up to the time of his death, December 28, 1892. He was one of the first councillors of Waterville and remained in office for thirteen years. He was a strong supporter of the Congregational church, and for several years deacon. He was married at Stamford, Ont., January 8, 1872, to Harriet, daughter of Francis E. England. He died at St. Catharines, Ont., in 1891. Issue, one daughter: Annie E., born June 6, 1877.

HENRY JESSE PENNOYER, superannuated excise officer, was born four and one-half miles north of Compton village, July 2, 1835. He is a grandson of Jesse Pennoyer, leader of the associates to whom the township of Compton was granted in 1802. His father, Jesse Pennoyer, jr., was born in Compton, in 1803, and died at Waterville in 1889. Our subject has always made the township of Compton his home, moving to Waterville in 1855. He was a farmer previous to 1875, when he was appointed excise officer, which office he held until 1893, when he was superannuated. He was one of the first councillors of Waterville, and for two years was mayor.

Also one of the first school commissioners. He is now a J. P., and chairman of the Sanitary Committee. Mr. Pennoyer was married in Lennoxville, June 17, 1862, to Mary Emma, daughter of the late Seth Huntington, of Hatley. Issue, five children: William Frederick, born February 22, 1864, died January 17, 1880; Mary Alice, born May 18, 1868, married W. H. Armstrong, one child, residence, Waterville; Lucius S. H., born May 26, 1876; Charles Henry, born June 8, 1878; Geneva May, born February 4, 1882. Mrs. Pennoyer died February 3, 1896, aged fifty-three years.

THE LATE DANIEL JONES was born in Sherbrooke, May 12, 1822. He went to Ascot when a boy and followed farming until 1875, when he moved to Waterville. He was accidentally drowned August 11, 1876, while trying to get his team out of the river, the horse having backed in. He was chosen one of the first councillors of Waterville. He was a son of the late William Jones, of Eaton Corner, the family originally coming from Wales. Mr. Jones was married at Stanstead, Que., June 3, 1851, to Annette Murray, of Compton. She was born May 16, 1829. No children.

THE LATE LARS MAGNUS JOHNSON was born in Dals Land, Sweden, February 13, 1852, died at Waterville in 1883. He came here in 1870 and worked in a furniture shop for a while, afterwards becoming a farmer. He was chosen one of the first councillors of Waterville. Mr. Johnson was married at Moes River, Que., June 24, 1880, to Abbie M., daughter of the late William P. Drake, of Ashland, N.H. No children.

THE LATE E. H. LANGMADE was one of the first seven councillors of Waterville. We have not been able to secure his portrait for use in the group, nor information for a short biography.

Mr. L. W. Wyman held the office of mayor during 1876 and 1877; he was followed in 1878, by Mr. H. J. Pennoyer for two years. In 1880 Mr. Wyman was again chosen mayor and held the office until he resigned in September, 1889, to accept that of secretary-treasurer. Mr. F. G. Gale was elected mayor October 7, 1889, and has since held the office with credit.

The past secretary-treasurers have been C. F. Wiggett, appointed in 1876; James Osgood, in 1877; and the present one, Mr. L. W. Wyman, appointed in 1889.

In 1876 the assessed valuation of Waterville was $54,430. The McIntosh neighborhood was added January 1, 1884, and was assessed at $12,370. The valuation roll now represents $161,735. In other words, the property of the municipality has nearly trebled in less than twenty years. There is comprised in this municipality 4,200 square acres. The tax levied in 1895 was eight and a half mills for municipal purposes, and five mills for school.

Waterville was set off from Compton for school purposes in 1883. At the first election of school commissioners, July 1, 1883, the choice fell upon L. W. Wyman, H. J. Pennoyer, C. O. Swanson, H. M. Bernard, and E. H. Langmade. These were organized with L. W. Wyman as chairman, and James Osgood as secretary-treasurer. In 1887 H. M. Bernard was chosen chairman; F. G. Gale in 1891; and the present chairman, L. Larson, in 1894. L. W. Wyman succeeded Mr. Osgood as secretary-treasurer in 1889.

The pioneer school teacher of Waterville was Seth Huntington. For many years an excellent elementary school was carried on here in the building now located next to the Anglican church. The efficiency of the teachers had gradually improved, until 1882, when the school was given the status of a model school.

The growth of Waterville requiring a larger building, in 1885 the present model school was erected. It stands in a central part of the village, on one of the four corners. Part of it is used as a public hall and council room. It is an imposing, substantial brick building, and one of the best school buildings in Compton county. The first principal in the new building was Miss Mary Armitage, with Miss Elizabeth Wyman as assistant. In 1886 Miss Elizabeth Hepburn became principal, and remained in the office for seven years, during which time the assistant teachers were: Miss Minnie Ball, Nellie Bayley, Nettie Bradley, Edith Miller, Maggie McIntosh and Susan Richards. In 1894 Miss Jane Reed, after Miss Hepburn's resignation, was appointed principal, with Miss Eliza Armstrong and Maud Fuller as assistants. This year Miss Reed is again in charge with Miss Fuller and Elizabeth Ball as assistants.

MODEL SCHOOL, WATERVILLE.

The school commissioners for 1895–96 are: Lars Larson, chairman; F. G. Gale, C. O. Swanson, E. A. Bishop, P. P. Holyan.

We herewith present an excellent photo-engraving of the Waterville model school from a photograph taken in the fall of 1895, showing the teachers and scholars in front. The average attendance is one hundred and twenty.

The Waterville of to-day largely owes its prosperity to the firm of Geo. Gale & Sons. Mr. George Gale and his two sons, Frank and Adelbert, have always labored hard in the interests of the place, erected costly and magnificent residences and other buildings, and in many ways their presence has been felt. At the present time it is one of the neatest and pleasantest villages in the Eastern Townships. The many fine buildings which we present by photo-engravings herewith, bear us out in this statement.

Of the business enterprises the foremost is the spring bed factory of Geo. Gale & Sons, described more fully elsewhere. We then find the Dominion Suath Company, with a good sized new factory; furniture factory of Peter Swanson; machine shop of R. O. Hopkinson; grist mill owned by C. J. Grant; good sized hames factory, recently opened by a Mr. Adams; two carriage shops; three blacksmith shops; two stores; a good hotel built by Geo. Gale & Sons in 1885, it is at present carried on by H. T. Sunbury.

No liquor license has been granted in Waterville for twenty-eight years. Previous to that time it had acquired quite a reputation as a liquor resort.

There are three secret societies in the village. The Royal Templars of Temperance,

Jas McGovern   F. G. Gale, Mayor   A. Cather
C. O. Swanson.   G. W. Powers, M. D.   H. M. Bernard.

COUNCILLORS, VILLAGE OF WATERVILLE, FOR 1895.

organized in 1883, is in a flourishing condition. This society succeeded the Good Templars, another temperance organization, established here in 1861. The Orange lodge, of which a complete history is to be found on another page, together with an engraving of their fine new hall. The Independent Order of Foresters organized a court here about 1893, and now have in the vicinity of fifty members.

Waterville has two churches, Anglican and Congregationalist. The Methodist minister from Hatley occasionally holds service in the school building.

The census of 1891 gives the following statistics for Waterville: Population, 516; families, 101; houses, 101; males, 254; females, 262; French-Canadians, 86; others, 430; religious—

HISTORY OF COMPTON COUNTY.

Roman Catholic, 100; Church of England, 152; Presbyterians, 21; Methodists, 62; Lutherans, 43; Freewill Baptists, 14; Congregationalists, 99; Adventists, 18; Universalists, 1; Jews, 3; other denominations, 1; not specified, 2.

The council for 1895 was composed as follows: F. G. Gale, mayor; and councillors C. O. Swanson, Alfonso Carbee, James McGovern, H. M. Bernard, James Logan and Dr. G. W. Powers. Secretary-treasurer, L. W. Wyman. We give a photo-engraving on the preceding page of the council together with a biography of each member.

RESIDENCE OF F. G. GALE.

FRANCIS GILBERT GALE, manufacturer and mayor, was born in Stanstead, near Smith's Mills, Que., June 12, 1855. He is a son of the late George Gale, inventor and patentee of the Dominion Wire Mattress. Mr. F. G. Gale is the youngest son and has recently purchased a full interest in the firm of Geo. Gale & Sons, for the American business. Mr. A. H. Gale, the other son, retains the foreign trade with head office in Birmingham, Eng. A more extensive history of the manufacture of these celebrated beds can be found under the history of Geo. Gale & Sons. Mr. F. G. Gale came to Waterville with his father in 1881, where he has since resided. He received his primary education in the schools of Stanstead and Hatley, finishing his studies at Dartmouth college, Hanover, N.H., graduating in 1876. Mr. Gale has been councillor twelve years, and mayor since 1889. For one year he was warden of Sherbrooke county. He is a member of the board of school commissioners, and from 1891 to 1894 was chairman. He is also president of the Coaticook River Water Power Company. He has always been a supporter of the Congregational church, and is now one of the trustees.

Mr. Gale is noted for his business ability and enterprise. He is always anxious to further the interests of Waterville, and to the firm of Geo. Gale & Sons is due most of the progress that has been made in the village. He was married in Eaton, December 31, 1885, to Olivia Iola, daughter of the late Benjamin Laberee. A biographical sketch of Mr Laberee may be found on another page. Issue, four children: Ethel Iola, born August 26, 1888, died January 20, 1891; Francis George, born March 15, 1890; died September 2, 1890; Royce Laberee, born August 12, 1892; Francis Gilbert, jr., born December 1, 1894. A photo-engraving of the fine residence and grounds of Mr. Gale is to be seen on preceding page

CHARLES O. SWANSON, Dominion Immigration Agent, was born in Grenstad, Sweden, June 5, 1844. He came to Canada in 1869 and settled at once at Waterville. At first he worked in the furniture factory of L. Emerson. He purchased the business May 1, 1871, and carried it on until 1891 when he sold to his brother, Peter Swanson. Mr. Swanson was the first Swede to settle in Waterville, and it has been largely through his efforts that others have come. They now number about one hundred and twenty-five. Mr. Swanson is public spirited and has always taken a lively interest in the affairs of Waterville. He has been one of the municipal councillors for several years, and was one of the first members of the board of school commissioners for the village. Mr. Swanson attends the Congregational church and is one of the trustees.

RESIDENCE OF COUNCILLOR C. O. SWANSON.

In 1892 he was appointed Immigration agent by the Dominion Government, which office he has filled with credit, having opened several townships in the North-West with new settlers, principally from the United States. He was married at Moes River, Que., October 24, 1872, to Ella C. (born May 27, 1852), daughter of the late B. F. Draper. Issue, two children: Lillian F., born August 12, 1877; Reginald W., born September 13, 1882. Mr. Swanson's residence is located in the centre of the village, and the photo-engraving here given shows it to be one of the tasty, pleasant homes for which Waterville is noted.

JAMES McGOVERN, retired farmer, was born in County Cavan, North of Ireland, April 2, 1840. Came to West Farnham, Que., in 1841, with his parents, where he lived the first twenty years of his life. In 1858-59 he was employed as time-keeper when the Stanstead, Shefford and Chambly Railroad was in course of construction, between Farnham and St. Johns, and until his removal to Waterville, was connected in various ways with railroad construction, on both the Massawippi Valley and Grand Trunk railways. In 1869 Mr. McGovern settled on a farm near this village. The years 1872 and 1876 he was road overseer, and in 1880-81 appointed school manager of his district. In 1886 Mr. McGovern moved into the village to enjoy the benefits of his hard toil, having been successful through life. For five years he has been a member of the local council, also connected with the Board of Health. Like many other citizens of Waterville, he is public-spirited, assisting in every way possible the growth of the place. He is a strong supporter of prohibition, and is a firm believer in the principles of the National Policy. He was married at New Haven, Vt., April 15, 1875, to Dora S., daughter of Lyman Cotton, of that place. Mr. Cotton came to Waterville in 1880, where he died in 1886. Issue, four children: Lyman B., born October 25, 1876; Albert J., born September 13, 1878; Walter E., born February 6, 1886; Annie D. F., born July 3, 1888. Herewith is an engraving of the pretty residence of Mr. McGovern, with himself and family in front.

RESIDENCE OF COUNCILLOR JAS. McGOVERN.

GEORGE WHEELOCK POWERS, M.D., C.M., was born in Franklin county, Vt., January 8, 1831. His father, Daniel W. Powers, died in Vermont in 1856, aged fifty-two years. Dr. Powers attended the Medical College, Castleton, Vt. In 1858 he went to Sutton, Que., where he practiced two years with Dr. Cutter. He then entered McGill Medical College, Montreal, and graduated in 1860. He returned to Sutton for two years. In 1862, at the request of local residents, he came to Eaton, Que., and for one year practiced in company with the late Dr Rogers, who at the end of that time gave up practice. Dr Powers remained in Eaton until 1883, having been successful. He went south in that year, returned to Lennoxville in 1884, but shortly returned south owing to the illness of his wife. He came back again from the south after his wife's death, where she was buried in her native land, and settled at Waterville in 1887, where he has since resided. He is a member of the local council, and a trustee of the Congregational church. He has been married three times. First at Cookshire in October, 1869, to Mrs. Martha A. King, daughter of Thomas Gould, of Brockville, Ont. She died February 8, 1883. Issue, two children: Jessie M., born November 28, 1871, died December 28, 1893; Gertie L., born in 1873, died in 1877. Second marriage at Atlanta, Ga., in October, 1883, to Mattie Green. She died May 28, 1887. Issue, one daughter: Fanny May, born November 9, 1884. Third marriage at Sherbrooke, Que., January 9, 1895, to Elizabeth A., daughter of Captain F. Bennetts.

HENRY MOUNTAGUE BERNARD, farmer, was born in Somersetshire, Eng., August 19, 1848. He came to Canada in 1866 and settled on a farm at Waterville in 1868. He attended the

HISTORY OF COMPTON COUNTY. 193

English public schools, and for two years studied law in England. Since coming here he has been school commissioner for nine years, and at present is one of the village councillors. He is a prominent member of the Orange Lodge, holding the office of recording secretary of Lord Erne, L.O.L.; Scribe R.S.C., and secretary of the County Lodge. Mr. Bernard was married at Compton, Que., November 9, 1872, to Adamena, daughter of Peter Young. Issue, six children: James, born January 23, 1874; Alice, born February 16, 1875, married James W. Hickey, residence, Stark, N. H.; Edith, born April 4, 1876; William, born December 25, 1879; Helen, born March 20, 1880; Ralph, born December 25, 1883.

ALPHONSO CARBEE, farmer, was born in Waterville, March 8, 1843. When seventeen years of age he went to the Western States, returning in seven years. Since then he has resided in Compton, Coaticook and Waterville. Mr. Carbee has always followed farming. For the past five years he has been a member of the municipal council of Waterville He was married in Compton, January 7, 1873, to Jemima, daughter of the late James Kerr. No children.

JAMES LOGAN, farmer, is a member of the Council, but his photograph and biography we are not able to give.

L. W. WYMAN, postmaster, and secretary-treasurer of the municipal council. His biography is to be found among those of the first councillors of Waterville. Mr. Wyman was chosen the first mayor. He resigned from the council and accepted the office of secretary-treasurer in 1889.

The Anglican church, Waterville.—This place was occasionally served by missionaries from Hatley, Stanstead and Sherbrooke, during the years intervening between 1818 to 1840. From 1840 to 1854, Rev. Charles Peter Reid, stationed at Compton, held regular services here, and it was during his ministry that the present church building, known as "St. John the Evangelist," was erected. This was the first and only church in Waterville for thirty-five years. On the next page will be found a photo-engraving of the same.

The first meeting for the erection of this building was held in October, 1843. Present, Rev. C. P. Reid, Jas. Bell, Lieut. W. F. Parker, Salvin Richardson, S. S. Wells, W. D. Lambkin, John McMillan, Geo. Moore, Frank Webster, W. Wiggett, and others. These started a subscription for the proposed building, and Lieut. Parker, W. Wiggett, and S. Richardson, were appointed the building committee. The site was given by the Hon. Hollis Smith. In the winter of 1844 stone for the foundation was drawn. In the winter of 1845 a large quantity of logs was given by Robt. Hawse, and sawed at Waterville. In the spring of 1845 the church was erected and closed in. In the spring and summer of 1846 the interior was completed, and the first service was held in October.

The first baptism was that of Wm. H. Wiggett, November 22, 1846. The first marriage in the church was that of Lucius Sutton and Eliza Ball. The first burial was that of Melissa Richardson, in 1849.

In 1854 Rev. C. P. Reid left Compton, and the Waterville mission was attached to Lennoxville. The following ministers are some of those connected with this church up to 1862: Rev. Thos. Pennefather, Rev. John Butler, M.A., Rev. Principal Nicolls, Rev. Aaron A. Allen, M.A., Rev. Edwin Loucks, and Rev. Wm. Richmond, M.A. In 1862 Rev. H. G. Burrage was appointed to Hatley and Waterville; Rev. A. J. Balfour, M.A., in 1872; Rev. Albert Stevens, M.A., in 1881; and Rev. Isaac Thompson in 1889. The latter reverend

13

gentleman remained in charge until December 31, 1892, when he was succeeded by the present pastor, Rev. Ernest A. Willoughby King, M.A.

Adjoining the church, on the west side, is an excellent lot, on which it is the intention to erect the future parsonage.

Since the organization of this church, for at least fifteen times, Messrs. Matt. Henry and Wm. Wiggett have been appointed church wardens.

During the first week of October, 1895, a series of services and meetings celebrated the jubilee of this church, with much enthusiasm, it having been built for fifty years. The municipality was represented by the mayor and councillors while Bishop Dunn and fifteen of the clergy showed their interest in the proceedings by being present.

The cemetery belong to St. John's church, consecrated by Bishop Mountain, with an enlargement consecrated by Bishop Williams, is still the only grave-yard available in this municipality.

ST. JOHN'S, CHURCH OF ENGLAND.

Under the guidance of Rev. Mr. King the church here is making good progress, and increasing in membership.

Congregational church, Waterville—On December 15, 1861, the Congregational church of Massawippi, Que., which had been organized some time previously, united in extending a call to the Rev. Cyril Pearl, to become their pastor. The reverend gentleman was a native of Maine, and had been trained and ordained to the work of the Gospel ministry in that State. Shortly after his arrival at Massawippi, there being need of Gospel services in Waterville, he began preaching, making it one of his stated appointments. The work prospered, and a Congregational church was organized July 1, 1862, the Rev. Mr. Pearl becoming its first pastor, Mr Amasa T. Martin and Mr. Alba Brown, the first deacons. At the organization of the church, the Rev. E. J. Sherrill, of Eaton, Que., preached, Rev. L. P. Adams, of Fitch Bay, Que., offered prayer, and Rev. Archibald Duff, of Sherbrooke, addressed the people. The following were received into fellowship at the time: Mr. and Mrs. A. T. Martin, Mr. and Mrs. Alba Brown, Mr. and Mrs. Wm. Johnston, T. D. Harris, Miss Richardson, Miss Watt, Mrs. Fowler, and Mr. and Mrs. John Glen. Mr. Pearl, strongly sympathizing with the North in the civil war then being waged in his native land, grew uneasy. He resigned his pastorate and returned home, serving some time at the front as chaplain.

The united congregations of Massawippi and Waterville then extended a call to the Rev. Jos. Forsyth to become their pastor, he accepted and was ordained and installed on August 10, 1864. Previously he had been a minister of the Wesleyan Methodist church, his last pastorate in that denomination being spent at Compton. The Rev. Archibald Duff, of Sherbrooke, and the Rev. E. J. Sherrill, of Eaton, forming with the church the ordaining council.

Mr. Forsyth continued as pastor of his united charges until his death, in September, 1856.

The distance between the two churches being too great to work them together to advantage, at the close of Mr. Forsyth's pastorate, they separated, Waterville alone extending a call to his successor. In the month of March, 1867, by invitation of the church, through the Rev. Arch. Duff, of Sherbrooke, district secretary of the Congregational Mission Society of Canada, Mr. George Purkiss, a native of England, then laboring as colporteur of the Montreal Auxiliary Bible Society, paid a visit to Waterville, and preached on the Sabbaths, March, 10 and 17, and on May 10 the church gave a call to Mr. Purkiss to become their pastor, who was at that time residing at Dickinson's Landing, Ont.

Mr. Purkiss, having accepted the call, moved to Waterville on June 25, and commenced his labors on the following Sabbath, June 30, 1867, and on July 24, was ordained and installed as pastor. The Revs. A. J. Parker, of Danville, E J. Sherrill, of Eaton, L. P. Adams, of Fitch Bay, John Campbell, of Melbourne, John Rogers, of Stanstead Plain, and Archibald Duff, of Sherbrooke, united in the examination and ordination of the candidate. The pastorate thus auspiciously begun continued without a break until 1889—a period of twenty-two years.

During these years of labor 133 persons were received into membership by Rev. Mr. Purkis, besides officiating at 255 baptisms, 143 burials, and 110 weddings. Laboring under many difficulties and with a small salary, God owned and blessed his labor of love

For the first eighteen years of its existence, viz , 1862–1880, the congregation were without a church home, worshipping in the village school. In 1880 an effort was made to erect a church, which was crowned with success, a neat and sufficiently commodious structure being erected at a cost of $1,617.72. The building committee, composed of Messrs. John McIntosh, jr., ex-M.L.A.; O. M. Swanson, L. M. Johnson, C. O. Swanson, Smith McKay, and L. W. Wyman, secretary, were so successful in their work that in handing the church over to the people they were able to do so free of debt. A photo engraving of the church is here given.

CONGREGATIONAL CHURCH, WATERVILLE.

In 1888, the church feeling the need of a better parsonage building, appointed the following as a building committee: Messrs. John McIntosh, jr., ex-M L A.; F. G. Gale, C. O. Swanson, James McGovern, A. A. Blount, Wm. Thwaites, and L. Larson, secretary. At a cost of $1,893 they had erected the tasty, two-story brick parsonage shown in the engraving.

The following year, after faithful service for twenty-two years, the Rev. Mr. Purkis resigned the pastorate of the church, and retired from the active work of the ministry, spending his remaining years in the peace and quiet of his daughter's home at Bowmanville, Ontario, where in April, 1894, painlessly and peacefully, he passed home to his Master and his reward. During his pastorate his congregation, none of whom were wealthy, had erected church property to the value of $3,500, and the year he left it assumed self-support, a small missionary grant having been received previously.

The Rev. Mr. Purkis was soon succeeded by the Rev. J. W. Goffin, of London, England, who remained, however, but two years, to be succeeded by the Rev. W. A. Dunnett, temperance evangelist, of Hamilton, Ont., who, finding himself unfitted for a permanent pastorate, resigned in six months. The next pastor, the Rev. Galen H. Craik, B.A., a native of Franklin, Huntingdon county, Quebec, assumed the pastorate in May, 1892, and has remained in charge since. Messrs. Larson and Johnston are at present the only deacons, two more to be appointed at the next annual meeting of the church and congregation. Offerings reported received by the secretary-treasurer, Mr. Larson, at the last annual meeting, $1,139, of which $800 were for church expenses, the remaining $339 being for denominational and benevolent objects, of which $100 was for foreign missions, $66 for the Congregational college, Montreal, and $53 for home missions. To this should be added the $150 raised at the appointment at Eustis, and applied on the minister's salary, making the total of money raised in the congregation $1,289, which with a membership of eighty-five makes an average of $15.17 per member—a sum that, considering the means of the people, that no special effort was put forth to raise money, and the treasurer of the church received and paid out every dollar of the total, makes a record hard to be equaled or surpassed.

CONGREGATIONAL PARSONAGE, WATERVILLE.

There are in existence in the church a Christian Endeavor Society of thirty members, a Sunday-school of seventy-five members, and a Ladies' Missionary Society. At present the prospects for spiritual work are good, many encouraging features having lately arisen that point to much blessing in the future.

SHERIFF JOHN McINTOSH, ex-M.L.A., whose portrait is presented herewith, was born in Laprairie, Que., October 27, 1841, of Scotch parentage. In the fall of 1860, in company with his parents, he came to Compton and settled on a farm about one and one-half miles north of Waterville. His father, John McIntosh, sr., lived there for twenty-five years, and then removed to Sherbrooke, where he resided up to the time of his death, which took place in 1894, while on a visit to Montreal. Sheriff McIntosh received his education at Laprairie high school, and became proficient in the use of French as well as English. After coming to Compton he followed farming for several years. On the establishment of the Canadian Meat and Produce Co., with headquarters at Sherbrooke, in 1875, he became connected with that company, having full charge of selecting and buying all cattle required for the operations of the company. After their dissolution, Mr. McIntosh entered largely into the export of cattle for the English market. He was a member of the Compton municipal council for six years, and of the Waterville council for ten years, also a member of the board of school commissioners. He is a prominent member of the Congregational church. In 1886 he was elected as the representative of Compton county at Quebec, defeating Hugh Leonard by over six hundred majority. In 1890 he was re-elected, defeating George Layfield by a still larger majority. After the dissolution of the Mercier Government in 1891, Mr. McIntosh was chosen as one of the members of the Hon. Mr. DeBoucherville's cabinet, and returned by acclamation at the general election following. In 1893 he was appointed commissioner for the Province of Quebec at the Columbian Exposition held at Chicago. Mr McIntosh's health having failed, he was offered the position of sheriff for the district of St. Francis, vacant through the death of Mr. Jos. L. Terrill. This he accepted in 1894, resigning in consequence his place in the cabinet, and as member for Compton county, greatly to the regret of all. His new duties required his moving to Sherbrooke, where he has since resided. For the past two years he has ably filled the position of president of the Eastern Townships Agricultural Association. He was married at Howick, Chateauguay county, Que., January 2, 1870, to Jeanette, daughter of the late William Greig, of Howick. Issue, eight children, six living: Maggie P, born May 6, 1872, married, residence, Waterville; Janet B, born June 7, 1874, died March 25, 1885; Elizabeth Alice, born April 12, 1876; Winnifred, born July 9, 1878, died September 13, 1895; John R, born June 29, 1880; James A, born March 19, 1885.

SHERIFF JOHN McINTOSH, EX-M.L.A.

GEORGE GALE & SONS, manufacturers of iron bedsteads and spring beds, was organized in 1877, comprising the late George Gale and his two sons, F. G. and A. H. Gale. On November 2, 1895, a separation of the business was agreed upon, Mr. F. G. Gale retaining Canada and the United States, while Mr. A. H. Gale takes the English and foreign business, with office and factory at Birmingham, Eng. The inventor of the Gale Spring Bed, and senior member of the firm, Mr. George Gale, was born in Williamstown, Vt., February 28, 1824. He came to Stanstead, Que., in 1830, with his parents. In 1843 he returned to Vermont and there learned the trade of millwright. Returning to Stanstead, he one year later moved to Barnston. During the gold craze of 1849 he went to California, remaining there two years. In that time he cleared $2,500. He returned again to Stanstead in 1854 where he remained until his removal to Waterville in 1880. During 1868-69 he built several bridges on the Tomifobia river, also repaired the large bridge between Rock Island and Derby Line at an expense of a few hundred dollars, which, civil engineers said, would cost nearly as many thousands. In the meantime he carried on a farm and saw mill in Stanstead, near Smith's Mills, and while on a trip to the Eastern States selling lumber he got his idea of the spring bed. Naturally of an inventive mind, he made improvements on his return home, which were patented. The first bed was made in 1873, and first patent issued in 1879. The beds were manufactured on a small scale in Stanstead. In order to increase manufacturing facilities the business was transferred to Waterville in 1880. Here Messrs. Geo. Gale & Sons have been very successful. The first year they occupied the old saw mill, situated on the opposite side of the river from their present factory. The second year the old machine shop was added for more room. The business having increased, in 1887, the large new factory was erected. This is a building 55 x 180 feet, four stories high, with an ell 28 x 48 feet. In the

FACTORY OF GEO. GALE & SONS.

fall of 1895 another addition was made to the building, to be used as a foundry for the manufacture of iron and brass bedsteads, which have heretofore been imported from England. This is 30 x 85 feet. There is also a railway from the station, half a mile long, extending through the main building, giving the very best of shipping facilities. Accompanying this sketch is a photo-engraving of the factory, from a photograph, taken in the summer of 1895. This is from a view just above the factory, at the dam, on the opposite side of the river. The ell of the factory is on the opposite side. The foundry erected after this photograph was taken, is at the side of the building, in the centre of the picture, and nearly in front of the freight car. After coming to Waterville, Mr. George Gale was always on the outlook to make improvements, leaving the management of the business almost wholly to his sons. The organization of the Coaticook River Water Power Company, was his idea. It has a paid up capital of $16,000 00. Dams were erected at Averill Ponds and Norton Lake in 1889, by this company, and in the summer, during low water, these places are drawn on for a fresh supply. Mr. Gale was married at Stanstead in 1847, to Dorothy Davis, widow of S. W. Mack, of Stanstead. Issue, four children: Albert, born in 1849, died in 1852; Adelbert H.; Francis G.; Fluella Lucretia, born in May, 1858, died in August, 1863. Mr. Gale died very suddenly at Stanhope, Que., January 26, 1892, while standing at the telephone talking, apparently in his usual good health. His wife did not long survive, dying on April 10, 1892, aged seventy-six years. Mr. F. G. Gale inherits his father's inventive faculties, and has made good use of them, greatly to the benefit of the firm. On July 3, 1895, he was granted a patent on what is known as "New Dominion Wire Mattress." Applications are also in for patents on what is called "Cuban Wire Mattress," and an "Oval Woven Mattress." The patents on the old "Gale Spring Bed," expired in 1894, and these three new lines were first offered for sale in 1895. The business of the firm is increasing, and the sale of the new styles above mentioned, show them to be the best thing of the kind on the market. Their combination beds, bedsteads, and hospital beds, are also in demand in all parts of the country. There is not another firm in the Eastern Townships with so extensive a market, as Messrs. Gale & Sons make shipments in quantities to all parts of the world. It is but fair to state that this firm, now so well and favorably known, have made Waterville and given it both a reputation and standing of which any new town might be proud. To accomplish all this, without a large fortune to begin with or fall back upon, particularly in the earlier years of the enterprise, speaks volumes for the ingenuity, the energy, and courage of these gentlemen.

LORD ERNE LOYAL ORANGE LODGE, 1591, was organized May 21, 1890, through the efforts of Leonard Van Luven, formerly of Battersea, Ont., but at that time and at present residing in Waterville, united with whom were the following charter members: Geo. Gardiner, James Rooney, James Lytle, Thomas Armstrong, James Campbell, Charles House, Geo. Flanders, F. Lewis, John Johnson. The lodge was opened under the patronage of the Right Hon. Lord Erne, Imperial Grand Master, who consented to become its patron and an honorary member. It was put into working order by Right Worshipful Provincial Grand Master Clark Gordon, of Sherbrooke. The following members elected officers for the first year: L. Van Luven, W.M.; James Rooney, D.M.; Rev. Isaac M. Thompson, Chap.; Geo. Gardiner, Rec. and Fin. Sec.; James Lytle, Treas.; D. McLean, D. of C.; Standing Committee—Mark Hodgson, Geo. Flanders, Thomas Armstrong, James Campbell, F. Lewis. The meetings were held in the town hall until the month of February, 1895, when the members moved into the large and handsome hall (a photo-engraving of the same is shewn on next page), which it was decided to build at a regular meeting held in September of the previous year. The membership having largely increased, and a warrant of incorporation obtained, and a considerable sum raised amongst the brethren and others, it was decided to at once begin building operations under the supervision of the following committee: L. Van Luven, F. Lewis and H. M. Bernard. The first stone of the foundation was laid October 22, 1894, and the hall was ready for occupation on February 11, 1895, on which day it was dedicated with the usual ceremonies by the Hon. N. C. Wallace, M.P., Comptroller of Customs, Most Worshipful Grand Master and Sovereign, assisted by Past Provincial Grand Masters, Wm. Galbraith, of Montreal, and Clark Gordon, of Sherbrooke, and other well known Orangemen from Montreal and the surrounding district. The Hon. N. C. Wallace was met at the station by the officers of L. O. L., 1591, and the mayor and councillors of the village of Waterville, and was presented with an address of welcome on behalf of the lodge, and with another by the mayor, on behalf of the village. On that day L. O. L., 1591, entertained the Hon. N. C. Wallace, R. H. Pope, M.P., the mayor and corporation, the visiting brethren, the Protestant clergy, and members of the learned professions, to a banquet; and in the evening a supper and entertainment was given in the hall in aid of the building fund, when its seating capacity, viz.: about 250, was taxed to the utmost. A flag staff (at that time the only one in the village) more than thirty feet high was erected on the hall, from which, on the proper occasions, floats a large, handsome Dominion ensign. July 12 has been yearly celebrated by successful picnics and entertainments, and November 5 usually by an oyster supper. In the month of March, 1896, the Grand Lodge of Quebec met in Waterville for the first time in the history of the village, and the county lodge has met here for the last three years. The officers of Lord Erne L. O. L., 1591, for 1896, are: Bro. W. H. Ward, W.M.; Bro. L. Van Luven, P.M.; Bro. James Orr, D.M.; Bro. James Lytle, Chap.; Bro. H. M. Bernard, Rec. Sec.; Bro. L. Van Luven, Fin. Sec; Bro. Wm. Edgecombe, Treas.; Bro. James Rooney, D. of C.; Bro. Lee Buckland, Lecturer. Standing Committee:—Bro. Adams, Bro. F. Lewis, Bro. H. Rinder, Bro. D. Johnston, Bro. Geo. Flanders. Auditors:—Bro. F. Lewis, Bro. H. M. Bernard. Sick Committee:—Bro. F. Lewis, Bro. D. Johnston, Bro. James Orr, Bro. H. Rinder, Bro. W. Edgecombe, Bro. James

HALL OF LORD ERNE LOYAL ORANGE LODGE, 1591.

Campbell. Trustees:—Bro. L. Van Luven, Bro. F. Lewis, Bro. H. M. Bernard. Medical Examiner:—Bro. R. A. D. King, M.D. Pianist:—Bro. H. Rinder. Past Masters:—L. Van Luven, Geo. Gardiner, W. H. Ward, and D. McLean. Membership at present sixty, twenty-seven of whom have the Royal Arch Purple degree. On October 14, 1893, the Royal Scarlet Chapter was opened. The following were elected officers for 1896:—Sir Kt. Comp. W. H. Ward, Wor. Comp. in Command; Sir Kt. Comp. L. Van Luven, Excel. Comp. in Command;

Sir Kt. Comp. J. Lytle, Chap.; Sir Kt. Comp. H. M. Bernard, Scribe; Sir Kt. Comp. James Orr, Treas.; Sir Kt. Comp. Lee Buckland, Herald at Arms; Sir Kt. Comp. H. J. McLung; Inside Herald; Sir Kt. Comp. Thos. Armstrong, Outside Herald.

ADELBERT HENRY GALE was born in Barnston, Que., April 30, 1854. He is a member of the firm of Geo. Gale & Sons, manufacturers and dealers in spring mattresses, matresses, pillows, iron beds, etc., and has been one of the principal founders of the present business, both in Canada and Great Britain, having taken an active part in its establishment and success. An engraving is here given of the residence of Mr. Gale, located at Waterville.

RESIDENCE OF A. H. GALE.

It is on rising ground and commands an extensive view of the Coaticook river, Waterville, and the surrounding maple grove country. Mr. Gale has been married twice. First at Waterville, Que., February 12, 1885, to Mary E. Ladd. She died April 5, 1886. Issue, one daughter: Mary E, born March 25, 1886. Second marriage at Bowmanville, Ont., January 3, 1890, to Katherine M., daughter of the late Henry Dobson, of Toronto, Ont. Issue, one son: Warren D, born October 15, 1890.

ALEXANDER McINTOSH, live stock exporter, at present with headquarters in Montreal, but until recently a resident of Waterville, was born in Laprairie, Que., December 24, 1855. Came to Compton with his father, John McIntosh, in 1861, who died in May, 1894. Previous to his moving to Montreal, in 1894, he was a farmer and general merchant, holding several public offices. Was married in Howick, Que., October 22, 1884, to Janet B., daughter of Robert Ness, Esq., member of the Provincial Council of Agriculture. Issue, five children: Robert B., born July 5, 1888; William A., born September 15, 1890; George N., born December 9, 1891; Mabel E., born November 7, 1885; Elsie M., born June 16, 1893.

LEONARD VAN LUVEN, agent Grand Trunk Railway, was born in Battersea, Ont., April 27, 1857. He received his education in the public schools of Ontario. For the past sixteen years he has been connected with the Grand Trunk Railway. In January, 1890, he came to Waterville as agent for the company, and has held the position since to the satisfaction of all. He is a prominent member of several secret societies, especially the Orange and Masonic Lodges. He has held many prominent offices in the Orange society, among them being W. M., L. O. L., 1591, County Master, Deputy G. C. of Quebec, delegate from the Quebec Grand Lodge in 1891 to Triennial Council in Toronto, and delegate to Grand Lodge British North America on various occasions. Mr. Van Luven was married at Battersea, Ont., September 17, 1878, to Jane Teachout. Issue, four children: Frederick C., born May 1, 1884; Karl, born May 30, 1886; Otto, born February 19, 1889; Vida, born June 29, 1894. His father, Henry Van Luven, was born in Dutchess county, N. Y., in 1794 (being the son of a U. E. loyalist), and was a veteran of 1812-15, taking part in the battle of Lundy's Lane, and several other engagements, having removed to Canada with his parents when a child. His mother was born in Ipswick, Eng., in 1816, and was the daughter of the late John King, master of H. M. frigate "Falcon," and who served under Lord Nelson, at the battle of the Nile.

JOSEPH RICE BALL, manufacturer, was born at Athens, Vt., July 24, 1846. He settled in Sherbrooke, Que., in November, 1893. Held the office of superintendent of schools in Vermont, is now superintendent of Methodist Sunday school at Sherbrooke, and member of the quarterly board. Is now, and has been since coming to Canada, member and manager of the Dominion Snath Company. Was married at Athens, Vt., October 18, 1870, to Augusta S., daughter of Caleb Bowles, of Bethlehem, N. H., who died in 1876. Issue, two children: Leon J., born April 19, 1876; Annie M., born January 10, 1872. Second marriage to Addie L., daughter of S. W. Stuart, of Bellows Falls, Vt., August 4, 1879. Issue, two children: Stuart, born December 4, 1888; M. Gussie, born April 17, 1881.

CHAPTER XIV.

TOWNSHIP OF CLIFTON.

Including History of Municipalities of East Clifton, Martinville, and Ste. Edwidge.

This is a tract of land in the southwest end of the County, and was erected into a township, named Clifton, July 13, 1799; and in part granted July 3, 1803, to Charles Blake, Daniel Cameron, Alexander Cameron, Duncan Cameron, John Cross the elder, John Cross the younger, Ann Hall the widow of Conrad Barnet, Mary Barnet the daughter of Conrad Barnet, Isaac Lemington Hall, Mary Catherine Christy Hall, and Ann Blake Hall. It appears that few, if any, of these grantees settled upon the lands thus granted, but probably sold them to other parties.

Two ponds, named respectively Lindsay's and Sucker ponds, each of which covers some 250 acres, lie within its limits; the former being in the southeast part, and the latter a little south of the centre of the Township. Around these ponds the land is wet and marshy, aside from which the swamps are of no great extent. Though hilly in some sections, it is mostly suitable for cultivation or pasturage. There is a large portion of the Township still a forest, from which the lumber is gradually being cleared each year, and used up in the different saw mills.

The first person known to have settled in the township of Clifton, was Isaac Thurber, in 1798, on lot 8, range 3. The only road then was a spotted or blazed line, also called bridle path, from Canaan, Vt., to Sawyerville, a distance of thirty miles. It bore nearly the same course as the present road, passing through East Clifton, leading from Sawyerville to West Stewartstown, N. H. Mr. Thurber only remained about two years, and was succeeded by Isaac Lindsay, who may be said to have been the first permanent settler. For nearly seven years he worked his farm, isolated from neighbors. There was no road and none of the conveniences or necessaries of life. The new land produced large crops, and thus he was encouraged to remain. Mr. Lindsay died in 1847. John Waldron moved to the lot adjoining Mr. Lindsay, in 1807. Jonathan Stone commenced on lot 9, range 4, in 1808. Mr. Lindsay's eldest son, Abram, purchased Waldron's improvements on lot 9, range 3, about 1819, where he cleared a good farm. He died in 1873. His widow, who is still in good health, aged eighty-six years, carries on this farm. The only member of the first settler's family living, is William Lindsay, of Eaton Corner.

John Waldron reared a large family, and three of the sons settled in Clifton—John, jr., James and Thomas. James was one of the first children born here, and is still living. Among the other early settlers were John Pope (grandfather of the late Hon. John Henry Pope), and Hosea Blair. The first settlers of this township suffered great hardships and privations, having no roads, mills or schools. It is told how Elder John Waldron, going without bread as long as he could, often carried a bag of wheat on his back to Colebrook, N. H., to have it ground. A grist mill was established at Sawyerville shortly after, and thus the distance to mill greatly lessened.

Road making was a very slow process, there being no organization provided by law, and all work was of a voluntary nature. The first effort towards building a road was a law of the settlers taxing each person owning or occupying 100 acres four days work each year. It is said this work was cheerfully and faithfully performed, and in many cases more than doubled.

It was not until 1851 that the required population of 300 souls was found in the municipality, entitling it to organize as a municipality. During the first sittings of the Sherbrooke council Clifton was divided among three municipalities, Eaton, Compton and Hereford. A few years later the whole of Clifton was united to Hereford for municipal and school purposes. When it was found in 1851 that there was a population of 300 souls, an effort was made for separate organization. The first to succeed was for school purposes. In 1853 the first Board of School Commissioners was elected, as follows: David H. Pope, Thomas Waldron, Thomas Pierce, Amasa T. Martin, and Benj. Donaldson; and H. E. Cairns appointed secretary-treasurer. For the first three years the meetings of the Board were held once in three months, at Eaton Corner, as there was no road between the east and west parts of the township. A. T. Martin was the first chairman, and Thomas Waldron is the only one of the first five now living.

In July, 1855, the township of Clifton was organized into a separate municipality, and the first election for councillors was held at Martinville, then called Martin's Mills, in the same month and same year. The following were elected:—David H. Pope, William Betts, Joseph Taylor, James Waldron, John Haines, Thomas Pierce, and John Corcoran. At the first meeting of the Council Thomas Pierce was chosen mayor, and H. E. Cairns secretary-treasurer. James Waldron is the only one of these seven now living. For a number of years there was no road, except a spotted line between East Clifton and Martinville, and the councillors were obliged many times to walk to the council meetings. The mayors who held office up to 1874 were:—D. H. Pope, Thos. Pierce, D. Hazeltine, Joseph Taylor, and Charles McClary.

About January 1, 1873, the east part of the Township petitioned the county council, praying for a division of the Township into two municipalities. This movement proved successful, and a new municipality was erected, known as East Clifton, taking effect February 1, 1874. The balance of the Township retained the name of Clifton.

The census of 1891 gives the following statistics of this Township, including East Clifton and the villages of Martinville and Ste. Edwidge: Population, 1,840; families, 349; houses, 334; males, 996; females, 844; French-Canadians, 1,019; others, 821; religions—Roman Catholic, 1,082; Church of England, 88; Presbyterians, 66; Methodists, 455; Baptists, 40; Freewill Baptists, 52; Congregationalists, 2; Adventists, 19; Universalists, 25; Protestants, 4; other denominations, 1; not specified, 6.

Bouchette, writing in 1831, gives the population of Clifton as eighty-three, with one school and one saw mill.

EAST CLIFTON.

The first councillors for this municipality were elected February 9, 1874, and the following chosen: Joseph Taylor, Joseph Mackay, Louis Ricord, Fabien Demers, John Cairns, Charles E. Gray, and Richard Evans. At the first meeting John Cairns was appointed mayor, and H. E. Cairns, secretary-treasurer. It will be noticed that Mr. Cairns was secretary-treasurer from 1855, and also held the same position in the two municipalities until 1883, when he resigned that of the western part, retaining the office for East Clifton to the present day.

The municipality of East Clifton has an area of 10,000 square acres, and a valuation of $100,000. The past mayors have been John Cairns and Richard Evans. The council for 1895 was composed as follows: H. A. Cairns, mayor; and councillors: Samuel Elliott, Geo. S. Hurley, Rob't Taylor, Thos. J. Waldron, William Mackay, and Eloi Crete.

There are four elementary schools. The school commissioners are: Geo. Hurley, chairman; Samuel Elliott, J. R. Macrae, and Wm. Bain.

There are two post offices: East Clifton and Charrington. East Clifton is principally a farming community, and not far distant is a station of the same name on the Maine Central Railway. Daily mail. Postal revenue, 1895, $109.80.

Charrington is three miles south of East Clifton. Daily mail. Near here is a saw and grist mill. Postal revenue, 1895, $14.75.

The early settlers of Clifton township, which for forty years were confined wholly to the present limits of East Clifton, had very few privileges of a religious character. Occasionally they were visited by a minister, but these were few and far between. The first preaching services were conducted by a Baptist minister named Rev. Mr. Ide, about the year 1835. A Rev. Mr. Sweatland, Methodist, preached a few times about 1838, and in 1840 or 1841 Rev. Mr. Gillies, Baptist, held regular services here once a month. In 1848 Rev. John Armstrong, Methodist, commenced regular services. These meetings were all held at first at the homes of the residents, and afterwards transferred to the school house. The Methodists increased in numbers and in 1866 the first church, and still the only church, was erected by this denomination. It is under the Sawyerville circuit, and services held every Sunday afternoon The Episcopal and Presbyterian denominations have each established a fortnightly appointment in East Clifton, their services being regularly held for some five or six years back, at the North school house.

One of the most prosperous parts of East Clifton is that known as High Forest, and located a short distance from Sawyerville. This place was first settled in 1860 or 1861. The first settlers were Edward Graham, John Lee, and Thomas Johnson, all of Lachute, Argenteuil county, Que. They were the only settlers for the first three years, but soon after were followed by others, until now this section is well settled by progressive and successful farmers. The first school here was opened about 1867.

HUGH EGBERT CAIRNS, third son of Hugh and Agnes (Watson) Cairns, was born August 26, 1826, at Rock Hill, near the town of Hillsboro, county Down, Ire. His father, with his family, emigrated to this County in 1843, arriving at East Clifton on the first day of June in that year. Hugh E. Cairns was married December 9, 1851, to Sarah Augusta, only daughter of John Waldron, of East Clifton, and granddaughter to John Waldron, one of the oldest settlers of this Township. Shortly after their marriage they moved on to a farm in the township of Eaton, about one mile from Sawyerville, where they remained two years, then purchased a farm in East Clifton, where they have since lived. In the year 1853, when the first board of school commissioners was elected in this Township, H. E. Cairns accepted the position of secretary-treasurer. This position he held until 1874, when Clifton was divided into two municipalities. From 1874 to 1883, he was secretary-treasurer for both. In 1883 he resigned that of the western municipality, but continues the same position in East Clifton until the present time. In July, 1855, when the first municipal council was elected, Mr. Cairns accepted the position of secretary-treasurer for that corporation, which he has held to the present day, in the same manner as for the board of school commissioners. In 1860 he was appointed justice of the peace. He has been superintendent of the East Clifton Sunday-school continuously from 1852 until the present time. He accepted nomination as a candidate for the representation of this County in opposition to the Hon. J. H. Pope twice, to wit: in 1874 and 1882, but was defeated each time by a large majority. Mr. Cairns' parents and forefathers for many generations were Presbyterians, but in 1847 he united with the Methodist church. He assisted largely in building the present Methodist church at East Clifton, was one of the original trustees appointed before the building was commenced, in 1865, and secretary to the board. He has held the position of class-leader since 1854. Mr. and Mrs. H. E. Cairns have four children : Hollis A., born January 1, 1853, married Sarah Agnes Harkness, of Compton, two children, Ralph C., born February 7, 1890, and Blanche G., born August 27, 1888. He owns and resides on the old homestead. He has been mayor of the council since 1885, having been unanimously appointed to the same position each year. Egbert Elmore, born September 1, 1854, married Eva M. Mayo, September 1, 1885, two children. They moved from Clifton to Bernardston, Mass., in 1892. Justice A., born June 11, 1857, married Hannah, daughter of the late Joseph Taylor, of East Clifton, June 27, 1882, one child. They sold their farm here in 1890, and purchased a farm in Bernardston, Mass. Augusta Maria, born August 19, 1865, married Byron S. Curtis, of Newport, Vt, September 18, 1895; Sarah Jane, born January 30, 1869, married Geo. Hodgen, April 11, 1892, residence, Buckland, Mass.

H. E. CAIRNS AND FAMILY.

WILLIAM MACKAY, farmer, was born in St. Sylvestre, Que., August 20, 1843, where his father, Joseph Mackay, lived and died December 28, 1874. In 1868 he came to High Forest, in East Clifton, about three miles from Sawyerville, where he located in the woods. He has cleared a good farm, erected neat and commodious buildings, and is a prosperous farmer. From nothing but woods, he has seen all this accomplished in twenty-eight years, and by his own hard work. For a number of years he has been a member of the municipal council, to the entire satisfaction of his fellow townsmen. He has been a member of the board of school commissioners. He takes a great interest in Orange Lodge No. 1308, Sawyerville, and at present holds the office of W. M. Mr. Mackay was married at St. Sylvestre, Que., January 2, 1866, to Margaret Macrae. She is a daughter of the late Wm. Macrae, who died in High Forest in 1885. By this marriage there were nine children, eight now living : Joseph Alfred, born March 1, 1870; William Edmund, born January 18, 1872; Arthur Theodore, born October 27, 1881; Chester Lawrence, born October 22, 1883; Esther Ann, born November 1, 1866, married John Curnew, no children, residence Lawrence, Mass ; Lucine, born May 29, 1868, married D. Williams, no children, residence St. Johnsbury, Vt.; Mary Alice, born December 24, 1886; Hetty Lilly, born January 27, 1879. The reader will here

RESIDENCE OF WM. MACKAY.

find an engraving of the residence of Mr. Mackay, in front of which he and his family may be seen. The two ladies in the upper corners are Mrs. Curnew and Mrs. Williams.

CHARLES D. TERRILL, farmer, was born in Stewartstown, N. H., August 15, 1817. He came to East Clifton in March, 1879, where he has since resided. An engraving is here presented of the residence of Mr. Terrill, where in front he and his wife may be seen. He has held the office of councillor, and is a member of the A. F. & A. M., and K. of P. He was married at Canaan, Vt., April 24, 1870, to Melinda, daughter of William Williams, of East Clifton. No children.

EDWARD GRAHAM, farmer, was born in county Monaghan, Ireland, July 5, 1855. In October of the same year his parents came to Canada and he lived in Argenteuil county, until December, 1861. In that year he moved to his present farm in High Forest. He was one of the first settlers of that section, and when Mr. Graham came here there were no roads, and where fine farms may now be seen, there was then nothing but woods. On the next page is an engraving of the home place with Mr. and Mrs. Graham and three of their children in front. This is as pretty a farm house as can be wished for, surrounded by large new barns, showing at a glance how successful he has been in a few years time. Our subject has been school commissioner, and held minor town offices of trust. He was married at Lachute, Que., July 6, 1857, to E. McCormick.

RESIDENCE OF C. D. TERRILL.

Issue, six children: John, born May 5, 1858, married Charlotte McVetty, of High Forest, May 30, 1893, three children, residence, Sawyerville; William D., born September 27, 1865; Richard G., born August 9, 1859, died June 27, 1891; Elizabeth, born November 26, 1861, married Kingston Birch, two children, residence, Sawyerville; Susan Caroline Violet, born June 30, 1863, married Arthur A. Laberee, residence, Sawyerville; Martha Lena, born August 27, 1867.

CLIFTON.

This municipality, now more generally known as Martinville, was again divided on January 1, 1896. After the setting off of East Clifton in 1874, the west part continued as one municipality, growing in population all the time. One section, known as St. Edwidge, is nearly all peopled by French Canadians, while Martinville is composed of English speaking people. Early in 1895, these two sections having sufficient population for two municipalities, steps were taken for a separation. Both had got along in a friendly manner, but as the two classes of people differed so much in their modes of thought and action, it was thought best for both, that they should manage their affairs separately. This was granted by the Provincial Parliament in the fall of 1895, the English portion retaining the

RESIDENCE OF EDWARD GRAHAM.

name of Clifton, while that of the French Canadians adopted the name Ste. Edwidge de Clifton. The history of the latter municipality is taken up at the end of this chapter.

The municipal affairs of Clifton, previous to January, 1896, were carried on amicably, with council meetings held at St. Edwidge. Charles McClary was chosen mayor, in 1872, previous to the setting off of East Clifton, and continued in this office until 1893. Gilbert Marchesseault was mayor for two years, when he was followed in 1895 by C. N. Cass, the present mayor of the new municipality of Clifton. Mr. H. E. Cairns continued as secretary-treasurer of East Clifton and Clifton until 1883, when he resigned from the latter, and Mr. G. Boulay was appointed. The council of Clifton for 1895 was composed as follows: C. N. Cass, mayor, and councillors G. Marchesseault, John Johnston, Lyman Smith, Adelard Plante, Antoine Rabouin, and Henri Désoicy; G. Boulay, secretary-treasurer.

The present municipality of Clifton, or Martinville, comprises fifty-five lots. Has a valuation of $96,000, and a population of four hundred and fifty.

The first settler in Martinville was Daniel Martin, after whom the place is named. For several years it was known as Martin's Mills. He came here about 1838, and at once realized the value of the water-power here. The Salmon river passes through the village. He built a dam, and erected a saw mill. The latter was partly over the dam, and had an old-fashioned upright saw. He first erected a bridge across the river, which was covered with poles for a flooring. He also built the first house, which is now occupied by Wm. Furse. Daniel Martin did not live long, as he died within a few years, from injuries received from a fall, while repairing roof of mill. His brother, Amasa Martin, took over the property and carried it on thereafter. The second pioneer was Thomas Pierce, a great hunter, and brother of Wilder Pierce, of Stanstead. He came to Martinville with his family in the winter of 1842, and settled on the Eaton road, about one mile from the village. He, as well as the other settlers, came in the winter time, as this was the only way to get through, there being nothing but a bridle path from Compton. In 1843 John Haines arrived with his family and settled on the Ste. Edwidge road, in what is now known as the Haines neighborhood. On January 19, 1846, John T. Cass came to Martinville, also with his family. He, as well as the three families before mentioned, came from Stanstead. Mr. Cass settled nearer the present village, not far from Haines. Other settlers soon followed until this is now a thriving part of the County. They at first suffered all the hardships of pioneers, living in log houses for several years.

The road through to Moes River was opened about 1845. In 1869, Carlos N. Cass, a son of John T. Cass, in company with E. B. Bean, purchased the saw mill of Amasa Martin. In 1870 Cass bought out Bean, and in May, 1871, his brother, Orville A., purchased an interest in same, and the business to this day is carried on by Cass Bros. The present saw mill was built in 1872. About 1872 Amasa Martin erected the frame for a grist mill, which commenced running about 1875. In 1876 the grist mill was also purchased by Cass Bros. These are the only power mills in the place.

The post office here was opened in 1858, and a small store at about the same time. From Compton station, eight miles distant, the mail is brought daily. A new road to Johnville, on the Canadian Pacific Railway, has been opened within the last two or three years, which makes the latter the nearest railway station by several miles. The postal revenue for 1895 was $265.

The industries of this place are a saw and grist mill, two blacksmith shops, cheese factory, carriage shop, butcher, etc.; three stores kept by C. Smith & Son, E. Green, and Mrs. F. Pierce. The latter is postmistress.

There are three Protestant elementary schools in the new municipality, and by the act of incorporation a new board of school commissioners is to be elected in July, Ste. Edwidge and Clifton being united until then for school purposes.

At the election of councillors on January 2, 1896, the following were chosen:—L. A. Smith, C. N. Cass, J. A. Sherman, Wm. Sherman, Archie Thompson, Noah Hinds, and C. L. Caswell. At their first meeting C. N. Cass was chosen mayor, and John Johnston secretary-treasurer.

In 1874 the only church in the village was built. It belongs to the Methodist denomination, and is under the charge of the Compton circuit. Services are held every Sunday afternoon. No other denominations hold services here now. Rev. Mr. Gillies, Baptist minister at Sawyerville, occasionally held services here during his ministry.

LYMAN A. SMITH, butcher and farmer, was born in Eaton, August 18, 1853. His father is Thomas Smith, still living in Eaton. On next page is presented an engraving of the residence of Mr. Smith, and in front he and family may be seen. He was married in Eaton, November 29, 1877, to Emma, daughter of James Mills. Mr. Mills died in Bury in 1858. Issue, two

HISTORY OF COMPTON COUNTY.

RESIDENCE OF L. A. SMITH.

children: Hollis Austin, born April 23, 1882; Lula Emma, born October 3, 1885. Mr. Smith for several years was one of the councillors, and a school commissioner in the old township of Clifton when it was connected with Ste Edwidge. On the coming into force of the new township of Clifton, in January, 1896, comprising Martinville alone, he was elected by acclamation one of the first councillors. He is also a steward in the Methodist church, and Sunday-school superintendent.

CARLOS N. CASS, grist and saw mill owner and lumber dealer, was born in Stanstead, January 20, 1838. He came to Martinville in 1846, and previous to going into his present business was a farmer. He has held the office of councillor for thirteen years, and in 1895 was mayor of Clifton. He also was elected mayor of the new town of Clifton created in January, 1896. Mr. Cass has always taken a leading part in the work of the Methodist church in his place, and is now one of the trustees and a class leader. His father, John T. Cass, died in Martinville, February 4, 1877. Mr. Cass has been married twice, first at Compton to Sarah A. Clark, January 3, 1866, died February 27, 1868; second marriage at Compton, March 2, 1870, to Lora A. (born June 5, 1849), daughter of Nathan Pierce, who died in Compton, July 22, 1884. Issue, four children: Delbert Oren, born March 19, 1883; Merna A., born January 11, 1871; Hattie Elinor, born July 22, 1874; Bella May, born October 5, 1885. The engraving accompanying this sketch is of the residence of Mr. Cass, located just east of his mills. The group in front is Mr. and Mrs. Cass and family.

RESIDENCE OF C. N. CASS.

GEORGE GROOME, farmer and mason, a resident of Martinville, was born in England, November 5, 1822. He came to Compton county in 1836, and previous to moving to Martinville, lived in Bury and Eaton. He married Celistia S. Coates, who was born in Eaton May 18, 1824. Issue, five children: James E., born January 10, 1848, married Susan Caswell, residence, Clifton, four children; Herbert E., born March 22, 1855, married Villa Rice, residence, Lancaster, N. H., four children; Persis L., born November 11, 1852, married Lischer Griffin, three children; Alzina E., born November 11, 1867, married Wilkes Pope, two children; Alice J., born March 25, 1862, married Lysander Davis, two children. The three daughters live in Clifton.

ALONZO T. MERRILL, farmer, resident of Martinville, was born in Stockholme, N. Y., January 14, 1843. Came to Clifton in 1844. Has been school commissioner, and is now valuator and rural inspector. Was married in Eaton, April 28, 1868, to Eunice Lacy. Issue, five children: Willie A., born April 28, 1875; Alice M., born March 3, 1869; Celia F., born October 4, 1878; Ida B., born May 26, 1884; Annie C., born March 27, 1890.

BENJAMIN N. HAINES, farmer, resident of Martinville, was born in Stanstead, May 4, 1835. Moved to Martinville in 1843. Has held office of councillor. His father, John Haines, died 1877. He was member of first council of Clifton. In Compton, December 30, 1863, Mr. Haines married Sarah F., born July 13, 1840, daughter of Thomas Pierce, first mayor of Clifton. They have one adopted daughter: Emma Louisa, born March 11, 1873.

JAMES E. GROOME, farmer, a resident of Martinville, was born in Eaton, January 10, 1848. His father, George Groome, is still living in Martinville. Mr. Groome was first married to Augusta Barrey. Second marriage to Susan E. Caswell. Issue, four children: Lydia J., born January 25, 1876; Chloe Mary, born July 12, 1886; George Mason, born September 18, 1889; Eva Rose, born April 24, 1892. Our subject holds the office of chaplain in the R. T. of T.

DENSMORE C. PIERCE, a resident of Martinville, was born in Compton, April 23, 1851. Married Emma J. Rogers, of Eaton. Issue, four children, three living: Sternie E., born June 7, 1885; Della M., born January 25, 1878; Dora E., born August 22, 1882.

EDWIN BUTLER, farmer, was born at Lennoxville, March 9, 1865. In 1867 he moved into the township of Eaton and afterwards to the township of Clifton. Was married January 12, 1892, at Lennoxville, to Anna M., daughter of Frederick D. Burton, of Ascot, and widow of Fred. Broadbelt. Issue, two children: Clifford Stanley, born February 24, 1895; Mabel Elizabeth, born October 22, 1892. The step-son, Henry W. Broadbelt, was born July 10, 1888. John Butler (father) was married in England in 1852, and died in the township of Eaton, 1894.

ORIEN A. ADAMS, millwright, son of William P. Adams, who died in 1895, was born November 15, 1852, in Newport, Vt.; came to Martinville in 1888. Married Lucy J., daughter of Roderick Hunt. Issue, two children: Frank and Jane.

WILLIAM AUGUSTUS PIERCE, farmer, was born in Stanstead, August 31, 1834, moved to Martinville in 1841. Married in Clifton, June 11, 1861, to Maria Merrill, born January 2, 1845. Issue, three children: Wilder W., born August 21, 1863, married Emma Merrill, residence, Martinville, two children; Wilber A., born February 17, 1872; Frank B., born February 8, 1881.

HISTORY OF COMPTON COUNTY.

JOSIAH J. PARSONS, farmer and mason, resident of Martinville, was born in Bury, September 22, 1841. Married Effie May Parker, of Kirby, Vt. Issue, six children: Guy D., born August 26, 1877; Merriett P., born January 3, 1885; Thirza M., born March 4, 1876; Tina E., born May 14, 1882; Dessie E., born June 20, 1887; Isabelle E., born December 10, 1892.

FREDERICK E. SMITH, general merchant at Martinville, was born in Eaton, March 27, 1871. Married December 16, 1891, to Hattie Alice, daughter of Carlos R. Bailey, of Clifton.

JOSEPH LEMAY, farmer, was born in Halifax, N. S., and came to Clifton in 1867. Was married here in 1868 to Rozalie Paire. Issue, fifteen children, seven living: John, Francis, Zoëlle, Delina, Marianne, Florence, Clarida.

LISCHER DEMMON GRIFFIN, farmer and patent medicine manufacturer, is a resident near Leavitt's Mills, Clifton. He was born in Morgan, Vt., December 11, 1847; came to Canada in 1857 with his parents, Silas and Julia A. (Parker) Griffin, jr., who settled near Johnville, in Eaton, in 1865. Silas Griffin died March 10, 1876. His wife died in Charleston, Vt., August 1, 1895. Mr. Griffin moved to his present farm in 1875, and now holds the office of school commissioner. He was married at Moes River, July 15, 1869, to Persis L. Groome. Issue, three children: George Westley, born June 29, 1870, died December 20, 1883; Josie Ednah, born June 25, 1878, died December 4, 1883; Lischer Raymond, born March 15, 1890.

LATE FREDERICK PIERCE, born in Brompton, Que., December 3, 1829, died May 2, 1895. Came to Martinville in 1876. At time of his death he was postmaster and mail contractor, and general merchant at Martinville. He married Amy L., daughter of Otis Chillson, Esq., of Massawippi, Que. One adopted daughter, Mary E., born May 11, 1861, married Joseph Cox, two children.

JAMES MACKEY, farmer, was born in St. Sylvestre, Que., January 11, 1844. Came to Clifton in 1868. Married in Sherbrooke in 1877 to Jessie M. Alderich. Issue, one child: Alexander A., born March 12, 1878.

JOSHUA MARTIN, farmer, was born May 20, 1832. Came to Compton in 1853, and later moved to Clifton. Married September 2, 1856, to Mary J. Paul, of Compton. Issue, nine children: Joseph, born July 28, 1860, married Isabel Plumbley, two children; James A., born November 12, 1862, married Idella Merrill, two children; John, born December 22, 1864, married Jennie M. McDonald, two children; Levi H., born May 9, 1867; Joshua, born May 7, 1869; Fred. C., born November 4, 1881; Ellen A., born October 30, 1870, married Clarence F. Cass, one child; Eliza J., born July 2, 1873, married George Merrill, one child; Hattie J., born December 23, 1878.

BENJAMIN COOK BAILEY, farmer, was born at Compton, March 2, 1832. Resided at different times in the townships of Eaton, Clifton and Compton. Formerly carried on the trade of shoemaker. Has held the office of road inspector. Married at Morgan, Vt., March 27, 1855, to Thirza Jane, daughter of the late W. C. Parker. Issue, four children: Clarence C., born December 27, 1855, married Hannah Butler, residence, Clifton, one child; Gladys O., born September 7, 1894; Lillian R., born February 16, 1866, married George H. Parker, residence, Compton. Two children (twins), died in infancy, Loren E. and Laura E., born January 8, 1860. Joseph Bailey, father of the subject of this sketch, died in Compton in 1846.

ABNER W. PARSONS, farmer, resident of Martinville, was born in Compton, August 2, 1823. His father, Joseph S. Parsons, was born in Gilmantown, N. H., in 1796, and moved into Compton with the early settlers about 1820, where he died in 1859. Our subject was married July 16, 1850, to Thankful D. Hyatt, of Ascot. Issue, four children: Joseph, born August 11, 1854; Willie, born June 2, 1857; Ella R., born July 29, 1852, married Garvin Goudie, three children; Maraetta, born November 22, 1860, married Henry Merrill, two children.

LATE NELSON D. HITCHCOCK, in his lifetime of Martinville, died December 14, 1893. He married Miss R. C., daughter of John Haines, a councillor of Clifton for many years. She was born in Stanstead in 1840, Issue, three children: Guy, born September 9, 1876; Nora, born March 5, 1871; Effie, born June 25, 1878.

LATE DANFORTH HASELTINE, born in Cookshire, December 7, 1826, died in West Clifton, July 13, 1894. In his life time he was a school teacher, later mill owner and lumber manufacturer. He always lived in the county. He held the offices of school commissioner and councillor. For twenty-eight years he was trustee of the Methodist church at Bulwer. On November, 17, 1858, at Sherbrooke, he married Mary McClary. Issue, two children: Charles Franklin, born August 9, 1872; Cleora Frances, born July 13, 1866.

WILLIAM JAMES MAYHEW, farmer, born in Bury, July 18, 1866; moved to Clifton in 1872. First marriage at Martinville to Cynthia M. Groome. Issue, one child: Lillian Etta, born November 8, 1883, died January 8, 1894. Second marriage January 2, 1895, to Lydia J. Groome. Mr. Mayhew's father, James, was born in Bury, February 28, 1841, and his mother (Elizabeth Parsons) in England, December 23, 1835. They were married in Eaton, August 6, 1861.

SAINT EDWIDGE DE CLIFTON.

This is a new municipality created out of Clifton, on January 1, 1896, by Act of the Provincial Parliament passed in 1895, and comprises lots one to seventeen inclusive of the fifth, sixth, seventh, eighth, ninth, tenth and eleventh ranges of the old municipality of the township of Clifton.

The first settler in this municipality was Charles McClary, the present member for Compton in the Quebec Legislature. When he moved here with his wife in 1855, there was no road nearer than eight miles. He commenced on his present holding when it was nothing but woods, and has made for himself a good farm. Jos. A. Courtemanche, who worked for Mr. McClary, a short time after took up land for a farm next to his, and thus the settlement of this place commenced.

St. Edwidge de Clifton now contains about eight hundred souls, mostly of French descent, with one Catholic church, over which ably presides Rev. Wilfred Morache. There are also in the municipality eight elementary schools. The school commissioners are Pierre Gosselin, chairman, Auguste Gervais, Ferdinando Scalabrini, Antoine Raboin, and Celase Rivard; G. Boulay, secretary-treasurer.

St. Edwidge Post Office is a thriving little village, with saw and grist mills, good store, cheese factory, and other small shops. It is ten miles from Coaticook, and the same distance from Compton. Daily mail. G. Boulay, postmaster. Postal revenue, 1895, $203.

CHAPTER XV.

Township of Newport.

Under the hand and seal of Robert Shore Milnes, baronet, lieutenant-governor, etc., a warrant was issued for the survey of a tract of land, bounded north by Bury, east by Ditton, south by Auckland, and west by Eaton, which, when sub-divided into 308 lots, beside the allowance for highways, was erected into a township named Newport, July 4, 1801. One-fourth of this Township was granted to Edmund Heard and his associates, viz.: Samuel Hurd, Longley Willard, Edmund Heard, the younger, Nathaniel Beaman, the younger, Peter Trueman, John Squires, William Heard, William Hudson, Elisha Hudson, and Caleb Sturtevant.

From records in existence relative to the first settlement of this township, the following has been gleaned: In 1791 Alured Clark, then governor of Lower Canada, issued a proclamation for granting the waste lands of the Crown into townships of ten miles square, to applicants, in free and common soccage. In consequence thereof, Stephen Williams, of Danbury, Vt., petitioned for a township by the name of Newport, to be granted to himself and forty associates, the prayer for which was approved. But the said Stephen Williams neglected to come forward, as was expected, but Edmund Heard, one of the associates, did, in 1793, in company with Josiah Sawyer, set out from Missiskoui Bay, on Lake Champlain, with provisions, tools, etc., through the woods, ninety miles from inhabitants, to the westward, and after traveling and exploring the woods thirty-one days, arrived on a hill, now called Pleasant Hill, in Newport. Here he and the said Sawyer commenced to make improvements, distant twenty-five miles from inhabitants to the south, and seventy miles from the French settlements to the north. In the year 1794 Sawyer moved in his family, and in 1795 Heard moved in his family also. Finding that the said Williams did not come forward, Edmund Heard, on June 24, 1797, petitioned the goverment that the said township be granted to him and his associates. Accordingly, on March 22, 1800, an order of council was passed in his favor. It was not until July 4, 1801, that the letters patent for the land were issued.

In this township was probably held the first public municipal meetings of any in the Eastern Townships. By again referring to these old records, we find there was a meeting held of the associates and inhabitants of the township of Newport, by notification, at the house of Asa Waters, on September 28, 1799, at which Asa Waters was chosen moderator, and Edmund Heard, clerk. Messrs. Samuel Hurd, Wm. Hudson, and John LeBourveau were appointed "as a committee to form some necessary regulations for the inhabitants of said township." These regulations were unanimously accepted at a public meeting held October 3, 1799. By assessing the inhabitants through these annual meetings, several roads were made in Newport. The minutes also show that they assisted in 1802 in building a road from the house of John Ward, in Ascot, to Nicolet or Three Rivers. The amount so contributed was twelve and a half days work each, of four men, amounting to $50. In 1803 they raised $107 to improve and alter the road to Connecticut river, passing through Clifton. Payments were made sometimes in money, but generally in wheat. One bushel of wheat equaled one dollar, and was generally the commodity of exchange, rather than money. The last of these records is signed by David Metcalf, clerk, under date September 12, 1814. It was the next year that many of the inhabitants commenced to leave owing to failure of crops, and not until after 1820 did the old settlers return, or new ones come in. No further municipal records are known of until 1841, when the Government established district councils. The manner in which the records above referred to were kept up indicates that the first settlers of Newport were an order-loving and efficient class of men.

In 1815 Captain Samuel Hurd, who had been one of the most active and public-spirited men in the settlement from the first, was unfortunately drowned at Brompton Falls. This melancholy event cast a gloom over the minds of the people of Newport, who now realized how much they had depended on him; and over the prospects of the settlement of which he had been a ruling spirit.

The present municipal records of Newport date back to 1855, when the first principles of the present law came into force. On July 23, 1855, the following councillors were chosen: Alden Learned, Charles Sawyer, Samuel Hurd, Wm. G. Planche, Gilbert T. Williams, Charles B. Hawley, and Wm. Stevenson, jr. Since then the following gentlemen have held the office of mayor: Alden Learned, Samuel Heard, Wm. G. Planche, Joshua Nourse, C. D. Chaddock, W. W. Bailey, Geo. G. Hurd, S. N. Hurd, and E. Learned. There have been only two secretary-treasurers in the township: Charles H. Harvey, who held the office from the first until the appointment of Mr. R. H. Wilford. The council for 1895 was formed as follows: A. S. Farnsworth, mayor, and councillors Geo. W. L. French, John Kidd, H. B. Learned, N. C. Rand, Edward Dawson, and Robert Halliday.

Newport contains 61,600 square acres, and has a valuation of $355,536. The industries of the township are G. W. L. French's saw and grist mill, Lyon's clapboard and shingle mill, T. F. French's shingle mill, at Island Brook; and G. S. D. Rand's saw, shingle and grist mill at Randboro. A large part of the east end of the township is still well timbered. The west end is nearly all settled, with good farms, and progressive farmers.

The associates and first inhabitants located in the south-west corner, around Randboro. The first settlement made at Learned Plain was by Alden Learned, after whom the place is named. He was a son of Ebenezer Learned, one of the first settlers in Eaton, who located at Cookshire. Mr. Alden Learned spent his boyhood days around Cookshire. In the fall of 1823 he made the first opening at Learned Plain, and there he labored alone for nearly ten years. Not until 1830 did other settlers begin to arrive; shortly after the first school was started. It was principally by the efforts of Mr. Learned, and under his guidance, that the roads to and through Learned Plain, in all directions, were first built. He met with and over came strenuous opposition. It was through him the road to Ditton, now known as the Island Brook road, was first built. On this road is a small stream called Christmas brook, so named by the surveyors having reached thus far on a Christmas Day.

At Randboro and Island Brook are Anglican and Methodist churches, while the latter place also has a Roman Catholic chapel. The history of the Methodist and Catholic denominations is to be found in the history of these churches in the township of Eaton. That of the Anglican is here given.

Christ's church, Island Brook—This church is a wooden structure, consisting of nave and chancel. It was built in 1875, the principal movers in the work of building being Messrs. S. Wood, Wm. Dawson, R. H. Wilford and James Weston. The Rev. E. C. Parkin was missionary of this district at the time. The cost of the building was upwards of $1,000. It has just been thoroughly renovated inside, and is now a very pretty and thoroughly churchly structure. Messrs. Geo. W. L. French and R. H. Wilford are the present wardens, and the Rev. A. H. Moore, B.A., is the incumbent. Past incumbents: Revs. E. C. Parkin, A. H. Judge, A. H. Robertson, T. Rudd, and H. A. Dickson, M. A.

St. Matthew's church, Randboro—This church owes its existence to the real missionary ardor of Rev. A. H. Judge, and to the able support given to his efforts by Asher B. Jones, sr., Wm. Loveland, Augustus Hurd, R. Dawson and Asher B. Jones, jr. The church, which is a pretty Gothic one, was built of wood in 1883. In 1893 the interior was ceiled in hard wood, and the church is now an exceedingly pretty one. The present wardens are Messrs. H. H. Hunt and C. H. Loveland. Rev. A. H. Moore, B.A., resides at Randboro, having both the Island Brook and Randboro churches under his charge.

The statistics given by the census of 1891, are as follows, for the township of Newport: Population, 1,121; families, 225; houses, 221; males, 595; females, 526; French Canadians 99; others, 1,022. Religions—Roman Catholic, 254; Church of England, 303; Presbyterians, 89; Methodists, 347; Bible Christians, 1; Lutherans, 1; Baptists, 51; Freewill Baptists, 21; Congregationalists, 28; Adventists, 22; Universalists, 2; not specified, 2

In this township are located five post offices—Island Brook, Learned Plain, Randboro, Maple Leaf, and New Mexico.

Island Brook is located eight miles east of Cookshire, the nearest railway station. Has a daily mail. Postal revenue, 1895, $187.50. Settlement was commenced here about 1870, and for a while progressed rapidly. North river passes through the place, on which are several mills. Just below the village it descends in a quick chute of sixty or seventy feet. Here is located the town hall and office of the secretary-treasurer, also a Royal Templars' hall.

Learned Plain is four and a half miles east of Cookshire, the nearest railway station. It is the centre of good farming lands. Mail daily. Postal revenue, 1895, $41.

Randboro is two miles east of Sawyerville, and eight miles south of Cookshire. Here are saw and grist mills, store, cheese factory, etc. Daily mail. Postal revenue, 1895, $113 90.

Maple Leaf is two miles east of Randboro and ten miles from Cookshire. It is the centre of a farming community. Mail daily. Postal revenue, 1895, $17.

New Mexico is six miles from Sawyerville, and four miles from Island Brook. Farming community. Mail tri-weekly. Postal revenue, 1895, $14.

EBENEZER LEARNED, farmer, was born at Learned Plain, where he still resides, December 7, 1831. His father, Alden Learned, after whom the post office is named, was born at Cookshire, March 31, 1803. In the fall of 1823 he took up land on lot 1, range 3, Newport, located where our subject now lives. He was the first settler in that section, and although he done well, suffered all the necessary hardships. There were no roads, and all provisions, etc., had to be brought in by a spotted line. Up to 1830 he lived in a shanty, but in that year he built a log house, and on February 24, 1831, married Sally Mallory. They had a family of five children, viz.: Ebenezer, Samuel, Sarah M., Royal, and John M. After living in this log house ten years Mr. Learned erected the brick house now occupied by his son Ebenezer. The clay he hauled from the brook on H. Metcalf's farm, and sand from near the Cookshire cemetery, making his own bricks. He was a man of strong mind and good judgment, which has descended to the present generation. He was closely connected with the development of Newport, and one of the leading men in municipal affairs. He was a justice of the peace, and captain of the Newport Militia. In May, 1868, his wife died. He lived until his eighty-second year, when he died suddenly of apoplexy. Our subject, Ebenezer Learned, has held all of the municipal offices, such as school commissioner, councillor, mayor, and minor offices, to the perfect satisfaction of his townsmen. At present he is one of the valuators, also auditor, and has been postmaster for over twenty-six years. He is also a trustee in the Congregational church. We give herewith an engraving of the residence of Mr. Learned, in front of which he may be seen, also Mrs. Learned and

HISTORY OF COMPTON COUNTY.

RESIDENCE OF EBENEZER LEARNED.

their two daughters, Mrs. T. F. French and baby, and Mrs. B. Lebourveau. He was married in Eaton, September 30, 1857, to Helen Isabella, daughter of the late Andrew Brown. Issue, five children: Homer B., born May 27, 1858, married Elizabeth Beattie, four children, residence Learned Plain; Elsie Maria, born November 12, 1859, married Edgar G. Smith, three children, residence Eaton; Evelyn Eliza, born October 20, 1862, married Joseph C. Smith, two children, residence Eaton; Emma Mary, born August 14, 1867, married Thomas F. French, one child, residence Island Brook; Sarah Helen, born December 9, 1871, married Benjamin Lebourveau, residence Eaton. Additional history about early records of the Learned family may be found with that of J. F. Learned, Cookshire.

HOMER B. LEARNED, farmer, was born at Learned Plain, on the farm which he carries on with his father, May 27, 1858. He is an only son of Ebenezer Learned, and grandson of Alden Learned, after whom the place received its name. He was chairman of the school commissioners for three years, and is a member of the council, also secretary of the P. of I. Association. Was married in Brompton September 21, 1880, to Elizabeth, daughter of Wm. Beattie, of Brompton. Issue, four children: Wm. Gordon, born December 9, 1883; Ronald Brown, born September 17, 1887; Frank Beattie, born May 30, 1890; Genie Helen, born December 14, 1881. Herewith is an engraving of the residence of Mr. Learned, with himself and family in front. It is one of the most attractive homes in the township.

RESIDENCE OF H. B. LEARNED.

ARTEMAS STEVENS FARNSWORTH, farmer, mayor of Newport, and warden of Compton county for 1895, was born near Flanders, Eaton, December 3, 1855. He has always resided in Eaton and Newport, his present farm being located near Flanders, in the township of Newport. He is a son of David Albert Farnsworth, of Eaton. He has been one of the councillors for eight years, and mayor for three years. He is agent for the B. A. L. Co. Mr. Farnsworth takes a great interest in public affairs, and his fellow citizens have confidence in him. He was married in Newport, October 9, 1884, to Luvia A., daughter of Lewis L. Bowker. Issue, four children: Lewis Bowker, born January 20, 1886; Chas. Albert, born December 21, 1887; Agnes Stevens, born May 6, 1890; Henry Alton, born November 14, 1892.

GARDNER STILLMAN DODGE RAND, farmer, and mill owner, resident of Randboro, was born in this Township, May 8, 1830, and always resided here. His father, Artemas D. Rand, came to Newport with his parents, when a small boy, from Connecticut, and died here in 1877, aged eighty-three years. He served in the war of 1812, on the British side. Our subject held the offices of councillor and school commissioner for several years. He married Celestia Annett, daughter of Russell Williams, of Eaton. Mr. Williams died in 1867, aged sixty-two years. Issue, seven children: Flora A., born June 3, 1855, married Austin S. Rand, residence, Randboro; Corrilla F., born May 15, 1857, married A. G. Jones, residence, Randboro; Hollis G., born November 24, 1858, married Florence H. Mildram, of South Braintree, Mass.; Alice Adella, born August 30, 1861, married Moses H. Cairns; Luna M., born December 11, 1865, married Benjamin S. Seale, residence, Maple Leaf, one child; Lucia A., born May 30, 1867, married Moses H. Cairns, residence, Randboro; Myrtie M., born October 30, 1875.

HERMAN ALTON STEVENSON, farmer, resident of Learned Plain, was born June 6, 1867, on the farm where he now lives. He is school commissioner, organizer for the Patrons of Industry, and a prominent officer of the I. O. F. Married at Randboro, September 27, 1893, to Ella Kate Hodge. Issue, one child: Beulah Ella, born May 30, 1895. His father, Wm. Stevenson, was born in Hereford, September 11, 1822, moving to Learned Plain in 1827. He held the office of councillor for fourteen years. Married January 1, 1851, near Randboro, to Matilda R. Hurd. Issue, seven children, six living: Horace N., born March 10, 1858, married Rose Goodenough, residence, Learned Plain, three children; Mary E., born March 1, 1846, married Elijah Leggett, residence, Auckland, two children; Lucy A., born August 28, 1851, married Herman F. Gates, residence, Cookshire, one child; Sarah J., born July 6, 1854, married Isaac Goodenough, residence, South Ham, four children; Edith M. M., born April 21, 1863, married Thomas P. Studd, residence, Ware, Mass.

COURT ISLAND BROOK, No. 605, I. O. F., was instituted on August 5, 1890, by John W. Stocks, H.S. Meetings have been regularly held at Island Brook, usually with good attendance, and the Court is in a flourishing condition. The first officers were: A. F. Bowen, C.D.H.C.R.; H. N. Stevenson, C.R.; G. W. L. French, V.C.R.; M. W. Bowen, R.S.; H. A. Stevenson, F.S.; Wm. Morrow, treasurer; F. Burns, chaplain; T. French, S.W.; R. Lavallier, J.W.; Wm. J. Kerr, S.B.; E. Phelps, J. B.; E. E. Bowen, P.C.R.; A. E. Orr, M.D., physician. The foregoing officers with the following, comprised the charter members: Arthur H. Dawson, Alvin M. Lebourveau, Herman F. Gates, Benj. Lebourveau, Frederick G. Goodenough, and Austin A. Stevenson. The following members have been initiated since organization: Wm. Thompson, W. P. Hodgkins, C. W. Stevenson, H. J. Nourse, John A. Quinn, Wm. Nourse, John Nourse, Mark Holbrook, W. H. Gates, W. H. Raney, Richard Seale, Joseph A. Seale, Arthur W. Alden, Arthur A. Allison, A. W. Burns, Arthur Dawson, Isaac Westgate, James Simpson, Augustin

Sherman. The officers at the present time are: H. A. Stevenson, C.D.H.C.R.; Herman F. Gates, C.R.; G. W. L. French, V.C.R.; H. J. Nourse, R.S.; W. H. Gates, financial secretary; Mark Holbrook, treasurer; F. G. Goodenough, chaplain; A. F. Bowen, S.W.; R. Lavallier, J. W.; W. Morrow, S.R.: E. E. Bowen, J.B.; Benj. Lebourvean, P.C.R. Herewith is found an engraving of the officers and most of the members of this court.

EZEKIEL ELLIOTT BOWEN, blacksmith and farmer, was born in Compton, June 19, 1842. He has lived in Ascot and Moes River, and is now a resident of Island Brook. His father,

MEMBERS OF COURT ISLAND BROOK, No. 68, I. O. F.

Israel Bowen, died at Island Brook, December 18, 1887, aged seventy-seven years. Mr. Bowen was married at Huntingville, Que., March 26, 1863, to Susan, daughter of Lyndolph Caswell, Esq., who died at Johuville, May 29, 1888, aged eighty-four years. Our subject has held the office of school commissioner, and is a member of the I. O. F., holding the office of financial secretary. By the above marriage there are three children: Maurice W., born May 4, 1871, married Jennie I. Chandler, of Bartlett, N. H., January 1, 1896, residence, Robinson; Henry L., born July 2, 1872, married Lizzie M. Tracey, of Bartlett, N. H., May 22, 1895, residence, Bartlett, N. H.; Inez E. B., born June 17, 1876.

EDWARD TIMOTHY ANNABLE, farmer, was born in Newport, November 16, 1843, where he still resides. Previous to taking up farming, he worked at his trade as shoemaker. He is a son of the late Charles Annable. Married first at Compton, Que., June 22, 1868, to Amelia, daughter of Alvin Farwell; second marriage at Newport, Que., January 12, 1876, to Mary Anne, daughter of John Halliday; third marriage at Dudswell, Que., June 11, 1889, to Carrie, daughter of Benjamin Smith. Issue, one son: Frederick Gilman, born October 17, 1893.

RICHARD HAWLEY WILFORD, general merchant, was born at Cookshire, October 3, 1829. He is a son of the late Richard Wilford, who died in Cookshire in November, 1853. For many years Mr. R. H. Wilford resided in Cookshire, but on the opening up of Island Brook, and rush of settlers to the territory thereabouts, several years ago, he moved to that place and opened a general store. Herewith we present an engraving of the store, to which the house is attached, and in front may be seen Mr. Wilford and his youngest son Harold. For a number of years he has held the appointment of postmaster, and is also secretary-treasurer for the municipal council and the school commissioners. He was postmaster at Cookshire for seventeen years previous to going to Island Brook. Mr. Wilford is a man highly respected by all. He was married at Cookshire, April 16, 1862, to Eliza J., daughter of the late Japheth W. Dexter, of Orono, Me. Issue, five children, three living: Agnes M., born December 14, 1862, died May 3, 1865; Frederick R., born April 27, 1866, married Maud M. Deacon, of Lindsay, Ont., residence Cookshire; Agnes M., born May 15, 1869, married Robert A. Darker, residence Cookshire; John W., born November 23, 1873, died January 3, 1896; W. Harold, born December 3, 1878.

POST OFFICE AND STORE OF R. H. WILFORD.

WILLARD S. RAND, farmer, was born in the township of Newport, November 28, 1854, and has always lived here. He has held the office of school commissioner, and is now valuator. Married at Lennoxville, December 11, 1878, to Sarah McCurdy. Issue, one son: Scott G., born August 13, 1881.

JOHN WILLIAM PLANCHE, farmer, was born at Currier Hill, Eaton, April 9, 1843. At present he is postmaster at Maple Leaf, having been a councillor for several years. Married at Eaton Corner, October 6, 1868, to Leonora Williams. Issue, three children: Frederick A., born March 1, 1871; Eva M., born July 20, 1869; Florence J., born March 29, 1878.

NEWELL C. RAND, farmer, was born April 21, 1850, in the township of Newport, where he has always lived. He holds the office of councillor, and is secretary of the P. of I. Married at Lennoxville, November 19, 1873, to Laura McCurdy. Issue, four children: Alonzo A., born September 19, 1883; Marshall N. W., born August 22, 1888; Mary M., born March 9, 1879; Edna S. E , born November 30, 1885.

JOHN FRENCH, farmer, was born March 19, 1824, in Cornwall, Eng. He came to Canada and settled on his present farm, located near Flanders, in the township of Eaton, in 1843. Accompanying this sketch is a reproduction of a photograph of the home place with Mr. French and his whole family in front. In the upper left hand corner are the portraits of John W.

RESIDENCE OF JOHN FRENCH.

and Charles D. French, sons of our subject. They are two enterprising young men who have taken a deep interest in telephone lines and electric light plants. About 1891 they built an extensive line of telephone through Eaton, connecting with points in Newport, Bury, Scotstown, and elsewhere. This they sold to the Bell Telephone Company, in 1893. In the same year they put in an an electric light plant for Sawyerville, which they still run successfully. In 1895 they built the telephone line from Sawyerville, through East Clifton, to Beecher Falls, Vt., by contract for the Canadian Telephone Company. By their past enterprise we may expect to hear favorably from them in the future. Our subject, Mr. John French, was married in Eaton, October 14, 1858, to Emma J., daughter of George Parsons, deceased. Issue, nine children: Frederick W., born July 31, 1859, married Eliza Jane Bridgette, residence, Sawyerville, one child ; John W., born June 27, 1866; Charles D., born June 19, 1870;

HISTORY OF COMPTON COUNTY.

Abel E., born March 7, 1876; Ella J., born January 29, 1861, married Benj. Farnsworth, residence, Flanders, one child; Alice M., born October 28, 1862, married Eugene Baldwin, residence, Dixville, one child; Annie E., born Aug. 20, 1864; Emma C., born August 3, 1873.

EDMUND HASKELL HURD, farmer, a resident of Maple Leaf, was born here in 1836, a son of Edmund Hurd, who came from Massachusetts, and died in 1852. First marriage in Ascot, September 24, 1863, to Eliza McCurdy, deceased. Issue, four children: Laura Abigail, born April 26, 1865, married Valentine Swail, 1886, two children, residence Newport; Mary Maria, born November 5, 1870; Sarah Eliza, born November 26, 1875, married December 27, 1893, Augustus Hurd, jr ; Jessie Minerva, born October 4, 1878. Mr. Hurd's second marriage was to Adeline Whitcomb, at Sawyerville, February 17, 1892.

RESIDENCE OF R. L. TODD.

GEORGE GIBEON HURD, farmer, a resident of Randboro, was born here December 8, 1839, and always resided in the same place. He held offices of warden of county, mayor, councillor, and is now a school commissioner. His father, Luke Hurd, died in Newport, in 1873. Mr. Hurd was married twice; first to Mary I. Sawyer, in Eaton, 1861; second, in 1876, to Achsah Hodge. Issue, two children: Alonzo G., born February 12, 1882; Julia L., born June 8, 1893.

RALPH LINDSAY TODD, farmer, was born in Eaton, February 15, 1830. He has resided in Eaton and Compton, and moved to Island Brook, his present home, several years ago. Mr. Todd has always taken a great interest in public affairs, and been a member of the council both in Eaton and Newport. That office he has held for thirteen years, besides others, to the credit of both himself and the township. He is a son of the late John Todd, who died at Compton, in 1867, at the residence of his son. Mr R L Todd was married in Newport, January 14, 1855, to Rosetta Ann, daughter of the late Eliphalet Lyon. Issue, ten children, nine living: Herbert L., born November 8, 1855, married Alberta Coates, two children, residence, Eaton; Benjamin Franklin, born December 27, 1861; George Otis, born May 3, 1869; Nahum Day, born November 1, 1871; Amos Eugene, born June 23, 1873; Artemas N., born June 30, 1878; Florence E., born November 21, 1856, married Hollis B. Coates, no children, residence, Birchton; Beatrice E., born January 12, 1859, married Wellington Warner, one child, residence, Eaton; Gertrude Blanche, born January 28, 1867, married Henry H. Weston, three children, residence, Cookshire; Amanda A., born September, 1863, died December, 1894 A photo-engraving of the residence of Mr. Todd is here given. The place is located about half a mile west of the Island Brook post office. In front of the house he and his family may be seen.

HORACE METCALF, gardener, was born in Corinth, Vt., June 18, 1817. He is a grandson of Samuel Metcalf, who was one of the minute-men of Massachusetts, and served in the Revolutionary war. His father, David, was born September 15, 1766, in Oakham, Mass., died in Corinth, Vt., November 7, 1847; married Candace, daughter of John and Mary Stratton, October 5, 1793. She was born in Rutland June 15, 1777, died in Eaton, Que., June 17, 1855. In 1799 David Metcalf with wife, and her parents, came to Canada and settled on a farm near Randboro, where eight children were born to them. Owing to the universal short crop of 1816 he abandoned his farm and removed to Corinth, Vt., in the spring of 1817. Horace learned the carpenter's trade, at which he worked summers and taught school winters, and later lectured upon electricity. He came to Cookshire in 1852 and taught the village school from December, 1852, till the spring of 1854. Married, November 23, 1854, Eliza, daughter of Thomas K. Oughtred, for many years government school teacher in that place. She died September 6, 1889. Issue, three children: Alice Amanda, born May 19, 1856, married May 19, 1881, David M. Morgan, residence Learned Plain, one child, Mary Rachel, (born June 20, 1883, at Moes River, Que.); Mary Eliza, born May 24, 1859, married, March 18, 1896, to Dennis E. Lawson, of Littleton, N. H.; Horace Edward, born March 22, 1869, present residence Littleton, N. H., occupation, granite cutter. Mr. Metcalf removed to Learned Plain in 1866, where he now resides. He has always taken a prominent part in temperance work, has been a teetotaler since 1832, and believes himself to be the oldest teetotaler in the county.

LATE HEZEKIAH L. AUSTIN, farmer, was born in the State of Maine, July 30, 1820. From the age of nineteen until he was thirty years old he followed the sea for a living; he then returned to his native place, remaining there until 1863, when he moved to Newport, where he lived until his death, April 5, 1892. In Newport he held the office of councillor, school commissioner and road inspector. Married at Dixfield, Maine, July, 1851, Sarah E., daughter of Thomas Harlow. Issue, five children: George C., born June 2, 1859; Byron W., born May 30, 1863, married Cora I. Sunbury, of Maple Leaf; Emma J., born May 21, 1853, married John B. Hurd, residence, Maple Leaf, one child; Flora A., born August 18, 1856, drowned April 25, 1865; Florence M., born September 30, 1869, married Edward Dawson, residence, New Mexico, Que.

LUTHER FRENCH, farmer, mill owner, and lumber manufacturer, was born in Cookshire, July 11, 1828. He is a son of Levi French, one of the associates and first settlers in Eaton, who came from the United States about 1796, and died in Eaton in March, 1858. Our subject has always lived in the County, with the exception of one year, and he moved from Eaton to Island Brook, his present home, January 17, 1876. On the next page is an engraving of the home of Mr. French, in front of which are to be seen Mr. and Mrs. French, their son, and Mr. and Mrs. L. J. French, and children, of Cookshire. The house is situated close to the mill, opposite the post office. He was married at Learned Plain, February 18, 1852, to Margaret, daughter of William Stevenson. Mr. Stevenson died at Learned Plain, February 28, 1872. Issue, eight children: George W. L., born November 17, 1852, married first, Ida Jane Willard, deceased, second, Mary Lathrop, one child, residence, Island Brook; Levi E., born December 12, 1858; Clyde W., born March 4, 1861, married first, Hannah Hood, second, Annie McFarlane, one child, residence, Sawyerville; Elon R., born September 6, 1863, married Estella Lindsay, residence, Sawyerville; Thomas F., born June 22, 1866, married Emma M. Learned, one child, residence, Island Brook; Horace W., born March 23, 1854, died November 2, 1856; Alice M., born February 11, 1856, died December 26, 1875; Anna M., born August 11, 1869, died September 27, 1871.

RESIDENCE OF LUTHER FRENCH.

LIEUTENANT GEORGE WASHINGTON L. FRENCH, mill owner and lumber manufacturer. Born at Cookshire, November 17, 1852, always lived in county. Moved to Island Brook, January 17, 1878. Mr. French is a son of Luther French, and a grandson of one of the first settlers and associates who settled in Eaton, coming from the United States. Since moving to Island Brook he has held several offices of trust, and has been councillor and school commissioner for the township of Newport for several terms, at the present time holding the office of councillor, and that of chairman of the school commissioners. He carries on a large and profitable business as saw mill owner, at Island Brook. Mr. French is First Lieutenant of No. 1 Troop, Cookshire Cavalry, Fifth Dragoons, and holds the office of justice of the peace for the district of St. Francis; also V. C R. of the I. O. F., and is a member of A. F. & A. M. Our subject has been married twice, first at Grove Hill, Newport, October 16, 1879, to Ida Jane, daughter of the late Gardner Marshall Willard, of Dudswell. Mrs French died July 25, 1880. Issue, one daughter: Ida Jane, born July 13, 1880, died September 10, 1892. Second marriage at Lake View, Dudswell, August 24, 1887, to Mary Lovisa Alberta, daughter of the late Lieutenant Horace Lothrop, of Dudswell. Issue, one daughter: Alice Maud May, born October 28, 1888 Given herewith is an engraving of the home of Mr G. W. L. French, which is one of the most attractive residences in Island Brook In front may be seen Mr French and family, his father and mother, and several relatives and friends.

RESIDENCE OF LIEUT. G. W. L. FRENCH.

HISTORY OF COMPTON COUNTY.

SAMUEL NEWEL HURD, J. P., general merchant and postmaster, Randboro, was born in Stanstead, February 24, 1837. Came to Randboro, where he has always lived, in 1838. He has held the office of councillor for twenty-three years, mayor twelve years, and school commissioner for several terms. He is a son of Luke Hurd, who died in 1873. On June 28, 1860, in Newport, he married Persis Dorcelia, daughter of Gilbert P. Williams. Issue, one son: Phineas N., born February 6, 1862, died November 2, 1883.

LEWIS L. BOWKER, farmer, was born in the State of Vermont, October 28, 1821, came to Canada and settled in Compton county, in 1836. His father, Lyman Bowker, died at Newport, Que., December 1, 1867. Was married October 21, 1845, to Lucy Minerva, daughter of Edmund Hurd. Issue, four children: Edmund H., born June 27, 1849, married Minerva Ferguson of Springfield, N. Y., one child; Lyman J., born July 5, 1853, married Clara Harvey, of Newport, Que., two children; Herbert R., born December 1, 1857, married Ormesinda Farnsworth, of Eaton, one child; Luvia A., born September 2, 1855, married A. S. Farnsworth, of Newport, four children.

THOMAS PAINTER, farmer, born in Gloucestershire county, Eng., August 14, 1835. Came to Ditton in 1870, and later moved into Newport. Married in London, Eng., November 10, 1867, to Elizabeth Jane Gray. Issue, eight children, six living: Arthur A., born September 22, 1871, married, 1896, Mary Sizeland, residence, Cookshire; Oscar T., born June 12, 1878; Ernest C., born February 13, 1881; Agnes, born October 26, 1868, married George Wooley, one child, residence, Cookshire; Wm. Henry, born August 6, 1888; Alice, born August 23, 1874; Lucy E., born December 25, 1885, died March 10, 1886.

RESIDENCE OF D. MUNN.

DEMMON MUNN, farmer, was born in Hereford, December 29, 1835. When twenty-one years of age he moved into Eaton, and six years later purchased his present farm in Newport, located about two and one-half miles from Sawyerville. His father, James Munn, died in Newport in March, 1874. During his lifetime he was a prominent man, holding several public offices with credit to himself. Presented herewith is an engraving of the residence of Mr. Munn, in front of which he and his family may be seen. He has married twice, first to Abigail, daughter of Paul Phelps, at Grove Hill, Newport, April 17, 1861. Issue, three children: Edwin E., born October 15, 1865, married Martha E. Dwinnells, residence, Manchester, N. H.; Alva M., born November 19, 1862, died August 25, 1881; Effie Maria, born February 23, 1868, died September 20, 1881. Mrs. Munn died September 7, 1881, aged forty-two years. Second marriage in Newport, September 27, 1882, to Elizabeth M., daughter of William Cairns. Issue, two children: Fred Sanborn, born October 25, 1883; Mary Ella, born February 21, 1885. Mr. Munn at present is a member of the board of school commissioners, and has held office as councillor for several years. He is a deacon in the Baptist church at Sawyerville. He has been a successful farmer, and quick to make use of the latest improvements in farming.

LATE ROBERT BUCHANAN, farmer and carpenter, died at New Mexico, in July, 1895. He was born in 1828, at Autrin, county of Armaugh, Ireland. Came to Canada in 1831, and to Compton county in 1871, settling at New Mexico. His previous occupation was that of ship carpenter. He married Catherine, daughter of James Rogers, of Quebec city. Issue, five children, four living: Robert, born May 29, 1871; Mary, born April 25, 1855, married Edgar Harvey, of Sawyerville, seven children; Annie, married Willard Parker, residence, Sawyerville, two children; Betsey, married William Douglas, residence, West Concord, Vt., three children.

HENRY MORROW, farmer, was born in the county of Derry, Ireland, in 1821. Came to Canada in 1844, and settled in Newport in 1871. He is a prominent member of the L. O. L. Was married in Argenteuil county, in 1855, to Ellen Wilson. Issue, eight children: William W., born December 5, 1856; married Hattie J. Cable, residence, Island Brook; John A., born April 18, 1861; Harry, born June 16, 1863; James, born February 19, 1865; David, born August 4, 1870; Edward, born March 18, 1873; Archie L., born May 25, 1876; Ellen, born March 11, 1868, married Chas. H. Nichols, one child, residence, West Milan, N. H.

AUGUSTUS HEBER ALDEN, farmer, son of John Alden, of Cookshire, was born at Port Hope, Ont., May 27, 1849. Came to Cookshire with his parents before he was a year old, where he remained until he attained the age of nineteen, removing from there to Bury, and afterwards to Newport, where he now resides. Married, at Bury, January 15, 1872, to Elizabeth Jane, daughter of James Mills (deceased). Issue, four children: Anthony Wellington, born October 27, 1872; Charlie Stanley, born May 8, 1878; Fred Oliver, born January 20, 1882; Lucy Ann, born May 30, 1889. Mr. Alden has held, for many years, the position of road inspector, and is a past president of the Patrons of Industry.

MANLIUS HOLBROOK, farmer, came to Island Brook in 1871. Was born in Leamington, Vt., April 1, 1844. He held the office of corporal in Company E., U. S. Sharpshooters. Has been school commissioner. Is now president local association Patrons of Industry. Was married in Leamington, Vt., in 1868, to Persis Alvina Wheeler. Issue, eight children, six living: Horace, born January 1, 1869; Mark M., born September 19, 1870; Ernest W., born June 12, 1888; Florence May, born June 20, 1879; Olive Lucinda, born November 27, 1882; Alice Pearl, born December 19, 1889.

ANDREW SAMPLE, farmer, a resident of Learned Plain, was born May 19, 1861. Married Elizabeth Wilson. Issue, five children. His father, John Sample, was born in county Tyrone, Ire., December 25, 1812, came to Canada in 1832, and died in Cranbourne, Que., June 11, 1885. He was married August 24, 1836, to Rebecca Hamilton, of Cranbourne. Issue, twelve children, eight living: George, born September 5, 1853, married Margaret F. Reynolds, six children, residence, Levis; William I., born April 27, 1865; Matilda, born September 13, 1843, married Wm. Wilson, residence, Cranbourne, eight children; Rebecca, born August 23, 1849, married Alexander McClintock, residence, Bury, eight children; Mary J., born September 28, 1855, married

Charles Locke, residence, Eaton, five children; Margaret, born April 2, 1857, married Wm. Matson, residence, Bury, three children; Hannah E., born September 16, 1866.

JAMES GEORGE BARTHOLOMEW, farmer, was born in Buffalo, N. Y., May 15, 1851. In August of the same year he came to Canada with his father, James Richard Bartholomew, settling in Bury, and afterwards moving to Newport. December 10, 1878, he married Jane, daughter of James Robinson, of this place.

OLIVER PAQUET, farmer, was born in France, March 22, 1832. Came to Canada in 1832, and moved to Newport in 1862. He held the office of councillor for fourteen years. Married in Waterford, Vt, to Eunice Goodell. Issue, seven children, four living: John O., born October, 20, 1868; Eunice A., born September 21, 1862, married Charles Ward, three children, residence, Robinson; Sarah A., born June 14, 1871, married Amos H. Bennett, residence, Brookbury; Betsey E., born July 7, 1856.

HEMAN EBENEZER SUNBURY, farmer and carpenter, was born in Eaton, February 4, 1836, and has always lived in Compton county. He has held the office of councillor for fourteen years. Was married at Eaton Corner, August 31, 1858, to Roxena E. Gamsby. Issue, three children, two living: Fred. Walter, born March 20, 1864, married Mary A. Hammond, residence, Island Brook; Adeline Flavia, born December 3, 1873.

ROBERT WILLIAM LAVALLIER, farmer, was born in Newport, January 18, 1863, where he has always lived. Holds office of S. W., in I. O. F. Married in Bury, July 15, 1886, to Malvina Adeline Fisher. Issue, four children, three living: Levi Leroy, born August 30, 1887; Frederick Harold, born June 20, 1889; John Batiste, born March 13, 1892.

JAMES SIMPSON, farmer and stone mason, was born in the county of Argenteuil, Que., August 10, 1861. Came to Newport in 1875. Was married in Bury, January 14, 1884, to Connet Severson. She was born August 18, 1861. Issue, seven children, five living: Isabella Edith, born August 15, 1884; James John, born May 13, 1888; Lilla Maud, born March 29, 1891; Henry Charles, born February 3, 1894; William S. M., born March 11, 1896.

CHAPTER XVI.

Township of Westbury.

This tract of land is bounded northeast by Bury and Dudswell, south by Eaton, and northwest by Stoke, and contains 16,396 square acres of land. It was erected into a township named Westbury, and in part granted August 13, 1804, to Hon. Henry Caldwell, at that time receiver-general for Lower Canada, his heirs and assigns. In 1815 it was possessed by his son, John Caldwell, Esq.

This is a small, triangular-shaped township, the ranges and lots in which are of unequal length and irregular dimensions. With the exception of parts in the southeast, is considered of good quality. The St. Francis river flows directly through the township, and the Eaton river enters the St. Francis within its limits; beside which are small streams that have supplied power for several saw mills. Such of the land as was not settled was purchased by the British-American Land Company in 1835.

Mrs. Day, writing in 1869, says: "Certain local causes have operated to retard the prosperity of Westbury; one among which is a want of harmony among the people respecting the location of a bridge over the St. Francis, which would go far toward uniting the interests of the two sections. As there is no way of crossing this river but by ferry, at seasons of the year it is both difficult and unsafe to make the attempt." Since then a bridge has been built at East Angus, but the same difficulty is now met with, as there is the need of a bridge at what is known as the "Basin."

This township made slow progress until after the building of the Quebec Central Railway. The establishing of saw and pulp mills at East Angus, in 1882, by Wm. Angus, F. P. Buck and others, gave an impetus to the place. In 1891 a large paper mill was erected, and that place is now one of the most progressive and enterprising villages in the Eastern Townships, with water power almost unlimited.

In 1857 there was one post office only in the township, known as Westbury, with a tri-weekly mail to and from Sherbrooke. Reuben Hall was postmaster. At that time there was a population of about 200, and among the residents we find the names of Jos. Biron, carpenter; Prosper Cyr, tavern-keeper; Chas. Lathrop, saw mill owner; Chas. Lebourveau, millwright; Alonzo Rolf, saw mill owner; Jas. Ryther, saw mill owner; Geo. Stacey, saw and grist mill; Hiram Warner, butcher; John Willard, millwright; Daniel H. Winslow, assessor; John H. Winslow, road inspector.

The municipal records date back to 1855. Since then the following have held the office of mayor: H. M. Barlow, John Claxton, Wm. Chester, F. F. Willard, Albert Haseltine, D. B. Hall, and F. P. Buck. The secretary-treasurers have been Charles Barlow, Simeon Mallory, Horace Williams, Jeremiah Doremus, and F. F. Willard.

Present mayor, J. F. Wilson; secretary-treasurer, J. P. Woodrow; councillors, J. F. Wilson, F. F. Willard, Wm. Embury, Elie Duplie, P. Nedeau, Charles Laramie, and Jos. Chester.

There are three churches at East Angus: Episcopal, with resident pastor, Rev. R. Adcock; Methodist, supplied by Rev. C. W. Finch, from Cookshire; Catholic, built in 1895, Rev. E. F. Beadreau, resident priest. There are also Canadian and Catholic Order of Foresters, Royal Templars, and Patrons of Industry.

There are four elementary Protestant schools, and the same number of Catholic schools. The following is the Board of School Commissioners: F. F. Willard, chairman; D. B. Hall, J. T. Chester, John Brant, and R. C Cowling; secretary-treasurer, J. P. Woodrow. Property assessed in 1895, $156,496. Tax rate, seventeen mills.

Census of 1891 gave the following particulars of the township. Population, 973; families, 176; houses, 172; males, 525; females, 448; French Canadians, 558; others, 415. Religious—Catholics, 608; Church of England, 193; Presbyterians, 32; Methodists, 85; Baptists, 9; Congregationalists, 3; Adventists, 12; Universalists, 18; not specified, 10.

There are four post offices in the township: East Angus, a station on the Quebec

VIEW OF PULP AND SAW MILLS—ROYAL PAPER MILLS CO.

Central Railway, six miles north-west of Cookshire, thirteen miles from Sherbrooke, and 127 miles from Quebec. Population, 600. Great North-Western Telegraph. American Express. Post office revenue, 1895, $470.48. Nearest bank, Cookshire.

Linda post office, five miles north-west of Cookshire, one mile south of East Angus, and twelve miles from Sherbrooke. Population, 100. Nearest bank, Cookshire. Daily mail. Post office revenue, 1895, $14.50.

Westbury, four miles from East Angus, on Quebec Central Railway. Mail daily. Population, 150. Nearest bank, Cookshire. Sherbrooke distant eleven miles. Post office revenue, 1895, $19.90.

Westbury Basin, a station on the Quebec Central Railway, eight miles north-east of Cookshire, the nearest bank. Population, sixty. Mail daily. Post office revenue, 1895, $15.

ROYAL PAPER MILLS COMPANY.—The history of the mills of this company is the history of East Angus. Wm. Angus, of Montreal, after whom the place is named, purchased the site and water power of the present village, when it was a dense forest, and in March, 1882, sent men to make a clearing and erect the present pulp mill The same year the firm of Wm. Angus & Co. was formed, Mr. F. P. Buck, of Sherbrooke, being the silent partner. Mr. Angus had had considerable experience in the paper business, having been president for several years of the Canada Paper Company, of Windsor Mills. The first year there were erected the pulp mill, saw mill, dam, bridge, and railway siding. The late Alfred Ayerst, general superintendent, was in charge from the time the first tree was cut, until his death, in December, 1891. The first bookkeeper was Mr. T. McCaw, and he was followed in 1888 by Mr. F. A. Bottom, who held the position until the change of ownership. During these years Mr. Buck had the general management of the business. In 1891 Wm. Angus & Co. sold out to the Royal Pulp and Paper Company. The new company was officered by W. B. Ives, president; Wm. Angus, vice-president and secretary; F. P. Buck, treasurer; and J. D. Finlay, manager. In 1891 work was commenced in erecting a large paper mill on the south side of the river. The building was completed and the machinery first started in May, 1892. The construction of the building was by contract. Messrs. Loomis & Sons done the brick work; W. W. Bailey, wood work; and M. McCarthy, excavation and masonry. Plans were drawn by E. A. Ellsworth, architect, Holyoke, Mass. The work was under the charge of Mr. A. L. Husbands, civil engineer, of Cookshire.

In September, 1892, Mr. Finlay resigned as manager, and Mr. L. Jarratt selected in his place. Mr. Jarratt still holds the position. He is a practical paper maker, thoroughly understands his business, and gives general satisfaction. In January, 1893, the officers of the Royal Pulp and Paper Company were F. P. Buck, president; Wm. Angus, vice-president; and W. S. Dresser, secretary-treasurer.

In the spring of 1893 the Company went into liquidation. At the liquidator's sale the whole was purchased by Mr. R. H. Pope, M.P., for a new company known as the Royal Paper Mills Company. The officers of this company are: President, F. P. Buck; vice-president and general manager, R. H. Pope, M.P.; secretary-treasurer, F. W. Thompson. The directors are as follows: Hon. Frank Jones, Hon. Irving Drew, Hon. W. B. Ives, M.P., Geo. VanDyke, R. H. Pope, M.P., C. C. Cleveland, ex-M.P., F. P. Buck, Charles Sinclair, and Henry O. Kent.

In January, 1896, an application was made to the Provincial Government for increased capital stock from $400,000 to $800,000 This enabled them to purchase the property of the St. Francis Lumber Company, situated at the head and along the side of the St. Francis river and its branches. This latter Company owned 80,000 acres of private lands, and controlled about 185,000 acres of Government limits, which gives them an almost unlimited supply of timber. In connection with this amalgamation a new saw mill was erected at East Angus in 1895, size 36 x 120, two-story building, with capacity of sawing 70,000 feet per day. The refuse supplies the fuel required for running both the pulp and paper mills

The paper mill is a building 69 x 168 feet, three stories high, with machine and finishing room 56 x 204 feet, same height. There is an engine and boiler-room attached 48 x 72 feet. The machinery is all of modern construction. Capacity at present 12,000 pounds per day. New machinery is about to be added which will double the capacity.

The pulp mill is a two and a half story building, 100 x 150 feet, with capacity of 20,000 pounds per day. A chemical pulp is manufactured, about half of which is used in the paper mill

The company own in addition 120 acres in and around the village of Angus. They have thirty-five houses erected, bringing in a rental of about $175 each month, being occupied by their employees.

HISTORY OF COMPTON COUNTY.   231

In connection with the paper mill a large reservoir was built in 1895, and iron pipes laid for about two miles to some springs, giving the company an excellent system of water works. A new railway siding was also built at the same time, some three-quarters of a mile or more in length, besides additional yard sidings. They also have an extensive electric plant for lighting all of their buildings.

The company have in their employ over 300 men, divided as follows: Paper mill, 75; pulp mill, 75; saw mill and on the rivers, 150. Wages run from fifty cents to $3 per day.

In addition to the saw mill at East Angus they also own and have in operation the old Clark mills at Brompton Falls. Besides the large store-houses at Angus, they have

VIEW OF PAPER AND PULP MILLS- ROYAL PAPER MILLS CO.

one on McGill street, Montreal, and another on Front street, Toronto These are also sales-rooms, and have two travelers or agents in connection therewith. A ready sale is found for the out-put

We present herewith two engravings of the mills, taken from different sides of the river. The one showing the pulp mill and saw mill also has in the back ground a view of the Catholic church, and that portion of East Angus on the north side of the St. Francis river.

JAMES FREDERICK WILSON, merchant, and mayor of Westbury, whose portrait is presented on next page, was born in Compton, March 14, 1858. He is a son of the late Frederick Wilson. Mr. Wilson was a clerk for eleven years in stores at Lennoxville and Capelton. In 1884 he came to East Angus and accepted a position as manager of the Company's store, which he held until the fall of 1895, when he in company with James and E. J. Planche, of Cookshire, purchased the stock and good-will of said store, and are now carrying it on under the firm name of Planche, Wilson & Co. He was married at Haskell Hill, near Lennoxville, February 18, 1880, to Mary M., daughter of William Johuston, of Haskell Hill. Issue, four children: Clifford J., born January 19, 1881; William F., born October 5, 1882; Gordon, born May 3, 1886; George A., born April 7, 1889. Since coming to East Angus Mr. Wilson has held several public offices, among them being that of school commissioner and councillor. At present he is mayor of Westbury. He also holds the office of Dis. Dep. H. C. R., C. O. F.

JAMES F. WILSON.

JAMES PLANCHE, merchant, born in Leeds, Que., July 26, 1861, moved to Cookshire in 1885, owning bakery until 1895, when he moved to East Angus, forming partnership under name of Planche, Wilson & Co., general merchants. His father, J. P. Planche, died in Cookshire in 1893. Mr. Planche was married at Bowmanville, Ont., June 20, 1890, to Edith I., daughter of Rev. Magee Pratt. Issue, two children: Ford H., born November 21, 1892; baby, born June 2, 1895.

LATE HENRY SPOONER ROWE, was born in Norfolk county, Eng., June 22, 1824, came to Compton county in 1836, and died in Westbury, March 15, 1893. In his lifetime a farmer, and was a councillor for many years. Married in Marbleton, Que., June 5, 1857, to Eliza Ann Gilbert. Issue, ten children, nine living: Dennis L., born March 18, 1858, married Evelyn G. Bell, residence, Westbury, four children; Charles J., born February 11, 1864; Henry L., born January 8, 1869; Edward A., born November 3, 1878; Montague S., born July 28, 1880; Sarah A., born September 12, 1859, married Clarence C. Streeter, residence, Newark, N. J., one child; Betsey M., born August 29, 1861, married Oscar Woodrow, residence, Westbury, two children; Clarissa E., born September 15, 1873, married Henry Gilbert, residence, Dudswell, one child; Maria L., born July 8, 1875.

JAMES BRYANT, hotel-keeper, was born in Argenteuil county, Que., September 9, 1840. He moved to Westbury in 1864, where he followed farming until 1884. In that year he opened a boarding-house in East Angus, and in 1891 built that fine hotel known as the Angus House. In February, 1896, he sold the building and contents to L. R. Willard, of Sawyerville, but will still make his home in East Angus. His father, John Bryant, died in Westbury, in 1875. Our subject was married in Argenteuil, May 8, 1860, to Margaret Dixon, born in 1834. Issue, four children: Margaret A., born June 14, 1861, married H. Butler, 1887; Lizzie J., born December 4, 1862, married T. H. Currie, 1890; John H., born May 1, 1864, married I. Wearne, 1892; Mary E., born June 26, 1869; Mary A., born April 2, 1871, married J. H. Gorham, 1894. A niece of Mr. James Bryant has lived with him since her mother's death in 1876. On the next page we give an excellent reproduction of the Angus House, with Mr. Bryant and his family in front.

LOCKHART RAND WILLARD, hotel keeper, was born in Marbleton, April 12, 1857. Married in Cookshire, April 25, 1881, to Ellenor McDermott. Issue, four children, three living:

Luvia M., born March 24, 1882; Mabel E, born May 25, 1887; Gertie A, born April 23, 1889. In 1881 Mr. Willard purchased the hotel at Sawyerville where he remained until February of 1896, when he sold to William Keenan, and moved to East Angus, purchasing the hotel at that place from Mr. James Bryant.

SAMUEL MILLS, farmer, born in Framingham, Eng., February 18, 1818. He came to Bury in 1837 and ten years later moved to Westbury. Has held offices of councillor and school commissioner. Married in Bury, October 18, 1843, to Elizabeth Bush. Issue, six children: Isaac B., born November 5, 1849, married Catherine A. Embury, residence Westbury, three

ANGUS HOUSE.

children; Samuel J., born May 2, 1847, died May 11, 1884, married Maria A. Woodrow, residence Westbury, one child; Sarah E, born January 14, 1845, married John Brant, residence Westbury, one child; Ida E, born May 31, 1855, married Charles E. Martin, residence Eustis, Que.; Adeline V, born November 20, 1863, married Sylvanus B. Warner, residence East Angus; Mary A., born April 20, 1858, died February 8, 1889, married T. Staples.

DANIEL BROWN HALL, farmer, and postmaster at Linda, was born in Eaton, June 29, 1831. He moved to his present home and farm in 1862. We present on the next page an engraving of the residence of Mr. Hall, with himself, his son Elwin, and their wives. This is one of the neatest farm houses in Westbury, and is the result of many years of hard work, from clearing a new farm. He is a son of John Hall, who died here November 20, 1884.

Mr. Hall has been councillor for over twenty years, and mayor two terms. For the past thirty years he has been school commissioner, and for the last twenty-three years has held the office of postmaster. He was married at Eaton Corner, December 24, 1862, to Clarissa, daughter of the late Silas Harvey, of Newport. Issue, four children, three living: Elwin Morris, born September 16, 1866, married Jennie E. H. Mackenzie, of Leeds Village, June 21, 1892, one child, (Reuel E. M., born August 25, 1894). This son lives on the home farm, carrying on the same in conjunction with his father. Oren Austin, born September 3, 1869, residence, Boston, Mass.; Alberta Elvira, born July 25, 1864, married Rufus E. Laberee, two children, residence, Sand Hill.

RESIDENCE OF D. B. HALL.

FRANKLIN LOTHROP, farmer and postmaster, born in Dudswell, March 26, 1827, moved to Westbury in 1847. He has held offices of councillor and school commissioner. Married first in Compton, to Eleonor Winslow, second marriage in Westbury, to Lucern H. Woodrow. Mr. Lothrop has had seven children: Wilber A., born March 15, 1857. married Flora Wheeler, residence, California, two children; Abba A., born August 5, 1864; Mile M., born October 8, 1892; Scott E., born July 19, 1879; Lucy L., born February 2, 1851, married Albert Banfill, residence, Kansas, six children; Annette A., born May 13, 1853. married Dwight L. Crafts, residence, Massachusetts, three children; Mabel M., born September 17, 1883.

JAMES WOODROW, farmer, and secretary-treasurer of the municipal council and school commissioners, was born in Columbia, N. H., May 26, 1841. He came to Westbury in 1856, and has held the offices of councillor and school commissioner, and was postmaster for fifteen years. Married in Dudswell, May 25, 1868, to Mary, daughter of Saunders Shepherd. He died in 1883. Issue, four daughters: Annie L., born October 10, 1869, died January 7, 1885; Ada J., born November 11, 1871, married Albert Gilbert, residence, Dudswell, one child; Lois M., born April 16, 1874; Ella W., born September 17, 1877.

CHAPTER XVII.

TOWNSHIP OF HEREFORD.

Hereford is located in the south-western part of Compton county. It is bounded on the north by Clifton and Auckland, west by Barford, south and east by province line. It is subdivided into 308 lots, was erected into a township named Hereford, and in part granted November 6, 1800, to Jas Rankin and his associates, viz: Adam Kohlop, Samuel Pangbourne, Ephraim Wheeler, Reuben Brunson, Henry Casgrove, James Liddle, William Taylor, John Van Vliet, Theodore Stevens, Nathaniel Wait, Silas Town, Joseph Weeks, Daniel Tryon, Michael Hyar, Samuel Danford, Zeras White, Richard Dean, Ephraim Wheeler, the elder, James Sears, Doderick Fride, Henry Adams, and Wm. Johnston.

It appears, however, that the first settlers of Hereford were of that class, more significantly than elegantly, termed "squatters," who located on the lands without right or title. The first settlers came into Hereford probably as early, if not earlier, than into any other part of the Eastern Townships. We have records of settlements having been made at Coos, about twenty five miles further down the Connecticut river, as early as 1758. We also know that a son of Capt. John Pope was born in Hereford in 1793, the family having come here some time between 1783 and 1793. The settlers then could not be called "squatters," with the same meaning now given to the word ; the first settlers came in here and settled, when they could not tell whether they were in Canada or on United States soil, as surveys were not made until about 1800. We are led to infer, from history obtainable, that the original grantees either suffered their claims to lapse, or sold them to the occupants, or to other parties.

Bouchette, writing in 1815, says: "Greater part of Hereford may be called fairly good land, applicable to any kind of agriculture. In 1800 the southern half was granted to James Rankin and others. Well watered by several branches of the Connecticut river. Hereford mountain is in the fifth and sixth ranges, and in the northwest part of the township " Bouchette, writing in 1831, about Hereford, considered the wages high, " running up to $10 and $12 per month, with board." In 1815 the population did not exceed 200 souls, and in 1831 it was put down as 160 souls. In the latter year there were two schools with twelve to fifteen scholars each. Industries—two saw mills.

Owing to the isolated condition of Hereford, several reasons have operated to retard its progress. All business has been in the direction of the United States, and there the farmers have had to look for a market. It was to be expected that the feelings of the people should tend in the direction of preference for the United States government. Notwithstanding this, the inhabitants are as loyal subjects of Queen Victoria as are to be found anywhere. Since the building of the Hereford Railway, in 1889, there has been more intercouse between the centre of the county and that section, together with better business relations.

The settlement of the Township was slow until within the past twenty years. Hereford Gore has a considerable population of French-Canadians, brought there through the efforts of Mr. F. Paquette. He formed colonies of repatriated French-Canadians, and in this was successful; as his colonists have also been.

Hereford Gore is situated to the northeast of the Township, it being what remained of the tract called Drayton, after the boundary line was run. The commissioners engaged in this work, after leaving Hall's stream, took as the line of separation the height of land which divides the waters running north into the tributaries of the St. Lawrence, from those which flow south into the Connecticut river. It seems to have been a treaty stipulation that no water should be crossed till arriving at a certain point; and it is even said that in some instances where no water was to be seen on the surface of the ground, resort was had to digging in order to decide the matter. This explanation gives us to understand why the boundary line, after leaving the forty-fifth parallel, is so crooked and irregular.

"During the war of 1812, some border difficulties occurred, mostly relating to smuggling, and one man was shot while engaged in the unlawful work. At a later date have been the Indian stream difficulties, which grew out of the disputes concerning the boundary line. At a particular location on Indian stream, one of the head branches of Connecticut river, was a settlement very near the boundary, formed of persons from either side, led there by interest or convenience. Such as came from Canada, still considered themselves as Canadian subjects; while those who had come from the American side, as strenuously insisted on being within the limits of the State of New Hampshire; each party retaining in full their national and social prejudices. Being at such a distance from the courts of law which had nominal jurisdiction on either side, the matter had been in a measure compromised by a sort of tacit understanding that for the time being, the ground was neutral territory. A voluntary association had framed rules regulating their internal affairs, and chosen a prominent person from among their number to act as magistrate or umpire, among them. The population of the place came in time to receive large accessions of an ill-regulated and undesirable class of inhabitants, many of whom were counterfeiters or other refugees from justice. This state of things was not to continue. Such an asylum for unscrupulous characters as the settlement had become, could not long be tolerated. The arrest of criminals by officers sent from either side, and their delivery to those claiming them, was the signal for the opposition and rebellion of fiery spirits among the other party; till at length such a state of feeling prevailed as bid defiance to all efforts at control. Prejudices grew into bitter animosities; disputes led to violence and blows; blood was spilt; and the quarrel which became general, was only suppressed by the arrival of an armed force sent by the New Hampshire authorities. Soon after this, the boundary question was finally determined."

There are seven post offices in Hereford.

Paquette, situated in the Gore, is probably the largest settlement. It was started in 1861, by Mr. F. Paquette, who is now postmaster and has a general store. The place has made good progress, and been benefitted by the building of the Hereford Railway. The village proper is one mile from the station. Here is to be found a Catholic church, convent, academy, two general stores, grocery store, provision store, two blacksmith shops, harness shop, shoemaker, furniture shop, two tailors, and saw mill. The place is twenty-five miles from Cookshire, and twenty miles from Coaticook. Population in village about two hundred. There are both telephone and telegraph connections. Post office revenue for 1895, $152.80.

East Hereford is a station on the Maine Central Railway, five miles east of Hereford. Here are to be found four general stores and a saw mill. Population about one hundred and fifty. Postal revenue, 1895, $59.

Perryboro is located in the western part of the Township, and is principally a farming community. Here are two saw mills and a cheese factory. Population, seventy-five. Distant from Coaticook, six miles. Postal revenue, 1895, $18.

Hereford is on the road from Canaan, Vt., to Coaticook, distant from the latter place fifteen miles. Farming community. Population, one hundred and fifty. Postal revenue, 1895, $17.

Hall's Stream, a small farming community, two miles north of Comin's Mills. Postal revenue, 1895, $47.

Villette is nine miles from Coaticook. Farming community. Postal revenue, 1895, $19.

Comin's Mills post office is located on the boundary line. Here is a customs house, and it is a port of entry. Really forms part of the village of Beecher Falls, Vt. Postal revenue, 1895, $9.

The first municipal records in Hereford bear date January 16, 1860. The past mayors have been: Aaron Workman, Wm. Ellis, F. Paquette, C. O. Hibbard, Calvin Perry, Heman Nichols, and Edwin Bean. Past secretary-treasurers, Israel B. Luther, Aaron Workman, and Edwin Bean. The council for 1895 was composed as follows: Mayor, Alfred Lefebvre; secretary-treasurer, Philias Lapalme; councillors, Charles Geudreau, Nap. Paquette, Chas. H. Gray, Calvin Perry, John Heath, and Clement Dubé. The tax rate is twenty-eight and a half mills.

There are two school boards in the Township. Board of trustees as follows: Alex. Andrews, chairman; Frank Haynes and Ed. H. Birch; James Nish, secretary-treasurer. They have seven elementary schools. Board of commissioners: Albert Champeau, chairman; Philias Lapalme, Narcisse Beloin, Octave Lefebvre, and Nap. Beloin; Fred. Champeau, secretary-treasurer. The latter have under their control a model school, convent, and six elementary schools. Rev. Sisters of L'Assomption are teachers in model school and convent.

There is an Episcopal church at Hall's Stream, also South Hereford, with Rev. E. R. Wilson, incumbent; Advent church at Perryboro, supplied by Rev. G. H. A. Murray, of Dixville; Roman Catholic church, at Paquette, L. M. Hamelin, curé. At Hall's Stream there is an Advent Christian church, with D. W. Davis as pastor.

At Hall's Stream, Adventist teachings were first introduced nearly forty years ago, by A. Gordon, and have been advocated at times by others since then. Some ten years ago there was a church organized of seven members, with C. O. Hibbard as elder, and D. Keysar and H. Nichols as deacons. Since then accessions have been made until there are now over thirty-five members. In 1892 a neat and commodious church was erected. It is now in a fairly prosperous condition, with average attendance of about seventy-five.

In the township of Hereford are to be found four cheese factories, four saw mills, five grist mills, and two lodges of Patrons of Industry.

The census of 1891 gives the following statistics: Population, 1,814; families, 337; houses, 299; males, 1,005; females, 809; French Canadians, 1,294; others, 520. Religions — Roman Catholics, 1,344; Church of England, 153; Presbyterians, 9; Methodists, 80; Baptists 16; Congregationalists, 18; Adventists, 98; Universalists, 57; not specified, 39.

LATE EDWIN BEAN. On the next page will be found the portraits of the late Edwin Bean and his two sons, Leslie and Henry. Mr. Bean was born in North Hatley, Que., September 28, 1835, being a son of Mark Bean of that place. When he reached manhood he moved into the township of Barford, which adjoins Compton county, and later to Coaticook. In November, 1875, he with his family came to Hall's Stream, purchased a large farm where he lived until his death, August 30, 1894. Mr. Bean for many years was a justice of the peace, councillor and mayor of his township. He also held the office of sub-collector of Customs for the port of Hereford. He was married at Huntingville, Que., September 19, 1860, to Josephine, daughter of Simon Bean, of North Hatley. Issue, eight children, four living: Leslie E., born March 13, 1870; Henry, born February 26, 1874; Jennie, born August 20, 1872; Josie E., born December 18, 1880. Leslie Eugene was born in Coaticook, Que., going to Hall's Stream in 1875 with his parents. On reaching manhood he was appointed preventive officer of Customs, and January 1, 1891, promoted to sub-collector for the port of Hereford. He also carries on a large farm. He was married at Compton, October 23, 1895, to Clara I., daughter of John Carbee, Esq.

WILLIAM ANDREWS, farmer, was born in the county of Londonderry, Ireland, May 20, 1820. In July, 1849, he came to, and settled in the township of Hereford, where he now resides. His father, Burnett Andrews, died in this township in 1875. Has never married. His nephew, Richard W. Andrews, born in Barnston in 1845, resides with him. Mr. Andrews is one of the most prominent men of the township of Hereford, having held the offices of town councillor, school commissioner and town valuator.

Levi E. Bean.   Late Edwin Bean   Henry Bean

WALTER RUBIN STEVENSON, engineer at Beecher Falls, was born in Dudswell, Que., February 27, 1864. Came to Eaton in 1871. For several years was engineer for the Cookshire Mill Company, at Cookshire and Sawyerville. Married in 1891 at Cookshire, to Alice McDermott. Issue, one child: Fern E., born December 18, 1892.

JOHN HEATH, farmer, a resident of Hall's Stream, and son of Joseph P. Heath, was born in the township of Hereford, August 28, 1841, and has always lived here. When a young man Mr. Heath worked in the woods, and at river driving. By his energy he has now a fine farm in the valley of Hall's Stream. He is also one of the councillors of the township of Hereford. At Canaan, Vt., July 4, 1870, he married Hannah E., daughter of John I. Ingalls, of Canaan. They have no children.

WILLIAM MELROSE, dairy farmer and cheese manufacturer at Perryboro, was born in Leeds, Megantic county, Que., January 13, 1861. He came to Perryboro in 1864, with his parents, his father being one of the first settlers in this part of the town of Hereford. Mr.

Melrose has not resided continuously in Perryboro, although always taking a deep interest in his boyhood home. He is very fond of dairying and dairy cattle, and introduced some fine thoroughbred animals of the famous Holstein Freisian breed into the town. His brother, Charles, takes charge of the large farm and stock, as he is obliged to be away a great deal of the time, having interests and property in Hartford, Conn., to look after. Presented herewith is an engraving of Mr. Wm. Melrose, also one of his cheese factory. Late in the fall of 1895 he sold most of his real estate here. Mr. Wm. Melrose was married in 1891, to Miss Flora Gillette, of Hartford, Conn., where he resides at present.

WILLIAM MELROSE.

KNIGHTLY BIRCH, farmer, was born at Woolwich, Eng., June 25, 1826. He came to Canada in 1846 and settled in Perryboro in 1877, where he has since resided. Mr. Birch is a son of Captain George Birch, of the Royal Artillery, who was present at the Battle of Waterloo. He was married at Laprairie, Que., in October, 1850, to Maria, daughter of Charles Bradford. Issue, eight children: George, born April 30, 1853, married Miss Armstrong, residence, St. Johnsbury, Vt., three children; Kingston, born October 18, 1854, married E. Graham, residence, Sawyerville, two children; Charles, born November 25, 1860, married Miss Jones, residence, Perryboro, two children; William V., born October 5, 1862; Frederick K., born August 15, 1867, married Miss Jay, residence, Concord, N. H., one child; Edward H., born February 26, 1871; Caroline, born November 3, 1866, married G. Armstrong, residence, Danville, Que., six children; Matilda J., born June 3, 1865, married G. Taylor, residence, St. Johnsbury, Vt., two children.

JAMES NISH, farmer, was born January 30, 1835, in Terrebonne, Que., and came to Perryboro in 1859. He has held the offices of councillor and school commissioner, and at present is assistant secretary of Hereford, and secretary-treasurer of school trustees. Was married in Compton, September 2, 1862, to Janet Fenton. Issue, four children: William, born July 17, 1863; James F., born April 30, 1869; Jane, born January 18, 1865, married Wm. V. Birch, residence, Hereford; Ellen, born March 26, 1871, married John Robertson, residence, Coaticook.

A. M. CLARK, senior member of the firm of A. M. Clark & Son, mill owners and lumber dealers, was born in Vermont, December 30, 1841. He came

CHEESE FACTORY AT PERRYBORO.

to Canada in 1881, and to Perryboro, his present home, in 1891. During these ten years he operated a saw mill of about the same capacity, in Barford. Was married in Vermont to Agnes Batchelder. Issue, two children: Harry H., born March 2, 1865; Anice A., born November 2, 1881. Mr. Clark, with his son Harry H, formed the company above mentioned, and built the mill shown in the picture herewith, in 1891. At present they have a sawing capacity of 10,000 feet a day, employing twelve hands. They also manufacture shingle, and do custom grinding.

AMOS W. LAWTON, farmer, was born in Canaan, Vt, February 22, 1826. Came to Hereford in 1873. Married at Hadley, N. Y., October 15, 1853, to Fannie A. Goodnow. Issue, seven children, six living: Charles A., born October 6, 1857, married Addie A. Dunbar, residence Monson, Mass., one child; Lewis M, born June 19, 1867; Harbert A., born February 10, 1870, married Bertha M. Kingsley, residence Hereford; Adelia H., born July 18, 1855, married Alonzo Edmunds, residence Canaan, Vt., three children; Nora E., born March 3, 1861, married James A. Gray, residence Hereford, five children; Hannah M., born January 1, 1864, married Thomas Johnson, residence Hereford, two children.

MILL OF A. M. CLARK & SON.

HORACE EDWARD HODGE, farmer, a resident of East Hereford, was born in Eaton, November 11, 1835. When twenty-one years old he went to the United States, and after a few years returned and settled in Hereford. He was married first, on January 21, 1862, to Caroline Read, of Leamington, Vt. Issue, one daughter: Mabel, born May 15, 1863, died December 25, 1866. Mrs. Hodge died December 15, 1866. Second marriage at Compton, June 16, 1868, to Susan A. Blossom.

JAMES A. GRAY, farmer, a resident in East Hereford, was born in East Clifton, Que., March 11, 1856, and lived there until he moved to his present home. He has taken a great interest in the Patrons of Industry, and holds the office of president of Greenwood Association. His parents were Cormick C. and Honor (Higgins) Gray, who had eleven children. In West Stewartstown, N. H., December 7, 1878, he married Norah E. Lawton, (born March 3, 1861), of Hereford. Issue, five children: Melvin J., born July 4, 1881; Leo Ernest, born November 2, 1883; Charles A., born October 1, 1891; Fannie A., born January 27, 1880; May Esther, born August 11, 1889.

THE LATE ISAAC BROWN was born in England, and died in Colebrook, N. H., in 1855. He was a successful farmer in the township of Hereford. In 1846, at Canaan, Vt., he married Elizabeth H., daughter of William Woodrow, Esq. Issue, four children, one living: William H., born November 10, 1851.

JOHN W. KINGSLEY, farmer, living on Hall's Stream, was born in Eaton, November 9, 1839. He enlisted in the U. S. army in 1862, and took part in the battle of Gettysburg; after the close of the war settling in Weybridge, Vt., where he resided until 1880, when he came to Hereford. He is a prominent member of the G. A. R. Married at Weybridge, Vt.,

September 22, 1863, to Martha J. Merrill. Issue, five children : Frank B., born February 12, 1865, married Nettie E. Smith, residence, Hall's Stream, three children; Freddie M., born November 9, 1867, deceased; Gertrude M., born September 5, 1869, married Edmund G. Peck, deceased; Bertha M., born February 5, 1871, married Herbert Lawton, residence, Hall's Stream; Etta L., born June 17, 1877.

CHAPTER XVIII.

Township of Bury.

This tract of land was erected into a township named Bury, March 15, 1803, one-fourth of which was granted to Calvin May and his associates, viz.: John Abell, Asa Abell, Benjamin Akin, John Leach, Samuel Laflin, Nathan Pratt, Jehiel Smith, James Torrance, and Samuel Whitcomb. These grantees, however, like those in several other townships, never settled on or occupied the land thus granted, and it subsequently reverted to the Crown.

Bouchette, writing in 1815, says only one-quarter of this township had been surveyed. "A road was marked, blazed and mile-posts set through here, for a road from Kemp's road, Ireland township, through to Vermont, passing through Newport." Evidently this road was never completed or survey made use of.

The first settlers in Bury, of which we have any record, were a few "squatters," who came about 1831. The late Lemuel Pope moved into this township in 1835, and he said at that time there were only two residents, named respectively Moses Post and a man named Waite. It was about 1832 that the British American Land Company acquired by purchase all lands not sold or surveyed, in this district. In this way they became sole owners of the Township, and through their efforts it was first settled. In 1835-36 the first attempt at settlement was made. At this time a road was made to Robinson village from Taylor's farm, about two and a half miles east of Cookshire; also one through to Victoria. Nearly two thousand settlers came into this Township in 1836. The British American Land Company built log houses, and erected them for the new-comers at the rate of one each day. It was at this time Robinson village was started, the saw mill built, the store opened, and other shops established. Mr. Lemuel Pope was the leading spirit throughout this section in those early days, and at one time owned nearly all the land where the village of Robinson now stands.

Those early English emigrants came out under the auspices of the British American Land Company, but on finding things so different from what they had been accustomed to, and so entirely at variance with their preconceived notions, they got disheartened, and left their locations in search of more congenial quarters. But others with more pluck and forethought remained, and now the comfortable circumstances of their children attest their wisdom. The British American Land Company did much towards opening up the country and preparing the way for these settlers, encouraging them by building churches, establishing schools, constructing roads, etc., for their convenience.

Those who settled in that part known as Brookbury have done very well, the land proving to be of good quality. The following are names of those who first settled here: James Tite, John Bennett, Robert Batley, Frank Martin, Michael Warren, Jonathan Taylor, Samuel Baird, Elder John Warren, William Saunders, Samson Coates, George Downes, Samuel Burt, John Downes, Timothy Clark, Joseph Needham, Henry Joice, Charles Frances, John Grey, Benj. Butler, James Revel, William Rowe, Matthew McAdams, David Howe, Robert Jenkerson, and Patrick Kenny. With a few exceptions only, the foregoing sailed from Yarmouth Harbor, England, in June, 1836, and after a voyage of over ten weeks, arrived at Quebec in September.

They traveled by the way of Three Rivers as far as Sherbrooke, the men walking while the women and children rode in carts. The men left their families in Sherbrooke and came on into what was then an unbroken forest, to locate a farm and home, before bringing in their families. There were no roads from Robinson village to what is now known as Brookbury, and their only guide was a line of spotted trees; consequently all their household effects and provisions had to be brought in on their backs. A few of these families became so disheartened by the hardships they were compelled to endure, that they removed, some to Ontario and others to various parts of this province. The majority of those who were brave enough to remain acquired comfortable homes for themselves, and now their descendants are enjoying the fruits of their toil.

The first municipal records of this township bear date 1841. At that time there were also included in this municipality the townships of Westbury and Lingwick. At the first meeting Captain Thos. Bown was chosen as representative to the district of Sherbrooke council, and Nathaniel Ebbs was also chosen as town clerk.

The first school commissioners were elected January 10, 1842, as follows: Rev. Wm. King, Francis Martin, Asher Jones, Charles Hawley, and Angus McKay, jr.

In 1844 Captain Bown's time as district councillor having expired, the following were nominated as his successor: Lemuel Pope, Hammond McClintock, and John Gamsby. A poll being demanded the vote at the close stood as follows: Pope, 90; McClintock, 37; Gamsby, 8. Pope was therefore declared duly elected. From this time the records cease until July, 1855, when on reorganization under the new municipal and road act, this municipality comprised the united townships of Bury, Hampden, and Marston. The two latter townships were soon after detached from Bury. On July 23, 1855, the following councillors were elected: John Martin, Irvine Reed, Jesse Hunt, George Sherman, Lemuel Pope, William Saunders, and Gaymer Hunt. At the first meeting of the council Lemuel Pope was chosen mayor, and Lewis McIver, secretary-treasurer.

The following is a complete list of the mayors of Bury from 1855 to date: Lemuel Pope, Geo. R. Bird, Jessie Hunt, Lewis McIver (Mr. McIver, while in office the second time, died October 14, 1885, aged 72 years), Thos. Bennett, John Martin, Wm. Bown, and James Hunt, the present mayor, who was appointed in 1892. The past secretary-treasurers have been Lewis McIver, Nathaniel Ebbs, A. H. Vaughan, W. H. Mannix, Robert Cowling, Chas. Patton, Jno. Stubbs, John W. Bennett, and C. H. Tambs.

The council for 1896 is composed as follows: James Hunt, mayor, and councillors, James Hugh Leonard, Wm. Bown, Colin Morrison, Josiah Boydell, John Lefebvre, and Charles Murray. C. H. Tambs, secretary-treasurer.

In the Township there are one model and ten elementary schools. The present commissioners are: Charles Warren, chairman; Wm. Gaymer Hunt, Geo. Stokes, Henry Ord, and Wm. Bown, C. H. Tambs, secretary-treasurer. The model school is located at Robinson, with following teachers: Miss Elizabeth Hepburn, principal, and Mrs. A. J. Cook as assistant.

Although there are five post offices in the Township, Robinson is the only village, the others simply being the centre of farming communities.

Robinson, or Bury as the railway station is called, is one of the prettiest villages in the county. It embraces quite a large tract of land within its limits, but the houses are much scattered. The largest part is on a level plain, with pretty homes on each side of the street. The village has three carriage factories, with blacksmith shops connected therewith, two furniture shops, four large stores, saw mill, grist mill, and other small shops. The town hall is here located, also three churches, and Murray's hotel. There are three secret societies: C. O. F., R. T. of T., and I. O. O. F. The postal revenue for 1895, was $518.62.

Canterbury, which is near the town line of Bury, Lingwick and Hampden, is five miles west of Scotstown. Daily mail. Postal revenue, 1895, $22.

Brookbury is six miles distant from Robinson. Daily mail. Postal revenue, 1895, $58.

Crossbury is three miles west of Robinson, and on the town line of Westbury. Daily mail. Postal revenue, 1895, $4.

Keith is eight miles north of Robinson. Mail daily. Postal revenue, 1895, $24.

The Church of England was the first denomination to hold religious services in the township of Bury. In 1836, when there was such a rapid immigration, the minister at Cookshire commenced services at Robinson. By 1838 the work had grown so rapidly that the first resident clergyman, Rev. Wm. Arnold, was appointed. He was succeeded in 1839 by Rev. C. P. Reid, afterwards rector of Sherbrooke. In 1840 we find the Rev. F. Broome in charge, giving place in the following year to Rev. Wm. King, who stayed about six years, and was followed by Rev. Chas. Forrest. In 1847 Rev. John Kemp succeeded, and carried on a ministry of seventeen years in Bury, and Lingwick adjoining at varying intervals. The Mission has since been held by the following clergy: Revs. Thos. Richardson, appointed in 1864; R. Wainwright, 1869; James Boydell, 1871; C. Thorpe, 1875; P. Roe, 1877; A. J. Woolryche, 1878; F. U. Webster, 1882; W. C. Bernard, 1884; H. S. Fuller, 1887; and Rev. C. B. Washer, who is now in charge.

For a long time the services of this church were held in a building erected during the Rev. Wm. King's incumbency, which was a school and dwelling house under one roof. In 1860 a commodious church was built; in 1873 the edifice being too small, a chancel was added. In 1881 the present parsonage was built. St. John's church, on the Dudswell road, was erected during Rev. W. King's ministry, 1840-46. A church known as St. Thomas, was also constructed near the Bown school house, on the Victoria road, which, however, becoming dilapidated, was taken down, and the services transferred to the school house. It is proposed to rebuild on the old site. In 1893 extension of church work made it advisable to set off Canterbury and Lingwick and attach them to the new mission of Scotstown. The clergyman at Robinson now has the care of the village church, and the stations of St. John and St. Thomas, with two other stations served in week days.

The Methodist church, Bury, as a separate mission dates back to the year 1868 only. Previous to that time services were held by ministers from Sawyerville. A perusal of the history of Methodism in Eaton will give some information in regard to the Bury mission. The records show Rev. Wm. Adams as pastor from 1868 to 1872, and during his ministry the church at Robinson, as well as one at Brookbury, were built. The clergymen on this appointment since 1872 have been Revs. Hiram Fowler, A. M. De Long, James O'Hara, J. H. Fowler, Isaac Wheatley, B. Pierce, J. B. Hicks, J. H. McConnell, Henry Meyers, J. R. Hodgson, and the present pastor, W. H. Raney. The average attendance at all appointments is about 300. Number of church members, 110.

Roman Catholic church, Bury, is a mission only, with no resident priest, They have a church built several years ago, and regular services are held by the priest from Scotstown. who has this mission under his charge.

The Adventists hold regular services at Robinson and Brookbury, but have no church at present; Elder Wm. Blount is their pastor.

The following statistics are gathered from the census of 1891: Population, 1,621; families, 331; houses, 308; males, 856; females, 765; French Canadians, 64; others, 1.557. Religions—Roman Catholics, 155; Church of England, 740; Presbyterians, 275; Methodists, 331; Lutherans, 24; Baptists, 7; Freewill Baptists, 5; Congregationalists, 7; Adventists, 67; Universalists, 10.

LT.-COL. F. M. POPE

LT.-COL. FREDERICK M. POPE, mill owner and lumber manufacturer, was born in Bury, April 20, 1847. He is a son of the late Lemuel Pope, of Bury. He received his education at Bishops College, Lennoxville. He always took a deep interest in military affairs, and when a young man he attended the Montreal military school. In 1865 he received his second-class certificate, but at the request of those in authority he delayed finishing his studies and returned home, where he organized several companies of infantry. That was just previous to the threatened raid of the Fenians, which took place in 1866. He formed the first company of volunteers in Compton county, and it was through his efforts that several additional companies were formed in a few months' time. This was the beginning of the Fifty-eighth Battalion. He was appointed captain in 1866, and was on duty one month at Bury during the time of the Fenian raid. In 1867 he returned to the military school and received his first-class certificate. Largely through his efforts was the Fifty-eighth Battalion formed. He was appointed

RESIDENCE OF LIEUT.-COL. F. M. POPE.

adjutant to the battalion in 1867; and was on duty two weeks at Sherbrooke, at the second Fenian uprising in 1870. He received the appointment of major in 1872; brevet in 1876, and lieutenant-colonel of the Fifty-eighth Battalion in 1881. Lt.-Col. Pope commanded the militia during the Hereford Railway riots in 1888, and through his coolness, good judgment, and tact, brought the affair to a successful issue, without loss of life, for which he received special mention in the militia report. He was appointed to the district staff as brigade major for the Eastern Townships in July, 1889. Retired, retaining rank, in August, 1893, with gratuity; re-appointed brigade-major to the Eastern Townships, April, 1896. In civil matters Lt.-Col. Pope has filled many public offices with satisfaction to his fellow citizens. For six years he was a member of the council, and for six years chairman of the board of school commissioners. Appointed a J. P., May 5, 1883. He has extensive interests in saw mills and timber limits, shipping lumber to all parts of the country. At Bury, December 1, 1869, he married Elizabeth M., daughter of John George Edmond Lockett, Esq., of Pemberton Hall, Llangollan, Wales. Issue, three children: Osborne L., Maud E. A., and Ethel Alma. On the preceding page we give a miniature picture of Lt.-Col. Pope, and also a photo-engraving of his residence. The house and grounds are very prettily located at the west end of Bury village, and is one of the most attractive places in the county.

MR. AND MRS. ROBERT CLARK.

THE LATE LEMUEL POPE, Jr., was born in East Clifton, Que., September 24, 1815, and died at Bury, February 23, 1896. He was first cousin of the late Hon. John Henry Pope, their grandfather having settled in Hereford sometime previous to 1793. Lemuel Pope, the father of our subject was born in Hereford, Que., in 1793, and died June 5, 1859. He married Sarah Hughes, of Colebrook, N. H. She died in 1831. Mr. Lemuel Pope, jr., was one of the first settlers in Bury, coming here in 1835. In 1836 he accepted a position with the British American Land Company, but in 1839 resigned, going into trade. Since then he combined farming with the business of general merchant. He had great faith in the future of this country and invested heavily in land; at the time of his death owning about five thousand acres. His public services to the town were appreciated, he having been a member of the council for thirty years, and warden of the county one term. For the past fifty years he was a magistrate. He was a strong supporter of the Church of England, but also assisted other denominations. He gave the land on which the Methodist and Catholic churches, in Bury, are built. November 5, 1839, at Bury, he married Wealthy Adeline Hawley, who was born in 1819, and died June 15, 1885. Issue, three children: Frederick M., born April 20, 1847, married Elizabeth M. Lockett, three children; Helen M., born September 20, 1841, married Edmund Lockett, two children; Florence E., born September 19, 1852, married W. Allan Ramsay, deceased, two children. All residents of Bury.

ROBERT CLARK, farmer, was born at Halferne farm, parish of Crossmichal, near Castle Douglas, Kirkcudbrightshire, Scotland, January 1, 1824. He came to Compton Centre in 1862, but shortly after moved on to the farm in Canterbury where he now lives. Previous to coming to this country, Mr. Clark was a linen and woollen draper. He is a man of great energy, has been very successful as a farmer, and ably filled all positions to which he has been appointed. For many years Mr. Clark was Dominion immigration agent, and made several trips to England in quest of immigrants. He is a justice of the peace for the district of St. Francis, and has held the offices of postmaster and school commissioner. He was married December 10, 1850, at Marlpool, Derbyshire, England, to Eliza Wood, born October 2, 1821, and died July 8, 1887. Issue, four children: Martha, born April 19, 1852, married A. Lefebvre, residence Cookshire, six children; Mary, born August 22, 1853, married C. H. Parker, residence Scotstown, seven children; John, born June 9, 1859, died February 9, 1885; Eliza, born October 5, 1861, married W. G. Sharman, two children, died February 15, 1892. On the preceding page is a photo-engraving of Mr. and Mrs. Clark.

RESIDENCE OF J. BOYDELL.

JOSIAH BOYDELL, general merchant at Bury Station, was born in Toronto, Ont., in 1854. His father, Henry Boydell, who was formerly a lumber merchant in Liverpool, Eng., died in Toronto in 1856, and in 1860 the family returned to England. In 1869 our subject returned to Canada, coming to Compton county in 1871. For several years he was bookkeeper and clerk for Mr. A. L. McIver, of Robinson, going into business for himself in 1895. Mr. Boydell was largely instrumental in starting the I. O. O. F. at Bury, and holds the offices in that society of D. D., and P. N. G. In January, 1896, he was also elected one of the councillors of the township of Bury, after a keen contest. He married Harriet P. F. Ward, of Bury. Issue, four children: Arthur Henry, born October 29, 1886; Elizabeth Agnes, born May 16, 1888; Gertrude Eva, born September 22, 1891; Ethelwyn Trevor, born December 12, 1893. Accompanying this is an engraving of Mr. Boydell's home in Bury, with himself and family grouped in front.

LEWIS A. BENNETT, farmer, was born in Bury, May 7, 1858. With the exception of six years in Vermont; he has always resided in Bury township. His parents, Joseph and Mary (Butler) Bennett, are still living. Our subject was married in Brownington, Vt., January 14, 1886, to Laura Jane, daughter of Ezra S. and Laura P. Crandall, of the same place. Issue, one daughter: Enid Sylvia, born April 3, 1891. The engraving on top of next page shows Mr. Bennett and family in front of his residence, which is situated about two miles north of the Brookbury Post Office.

WILLIAM FRANCIS, farmer, was born in Brookbury, Bury township, April 1, 1840, where he has always lived. His parents were Charles and Georgiana (Rich) Francis. Charles Francis, sr., was born January 28, 1792, in Barnham, Norfolk Co., Eng., died in Brookbury, December 10, 1881; he came to Canada in 1836, together with his wife, three children, and four step-children, and settled in Brookbury, where two more children were born, William and Charles. They had eleven children in all; two, James and Hepzabah, remaining in England and not coming to Canada until several years after. The names of the three who came with their parents were Mary Ann, John, and Jemima. At the bottom of this page is an engraving of the residence of Mr. William Francis with himself and family at the left; the lady and children to the right are friends from Massachusetts, who were visiting Mrs. Francis at the time the photograph was taken. Our subject was married at Brookbury, November 24, 1866, to Amelia Jane, daughter of George Downes. He died April 14, 1871, aged fifty-six years. Issue, three children: Willis D., born December 1, 1876; George W., born March 4, 1885; Ella J., born October 8, 1869.

RESIDENCE OF L. A. BENNETT

JESSE ORLIN GILBERT, senior member of the firm of J. O. Gilbert & Son, mill owners and lumber dealers, was born in Dudswell, Que., September 4, 1842. In 1864 he moved into the township of Bury, and in 1876 settled where he at present lives. Mr. Gilbert and his son own and carry on a saw mill close to their home in Bury, and they also have a steam mill at Bishop's Crossing, in Dudswell, a few miles distant. Accompanying this sketch is an engraving of the home of Mr. Gilbert, in front of which he, his wife, and their children may be seen. Previous to 1876, when he went into the saw mill business, Mr. Gilbert was a farmer and carpenter. He has held several prominent offices, among them that of councillor, also Sabbath-school superintendent for several years. He was married in East Dudswell, November 22, 1864, to Lodema Mary, daughter of Oliver Bishop. Issue, four children: Frederick William, born November 19, 1868, married, January 23, 1895, Annie L. G. Ward, residence, Dudswell; Wilford Lewis, born

RESIDENCE OF WILLIAM FRANCIS.

RESIDENCE OF J. O. GILBERT.

July 12, 1875; Emma Jane, born August 14, 1871; Elsie Maria, born July 15, 1873, died February 21, 1889.

CHARLES WARREN, farmer, was born in Norfolk county, Eng., October 11, 1834. He is a son of the late Rev. J. Warren, and Eliza Gasking, and in company with his parents came to Compton in 1836. For twenty years thereafter he lived in Compton and Hatley, when he took up his residence in Brookbury, where he has since resided. His father died in Brookbury, September 27, 1889, aged eighty-one years. Mother died April 10, 1881, aged sixty-eight years. Mr. Charles Warren is president of the Patrons of Industry local association, a justice of the peace, and chairman of the school commissioners. He has been a councillor, and held other minor municipal offices. For several years he was clerk of the Advent church society, and formerly president of the Bury Farmers' Club. He has been a successful farmer, and has one of the pleasantest homes in Brookbury. A photo-engraving of his residence is here given. He was married in Hatley, Que., November 10, 1855, to Lydia, daughter of the late Kendrick Rowell. One child by adoption: Abba A. Willard, married Nehemiah Batley, one child, residence, Brookbury.

THOMAS STOKES, carriage maker, was born in Hampshire, Eng., February 13, 1835. His father came to Bury in 1836, settling near the present station, with his family. At that time there were only four other families in the township. They suffered all the hardships of pioneer life, but finally made a good home. The

RESIDENCE OF CHARLES WARREN.

250   *HISTORY OF COMPTON COUNTY.*

father died December 8, 1881. Our subject has always resided in Bury. He was a farmer until thirty years of age, when in 1865 he went into the carriage business with James Hunt, of Bury. They dissolved the partnership in 1879, and in 1880 Mr. Stokes built shops on the present site, where he has since carried on the carriage business. He was married at Robinson, Bury, in 1860, to Louisa, daughter of the late John Herring, of Bury. Issue, six children, five living: George W., born January 6, 1861, married Dora E. Stokes, one child; Carlos A., born May 4, 1869, married Beatrice Tambs; Maurice T., born March 31, 1872; Edgarton A., born May 24, 1877; Lilla A., born January 18, 1863, married Charles E. Baldwin, two children, residence Coaticook, Que.; Minnie E., born April 19, 1865, died July 9, 1887.

FACTORY OF THOMAS STOKES & SONS.

Accompanying this sketch is a good reproduction of the extensive shops of Thomas Stokes & Sons, the firm comprising the father and four sons. They may be seen standing in the foreground of the picture. This firm does an extensive business in carriages, wagons and sleighs. They also manufacture furniture, sash and doors, and carry on an undertaking business. Each member of the firm has charge of some special department in the business, which he superintends and has perfected himself in. Their shops contain all the latest improvements for turning out work of a high grade.

BENJAMIN N. WALES, M.D., C.M., was born in St. Andrews, Argenteuil county, Que. He is a son of Charles Wales, merchant, who died in St. Andrews in 1877. Dr. Wales was a student at McGill Medical College, graduating therefrom in 1874. In August, 1877, he located in

RESIDENCE OF B. N. WALES, M.D., C.M.

Sawyerville. After one year's residence in that place he moved to Robinson, Bury, where he has since resided. He has practiced here for eighteen years, and is now the senior physician in full practice in the county. The doctor is an expert cyclist, and makes his bicycle most serviceable in attending to his large practice. He is a general favorite. He was married at Sawyerville, October 23, 1878, to Emma T., daughter of the late Wellington Osgood. Issue, five children: Charles Wellington, born August 15, 1879, died August 16, 1880; Henry Osgood, born July 13, 1884; Julia Grace, born July 14, 1881; Anna Letitia, born September 1, 1887; Margaret Evelyn, born April 13, 1890. A photo-engraving of the residence of Dr. Wales is presented herewith. A miniature of himself is to be seen in the upper corner.

ERNEST TITE, farmer, was born in Brookbury, January 4, 1860, where he has always lived. He is a son of David and Rosamond (Burt) Tite. They are both living at Brookbury. Accompanying this sketch is an engraving of the residence of Mr. Tite, very prettily located opposite the post office on the Brookbury ridge. In front, he and family may be seen. He was married at Coaticook, Que., July 8, 1885, to Matilda M., daughter of Abram Waite, and widow of Chas. Pichett, Montreal, by whom there was one daughter, Geneviève. Mr. Waite died at Whitby, Ont., in 1884. Issue, two children: Nellie May, born July 9, 1886; Stanley Alexander, born July 2, 1889.

THOMAS BENNETT, Dominion Government land and immigration agent, was born November 14, 1825, in the county Cavan, Ire. He came to Bury in July, 1837, with his parents, who were among the first settlers. His father, John Bennett, died August 19, 1860. Our subject always followed farming until 1882, when he

RESIDENCE OF ERNEST TITE.

was appointed immigration agent, and moved to Brandon, Man. In 1889 he was transferred to take charge at Winnipeg of immigration at that place, where he remained until 1894, when he was sent to South Edmonton, N. W. T. He was one of the prominent men of Compton county, having been councillor for fourteen years, mayor six years, and warden three years. December 26, 1849, at Manchester, N. H., he married Jane Fields, of county Tyrone, Ire., who died in 1890. Issue, ten children, six living: John W., born February 4, 1851; James H., born September 26, 1852; George T., born October 18, 1859; Frederick F., born October 16, 1863; Cordelia, born April 30, 1854, married W. Saunders, residence, Brookbury, Que. Second marriage, Wilhelmina C., daughter of James Longmore, of Scotland. Issue, one daughter: Wilhelmina F., born November 11, 1893.

AMOS WALTER SAUNDERS, farmer, was born September 1, 1847, in Brookbury, where he has always lived. His father, William Saunders, came from England and settled here in 1836. Was councillor for twenty years. He died in Brookbury, February 18, 1890. Mr. Saunders was married in Bury, January 25, 1877, to Cordelia, daughter of Mr. Thomas Bennett, now of South Edmonton, N. W. T. Issue, six children: Llewellyn Walter, born March 17, 1879; James H., born June 8, 1883; Douglas J. S., born July 3, 1885; Thomas W. F., born September 6, 1889; Alden B., born November 14, 1891; Clarinda J. P., born August 28, 1880.

EDWARD LEONARD, farmer, was born in Fermanaugh, Ireland, in 1821. Came to Brookbury and settled on his present farm in 1845. For twenty-one years municipal councillor. First marriage at Sherbrooke, in 1852, to Mary Kenney, of Brookbury. Issue, seven children, four living: James H., born February 11, 1855, married Elizabeth Duffield, residence, Brookbury, one child; William E., born June 11, 1859, married Margaret Boyle, residence, Sawyerville; John O., born July 16, 1861, married Mary Pehleman, residence, Brookbury, six children; Susanne, born March 7, 1858, married Edward McCafferty, residence, Flanders, five children. Mrs. Leonard died June 19, 1876. Second marriage at Cookshire, January 28, 1880, to Honora V., daughter of the late Charles McCafferty, of Learned Plain.

WALLACE E. HOOKER, farmer, a resident of Brookbury, was born in Dudswell, Que., September 21, 1859. When twenty-one years of age he moved to Brookbury, and has always lived there. He is a prominent member of the P. of I. First marriage at Brookbury, November 1, 1880, to Emily M. Rich, died January 19, 1893. Second marriage at Brookbury, to Emily M. Clark, February 2, 1894. Issue, twin boys: Lloyd and Floyd, born January 2, 1895.

JOHN W. DOWNES, farmer, was born in Brookbury, January 29, 1845. He has always lived in Brookbury, except the four years he was in New Hampshire, as a weaver. October 26, 1872, in Nashua, N. H., he married Phebe M. Hooker, who was born November 12, 1848. Issue, one child: Lena Augusta, born June 27, 1878.

EBENEZER SHARMAN, farmer and carpenter, was born in Suffolk, Eng., November 30, 1824. He came to Canterbury, his present home, in 1836. He has held the offices of councillor and school commissioner. Was married January 1, 1850, in Bury, to Caroline Bennett. Issue, six children: James, born July 7, 1855, married Maria Mayhew, two children; Walter G., born October 30, 1863, married first Eliza Clark, second, Angeline McCoy, four children; Sarah, born March 13, 1853; Mary A., born August 16, 1858, married Henry Goodwin, residence, Scotstown, one child; Lucy J., born January 5, 1861, married Charles Bown, residence, Victory road, Bury.

DENNIS TITE, farmer, was born in Barnham, Norfolk county, Eng., May 29, 1823. Came to Brookbury in 1836, where he has since lived. Has held the office of councillor for several years. First marriage in Dudswell in 1846, to Emily Bishop. Issue, six children, four living: Alfred, born in February, 1852, married Sarah Stocks, residence Brookbury, four children; Lelia, born June 6, 1847, married Wm. Bodwell, residence Nashua, N. H.; Nellie, born in June, 1854, married Geo. Everett, residence Lime Ridge, three children; Gertrude, born in November, 1862. Second marriage in September, 1871, in Dudswell, to Calista O. Bishop. Issue, two children, both dead.

CHARLES HENRY WARD, contractor, was born in Bury, August 12, 1850, where he has always lived. First marriage in Bury, 1877, to Martha A. Ellis, who died in 1888. Issue, four children: Gertrude E., born February 22, 1879; L. Lillian, born June 26, 1881; Bernice H., born September 13, 1883; Persis A., born August 20, 1885. Second marriage, in 1890, to Eunice A. Paquette, of Newport. Issue, three children: George P., born May 30, 1891; Baby, born April 13, 1895; E. Mabel, born July 26, 1893.

JAMES WEIR, farmer, resident of Brookbury, was born in county Farmaugh, Ire., March 6, 1844. Came to Bury with his parents in 1849. Married in Highgate, Vt., October 22, 1866, to Letitia Boyd. Issue, ten children: James H., born December 27, 1869; Vernon J., born August 6, 1888; Winfield S., born March 1, 1890; Ellen J., born October 26, 1871, married O. S. Rich, deceased, residence, Brookbury, two children; Sarah E., born September 17, 1873, married Hubbard Turner, residence, Brookbury, one child; Mabel M., born January 15, 1876; Gertrude, born August 19, 1879; Susan E., born June 18, 1880; Letitia E., born April 4, 1882; Emma J., born May 13, 1884.

SAMUEL ORD, miller and farmer, was born in Bury, June 9, 1847, and has always resided there. Married in Marbleton, Que., August 15, 1877, to Adeline Batley, of Bury. Issue, six children: Riley Edson, born June 9, 1878; Minnie B., born August 25, 1879; Lottie A., born June 19, 1881; Mabel M., born January 12, 1884; Iva M, born September 30, 1890; Ethel W., born February 2, 1892.

JAMES HUGH LEONARD, farmer, was born in Brookbury, February 11, 1855, where he has always lived. At present he holds the office of councillor, vice-president Compton county P. of I. Association, and secretary Bury Farmers' Club. Was married at Cookshire, April 15, 1879, to Ann Elizabeth Duffield. Issue, one son: Edward Philip, born December 29, 1880. The father of Mrs. Leonard was from Belfast, Ireland; and her mother, Charlotte Besant, from Hampshire, Eng., is still living at Brookbury, aged eighty years.

HENRY ORD, farmer, was born in Bury (Dudswell road), where he has always lived, December 11, 1840. At present he holds the office of school commissioner. Was married at Robinson, June 21, 1864, to Mary Ann Moss. Issue, nine children: John A., born May 6, 1865, married Emma Tockeleton, two children; Charles H., born July 12, 1869; George A., born December 8, 1882; Annie A., born July 17, 1867, married Olsen, four children; Persis E., born July 17, 1872, married James Coleman, three children; Frances A., born October 17, 1874; Edith B., born March 1, 1877, married Rufus Lebourveau, one child; Jessie A., born November 22, 1879; Maggie A., born September 8, 1880.

JOHN LEFEBVRE, carpenter, miller, and farmer; was born in St. Giles, Lotbiniere county, June 6, 1838. Came to Bury in 1871. At present holds the office of councillor. Was married in Bury, January 1, 1881, to Mary Amelia Bown. Issue, three children, two living: Charles Joseph, born January 14, 1882; William, born June 22, 1885.

HISTORY OF COMPTON COUNTY.

CAPTAIN ALEXANDER LEWIS McIVER, trader and farmer, was born at Robinson, August 19, 1855, and has always lived there. He secured his education at Bishops College school, Lennoxville. Has been a councillor for years. Connected with the Fifty-eighth Battalion, and captain for the past fifteen years. He is a son of Lewis McIver, who came from Lewis Island, Scot., and died in Robinson, while Mayor of the township of Bury, October 14, 1884, aged seventy-two years. His mother, Sarah Pope, born in April, 1832, still lives in Robinson. Our subject was married at Toronto, June 4, 1884, to Miss Nina K. Fauquier, of Woodstock, Ont. Issue, one son: Eric, born April 8, 1894.

STEEN ANDERSON, farmer, was born in Norway, February 16, 1833. Came to Compton county in 1863, and settled in Bury. His previous occupation was that of a ship-carpenter. He has held the offices of school commissioner and municipal councillor in his adopted township, and, at the time of writing, still holds the latter office. Married at Rüsör, Norway, December 30, 1856, Anna Olsen, born June 4, 1833, daughter of Ole Knutsen. Issue, ten children, eight living: Anders, born May 9, 1858; Ole, born April 30, 1862; Fritjoff, born June 25, 1869; Helena Catherine, born May 29, 1864, married James Crawford, of Colville, Wash., four children; Anna Sophia, born June 6, 1867, married Alfred Clark, residence, Helena, Mont.; Belinda Matilda, born March 12, 1871; Rebecca Jane Maria, born September 21, 1873; Hardis Amelia, born October 14, 1880.

WILLIAM WRIGHT, farmer, was born in Stanstead, December 1, 1833. Came to Bury in 1857. Drove the stage from latter place to Sherbrooke for six years, afterwards was hotel keeper at Bury for four years, and since then has been a farmer. He was a member of the Cookshire cavalry for over twenty years, and was in active service in 1866, at Stanstead and at Frelighsburg, in 1870. He is senior member of the commissioners court for trial of small causes; a strong supporter of the National Policy and Liberal-Conservative party. Married at Eaton Corner, May 22, 1860, Sarah E. Strobridge, of Eaton. Issue, three children: Herbert B., born June 18, 1863, married Madge Henderson, of Brooklyn, N. Y., residence, Kyle, W. Va., one child; Henry G., born January 14, 1865, residence Seattle, Wash.; Chancy W., born December 18, 1869, residence, Kyle, W. Va.

WILLIAM BOWN, manufacturer, is a son of Thomas Bown, who died January 28, 1876, at the age of eighty-six years. Mr. Bown was born March 17, 1848, in the township of Bury, where he has resided ever since. He is a manufacturer of and dealer in lumber, also a builder and contractor. He is at present municipal councillor and school commissioner, also church warden in St. Thomas' church. Married December 30, 1874, to Mary Charlotte, daughter of William Herring, of Bury. Issue, four children: Walter Arthur, born November 29, 1875; Arnold William, born October 21, 1880; Ernest Roy, born November 11, 1893; Mary Edith, born August 30, 1877. Thomas Bown, above mentioned, was a captain in the militia and held several municipal offices in the township of Bury.

JOHN BENNETT, farmer, resident of Canterbury, was born at Sherbourn, St. Johns, Hampshire, Eng., June 15, 1818. Came to Bury with his parents in 1836, and always lived on the same farm. First marriage April 18, 1842, to Matilda, daughter of the late Thomas Maidment. Issue, six children, four living: Albert J, born April 25, 1844, married Lucia M. Andrews, one child; Frederick A., born January 6, 1855, married Rosette Crawford, three children; Caroline S., born March 14, 1858, married Robert Graham, residence, Clifton, three children; Charles, born November 8, 1859, married Louisa Asker, residence, Bury, three children. Second marriage September 30, 1862, to Althea Grenn, widow of John Andrews, of Eaton. Issue, one son: Reuben, born November 27, 1863, married Alice Gould. Mr. Bennett's first wife died March 25, 1860. He served as a volunteer in the Rebellion of 1837. Is a prominent member of the Church of England, having been warden several times.

GEORGE COATES, farmer, was born in Rockland, St. Peters, Norfolk, Eng., June 21, 1835. Came to Brookbury in 1836, where he has always lived. His father, Sampson Coates, died here May 29, 1876. Married in Bury, January 18, 1865, to Delia, daughter of Robert Batley, who died in January, 1890. Issue, nine children, eight living: Wesley J., born September 30, 1865, married Clara Brown, residence, Brookbury, one child; James S., born July 21, 1868, married Ezilda Vicent, residence, Robinson, two children; Charles G., born December 19, 1869; Willis R., born February 29, 1871; Samuel B. H., born October 20, 1874; Nehemiah G., born July 30, 1882; Walter W., born November 14, 1884; Rufus A., born February 22, 1887; Luella M., born December 28, 1875, married John Thompson, residence, Brookbury.

JOHN DOWNES, farmer. Came to Brookbury in 1836. Was born in Attleboro, Norfolk, Eng., April 4, 1816. In Bury, April 27, 1846, he married Sarah, daughter of Wm. Ward, who died here December 5, 1867. Issue, eleven children, six living: James, born July 3, 1847, married Naomi Clark, residence, Brookbury, four children; Albert, born March 9, 1852, married Hannah Bennett, residence, Brookbury, three children; Alfred E., born February 13, 1862; Henry, born January 1, 1868; Arthur A., born September 24, 1871, married Myra A. Warby, residence, Brookbury, one child; Sarah, born September 23, 1854, married Frank Butters, residence, Thompson, Minn., two children.

CHAPTER XIX.

TOWNSHIP OF LINGWICK.

This tract is bounded by the townships of Weedon, in Wolfe county, Winslow, Hampden and Bury. It was erected into a township, and in part granted March 7, 1807, to William Vandelvendon, Joseph Anger, Augustin Larue, Pierre Delisle the younger, Antoine Trudelle, Joachim Delisle the younger, Jean Baptiste Vésine the younger, Michel Tapin, Louis Vidal the younger, and Augustin Vésina the younger. For some cause there were no permanent settlements made here till a more recent date, and these grants reverted to the Crown. The whole afterwards became the property of the British American Land Company.

Salmon river enters Lingwick from Hampden, and flowing through the south and west parts of the township, turns north into Weedon. There are also two lakes of some size, named respectively Moffatt and Magill, and on the north-east boundary is the small lake McIver; besides which are small streams tributary to the Salmon river. The greater part of the land is said to be of good quality.

The first settlement made in Lingwick was the building of Victoria village, in 1836, by the British American Land Company. The history of this village is given under Chapter VI. In 1837 the first settlers, who were to remain in the township, arrived. They were John, Randal, and Henry Cowan, and a man named MacDowd; and James, John, Lijah, and Thomas Hanright. The Cowans were from the north of Ireland, and were half Scotch and half Irish; the Hanrights were Irish. They settled in Gould on the farms on which some of them are still living. These were shortly followed by a number of "Highland Scotch" from the island of Lewis. They were Donald MacKay, Murdo MacLean, Donald MacDonald, John MacLeod the horse (so called because he was the only Scotchman who had a horse for the first four years), Malcolm MacLeod, Donald MacLeod, Donald Matheson, Angus MacLeod, and John MacLeod the weaver. There being so many MacLeods and MacDonalds, the Scotch to the present day have many nick-names to distinguish one from the other.

These "Highlanders" had several reasons for seeking their fortunes in far-away Canada. They were poor, and had considerable trouble at home with their landlords; they wanted to own farms of their own. Some of them had been misled by stories of the advantages of the new country. They had been told that tobacco was grown in Canada as easily as barley; that when they wanted sugar they simply went out to the woods, bored a hole in a maple tree, and filled a bucket with syrup, which immediately flowed; after a little boiling this made splendid sugar. When they had all the sugar they wanted, they put a plug in the hole, till more was needed.

The first eight families were brought over by the British American Land Company, but the rest paid their way. They all settled on the road between Bury and Gould, as close together as they could. This was always the main thought with the Scotch settlers in those days. It was this that made them leave the farms close to Sherbrooke, which could be secured at the same price. They wanted to have a settlement of their own, where they could live like Highlanders, "shoulder to shoulder." None of them in those days thought of owning a larger farm than fifty acres.

The cabins built by the settlers the first year were very small. The season was so late when they came that the bark would not peel, and so they roofed them with split cedar, and some with spruce and fir boughs. They were floored with little poles, hewed on one side, and had one door and one window, being only one story high. The cabins had no fire places or chimneys the first winter. Flat stones were laid on the floor and against the end of the cabin furthest from the door. A hole was made in the roof to let all the smoke out that was inclined to escape. The roof was generally so badly constructed that whenever it rained outside it rained inside also. The kitchen utensils were a few dishes brought over from Scotland, and a pot or two. The furniture consisted of a table, a cupboard, or "dresser" as it was called, some clumsy home-made tools, and a bed or two.

The settlers lived the first year principally on oatmeal, advanced by the B. A. L. Company. They paid for this the following summer at the rate of $5 for one hundred pounds, by grubbing out a road from Bury to Gould. These Scotch families were all housed in four cabins the first winter. They were chopping all the time, and kept a fire going night and day. Each family had been given a sap kettle by the Company, and after leaching the ashes the lye was made into potash. In this way it helped to get seed grain and potatoes in the spring.

In 1841 the second crew of Scotch settlers came to Lingwick, twenty-seven families in all. They were instructed by the first settlers, profiting by their experience. They all passed through the same hardships of pioneer life. Scotchmen moved into Lingwick, several families at a time, for a number of years thereafter, being the principal proportion of the settlers.

Among the pioneers of Gould was the late James Ross, the first representative of Compton county at Quebec after Confederation. A biography of his life is to be found on another page.

In those early days large, gaunt, white wolves and bears were quite numerous. Further than killing a few sheep and calves they did very little damage, although known to chase the settlers once in a while. The government offered a bounty for killing the wolves which was the means of soon exterminating them.

The Cowans, previously mentioned as among the first settlers, were a little better off, and in what then could be considered comfortable circumstances. They, with the Hanrights, settled on the east side of the Salmon river. Henry Cowan was ferryman for the first fifteen years before a bridge was built. The Cowans and Hanrights were always willing to help the Scotch settlers whenever their Highland pride would permit them to ask for assistance. Instances were known where some of the settlers would go for weeks with nothing to eat but potatoes and salt. Messrs. Henry Cowan and James Hanright are both living, having seen this township reach a prosperous state, and all those around them doing well.

These two narratives give some idea of the loneliness and sorrows met with in those early days. In the winter of 1841 a little girl, daughter of Murdo Graham, North Hill, started for Gould with about half a bushel of potatoes on her shoulder, and was not expected to return until the next day. The following morning one of the inhabitants from Gould, on his way to North Hill, saw the girl leaning against a tree with the bag of potatoes beside her in the snow. He called, but receiving no answer went to her, and found that she was dead, frozen stiff. A few years after Murdo McDonald and his wife, an old couple living at North Hill, were found dead in the cellar. It appears the weather was very cold and they had gone into the cellar to sleep, taking the bed clothes and a pot full of coals down with them. Two days afterwards one of the neighbors heard the cattle lowing, and on investigation found that even the cat, which had also gone into the cellar, had been suffocated by the gas from the charcoal.

The first municipal records of Lingwick date back to 1855, when the first municipal councils were inaugurated. By referring to the minutes of council proceedings we find the following gentlemen have been mayor of the municipality: James Ross, John Keenan, Robert French, D. Buchanan, D. McKay, A. Ross, Geo. Layfield, K. Nicholson, A. McKay, and R. Y. Cowan. The past secretary-treasurers have been: A. Wait, Jas. Ross, Wm. Buchanan, Alex. McKinnon, John McKinnon, and R. D. Cowan. The council for 1896 is composed as follows: D. D. McDonald, mayor, Alex. McKay, R. Y. Cowan, Angus McKay, Neil McLennan, M. McIver, and M. H. McLeod; secretary-treasurer Geo. F. Cowan.

In Lingwick there is one model and eight elementary schools. Principal in model school is Miss Annie McDonald. The board of school commissioners is composed as follows: Wm. Wilson, chairman, Peter Young, Murdock McDonald, John Morrison, and E. C. McKay; secretary-treasurer Alex. McKay.

There are two churches only in the Township, both at Gould. The Presbyterian (Free) church was first built in 1845. This was pulled down, and a fine new brick church erected within the past three or four years. Just at present there is no settled Presbyterian minister. Over eight-tenths of the inhabitants of Lingwick worship in this church. There is also an Episcopal church in the vicinity of Gould. This was built in 1861. They have no resident clergyman, the incumbent at Scotstown, Rev. H. A. Brooke, holding service at stated periods.

Gould is the principal post office, of the four located in Lingwick. It is eight miles from Scotstown. Population about two hundred. This office was established some time previous to 1857. In that year the population was about one hundred, and among the inhabitants we find the names of John Keenan, bailiff; John Noble, hotel-keeper; Thomas Nurse, grist and saw mills; Austin Pennoyer, general agent; John A. Pope, general agent; James Ross, J.P., P.M., general merchant, potash manufacturer, and mayor; Abraham Wait, secretary-treasurer. Gould is now a thriving village, with several general stores, hotel, saw and grist mills, etc. No liquor license has been granted since 1890. There is a daily mail. Postal revenue, 1895, $249.

Galson is five and a half miles from Gould, and a post office for a farming community. Daily mail. Postal revenue, 1895, $51 50.

Red Mountain is nine miles south of Weedon station, on the Quebec Central Railway, and five miles from Gould. It is quite a village, with hotel, general stores, grist and saw mills, etc. Population, one hundred and twenty-five. Mail daily. Postal revenue, 1895, $25.

North Hill is nine miles from Weedon station, and the centre of a farming community. Mail daily. Postal revenue, 1895, $12.

The census of 1891 gives the following particulars about Lingwick: Population, 1,022; families, 184; houses, 171; males, 539; females, 483. French-Canadians, 72; others, 950. Religions—Roman Catholic, 76; Church of England, 77; Presbyterians, 844; Methodists, 13; not specified, 12.

THE LATE JAMES ROSS, ex-M. L. A., was for many years a prominent figure in the public life of Compton county. Born in Fearn, Rossshire, Scotland, in 1814, he received his early education at the Invergordon grammar school, came to this country when 15 years old, and for a few years was engaged in a mercantile house in Quebec. Later on he followed the sea, being captain of a vessel trading between Quebec and the West Indies. In 1842, he came to Cookshire, where for three years he carried on business in the stand afterwards owned by Mr. Rufus Pope, now one of the oldest buildings in the town. In 1845, he was attracted to the new township of Lingwick, where now stands the village of Gould—of which he was pioneer and founder, here he carried on business until his death in 1874. Concurrently with this he carried on a manufactory of pearlash, which in the absence of railways was transported to Montreal in wagons, the goods received in exchange being carried back in the same manner. Mr. Ross occupied at various times the position of mayor, secretary for schools and council, was lieutenant-colonel of the militia, and in every way in his power identified himself with the best interests of the place and people. It appears from an old county record that Mr. Ross, May 9, 1848, moved the resolution for the organization of the municipality of the county of Sherbrooke. At the Confederation of the Provinces he was elected representative for the county in the local house, a choice which his knowledge of the country's needs, his sterling integrity, his forcible and practical address, was thoroughly justified. He visited Great Britain in 1872, and again in 1873, to enlist the interests of his countrymen in the advantages of his adopted country as a field for emigration. This work, in which his heart and mind were much engaged, was interrupted by his too early death, in January, 1874. Mr. Ross was eminently literary, being probably one of the most widely read men of the Province. Debarred by the exigencies of fortune from pursuing a university course he bent every circumstance of life to the furtherance of his mental equipment. Trading to the West Indies he made himself master of the Spanish language. During his sojourn in Quebec he familiarized himself with not the language only, but also the literature of the French. Indeed he was said to be the

LATE JAMES ROSS, EX-M. L. A.

only man in Parliament in his day, who could speak four languages, Gælic, being equally with English, his native tongue. He possessed fine poetic tastes and genius. While yet a lad in Quebec, he received substantial recognition from the manager of one of the city papers, for poetic contributions. Some of his poems might still be found in old files of the *Sherbrooke Gazette*. In religion Mr. Ross was a Presbyterian, but while he loved the church of his fathers, he always had an open hand and a ready sympathy for churches of other denominations.

Unselfish, he employed every energy of his fertile brain towards the uplifting of his fellow citizens. Many an address on vital subjects, prepared amid the anxieties and trials of life in a new country, was giving to the youth of Lingwick to make up in some measure to them for the lack of other means of education. In 1838 Mr. Ross married Miss Marianna Browne, of Quebec. Issue, 14 children, 10 living: James and George, the eldest and youngest sons, respectively, have spent most of their lives in Montana; Alexander, now customs officer in Cookshire, for sometime carried on his father's business, and was mayor of the town until his removal to Cookshire necessitated his resignation of the office. He also served as warden of the county, in 1887-88. Charles, of the department of railways and canals, Ottawa; and Crawford, of the C. Ross Co., of Ottawa, Limited, are the other sons. Of the daughters, Jane C. was first married to George Pennoyer, of Sherbrooke, second marriage to Alexander McKay, of Gould; Malvina, wife of Rev. J. Macleod, of Vankleek Hill; Elizabeth, wife of H. A. Odell, of Sherbrooke; Belinda, wife of D. Macrae, of Toronto; Margaret, lady principal in the Boys' High School, Montreal. Mrs. Ross died suddenly in 1890, well and deservedly loved by a large circle of friends. She was a particularly amiable and benevolent lady, retaining to the last, marked traces of her early beauty. Mr. Ross' memory is held in great esteem by the older citizens of Lingwick, among whom his name is synonymous with all that is generous, reliable and upright.

HENRY COWAN, farmer, a resident of Gould, was born in County Meath, Ireland, August 20, 1814. He came to Canada in 1831, and to Lingwick in 1836. He was one of the first settlers in this township, and the house he lives in was the second frame house built in the township, while the barn was the first one erected east of Bury. He held the office of councillor for several years. In Bury, in 1839, he married Catharine, daughter of Donald Mackay. Issue, eleven children: Richard, born in July, 1840, married Mary Mackay, residence, Washington State, seven children; Angus, born February 15, 1847, married Jeannette Fife, of Lowell, Mass., residence, Gould; Henry, married Alice Little, residence, Washington State; Gordon, born in October, 1853, married M. A. McElwee, residence, Forest Hill, Cal., two children; John, born June 11, 1857, married Ann J. Murray, residence, Gould, three children; Harriet, married Wm. Buchanan, residence, Gould, three children; Mary A., married Roderick Macaulay, residence, Gould, seven children; Catharine, married Rev. Charles McLean, residence, Ardock, Dakota, four children; Margaret, born in 1851, married Edwin Phillips, residence, New York; Jennie, not married; Martha, married Robert Murray, residence, Lake Megantic, four children. Mr. and Mrs. Cowan are living, and are over eighty years of age.

NORMAN MURRAY, farmer, was born on the island of Lewis, Scotland, March 10, 1829. He came to Lingwick in 1842, with other settlers from Scotland, and is now a hale and hearty, prosperous farmer. He has held the office of school commissioner, and was councillor eighteen years. He married Jane Eliza Hanright, in Lingwick, in 1854. Mrs. Murray's father built the first frame house in Lingwick, and her mother, who died in 1881, was 104 years of age. Issue, eight children: Robert, born December 8, 1864, married Martha Cowan, residence, Lake Megantic, four children; Frederick W.; Daniel C.; David L.; Esther M., married Elgin Weston, residence, Lake Megantic, two children; Ann Jane, married John Cowan, residence, Lingwick, three children; Alice M., married Ebby Mackay, residence, Scotstown, three children; Malvina Murray.

JAMES AUSTIN PENNOYER, merchant, was born in Sherbrooke, August 28, 1868, going to Gould in 1870. April 18, 1894, he married Persis Lothrop. Mr. Pennoyer is a grandson of the late Charles Pennoyer, agent for the British American Land Company. His store is on the stand of the first store built in Lingwick, and it has always remained in the family, passing from his grandfather, James Ross, to his sons Alex. and Charles, and from them to the present occupant. Mr. Pennoyer is also postmaster at Gould.

CHARLES SMITH, farmer, was born in Lewis, Scotland, July 15, 1835. Came to Lingwick in November of 1841, with four brothers, three of whom moved, later, to the United States, and are now dead; the fourth, Norman, is living in Winslow. Mr. Smith is postmaster at Red Mountain. Was married in Lingwick, March 9, 1864, to Catharine Buchanan. Issue, eight children: Alexander, born December 11, 1864; John, born May 19, 1868; Kenneth, born January 26, 1870; Donald N., born December 12, 1872; Charles M., born October 13, 1878; George G., born March 19, 1883; Mary, born July 26, 1866; Margaret E., born August 16, 1874.

KENNETH D. McRAE, farmer and lumberman, was born in Lewis, Scotland, February 1, 1860. Came to North Whitton with his father, D. B. McRae, in May, 1874. Married Katie M. McLeod, of Loch Shell, Scotland. Issue, seven children: Malcolm D., born December 18, 1879; Samuel F., born October 8, 1885; Daniel L., born December 19, 1893; Flora Ann, born June 29, 1884; Effine, born May 4, 1887; Dolina M., born April 8, 1889; Lilly M., born August 25, 1890; Katie M, born May 2, 1892; Annie, born September 4, 1895.

ANGUS GORDON McKAY, farmer, a resident of Red Mountain, was born in Bury, June 16, 1852. He has held the office of councillor for six years. Married in Lingwick, December 27, 1876, to Annie McLeod, born February 20, 1853. Issue, five children: Donald Kenneth, born April 7, 1893; Margaret Jessie, born January 31, 1878; Jane Catharine, born March 19, 1880; Albina Mary, born October 14, 1882; Laura Grace, born March 20, 1887. Mr. McKay's father and grandfather came from Scotland among the first settlers.

DONALD MORRISON, farmer, born in Lewis, Scot., June 14, 1835, came to Red Mountain in 1858, where he has since lived. Married at the same place in October, 1871, to Margaret McRitchie, born June 16, 1837. Issue, six children: John, born May 28, 1876; Norman, born May 23, 1878; Murdo, born March 12, 1882; Donald, born March 3, 1884; Mary A., born July 17, 1872; Maggie Eveline, born June 7, 1874, died June 16, 1892; Catharine, born April 9, 1880.

JOHN J. MACKAY, carpenter, millwright and builder, was born at Red Mountain, November 15, 1859, where he now lives. Married at Gould November 20, 1890, to Flora McLeod Mr. Mackay was one of the crew of Scotch boys who worked on the Atlantic & Pacific railway, traveling through many of the western states, but finally returned to his old home.

GEORGE FRANKLIN COWAN, farmer, a resident of Gould, was born in Lingwick, December 15, 1865. He has always lived here. At Gould, October 25, 1893, he married Belinda Ross, daughter of James Hanright. Randal Cowan, the father of our subject, came to Lingwick in 1836. He married Susan Bennett, of Cookshire. Issue, thirteen children.

CHAPTER XX.

Township of Hampden.

Including History of the Town of Scotstown.

This Township is of irregular shape, containing only 20,270 square acres.

Settlements were first made to the north, and at about the same time as in Winslow, Whitton and Marston, by Scotch emigrants. After the building of the old International Railway, the settlement of the Township was rapid. The early history of the three Townships before mentioned is identical with that of Hampden.

On March 10th, 1874, the township of Hampden was first erected into a separate municipality, previous to that time having been included in the municipality of Whitton, Marston and Hampden. Thus it continued until 24th June, 1892, when Scotstown was incorporated by Act of the Legislature, and taken out of the township of Hampden for municipal purposes.

The Salmon river flows through this Township into Lingwick, besides smaller streams tributary to it, chief among which are Otter Brook, coming from the west of Marston, and Mountain Brook, having its source in the hilly sections of the Megantic mountains.

The school municipality includes the town of Scotstown. The board of school commissioners for 1895, was as follows: R. Scott, chairman, W. McDonald, R. Stevenson, H. Snell, and N. Murray; secretary-treasurer, D. B. McLennan. They have under their charge one model and five elementary schools. The model school is at Scotstown, and the teachers are John McMullen, jr., principal, and Misses Agnes and S. Sever, assistants.

The past Mayors have been J. Scott, Ænas McMaster, John Scott, C. H. Parker, D. D. McInnes, and Thos. Muir. Past secretary-treasurers: J. Brochu, J. Scott, D. B. McLennan, R. B. Scott, John Muir, John Black, and A. D. Parker. The Council for 1895, was composed as follows: Mayor, John D. Morrison, and councillors, D. D. McInnes, Kenneth Smith, Donald S. Morrison, M. J. McDonald, Godfrey Chouinard, and John Pringle; secretary-treasurer, D. L. McRitchie.

There are two post offices, now in the Township, Dell and McLeod's Crossing. Milan is just on the line between Hampden and Marston, and is described with the history of the latter Township.

Dell is a post office erected within a few years, located five miles and a half east of Scotstown. It is the centre of a farming community. Postal revenue, 1895, $43.50.

McLeod's Crossing is also a new post office on the C. P. R., likewise a farming community, and the centre for shipment of considerable pulp wood and ties, in the winter. Postal revenue, 1895, $70.50.

The churches in the municipality are all located at Scotstown.

The census of 1891 gives the following statistics for Hampden township, including the town of Scotstown. Population, 1,066; families, 196; houses, 159; males, 566; females, 500. French Canadians, 389; others, 677. Religious—Roman Catholics, 422; Church of England, 90; Presbyterians, 467; Methodists, 29; Adventists, 54; Salvation Army, 1; not specified, 3.

TOWN OF SCOTSTOWN.

The municipality of the town of Scotstown was created out of the township of Hampden, by Act of the Quebec Legislature, in 1892. The date of the first municipal records are August 3, 1892. It comprises 2,705¼ square acres, and in 1895 had a valuation of $100,000. For school purposes the town remains part of the township. The first and present mayor is Mr. C. H. Parker, and the secretary-treasurer since 1892, has been Mr. R. Scott. The councillors for 1895 were: W. F. Bowman, E. M. McKay, C. A. Leger, M. B. Macaulay, John Black, and Jos. Langlois.

RESIDENCE OF LT.-COL. M. B. MACAULAY.

Scotstown is well supplied with water power, the Salmon river passing through the town, with a good fall. Large saw mills are here located, while there is plenty of room and power for other industries. With these advantages the place is sure to make progress. The C. P. R. short line has a railway station here, and it is the centre for a large surrounding country. Postal revenue, 1895, $866.23.

The first hotel was built about the time of the completion of the old International railway, by the late Horace H. French. It is now owned and carried on by his son, C. W. B. French. There is another hotel, erected a few years ago, known as the Sherman House. This was not a success, and has been vacant for some time. No liquor licenses have been granted since 1890.

There are four churches at Scotstown. Church of England, with Rev. H. A. Brooke as pastor. Presbyterian Church, no stationed minister at present. Roman Catholic, Rev. A. Rousseau, parish priest. Advent Christian, pastor, Elder Samuel Clark.

The Advent Christian church was organized 21 March, 1887, but its inception dates back to July, 1886. It was organized with a membership of eight, and with Mr. R. B. Scott as ruling elder. A chapel 24 x 32 feet was built in the fall of 1887, on Albert street, and was dedicated free of debt. The present membership is 28.

LT. COL. MALCOLM B. MACAULAY, contractor and dealer in lumber, was born in Rosshire, Scotland, September 15, 1847. Came to Winslow in July, 1851, settled at Lake Megantic in 1879, and moved to Scotstown his present home, in 1890. On preceding page we give an excellent engraving of his home, prettily located in Scotstown. He left Winslow in 1864, enlisted in the army of the North, was ordered South, and remained there until the close of the war. Came back to Boston, Mass., in August, 1865. After living there two years he returned to Winslow in February, 1868, and has lived in the county since that date. His business has been principally railroad contracting, and farming. He had several contracts on the old International and Q. C. railways. He also put in the Cookshire water works and sewerage system. While in the Union army he served under General Thomas, and was in the battles at Nashua, Tenn., and Springfield, Tenn. He held the office of mayor of Whitton and also of Lake Megantic, each for four years, and many other public offices. He is a justice of the peace for the St. Francis District. He joined the 58th Battalion in 1869, as Lieutenant, having graduated from the Montreal military school that year. He has secured gradual promotion until now he holds the honorable position of lieutenant-colonel of the Battalion. His father, Malcolm Macauly, died at Coaticook in 1852. Our subject was married at Cookshire, December 25, 1879, to Emma M., fourth daughter of the late C. A. Bailey. Issue, five children, four living; Rupert Malcolm, born October 6, 1884; Colin Alexander, born October 27, 1893; Jane Maria, born September 28, 1886; Emily Christina, born May 25, 1888.

SCOTSTOWN HOTEL, C. W. B. FRENCH, PROPRIETOR.

CAPTAIN CHARLES WARD BAILEY FRENCH, hotel-keeper and farmer, was born in Cookshire, August 5, 1845. His father, Horace Hall French, was born on the old Hurd farm, Cookshire, July 16, 1812, and died at Scotstown, May 19, 1896. He married Harriet B. Ward, of Eaton, who died March 26, 1889, aged 73 years. Mr. H. H. French built the hotel in Cookshire, now owned by A. Learned, also the store now owned and occupied by S. J. Osgood, and later the hotel at Scotstown, now owned by his son. He was one of the chief supporters of the late Honorable John Henry Pope, and always deeply interested in public enterprises. Our subject, C. W. B. French, was educated at the Cookshire academy. He built the American House, Cookshire, but on the building of the Intercolonial railway, through Scotstown, he moved to this place in 1874, where he has since resided. He has held the position of Captain in the 58th Battalion, but is now retired, retaining rank. In 1894, on the resignation of Honorable John McIntosh, Mr. French came within one vote of receiving the nomination of the Conservative party, as their candidate for the Legislative Assembly. At present Mr. French is warden of St. Albans' Episcopal church, Scotstown. He has been married twice, first to

RESIDENCE OF C. H. PARKER.

Maria A., eldest daughter of the late C. A. Bailey, at Cookshire, May 31, 1867; she died February 2, 1880. Issue, three children : Herbert A., born January 7, 1880; Persis H., born November 22, 1875; Ellen B., born May 19, 1878. Second marriage at Scotstown, February 14, 1883, to Kate, daughter of Donald McIver, of Minnesota, U. S. Issue, six children, five living: Charles D., born March 26, 1884; John W., born October 22, 1888; Horace R., born March 10, 1890; Martha M., born March 2, 1887; Lottie M. M., born July 23, 1891. On preceding page will be found an engraving of the hotel at Scotstown, with Mr. French, his father, and family in front.

CARLOS HENRY PARKER, manager Scotstown Lumber Co., was born in Bothel, Me., September 26, 1850. He came to Bury in 1872, and two years later moved to Scotstown, where he has since resided. Previous to accepting his present position he was a millwright and lumber manufacturer. He is a son of Otis Parker, who died in West Stewartstown, N. H., in 1882. Mr. C. H. Parker was mayor of the township of Hampden for seven years, and warden of Compton county one term. Since the incorporation of the town of Scotstown in 1892, he has held the office of mayor. He is a prominent member of the R. T. of T., and holds the office of P. C. At Canterbury, September 26, 1878, he married Mary, daughter of Robert Clark, whose history will be found on another page of this book. Issue, seven children, five living: John Otis, born June 11, 1882; Persis Ann, born April 3, 1884; Archibald Sylvestre, born February 24, 1886; Winnifred Eliza, born January 4, 1888; Harold Leslie, born March 19,

RESIDENCE OF JOHN BLACK, SCOTSTOWN.

1890. On preceding page is a photo-engraving of the residence of Mr. Parker, and in front he and his family may be seen.

JOHN BLACK, manager Lumber Company's store, at Scotstown, was born in Rothesay, Island of Bute, Scotland, July 20, 1849. An engraving of his home and family, from a photograph taken in the fall of 1895, is given herewith. Mr. Black landed in Canada May 13, 1872, and for a short time he was clerk for Messrs. Brooks, Bacon & Co., in the large building opposite the E. T. Bank, Sherbrooke. In the same year, 1872, he accepted a position with the Glasgow Canadian Land and Trust Company, with head office in Scotstown. Mr. Black was one of the first settlers in the village, and has seen the place grow from woods and stumps to a thriving town. Our subject is agent for the G. N. W. Telegraph Company, and has been a councillor of Scotstown since its incorporation, previous to that time he was a councillor in the township of Hampden for two years. He is also treasurer of the Presbyterian church and the C. O. F. His father, Colin Black, died in Rothesay, in 1887, aged seventy-nine years, having been a sailor all his life and for many years captain of a merchant vessel. Mr. Black was married in Rothesay, February 15, 1871, to Annie, daughter of Angus McAlpine, who is still living in Rothesay, aged eighty-five years. Her mother died July 6, 1895, aged seventy-eight years, after a happy wedded life of fifty-six years. They were both members of the West Free church. Mr. McAlpine was for twenty years superintendent of police in Rothesay, and is now in charge of the Court House. Issue, five children: Margaret Barbour, first white child ever born within the limits of the present town of Scotstown, born February 16, 1874, married September 26, 1894, to Anthony Mahern, one child (Anne Ellen, born July 10, 1895), residence, Scotstown; John, born August 15, 1877; Angus Cleland, born October 1, 1881; Elizabeth Annie, born July 21, 1885; Colena, born March 5, 1887.

CHARLES A. LEGER, merchant tailor and dealer in gent's furnishing, was born at Ottawa, Ont., May 12, 1862. He attended the Ottawa University and graduated therefrom. In 1889 he came to Scotstown and has been successful in his business. The engraving which we give herewith is his shop, store and private residence, specially fitted up for the business by Mr. Leger, who may be seen standing in front. He takes a prominent part in the Liberal Association of Compton county, and for the past two years has been president of the same. When Scotstown was incorporated as a town Mr. Leger was one of the first seven councillors chosen, and still holds the position. He was married at Ottawa May 5, 1882, to Jane, daughter of the late F. X. Guertin, for several years one of the councillors of that city.

STORE OF C. A. LEGER.

EBENEZER MALLOY McKAY, blacksmith, was born in Bury, November 1, 1859. He came to Scotstown in 1884, previous to that time being five years in western states. He is one of the councillors of Scotstown, and is now an elder in the Presbyterian church. Was married in Gould, January 6, 1885, to Alice Maud, daughter of Norman Murray, of Gould. Issue, three children: Donald Russell, born September 16, 1892; Margaret Jane, born December 10, 1888; Carrie Sherburne, July 15, 1891.

DONALD A. MACKENZIE, harness maker and dealer, was born in Winslow, March 10, 1872, moving to Scotstown a few years ago. He is a member of the R. T. of T., being a past councillor, and at present financial secretary. He is a son of Allan Mackenzie, of Scotstown.

CHAPTER XXI.

TOWNSHIP OF WINSLOW.

Including History of Municipalities of North and South Winslow.

This tract of land, which forms the northeast corner of the county of Compton, contains about 73,000 square acres. It was erected into a township named Winslow, April 19, 1851, and has been subsequently divided into two distinct municipalities, viz.: North and South Winslow.

All of these townships, which were not surveyed or subdivided until after 1850, had been named and were outlined on the maps by the first surveyors, about 1800. Bouchette, the surveyor-general, writing in 1815, speaks of them as being projected townships.

Winslow is rather stony, but is, nevertheless, a good grazing country. It is watered by Felton river and its branches; and McIver lake lies on the Lingwick border; Trout and Maskinonge lakes lie on the Wolfe county line; while Lake St. Francis touches the county line of Beauce. This township was first settled about the time lumbering operations were begun in this part of the country by the late C. S. Clarke, for the supply of his mills at Brompton Falls. It was government land and opened by government roads. The settlers in the southern and larger part of the township are chiefly Scotch, those at the north, French-Canadians.

SOUTH WINSLOW.

Previous to 1849 no one had settled in South Winslow. In 1851 about twenty families, who had some time previously emigrated from Scotland and at first settled in Lingwick, moved into this municipality, and commenced clearing land. This was brought about by the Government offering free, fifty-acres of land, while Lingwick was owned by the British American Land Company, and the land there had to be paid for. The first year they managed to clear only enough to hold their claim. Potatoes, barley and other grain were planted. This seed had to be carried on the back by a spotted line from Lingwick, a distance of twenty miles. In the same way all provisions, tools, etc, had to be brought in, there being no road. Later on in 1851 thirty-four families came as far as Lingwick, with the intention of settling in Winslow. In 1852 some of them took possession of land, but others returned to work on the Grand Trunk Railway, which was then in course of construction between Richmond and Sherbrooke. About this time the Government, learning of so many settlers coming in, refused to grant any more free land. About 1860 the late Hon. John Henry Pope, then M. P. P., managed to get land for the recent settlers at half price, or thirty cents per acre.

In 1854 was commenced the building of a road through Winslow to Lambton; afterwards a road from Stratford through to Lake Megantic was built. Where the two roads crossed is the present village of Stornoway. In 1849 the first store was opened at Stornoway by a Mr. McClintock, of Bury. It was a log house, and about three years later was purchased by Mr. Colin Noble, now of Cookshire.

In the years 1851-52 a Presbyterian minister, named Rev. Mr. McLean, came to Winslow, being paid by Lady Mathewson, of Scotland, to preach to these people. He continued the services in a log shanty until the church which now stands a mile out of Stornoway was erected. About 1894 he was succeeded by Rev. Mr. McDonald, who remained until 1878, being followed by Rev. Wm. Mathewson; Rev. Angus McLeod was the next minister and remained until 1894, when the present pastor, Rev. Mr. McLennan, took the appointment.

In 1857 the frame of the first saw mill was erected by Donald McLeod, and afterwards sold to Messrs. Layfield & Pallister, who completed it. The mill is situated about one mile distant from Stornoway. Before this all sawing was done by the old fashioned whip-saw. Later on Pallister sold his share to Layfield. The latter shortly after built a grist mill, and the mills are now carried on by his son, Alex. Layfield.

The first hotel was built in Stornoway in 1853, by the late Thos. Leonard. It was burnt down, rebuilt, and again destroyed by fire. The third building erected was the present hotel. It is carried on by the son, James Leonard. No license for liquor has been granted since 1892.

The first school records are dated July 2, 1854. The following were then elected commissioners: Alex. McLeod, Angus McLeod, Angus Smith, John Wm. McDonald, Rev. E. McLean, chairman; Donald Campbell, secretary-treasurer. The first school house was built in 1855. Since then six more have been opened. The present board of school commissioners is composed as follows: Malcolm McLeod, jr., chairman, Murdo N. McLeod, John C. Matheson, Alex. McDonald, and Malcolm Campbell; John A. McDonald, secretary-treasurer.

The first municipal records of Winslow are dated August 6, 1855, and the municipality then included the townships of Winslow and Whitton. There were present at the first meeting councillors McIver, Noble, McLeod, McDonald, and Belliveau. Councillor Colin Noble was chosen mayor. He held the office from 1855 to 1857, again from 1864 to 1866, and from 1868 to 1872. The other past mayors have been Donald Benton, Angus Smith, Thos. Leonard, Henry Layfield, Daniel McIver, and Malcolm Smith. The present mayor, Mr. Hugh Leonard, has held that office since February 1, 1875. The past secretary-treasurers have been as follows: Donald McLeod, Donald Campbell, Malcolm Campbell, William McAulay, Donald D. McLeod, John A. McDonald, and Peter Matheson. The council for 1895 was composed as follows: Mayor, Hugh Leonard, and councillors, George McRae, Angus Campbell, Augus P. McIver, Norman P. McLeod, and Alcide Belliveau.

Stornoway is the principal post office and only village in South Winslow. It derives its name from the capital of Lewis Island, Scot. It is nine miles from Spring Hill, the nearest railway station. Population, about two hundred and fifty. Daily mail. Postal revenue, 1895, $234.50.

Tolsta is the only other post office. It is four miles from Stornoway. Population about one hundred. Daily mail. Postal revenue, 1895, $19.

NORTH WINSLOW.

This is the northeastern section of the Towuship, and inhabited principally by French-Canadians. The first settlements were made here at about the same time as in South Winslow, only that the settlers came from the opposite direction, Beauce county. The only post office and village in this municipality is St. Romaine, six miles from Stornoway, on the road to Lambton. Population, four hundred. Here are found several saw mills, grist and carding mill, general stores, etc. Daily mail. Postal revenue, 1895, $190.

The mayor of North Winslow in 1895 was A. Campeau, and secretary-treasurer was A. Brun.

The census of 1891 gives the following statistics for the whole township of Winslow:

Population, 1,499; families, 265; houses, 250; males, 760; females, 739. French-Canadians, 995; others, 504. Religions—Roman Catholic, 1,024; Church of England, 4; Presbyterians, 471.

HUGH LEONARD, mill owner and trader, and mayor of South Winslow, was born in Bury, November 29, 1847. When two years of age his parents moved to Lingwick, and three years later went to Stornoway, where the family has since resided. His father, Thomas Leonard, died here July 2, 1872. He was a man of force of character, which has been inherited by his sons He was mayor of South Winslow one term. Mr. Hugh Leonard is interested in several saw mills throughout the country, and noted as being one of the best business men of this section of the country. He has recently developed a chrome iron mine on the Quebec Central Railway, which is paying well, with large orders for shipment to the United States. In public affairs Mr. Leonard is one of the most prominent men in the country. He has been mayor of South Winslow for the past twenty-two years, and warden of the county of Compton one term He is a justice of the peace for the district of St. Francis. Twice he has unsuccessfully contested the county in the interests of the Liberal party. First, in 1878, opposing the late Hon. John Henry Pope. Second, in 1886, at the first election of John McIntosh, present sheriff of the district. Mr. Leonard always commanded respect from his opponents, although they could not agree politically.

DONALD B. McLENNAN, book-keeper for the Scotstown Lumber Company, and secretary-treasurer of the school commissioners of Hampden. Born in Valtos, Uig, Lewis, Scotland, October 16, 1855. He came to Scotstown in 1878. Previously engaged as general merchant. A Past Chief Ranger of the C O. F., now holding office of Chaplain. Married at Kirk Hill, Ont., October 26, 1893, to Annie Nicholson, of Lingwick. Issue, two children: Ann Buchanan, born January 12, 1895; Nicol Angus, born March 25, 1896.

DONALD SMITH, farmer, was born on Lewis Island, Scotland, August 10, 1844. With his father he came to Winslow in 1855, and the family as a whole have been successful. Our subject was married in Winslow, April 20 1870, to Marion Campbell. Issue 7 children: John D., born May 8, 1879; Murdo R., born March 31, 1883; Isabella, born January 11, 1873; Katie A., born March 5, 1875; Margaret, born May 29, 1877; Christy, born February 18, 1881; Alice, born November 23, 1891.

CHAPTER XXII.

TOWNSHIP OF WHITTON.

Including History Village of Lake Megantic, and North and South Whitton.

This projected township was subdivided and erected March 4, 1863, and contains 73,500 square acres. It is of very irregular shape. The Little Megantic mountains lie in the north part. The principal stream is the Chaudière, which separates it from Beauce county on the south-east. There are several small lakes within the township, the principal of which are the Three Mile, Moose, and Muskrat, the outlets of which discharge into the Chaudière. In the western part are the head waters of the Felton river, which flows into Winslow, and thence into Lake St. Francis.

In the early history of Winslow township, we have the same experience and same class of settlers as in Whitton, and for a number of years the settlers did not know whether they were in Winslow or Whitton. The Drum-a-Vack district, which lies between Spring Hill and Lake Megantic, was first settled, in 1859, by Angus McRae, Murdo and Rory McLeod, and John Murray. In those early days one of the first enterprises was a company organized to catch fish in Lake Megantic and ship fresh to Boston. The company had their head office at Bury, Que., and was under management of a Mr. DeCourtney. It was a complete failure financially, still operations were continued for three years, and brought considerable money to the settlers. There are evidences yet to be seen of that undertaking in the shape of old crib-work and stakes, where net-pounds were made at great expense. The company also built a good house at Sandy Bay (now Echo Vale), the lumber being sawed by a whip-saw. This served as a rendez-vous for United States "skedaddlers," during the civil war in that country. In it the late John Boston McDonald commenced business in 1861-62.

In 1861 the combined townships of Whitton, Hampden, and Marston were erected into one municipality, and John Boston McDonald chosen mayor. He continued in office until 1868, being followed by Allan McLeod, the present mayor of Marston, until 1870. Donald Smith was mayor up to 1872, and Wm. McLeod until 1874, when the three townships were divided into as many different municipalities. The first records for Whitton are dated 1874. The past mayors of Whitton have been: Norman McDonald, Malcolm Matheson, M. B. Macaulay, J. B. McDonald, Wm. D. McAulay, A. S. McDonald, and D. P. Matheson. Past secretary-treasurers: Mal. McAulay, Mal. Matheson, and John Buchanan. The present council is composed as follows: Kenneth W. McLeod, mayor, and councillors, Finlay McLeod, Norman Beaton, Robert McLeod, John R. Macaulay, Rory Smith, and Murdo N. Murray.

There are six elementary schools.

Spring Hill is the largest of the three post offices in Whitton outside of Lake Megantic village, which lies in this Township, but is a separate municipality, and has a history of its own, which may be found following that of this Township. Spring Hill is on the line of the Canadian Pacific Railway. Has a population of about three hundred. Here is to be found a large saw mill, and a centre for the shipment of pulp-wood and lumber. Postal revenue, 1895, $172.

Whitwick is three miles from Milan, and located in the east end of the Township. It is the centre of a farming community. Population, seventy-five. Daily mail. Postal revenue, 1895, $31.

Echo Vale, known also as Sandy Bay, is a flag station on the Canadian Pacific Railway. Daily mail. Postal revenue, 1895, $80.50.

Whitton has been divided into two municipalities known as North and South Whitton. The population of North Whitton is composed nearly altogether of French Canadians. In this municipality there is only one village and post office. It is known as Ste. Cecil de Whitton. It is nine miles from Lake Megantic, the nearest railway station. There is a population of sixty. General store, and saw and grist mill. Daily mail. Postal revenue, 1895, $103.

The mayor for North Whitton in 1895 was Pierre Rosa. The secretary-treasurer is A. Brun, with post office at St. Romain, in North Winslow.

The census statistics of 1891 give the following particulars for the whole township of Whitton, not including Megantic village. Population, 983; families, 171; houses, 163; males, 504; females, 479. French Canadians, 460; others, 523. Religions—Catholic, 486; Church of England, 31; Presbyterians, 454; Methodists, 11.

LAKE MEGANTIC VILLAGE.

Lake Megantic and Agnes villages are virtually one, although bearing two names. The Chaudière river divides them, also the boundary line between Compton and Beauce counties. Agnes was first settled, and one of the pioneers was Capt. J. S. Wilson, now postmaster at that place. He gives the following description of the settlement of the two villages.

"In May, 1876, I first came to Lake Megantic in connection with the Canadian Land Reclaiming and Colonizing Company. At that time John Boston's house was the rendez-vous of any one coming to the lake, and at that house all were made welcome, whether strangers or not, for John was a most liberal and hospitable individual. From thence proceeded to Sandy Bay, where stood an old barn, and as there was no road for vehicles to the Chaudière, all goods were left in that barn until communication was had with those living at the Chaudière. This was done by firing two shots, on hearing which a boat was sent to Sandy Bay to convey any goods or passengers who might be in waiting.

"At that time 'The Chaudière,' as it was then called, was a pleasant place at which to live. Where the saw mill now stands at the outlet of the lake was a little bay, well sheltered and bordered with shrubs, which extended round as far as the bridge, and in summer was one mass of blossoms; a small log camp stood in what is now the mill yard, and as no clearing had then been attempted, the forest trees still stood in their primeval beauty. Certainly there were no roads on either side of the river, but at that time we could, and did dispense with them, and got along wonderfully well. The fish were at that time plentiful; lunge, bass and trout could be caught above the bridge with the greatest ease. Trout of three and four pounds being no rarity.

"In 1877, I received money from the Government to cut a road through the bush to Ness Hill, and so give us communication with the outer world; this was done and that road is now the main street in the village of Megantic. In the Spring of 1877 the roads from Sandy Bay were not passable for a fortnight, consequently, no flour or other stores were to be had, and all hands at the Chaudière had to live on potatoes of which we had a sufficiency. When we could use the roads, such as they were, I drove to Stornaway, eighteen miles distant, and got a barrel of flour for which I paid eleven dollars cash, which was one dollar less than the credit price. White sugar, sixteen cents per pound; tea, ninety cents to one dollar per pound, all other goods in proportion, except beef, of which I brought a carcase at three cents per pound.

"In that year, (1877), a post office was applied for and opened at Agnes, and I was appointed postmaster. It was originally named Moutignac, but at the request of the then owner of the land on which it stood, Dominique Morin, the name was changed to Morinville; afterwards, as I understand, on a visit made here by Lady Macdonald, in 1878, she stood on the centre of the bridge connecting the two counties, and at the request of the Hon. J. H. Pope, named the settlement after herself 'Agnes,' which name the village on the Beauce side of the Chaudière still retains.

"This post office was originally served by the old 'Lake Megantic' post office, J. B. McDonald, postmaster, and which was afterwards removed to Robert McLeod's."

Malcolm Matheson was the first one to settle in the present village of Lake Megantic. He came here May 23, 1873, from Lennoxville, and erected a house. In August of the same year he was followed by Telesphore Legendre, of Legendre Bros., Stornaway, who erected a saw mill, sixty by forty feet, now owned by the Montague Paper Company, and situated at the outlet of the Lake. In the fall of 1878 Messrs. Alexander Ross and Jerry Ham came to Megantic, and erected the present hotel known as the "Prince of Wales." Telesphore Lemay and Antoine Roi were the fourth batch of settlers.

In 1878 the old International Railway, now the C. P. R. short line, was completed through to Lake Megantic, and commenced running passenger trains the following spring. In 1881 the bridge over the Chaudière was built. After the railway commenced running the growth of the place was rapid, and in 1885 they applied to be set off as a separate municipality from the township of Whitton, to be known as Lake Megantic village, taking the name of the Lake on the borders of which the place is located. The first mayor was Lt.-Col. M. B. Macaulay, followed by J. A. Chicoyne, present M. L. A. for Wolfe county, F. Chartier, J. A. Millette, J. A. Fournier, D. Graham, A. B. Gendreau, A. Becigneul, and Nap. Lemieux. Mr. J. N. Thibodeau was chosen secretary-treasurer, and has held the office to the present time. The council for 1895 was composed as follows: Geo. M. Stearns, mayor, and councillors, Nap. Lemieux, Teles. Lemay, Jos. Dion, Jos. Laroche, Archibald Renne, and Charles L'Heureux.

There is only one church in Lake Megantic village, and that is of the Presbyterian denomination. It was built in 1889. In Agnes, however, is located Roman Catholic, Methodist, and Anglican churches, being attended by people from Megantic.

Megantic village is largely composed of French Canadians, while the reverse is the case in Agnes.

The village has a large convent erected in 1895, and a Catholic model school. There is also one Protestant elementary school, at which the average attendance is about twenty-eight.

The industries of Lake Megantic village are a large pulp mill, and a mill used exclusively for preparing wood to be ground into pulp. These are owned by the Montague Paper Company, of Massachusetts, who in the fall of 1895 also purchased the extensive saw mills of F. Dudley. There are other saw mills, stores without number, sash and door factory, four hotels, and a branch of the People's Bank of Halifax. This is a junction point between the Canadian Pacific and Quebec Central railways, the latter having been opened for traffic in 1895. There are two steamboats on the lake, one making regular trips each day, during navigation. Recently there has been a good system of water-works put in by Mr. A. B. Gendreau, which supplies the village with excellent spring water. It is also a sub-port of entry of Canadian Customs, under Cookshire; and here is to be found a U. S. consular agency.

The village is well supplied with societies, among which are to be found the I. O. F., C. O. F., Catholic O. F., St. Joseph Society, and a lodge of the R. T. of T.

From the census of 1891 we secure the following statistics: Population, 1,173; families, 225; houses, 223; males, 644; females, 529. French Canadians, 976; others, 197; Religions—Roman Catholics, 1,000; Church of England, 23; Presbyterians, 75; Methodists, 22; Congregationalists, 7; Universalists, 7; Protestants, 4; Jews, 7; not specified, 28.

KENNETH W. McLEOD, farmer, and mayor of Whitton, was born in Winslow, May 4, 1857. His father, Angus W. McLeod, came from the Island of Lewis, Scotland, with the first settlers, and passed through all the trials and hardships, so usual with those early pioneers. He has, however, raised a large family, and is now living in Whitton enjoying the fruits of his labor. Mr. Kenneth McLeod, though a comparatively young man, is one of the principal public men of the township, and takes a great interest in public affairs. For seven years he has been a school commissioner, councillor sixty-six years, and mayor two years. He has been married twice. First, April 10, 1880, to Catherine MacIver; she died November 29, 1891. Issue, four children: John Angus, born April 10, 1881; Mary Ann, born October 5, 1883; Flora, born August 9, 1885; Annie, born November 28, 1887. Second, to widow Annie MacLeay; she had two children: Catherine, born March 2, 1883; Dollie S., born September 28, 1884. By this second marriage there is one son: Lyster J., born June 16, 1894.

MALCOLM MACKAY, farmer, born in Lewis, Scotland, in April, 1813, came to Lingwick in 1841, and fourteen years later, went to Lake Megantic, being the first settler at Victoria Bay. Was married at Cookshire, March 20, 1844, to Anna McIver. Issue six children: John, married Cora Boyes, residence, Warren, N. H., one child; Murdo J.; Rory, married Mary Mackay, residence, Marston, three children; Catherine, married James Colby, residence, Warren, N. H., three children; Isabella; Euphemia, married Fred. F. Stone, residence, Warren, N. H., two children.

NORMAN BEATON, farmer, was born on the Isle of Lewis, Scotland, November 2, 1835. He came to Canada and settled in Whitton in 1851. His father, John Beaton, was the pioneer of Whitton, and died only a few years ago on the farm he first settled on, aged ninety-four years. The subject of this sketch has filled the offices of councillor, school commissioner, and elder in the Presbyterian church. He was married in 1862, in Whitton, to Jane (deceased), daughter of Malcolm Macaulay, Esq. Issue, seven children: Malcolm, born May 12, 1863; Donald K., born July 15, 1875; John Z., born December 5, 1877; Angus, born July 8, 1880; Margaret, born December 22, 1861; Jane, born June 15, 1873. His second marriage was to Flora McIver. All of Mr. Beaton's boys are working in the United States, Donald K. holding a position as stone cutter, at Barre, Vt.

CAPTAIN JAMES MILLER, master mariner, born in Dundee, Scot., October 2, 1835. He is well known in the steamship service between Great Britain and America, and has made over 500 crossings. He is considered an extremely careful and first class navigator. His father was Alexander Miller, of Dundee, Scot., a lawyer of note. His grandfather was a merchant in Hawick, Scot., and was provost for some time. In 1882 he erected the fine residence here reproduced. Capt. Miller moved his family from Liverpool, Eng., to Lake Megantic, where they have since resided. He has here a farm of 275 acres, with good lacation, situated about two miles from Lake Megantic village, and known by the name of "Ravensby." In front of the house, and at the top of the engraving, may be seen Capt Miller and his family. He was married in Liverpool, Eng., to Miss Margaret White. Issue, eight children: Alexander, James, Mary Elizabeth, William, Margaret, Isabella, Walter, John.

RESIDENCE OF CAPTAIN JAMES MILLER.

JAMES KELLY, retired British soldier, was born in Lisburn county, Antrim, Ire., August 22, 1824. Came to Canada in June, 1874, and to Winslow in March, 1876, moving shortly after to Lake Megantic, where he has since resided. He has been chairman of the board of school commissioners, and is first lieutenant No. 9 Company, Fifty-eighth Pattalion. Accompanying this is an engraving of the residence of Mr. Kelly, at Lake Megantic. The two young ladies in the upper corners are his two daughters. Mr. Kelly has been connected with the British army since 1842. For fifteen years in the East Indies Present at the siege of Moultan, December 27, 1847 to January 22, 1849, the final surrender of the fort, under General Wish. Again, at the battle of Gujerat, under Lord Gough, and the surrender of the Sepoys at Rawul Pindi under General Gilbert; the occupation of Attock and Peshawur, and the expulsion of the Ameer Dost Mohammed Khan beyond the Khyber Pass in 1849. At the battle of Budlie Keseria, the taking of the Heights of Delhi, 1857, the subsequent seige operations before Delhi, the storming of the city on September 14, and the occupation of the Palace on September 20, 1857. Served in the campaign of Oude and Rohilcund, 1858 and 1859. Mr. Kelly was married in 1864, at Thatcheu, county Berks, Eng., to Sarah A. Loder. Issue, 3 children: Elizabeth J., born June 8, 1865; Wm. James, born September 30, 1867; Katherine, born November 14, 1869.

GEORGE H. KERR, general merchant, was born in Quebec, March 26, 1866. He is a son of Robert Kerr, of Sherbrooke, who was at one time mayor of

RESIDENCE OF JAMES KELLY.

HISTORY OF COMPTON COUNTY.

GENERAL STORE OF G. H. KERR.

Quebec city. He came to Lake Megantic in 1893, and in 1895 leased the large store on Main street, occupied for many years by Mr. M. J. Smith. Mr. Kerr carries one of the largest stocks for a general store of any merchant in Megantic, and does a good business. The engraving given herewith shows Mr. Kerr standing at the side of the wagon. In addition to that of general merchant he is auctioneer and does a large business throughout this section. He was married in Leeds, Que., in 1888, to Maggie Cameron. Issue, two children: Gordon R. C., born September 11, 1889; Ethel V. M., born September 19, 1891.

NAPOLEON LEMIEUX, general merchant, was born at Ste. Anne La Pocatière, Que., December 1, 1844. He came to Lake Megantic in 1877, and has prospered as a general merchant. The fine brick block which he built and occupies, is the finest store in the place. An engraving of the same accompanies this sketch. Mr. Lemieux has been councillor for several years, mayor of the village, and warden of Compton county one term. He is very popular wherever known. A prominent Conservative, and president of Compton County Liberal-Conservative Association one year. He received strong support in 1895 for the nomination of the Conservative party for the Legislative Assembly. He was married in 1865, at Ste. Foye, Que., to Miss Mary P. Routhier. Issue, two children: A. J. N. Lemieux, born May 6, 1870; Mary Z. P., born February 28, 1867.

DOUGLAS G. MACKENZIE, merchant, was born in Melbourne, Que., in February, 1873. He is a son of Andrew Mackenzie, flour and grain merchant, at Richmond, Que. His mother was Catherine Macdonald, only daughter of Capt. Kenneth Macdonald, of Clarenden, Jamaica, W. I. Mr. Mackenzie came to Lake Megantic in 1890, and for four years was assistant agent at the station here for the Canadian Pacific Railway. He then opened his present store, of which we give a photo-engraving on following page, where he may be seen in front. The building is located in a central part of the village, and he gets his share of the business. He deals chiefly in groceries, flour, grain and feed. Settled around Megantic are many Scotchmen, and, as the name implies, our

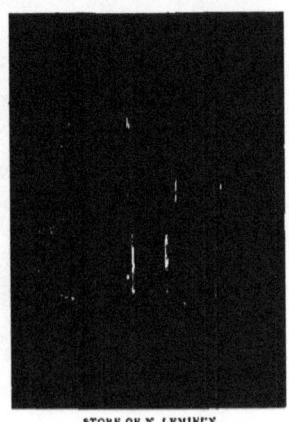

STORE OF N. LEMIEUX.

HISTORY OF COMPTON COUNTY.

STORE OF D. G. MACKENZIE.

subject is one of the "clan," he therefore has made many friends, while his genial manner has attracted a large share of business to his store.

MALCOLM MATHESON, general merchant, whose portrait is here reproduced, was born in Aird Uig, Lewis, Scotland, February 2, 1848. He came to Stornoway in 1870, and shortly after went to Providence, R. I. Ill health soon compelled him to leave there, and he moved to Montreal. In that city he held responsible positions in the dry goods stores of S. Carsley and Henry Morgan & Co. In May, 1877, he started a general store at Lennoxville, but the following year removed to Lake Megantic, where he has since resided. Here he has been lumbering and in trade, on an extensive scale. On October 2, 1872, at Sherbrooke, he married Margaret Buchanan. Issue, ten children, five living : John H., born May 21, 1874; Hector N., born August 21, 1882; Oliver C., born November 29, 1886; Christie Ann, born August 16, 1877; Catherine D. A., born April 9, 1889. Mr. Matheson, in company with the late celebrated Donald Morrison, cut the first tree for improvement, in Lake Megantic village, on May 26, 1878.

That summer he built the first building—it being 25 x 35, two and a half stories high. The boards were rafted nine miles from Moose Bay, shingles and dry pine were brought from Stornoway, distance eighteen miles, while the doors, windows and nails were hauled by team fifty-three miles from Robinson, Bury. There was then no road within one and a half mile of the village, and he had to build a small boat to carry the provisions from Sandy Bay, distant two and a half miles. He has been successful in business and acquired considerable property throughout the county. He has held many public offices with great satisfaction to his fellow townsmen, but his business has obliged him to refuse re-election in many cases. He was secretary-treasurer of Whitton in 1879, and mayor in 1880. In 1881 he resigned as councillor. For nine years he acted as school trustee, but in this he also refused re-election. He was largely instrumental in building the Presbyterian church, and acted as trustee and manager of the property for several years. He holds the office of C. R. in the I. O. F., and a like position in the C. O. F., having been a charter member of both lodges. He is a Mason, Orangeman but first, last and always a Highland Scotchman.

MALCOLM MATHESON.

DONALD P. MATHESON, farmer, butcher and dealer in agricultural implements, was born in Lingwick. He has been mayor of Whitton for four years, councillor six years, and is now secretary-treasurer. He was married in Sherbrooke, February 29, 1881, to Isabelle Murray. Issue, four children: Waldo Peter, born November 20, 1887; John N., born June 1, 1890; Annie F., born February 14, 1883; Mary I., born August 10, 1885.

LOUIS PHILEAS VILLENEUVE, was born at Quebec, September 14, 1848. In February, 1895, he came to Lake Megantic, and purchased the Grand Central Hotel. He was married at Quebec, February 2, 1871, to Emedine Pelletier. Issue, seven children: Nelson, Albert, Arthur, Osilda, Bella, Maria, and Emedine.

WALTER HAND, hotel proprietor, was born in Staffordshire, Eng., May 13, 1868. Came to Canada in 1884, and for several years resided at Waterville and Sherbrooke. In 1891 he moved to Lake Megantic. He was married at Lake Megantic, in 1893, to Miss Elizabeth N. Ball.

ELGIN RUFUS WESTON, millwright, was born in Marbleton, Que., March 10, 1860. He is C. R. of the I. O. F. Was married at Gould, December 21, 1887, to Maria, daughter of Norman Murray, of that place. Issue, two children: Ellsworth, born December 22, 1888; Sylvia G., born June 27, 1891.

DONALD MACKAY, stationary engineer and miner, was born in Lingwick, October 5, 1854. Never married. In 1878, he left Canada, and did not return until 1893, when he settled in Lake Megantic. During this time he traveled through all the western states. His father, Donald Mackay, was one of the pioneers from Scotland, and died in 1891, leaving six children, all living in Compton county, and only one a farmer.

WILLIAM D. MACKENZIE, resident of Lake Megantic, son of John Mackenzie, was born in the township of Newport, March 17, 1873. He holds the office of S. C. in the R. T. of T.

JAMES SCOBIE WILSON, retired sea captain, was born in Kincardine, Perth county, Scotland. He came to Megantic in 1876, being one of the first settlers. For a number of years he followed the sea and commanded a ship in East India and China trade, being at that time senior captain in employ of the British and Eastern Shipping Company. Captain Wilson was appointed postmaster at Agnes in 1877, and still holds the same position. Was married in London, England, in July, 1858, to Elizabeth C. Alltham. Issue, ten children: Henry J.; James B.; George A.; William Graeme Ditchfield; Ernest S.; Lydia E.; Elizabeth C. A. M.; Florence G.; Martha L.; Annie E., married Nicholas Swan, residence, Montreal, two children. Of the above children, William G. D. was the first child born in Ditchfield, of English speaking parents.

HENRY WILLIAM ALBRO, U. S. consular agent, was born October 27, 1841, at Peterboro, Ontario. In 1850, his father, Samuel W., died, and he shortly after went to Nova Scotia. In 1876, he moved to Lake Megantic. For five years and a half, he held the position of freight agent for the Canadian Pacific Railway. Mr. Albro holds now, and has for a number of years, the position of United States consular agent at Megantic. During his residence here, he has held the position of secretary-treasurer for the protestant board of school trustees, for the townships of Ditchfield and Spaulding. In 1865, at Liverpool, N. S., Mr. Albro married Mary Collins, daughter of Francis W. Collins, now deceased. Issue four children: Henry Samuel; Kate de Wolfe; Agnes; Alice Maud.

CHAPTER XXIII.

Township of Marston.

Including History of South Marston.

This tract of land is situated on the west side of Lake Megantic. Bouchette writing in 1815, says: "The waters abound with excellent fish, and the country around this sequestered and romantic spot, is the resort of almost every species of game." The land, though somewhat rough, is comparatively level, with the exception of the south-west part, into which the Megantic hills extend. The principal stream of water is the Megantic river, which has its source among those hills, and receiving many small tributaries by the way, flows north-east into Victoria Bay, on the west side of Lake Megantic. There are other small streams, some falling directly into the lake, while others in the west and north-west of Marston, which are the outlets of small lakes in that region, find their way to Salmon river, in Hampden. The largest of these is Otter Brook, which issues from Otter lake, in Marston.

The following narrative by one of the four pioneers here mentioned, Mr. William McLeod, gives as complete and accurate an account of the early settlements around Lake Megantic, as we have been able to obtain.

"In the year 1852, William McLeod, Rory McIver, Murdo McIver, and John McIver, all four of the township of Lingwick, with the aid of a pocket-compass, started eastward in quest of Government lands. The township of Marston, where they finally located, was not then surveyed, but those dauntless pioneers took their course through Winslow and Whitton, until after three days, they struck the shore of Lake Megantic, at Black Point. Here they made a raft and explored the shores of the lake as far south as Rocky Point. They spent a week in the vicinity and found fish and game very plentiful, then retraced their steps. Early in the following spring they again sought the Megantic region, and carried three bushels of potatoes. They chopped and cleared an acre and planted the potatoes. The distance from Lingwick to Lake Megantic is thirty miles. It took from two to three days to make the journey by a blazed line. The winter of 1853 these four men took a month's provision with them on their backs and came to the lake. Marston was then surveyed, when they took lands which they have since owned. They made a clearing on their respective lots, in the spring of 1854. Each brought, in addition to the necessary provisions to keep body and soul together, a bushel of barley, which was sown, together with what potatoes they got from the acre planted the previous year.

"It was not, however, until May 20, 1856, that they brought in their families. In the fall commenced the work of making hand-mills. John McIver was an expert, and when the stones were cut and leveled off Mr. McIver set the mill up. William McLeod was a Hudson Bay man, also fisherman, and he laid in a good stock of lunge for the winter. Rory McIver wintered three cows on one ton of barley straw and brush, and often parties would go once a month to Winslow, sixteen miles, on snow-shoes, to get tea, tobacco, and such articles as could be carried.

"The spring of 1857 brought one addition to the number. Malcolm Mackay came and located at Victoria Bay, a most uninviting spot then.

"The following year, the road was opened to within two miles of the lake shore, and nine settlers came to the lake, all of whom took up lands in Whitton. Fish was easily got in those days, and so was game. William McLeod, in the fall of 1857, took one hundred and sixty-one lunge in two nights, from Rocky Point. One of them weighed thirty-three pounds —the largest ever caught in Lake Megantic."

In 1870-71, the first French Canadian settlers came to Marston, and located in the southern part. A complete history of the settlement of South Marston is to be found at the close of this chapter.

The first municipal records of Marston bear date February 16, 1874. Previous to that time it had formed part of the combined townships of Whitton, Marston and Hampden. In 1879, owing to the large increase of French Canadian settlers in the southern part, it was amicably arranged that the Township should be divided. Since then there have been two municipalities in the Township.

The past mayors have been, J. F. McIver, to 1885; D. L. McLeod, three years, and the present mayor Allan McLeod, the rest of the time. Allan McLeod was secretary-treasurer from 1874 to 1885, when he was succeeded by J. F. McIver. The council for 1895, was composed as follows: mayor, Allan McLeod, and councillors, D. L. McLeod, Donald Beaton, D. A. McDonald, Léon Beaudry, William Murray, and Rodrick McDonald.

The school commissioners are J. F. McIver, chairman, Colin McLeod, Norman McDonald, Donald Beaton, and D. L. McLeod; Murdock McKenzie, secretary-treasurer.

There is a temperance hotel at Milan, liquor licenses have never been granted in the municipality.

There is a Presbyterian church at Marsboro, but at present no resident pastor.

In North Marston there are two post offices, Milan and Marsboro. Milan is also known by the name of Marsden. It is located on the Canadian Pacific Railroad, and the boundary line between Marston and Hampden It has a population of about 250. Here are several stores, saw mill, hotel, etc. Postal revenue, 1895, $134.

Marsboro is seven miles from Lake Megantic village. It is the centre of a farming community. Daily mail. Postal revenue, 1895, $25.

The census of 1891 gives the following particulars for the whole township of Marston: Population, 1,117; families, 189; houses, 175; males, 587; females, 530; French-Canadians, 529; others, 588. Religions—Roman Catholic, 538; Church of England, 4; Presbyterians, 559; Methodists, 15; Baptist, 1.

SOUTH MARSTON.

This municipality was erected September 6, 1879. The first councillors were: F. B. de Grosbois, Joseph H. Morin, Thomas Cameron, Israel E. Myers, Jean Guay, Romaine Cousineau, and Barthelemi Bergeron. It contains 19,980 square acres. Has a valuation of $67,501.

Between 1862 and 1872 portions of the township of Marston were granted to three colonization societies, known under the name of Compton, Montreal, and the Glasgow Land Company. In 1894 the Montague Paper Company purchased all of the interests of the latter company in the township. The only one which accomplished anything in the way of colonization was that of Montreal. In the winter of 1870-71 they erected a log house 20 x 22 feet, and called the place Piopolis, (city of Pius IX). On April 21, 1871, the first French Canadian settlers in Marston, and the pioneers in South Marston, reached Piopolis. They were seven in number, all young men, with very little, if any, experience in farming, having come from

Montreal. Eight days after they were followed by another lot, and additions were gradually made to their number. The hardships of those early settlers were great, and so discouraged them that out of the first twelve, all but two left the place. One of them, Alfred Gaumont, died in 1879, the other, Odilon Martel, resides at Piopolis village, he prospered and owns several farms.

In 1879 the settlers of South Marston had largely increased, and as they were all French-Canadians, located in one section, while the other part was settled by the Scotch, it was mutually agreed that the interests of both sections would be improved by a separation for municipal purposes. This was not brought about by any ill-feeling having arisen between the two nationalities, for they were all on friendly terms. According to reports in the hands of the parish of Piopolis, in 1876, there was a population in South Marston of 293 souls, with 72 families, and 197 adults.

The first mass at Piopolis was celebrated April 30, 1871, by Rev. Mr. Seguin. A few days after the arrival of the first settlers, they commenced the erection of a house, to be used as a chapel and residence for the priest. Rev. Mr. Seguin was followed in the fall by Rev. Pierre Champagne, who in turn gave way to Rev. Jos. Aubin, in 1872. The first baptism took place June 16, 1872, the child, a son of Edouard Beaulé, was born the day previous, and probably the first birth in the new colony. On June 18, 1872, the first burial took place. The first marriage was on April 20, 1874. Rev. J. Aubin was succeeded late in 1874, by Rev. J. B. A. Cousineau, who is now the resident priest at Agnes and Lake Megantic. The latter had energy, perseverance, a pleasant disposition, and tact. He was well liked, as he is to-day, by all creeds and nationalities. Through his labors the Catholic church made good progress, not only in Piopolis, but throughout a large surrounding territory. Through his efforts the Catholic missions of St. Leon, of Marston, St. Augustin, of Woburn, St. Paul, of Scotstown, and others were established. Rev. Mr. Cousineau did not confine his efforts wholly to the church, but in municipal matters, securing government help for new roads, and looking after the proper expenditure of such money, he materially assisted the early settlers. In October, 1886, he was transferred to the Megantic and Agnes mission, where he has since remained. He was succeeded at Piopolis by the Rev. A. A. Gagnon, who was also followed, September 30, 1890, by the present parish priest, Rev. J. E. Simard. The latter is greatly interested in his work, and to him are we indebted for these particulars, which required considerable research and work on his part.

The first school was established at Piopolis in 1873. There are now, in South Marston, three elementary schools. The commissioners for 1895 were R. Cousineau, D. Cousineau, P. Goupil, Donat Trudeau, and Edmond Grenier, chairman; secretary-treasurer, Elzéar Fournier.

The past mayors of the municipality have been Israel E. Myers, F. B. de Grosbois, Edmond Grenier, J. H. Morin, Arthur Grenier, Edmond Grenier, and Jean-Baptiste Brault. There was only one secretary-treasurer previous to the present occupant, he was Arthur Grenier. The council for 1895 was composed as follows: mayor, Edmond Grenier, and councillors R. Cousineau, Pierre Goupil, D. Cousineau, Jos. Lessard, Nap. Beaudry, and Alfred Desrochers. Liquor licenses have never been granted.

In South Marston are two post offices. The oldest and largest is Piopolis. This was established about 1873. In the Catholic parish of Piopolis there are now three hundred and twenty-four people, divided among fifty-two families. There is a daily mail. Population about one hundred and fifty. Postal revenue, 1895, $78.50.

Valracine is eight miles from Milan, the nearest railway station. It is the centre of a farming community with small population. Here is located a Roman Catholic church, under the charge of Rev. J. D. Bernier. Daily mail. Postal revenue, 1895, $70.00.

ALLAN McLEOD, farmer, mayor of Marston, and warden of Compton county for 1896, was born in North Ely, Shefford county, Que., September 1, 1843. His father, Wm. McLeod, was one of the first pioneers to settle in the Lake Megantic district, and Mrs. Wm. McLeod the first white woman to go into the territory. He now resides with his son, John. He was councillor for eleven years, and the last mayor of the united townships of Whitton, Hampden and Marston. Mr. Allan McLeod, our subject, was secretary-treasurer of Marston for thirteen years, and mayor for the last eleven years. He sat in the county council for one or two terms, twenty-five years ago, when the famous By-Law 37 was passed. He is one of the few left who were then present. He was married at Lake Megantic, December 29, 1869, to Anna, daughter of Murdo MacDonald, of Hampden. Issue, six children: Murdo C., born July 17, 1870; William A., born July 15, 1872; Donald J., born July 5, 1874; Katie J., born June 28, 1876; Colin A., born September 12, 1878; Mary A., born May 30, 1886. Mr. McLeod is a man of good judgment, a successful farmer, and well read on general topics of the day. He is a justice of the peace for the district of St. Francis. His son, Wm. A., is local editor of the *Lake Megantic Chronicle*.

LIEUTENANT DUNCAN L. McLEOD, merchant and lumber dealer, was born in Lingwick in 1848. At present he is school commissioner and councillor, also lieutenant in the Fifty-eighth Battalion. Was married in Winslow, May 19, 1874, to Anna McDonald Issue, seven children: Annie Maggie, born May 8, 1875, died June 17, 1879; Murdo Alexander, born March 3, 1877; Norman Malcolm, born June 19, 1882; Mary Ann, born July 15, 1879; Ida Bella, born May 29, 1884; Margaret Agnes, born January 27, 1889; Catharine Lamont, born June 25, 1891. Mr. McLeod was the first settler in Milan. He has been mayor of Marston for several terms.

CAPTAIN JOHN F. McIVER, farmer, was born in Lewis, Scot, January 30, 1835. Came to Compton county in 1841, and has resided in Lingwick, Winslow and Marston He has been councillor, mayor for ten years, and is now secretary-treasurer of the township of Marston. First marriage, in March, 1853, to Anna McLeod, died 1871. Issue, two children: Ella, married Ellsworth Crossman, residence Portland, Me, two children: Anna, married Frank Cardozo, residence South Barbara, Cal., two children. Second marriage at Winslow, March 17, 1874, to Isabella McLeod. Issue, ten children: Christina, born March 8, 1875; Murdo, born December 24, 1876; William, born July 17, 1881; Rachel, born December 31, 1878; Isabella, born October 19, 1883; Margaret, born April 8, 1886; Catherine M., born July 28, 1888; Mysie, born November 10, 1890; Ida, born June 1, 1893; Ruth, born August 30, 1894.

DONALD STEWART, retired farmer, was born in Lewis, Scotland, in 1812. He came to Compton county in 1850, and was the first settler in Middle district. The first potatoes he planted he carried on his back eighteen miles from North Hill. He was married in 1849, to Anna McIver. Issue, nine children: George; Donald; Alexander; Angus; Mary; Isabella; Anna, married William Dwyer, residence, Sheffield, Vt., ten children; Catherine; Johanna.

DONALD K. MORRISON, farmer, born in Lewis, Scotland, in 1836, came to Marsboro, in 1871. Married in Lewis in 1860, to Katie Stewart, who died in May, 1875. Issue, twelve children, seven living: Murdo, born April 14, 1866; Annie, born October 1, 1869, married Norman McDonald, residence, Springfield, Mass., two children; Christy, born March 17, 1871; Mary Ann, born May 7, 1873; Jessie, born May 6, 1875; Katie E., born June 20, 1877; Sophia L., born August 6, 1881.

CHAPTER XXIV.

TOWNSHIPS OF DITTON, CHESHAM, EMBERTON, AUCKLAND AND CLINTON.

TOWNSHIP OF DITTON.

It is thought by some Ditton derived its name from a writer of note who died at Lordes in 1715. No particular reason, however, is given for this surmise.

This tract of land is bounded on the north by Hampden, east by Chesham, west by Newport, and south by Emberton. It contains three hundred and eighty lots of the usual dimensions. It was constituted a township named Ditton, in May, 1803, and in part granted to Minard Harris, yeoman, and his associates, viz.: Stephen Bigelow, Anson Bradley, David Bradley, Christopher Babity, Alexander Brimmer, William Chamberlain, — Eastman, Andrew Henry, Obadiah Jones, Edmund Lamb, Joseph Laret, Charles Lewis, David Morrow, Reuben Ross, Thomas Shadruck, and Ziba Tuttle.

Notwithstanding these grants no settlements were made at the time indicated. Though the land is of an excellent quality it was not until 1862 that any attempt at settlement was made. In 1861 Mr. O'Dwyer, P. L. S., was sent by the government to lay out a road, which was to run from the present town of Scotstown, through Hampden, Ditton, Chesham and Woburn, to the river Arnold.

About 1862 Luther H. Weston, of Cookshire, moved to Ditton and took possession of several lots. He had to carry all his provisions by the Victoria road to Scotstown, and thence by a canoe up the Salmon river to Ditton. He there built a small house, the first one in the township.

In 1864 Richard Dawson moved to Ditton. His wife was the first woman to go there, and on May 26, 1865, there was born to them the first child in Ditton. He was named John Henry Ditton Dawson.

In 1864 it was discovered that Ditton was not only rich in soil, but also in more or less rich deposits of gold. The late Hon. John Henry Pope acquired considerable property on the streams where the gold was found, and for over twenty years successfully carried on gold mining. For the past five years the mining has come to a stand still, gold not being now found in paying quantities.

In October, 1864, L. H. Weston built a saw mill. Up to 1867 Weston and Dawson were the only inhabitants of Ditton, but in that year several families arrived.

In 1868 the post office was opened under the name of West Ditton. Gardner Boynton was the first postmaster. He also opened a small store. On August 25, 1868, sixteen families of Norwegians arrived. Shortly after they got discouraged, and left one by one for the western states. In 1869 prospectors were quite numerous, looking for gold. One piece found was valued at $135.00.

In 1869 the Compton County Association was formed, having for president Hon. J. H. Pope; and secretary, J. I. Mackie, Notary. Their object was to promote immigration, and with that object in view, in 1870 they erected thirteen houses in different parts of the township, for the use of new settlers. In 1871 Rev. Mr. Parkin, Anglican minister at Cookshire, commenced the erection of a church, but meeting with poor success left it unfinished.

About 1870 Rev. Mr. Gendreau, priest at Cookshire, became interested in settling this part of the County. He at once interested his fellow French Canadians throughout the province, and from that time on the growth of the Township was rapid. French Canadian settlers, who had gone to the United States, were influenced to return and settle here, while many from the old French parishes also moved to Ditton.

In September, 1873, the erection of the first Roman Catholic chapel was commenced, and by October 8 had advanced so far towards completion that Rev. Father Gendreau held services therein. That same day the funeral of the first woman to die in Ditton took place. About 1875 Rev. Mr. Gendreau was replaced at Cookshire by Rev. Edouard Blanchard (now of Malone, N. Y.), who held services at Ditton once a month. December 5, 1875, Rev. Victor Chartier was placed over the parish of Ditton, with church at La Patrie.

On February 14, 1876, the first municipal records for Ditton are dated. That part of the township of Clinton, which is in Compton county, also forms part of the municipality of Ditton. Valuation is $156,900, on which there is a tax of 16½ mills. The mayor and councillors for 1895, were as follows: P. L. N. Prevost, mayor, A. W. Giard, Joseph Megré, Joseph Dubrenil, Theophile E. Choquette, Isaië Beaudry, and Pascal Paquette. Dr. Charles F. X. Prevost is secretary-treasurer. The names of the past mayors are as follows: J. A. Chicoyne, now M. L. A. for Wolfe, February 29, 1876, to March, 1878; George Forbourne, sr.; Alfred A. Gendreau, P. L. N. Provost, 1880 to 1889; F. X. Vincent; Louis Dansereau; Allan W. Giard, three years. The past secretary-treasurers have been: Joseph D. A. McDonald, Paul Allaire, R. R. Dumoulin, F. X. Rivard, B. Lalime, Dr. Chas. N. Gauvrean, Christopher Thibeault, J. P. Charbonneau, Dr. Chas. F. X. Prevost, since July 19, 1885.

Rev. N. A. Garriepy is priest of the only church in the township, which is located at La Patrie.

There are at present seven elementary schools. The school commissioners are: J. Gobeil, chairman, A. W. Giard, M. Foucher, A. Bonin, J. Lacasse, jr.; Dr. C. F. X. Prevost, secretary-treasurer.

La Patrie is the leading village of the Township, and one of the most thriving in the County. Here is located the town hall, temperance hotel, five merchants, physician, two blacksmiths, carriagemaker, butcher, two millwrights, shoemaker, carpenter's shop, cheese factory, etc. It is nine miles from Scotstown, the nearest railway station. There is a population of over two hundred, with a daily mail. Postal revenue for 1895, $293.00.

West Ditton is the only other post office in the Township. It is ten miles from Scotstown, and eighteen miles east of Cookshire. Population fifty. Daily mail. Postal revenue, 1895, $10.

Census of 1891 gives the following statistics for the township of Ditton and Clinton: Population, 827; families, 153; houses, 148; males, 431; females, 396; French Canadians, 785; others, 42. Religious—Roman Catholics, 801; church of England, 31; Lutherans, 15; Baptists, 3; other denominations, 5.

TOWNSHIP OF CHESHAM.

This township is bounded on the north by Marston, east by Woburn and Clinton, west by Ditton and Emberton, and south by the province line. When the other townships were surveyed and granted, Chesham was put down as only a projected township. It was not until

1853 that it was sub-divided, by W. O'Dwyer, Provincial Land Surveyor. In 1869, it was erected into a township by Letters Patent.

The year following the survey, nearly all the lots containing a rivulet or stream of water, were purchased by different parties having the "gold fever." The western part of this township is drained by the Salmon river, while the brooks that rise in the east find their way into the Arnold. Those in search of gold soon lost courage and one by one left the country. Saddle mountain is in the south-east part.

The first seed planted in Chesham was by Mr. P. U. Vaillant, in the spring of 1874. Soon after this the French Canadian repatriation scheme was put into effect by the government; four hundred and fifty acres were cleared and fifty houses built, for use of settlers. In 1875, there was a population of only about seven persons, but under the repatriation law, there was rapid immigration, and by December 13, 1876, there was a population of five hundred and eighty-seven souls. The first child born in Chesham was a daughter to the wife of François Luc, on February 6, 1874.

The first municipal records bear date February 12, 1877. Previous to that Chesham was included in the municipality of Ditton and Clinton. Chesham has an area of 53,300 square acres. Property assessed in 1895, $72,480. Tax rate, 30 mills. Present council is composed of the following gentlemen: Elzear Roberge, mayor, Israel Gondreau, Chas. Lambert, Léandre Marin, Pierre Dubuc, Meril Lapierre, Geremi Danjou; secretary-treasurer, A. R. Dumoulin. The past mayors have been: Frs. Poulin, Jacques Larochelle, Ant. Belanger, Jos. Roberge, Cyprien Perrier, F. X. Dufresne, and Jean Goulet. Past secretary-treasurers: Theophile Lachance, Frs. Poulin, F. X. Dufresne, and Elzear Roberge. The Township is well supplied with elementary schools. No liquor license has been granted for eight years.

The first Roman Catholic service was held on June 17, 1875, when mass was celebrated in the open air, with a rock for an altar. Shortly after a "chapel" was erected at the present village of Notre Dame des Bois, and there is now here a large parish under the charge of Rev. D. Bellemare.

There is one village and post office only in Chesham. This is Notre-Dame-des-Bois, and located in about the centre of the Township. It is fourteen miles from Milan, the nearest railway station. There is a population of about one hundred. Daily mail. Postal revenue, 1895, $111.50. Here are located saw and grist mills, hotel, two general stores, blacksmith shop, etc.

By the census of 1891 the following particulars are given of Chesham: Population, 621; families, 109; houses, 101; males, 338; females, 283. French Canadians, 603; others, 18. Religions — Roman Catholic, 620; other denomination, 1.

TOWNSHIP OF EMBERTON.

This township is thought to have derived its name from an illustrious English statesman named Pemberton, as it is thus found on some maps. By referring back to Bouchette's works, we find it named Emberton, and thus it has always been legally known.

This is a small border township containing only 41,000 square acres. It is bounded on the north by Ditton, east by Chesham, west by Auckland, and south by the province line. It was a projected township only until 1864, being subdivided in that year by Mr. W. O'Dwyer, land surveyor. It was erected into a township by letters patent, September 1, 1870.

Those first attracted to Emberton were in search of gold, which had been found on the Little Ditton river. This river has its principal head in Emberton, and in 1866 nothing more was wanted to attract prospectors. As gold was not found in the quantity expected, this did not prove

HISTORY OF COMPTON COUNTY.

a source of permanent settlement. The first work on land was done in October, 1870, by the St. Hyacinthe Colonization Society. In the spring of 1871 there arrived the first settler, Alfred Cardinal, a young man full of courage and energy. He remained the solitary inhabitant of Emberton until 1873, when he got tired of waiting for settlers and moved to Ditton. About this time he was married, and a few weeks after was lost in the woods while hunting, and frozen to death. His body was found after a two days' search, within a few hours after his death. He was not over two miles from his home.

In August, 1873, a Belgian immigrant named Honore Dion, took the place of Alfred Cardinal, who had then moved to Ditton. Dion brought his family with him, and on October 24, 1874, was born the first child in Emberton. This man and his family to the number of eight, were the only inhabitants of Emberton, until the effects of the laws of repatriment began to be felt. Ditton and Chesham received the first settlers under this law, and it was not until September 29, 1875, that this township received the first patriot in the person of Ulric Chaille, who came from North Adams, Mass. Since then immigration has been gradual.

The first municipal records are dated February 11, 1878. The south part of Ditton is included in Emberton for municipal purposes, being known as "Emberton and Ditton South." The valuation for 1895 was $70,398, on which a tax was levied of ten mills. The past mayors have been: A. Voyer, A. B. Gendreau, Leon Beliveau, A. Daigneau, Charles Martin, Silva Chailler, T. Beaulieu, and C. Bellerose. Names of past secretary-treasurers: A. Daigneau, D. LeBel, A. Rolin, S. Rolin, S. Chailler, and Ed. Gagnon. The present council is composed as follows: mayor, Chas. Martin, and councillors, H. Mercier, R. Gagné, Joseph Beck, A. Labbé, M. Labbé, and F. X. Beaudette; secretary-treasurer, Ed. Landry.

In the municipality there are four elementary schools. Names of school commissioners: Rev. A. Tremblay, chairman, B. Corbeil, H. Mercier, James Lanzon and Elisée Beaudoin.

There is one church only in the municipality. That is at Chartierville, and is known as St. Jean Baptiste, with Rev. A. Tremblay as curé.

The township is purely agricultural, with good land, well watered. There is one cheese factory at Chartierville; a hotel, but license has never been granted in the municipality.

There is but one village and post office in Emberton. It is near the boundary line of that township and Ditton, and known as Chartierville. It is nine miles from La Patrie, and eighteen miles from Scotstown, the nearest railway station. The place has a population of about two hundred, with a daily mail. Postal revenue for 1895, $80. Here are to be found a saw and grist mill, three general stores, blacksmith shop, etc.

The census of 1891 gives the following statistics for the township of Emberton: Population, 422; families, 85; houses, 74; males, 244; females, 178; French-Canadians, 412; others, 10. Religions—Roman Catholic, 422.

TOWNSHIP OF AUCKLAND.

This is a tract of land bounded on the north by Newport, east by Emberton and the province line, south by Hereford, and west by Clifton, containing 61,717 acres of land. It was erected into a township named Auckland, and in part granted, April 3, 1806, to Fleury Dechambault, Gilette Dechambault, Joseph Montarville, Louis Dechambault, Charlotte Dechambault, Elizabeth, widow of Dr. John Gould, George King and Elizabeth King, children of Godfrey King, deceased, Nicholas Andrews, Samuel Andrews, and twenty-five others. Notwithstanding this grant no settlement was made until a more recent date.

Bouchette, writing in 1815 and again in 1831, says no part was settled at that time. He further adds, "a sort of foot-path runs through it, by which the Indians frequently make their way to river Chaudiere" from the river Connecticut.

The headquarters of the Eaton and Clifton rivers flow from the north and west parts of the township, the other creeks flowing into Hall's stream, from the head of which the boundary line becomes very crooked, as it follows, by agreement of the commissioners to determine it, the natural water shed, so as to cross no streams.

Previous to January 1, 1870, Auckland formed part of the municipality of the united townships of Ditton, Newport, Clinton, Chesham and Auckland. On December 8, 1869, the county council granted a separation for municipal purposes.

The mayors of the municipality of Auckland, since 1870, have been George Beloin, Ludger Fauteux and Joseph Agagnier. The secretary-treasurers have been Moïse Roy and Ludger Lazure.

The present members of the council are Joseph Agagnier, mayor, and councillors, C. Hébert, F. D. Gagnon, Eugène Inkel, A. Beaudoin, D. Favreau, and O. E. Durocher. Secretary-treasurer, George Beloin.

There are seven elementary schools in the township under the charge of the following school commissioners, Eugène Inkel, chairman, D. Breault, G. Fortin, F. X. Lapierre, and A. Gagnon ; secretary-treasurer, George Beloin.

This township is composed almost wholly of French Canadians, the few English families residing in the northern part. There are four saw-mills in the township. For the year 1895-96, there was a valuation of $116 000.

There are two post offices in the township located at the south end, St. Malo and Malvina. The former is the larger of the two, and contains saw and grist mills, stores, etc. Here is located the only church in the township, belonging to the Roman Catholic denomination. Rev. L. E. Gendron is the pastor. This post office has a daily mail. Postal revenue, 1895, $105.

Malvina is three miles south of St. Malo, a station on the M. C. Railway. There is a is a saw mill, general store, etc., located here. Daily mail. Postal revenue, 1895, $79.50.

The census of 1891 gives the following statistics for the township of Auckland. Population, 677 ; families, 111 ; houses, 95 ; males, 364 ; females, 313 ; French Canadians, 636 ; others 41. Religions—Roman Catholics, 647 ; church of England, 4 ; Methodists, 16 ; Baptists, 3 ; Adventists 1 ; Protestants, 2 ; not specified, 4.

TOWNSHIP OF CLINTON.

About half of this Township only, lies within the county of Compton, it being nearly equally divided with Beauce county. It is bounded on the north by Marston, east by Beauce county, west by Chesham, and south by Woburn.

This is a small, irregularly shaped tract of land, containing but four ranges of unequal length. It was erected into a township named Clinton, May 21, 1803, and in part granted to Frederick Holland and his associates, viz : Louis Deguise, Augustin Robitaille, Joseph Larue, Louis Joseph Roux the younger, Joseph Martin the elder, Joseph Tapin, Charles Tapin, Joseph Vezina, and Pierre Delisle the younger.

These associates never settled in the Township, and their land all reverted to the Crown. There are now very few inhabitants, although the section is well timbered and said to be good land.

Arnold river, coming from Woburn on the south, which enters Lake Megantic, in Clinton, is the principal stream of water ; others from the south-west being very inconsiderable. The former derives its name from the U. S. General Arnold, who, in 1775, passed his troops down it on their way to Quebec.

There is no village or post office in the Township, and for all municipal purposes it is added to Ditton. The population is so small that in the census of 1891, all statistics in regard to this territory were included with those of the township of Ditton.

PIERRE LOUIS NAPOLEON PREVOST, farmer, insurance agent, and mayor of the township of Ditton, was born in Quebec city, May 11, 1856. He came to Ditton in 1876. He received a complete classical education at the Quebec Seminary, and passed with great success his first examination in the faculty of Arts, at Laval University, Quebec. His father, Pierre Norbert Prévost, has been a clerk in the Department of Education, at Quebec, for the past twenty-eight years. Our subject has taken a great interest in public affairs. He has been a member of the Council since 1878, and mayor for ten years, scattered over this period of time; county delegate three terms, one of the school commissioners of Ditton, and church warden. For several years Mr. Prévost was one of the writers for *Le Pionnier* and *Le Peuple*, of Sherbrooke, and contributed several articles on the early history of the counties of Compton, Sherbrooke and Wolfe. He was married at La Patrie, September 4, 1877, to Céline Morel de la Durantaye. Issue, nine children: Marie J. A. C., born July 22, 1879, died 1886; Pierre L. J., born July 19, 1882; Joseph C. N., born August 22, 1888; Louis J. D., born April 8, 1890; Marie Séraphine, born April 26, 1881; Anne Clémentine, born May 3, 1884; Marie Adelaïde R., born March 13, 1886; Marie Joséphine, born July 2, 1892; Marie C. Céline, born July 6, 1894.

ELZEAR ROBERGE, general merchant, farmer, and mayor of Chesham, was born at St. Norbert d'Arthabaska, Que., June 25, 1864. He was married in Chesham, July 6, 1886, to Marie Anna Demerise LaPlante. Issue, one son: Harvay, born March 3, 1889. Mr. Roberge came to Chesham November 16, 1875, when eleven years of age, with his parents. He worked on his father's farm until 1887, when he started a general store at Notre Dame des Bois, where he has secured the confidence of the people and is one of the progressive business men of the county. For seven years he was secretary-treasurer for the township, but increase of business forced him to resign, when he was chosen by acclamation a member of the Council in 1895, and the same year appointed mayor.

JOSEPH GAGNIER, farmer and mill owner, was born in Laprairie, Que. March 31, 1842. In the year 1868, he came to Auckland and settled at St. Malo, where he has since resided. He was elected a member of the council in 1870, and has held the office of mayor since 1875. His photo is to be found among those of the County council. He was married at St. Jean Chrysostome, Chateauguay county, September 9, 1867, to Francoise Gagnier. Issue, three children: Joseph Albert, born September 17, 1868, married Albina Audet, no children; Alfred André, born April 28, 1870, married Florestine Crete, one child; Marie Louise Rose Delina, born August 24, 1872, married Barnard Beauchemin. The three families reside at St. Malo.

ELIJAH LEGGETT, farmer, resident of the township of Auckland, was born in the township of Newport, September 12, 1841. His parents were Robert and Mary A. (Folsom) Leggett, father died in 1889, mother in 1850. Our subject now holds the office of school commissioner. In the township of Auckland on February 16, 1870, he married Mary Elizabeth Planche. Issue, two children: Willis Frank, born August 17, 1885; Effie Matilda, born October 17, 1878.

LEWIS CABLE, farmer, was born December 24, 1835, in England. He came to Bury with his parents in 1837, and has always lived in the county, although he moved to Eaton, and later to his present home in Auckland. On December 24, 1861, he was married in Eaton to Mary Ann Jordon. Issue, nine children, seven living: Celia S., born January 2, 1862, married, Ira L. Fisher, residence, North Woodstock, N. H.; Archie George, born October 16, 1864, died July 19, 1889; Hannah S., born February 24, 1868, married Asher Jones, residence, Newport; John S., born August 16, 1869; Hattie J., born July 30, 1871, married William Morrow, residence, Newport; Fanny M., born April 14, 1874, died December 25, 1893; Alice C., born August 9, 1876; Delia L., born June 2, 1878; Florence C., born August 16, 1881.

CAPTAIN DONALD BEATON, farmer, was born on the Isle of Lewis, Scot., March 12, 1833. His father, John Beaton, who died at the advanced age of ninety-seven years, came to Compton county with a wife and nine children during the summer of 1851. He was the first man to fell a tree in Whitton. Our subject lived in Whitton until 1878, when he moved to Marston, his present home. He has held the office of councillor twenty years, mayor four years, also school commissioner. At Stornoway, 1862, he married Mary, daughter of John W. Macdonald. Issue, eight children: Angus M., born March 3, 1873; William, born May 30, 1874; Mary, born in January, 1863, married L. Mackinnon, residence, Chicago, Ill., three children; Margaret, born April 1, 1866; Euphemia, born April 2, 1868; Catherine, born May 3, 1870; Christina, born June 15, 1871; Jeanette, born September 15, 1873.

ELZEAR FOURNIER, general merchant, resides in Piopolis. He was born in Trois Pistoles, Temiscouata county, Que., July 22, 1835. Came to Piopolis in 1881, previous to that time having been a sailor and railroad contractor. Mr. Fournier has been president of the Liberal-Conservative Association of Compton county, and is now secretary-treasurer of South Marston, which office he has held for the past eight years, also postmaster for the past two years. November 24, 1862, in Trois Pistoles, he married Mathilde Rioux. Issue, four children: Charles, born August 19, 1865, married Philomene Rioux, residence, Farnham, Que.; John, born October 14, 1870; Alice, born December 14, 1866, married Arthur Grenier, residence, Montreal, five children; Isabelle, born March 28, 1875, married Hector l'Heureux, residence, Montreal.

CORRECTIONS.

Page 23, line 40, read lonely for *lovely*.
Page 24, lines 33 and 35, read Moe for *Mol*.
Page 29, line 45, read Ditton for *Dilton*.
Page 41, line 10, read 1831 for *1848*, and 1848 for *1841*.
Page 43, line 6, read Wm. for *W. M.*
Page 44 and others, read Lime for *Line*.
Page 50, read R. Y. Cowan for R. *Ig.* Cowan.
Page 52, line 10, read Flanders for *Clanders*.
Page 53, line 34, read Milan for *Millon*.
Page 54, line 35, read hotel bar for *hotellier*.
Page 55, line 29, read Chaddock for *Claddock*.
Page 55, line 42, read A. O. Kellum for *N.* O. Kellum.
Page 56, line 27, omit the word *one*, second in line.
Page 104, line 38, read 1797 for *1897*.
Page 116, line 2, read 1810 for *1880*.
Page 139, line 36, read Que. for *Me*.

GENERAL INDEX.

INTRODUCTION 5
CHAPTER I. The Eastern Townships. Origin of name—The Townships so-called—When first settled—Their advantages 7
CHAPTER II. District of St. Francis. When created—Boundary—Dates of enquêtes, courts, etc.—Names of past and present Court officials—Its educational advantages 12
CHAPTER III.—Early history (1692-1791). Indian fight between the Iroquois and Abenaquis Indians—Roger's attack on the St. Francis village—Arnold's expedition to Quebec 15
CHAPTER IV. Buckingham county (1791-1829) . 24
CHAPTER V. Sherbrooke county (1829-1853) . 27
CHAPTER VI. Compton county (1853-1896) . . 33
CHAPTER VII. Political history (1792-1896) . . . 39
CHAPTER VIII. Municipal history. Early records - Council proceedings—Members county council. 47
CHAPTER IX. The militia. Early history—Organization—First troops—Hereford Railway riot—Present officers 54
CHAPTER X. Railways of Compton county. Grand Trunk—Canadian Pacific—Maine Central—Quebec Central 59
CHAPTER XI. Township of Eaton. Including history town of Cookshire and village of Sawyerville 65
CHAPTER XII. The late Hon. John Henry Pope. A life example for the youth of to-day—Written by Hon. C. H. Mackintosh, lieut.-governor Northwest Territories 155
CHAPTER XIII. Township of Compton. Including history of the villages of Waterville and Compton 166
CHAPTER XIV. Township of Clifton. Including history of municipalities of East Clifton, Martinville, and Ste. Edwidge............ 203
CHAPTER XV. Township of Newport . 214
CHAPTER XVI. Township of Westbury 228
CHAPTER XVII. Township of Hereford ... 235
CHAPTER XVIII. Township of Bury 242
CHAPTER XIX. Township of Lingwick 256
CHAPTER XX. Township of Hampden. Including history town of Scotstown........ 262
CHAPTER XXI. Township of Winslow. Including history municipalities of North and South Winslow 268
CHAPTER XXII. Township of Whitton. Including history village of Lake Megantic, and North and South Whitton 271
CHAPTER XXIII. Township of Marston. Including history of South Marston 279
CHAPTER XXIV. Townships of Ditton, Chesham, Emberton, Auckland and Clinton 283

ENGRAVINGS.

Agagnier, Jos., portrait	51	Carbee, A., portrait		189
Angus House	233	Carr, Guy, group		178
		Carr, Guy, residence		179
Bailey, A. A., portrait	136	Carr, Guy, monument		179
Bailey, A. H. W., portrait	112	Cass, C. N., portrait		50
Bailey, Cyrus A., residence	108	Cass, C. N., residence		210
Bailey, C. C., residence	111	Channell, L. S., portrait		139
Bailey, Mr. and Mrs. H. H., portraits	110	Clark, A. M., & Son, mill		240
Bailey, W. W., residence	109	Clark, Mr. and Mrs. Robert, portraits		246
Bean, Edwin, portrait	238	Coates, Barlow, residence		90
Bean, Henry, portrait	238	Compton county, map of		2
Bean, Leslie E., portrait	238	Compton county council, groups	50 and	51
Bennett, L. A., residence	248	Cook, George W., residence		116
Bernard, H. M., portrait	189	Cookshire Flour Mill Co., mill		125
Black, John, residence	266	Cookshire Mill Co., store		132
Bowen, A. F., group	89	Cookshire Mill Co., mill		133
Boydell, J., residence	247	Cooper, S., portrait		136
Bridgette, R., residence	92	Cooper, S., residence		119
Brouillette, C. G., residence	152	Court Cariboo, C. O. F., group		135
Brown, B. F., residence	89	Court Island Brook, I. O. F., group		219
Bryant, Jas., Angus House	233	Court Sawyerville, I. O. F., group		153
		Cowan, R. Y., portrait		50
Cairns, H., residence	146	Cromwell, A., residence		130
Cairns, H. A., portrait	51			
Cairns, H. E., group	206	Darker, R. A., portrait	131 and	136
Cairns, late Robert, portrait	145	Desruisseaux, Olivier, group		88
Cairns, Robert, residence	148	Desruisseanx, O., residence		94
Cairns, Robert, group	149	Dinsmore, S., residence		87
Campeau, R., portrait	50	Doe, L. E., residence		180

INDEX--Engravings.

	Page
Evans, J. A., portrait	151
Farnsworth, A. S., portrait	51
Farnsworth, Benj., residence	87
Francis, Wm., residence	248
French, C. W., residence	138
French, C. W. B., Scotstown Hotel	264
Frizzle, E., residence	91
French, E. R., residence	150
French, G. W. L., residence	224
French, Hiram, portrait	77
French, John, residence	221
French, J. D., residence	93
French, J. L., residence	117
French, Luther, residence	224
Friendship Lodge, A. F. & A. M., past-masters	136
Gale, A. H., residence	201
Gale, F. G., residence	190
Gale, F. G., portrait	189
Gale, George. & Sons, factory	198
Gauthier, L. J. D., residence	130
Gilbert, J. O., residence	249
Gillies, Rev. Arch., portrait	144
Graham, Edward, residence	208
Grenier, B., portrait	51
Harvey, A. W., residence	147
Harvey, Chas. H., residence	146
Hall, D. B., residence	234
Hodge, Capt. A. T., portrait	82
Hodge, H. M., residence	81
Hodge, J. A., residence	79
Hodge, S. A., farm buildings	78
Hodge, V. F., portrait	50
Hodge, V. F., residence	80
Hunt, Jas., portrait	51
Hurd, Tyler W., residence	124
Husbands, A. L., residence	129
Johnson, L. M., portrait	185
Johnston, Thomas, residence	95
Jones, Daniel, portrait	185
Kelly, Jas., residence	275
Kerr, G. H., store	276
King, R. A. D., M. D., C. M., residence	175
Laberee, Benj. R., portrait	82
Laberee, J. H., portrait	83
Laberee, Jos., residence	148
Laberee, R. E., residence	84
Learned, A., Cookshire House	113
Learned, Ebenezer, residence	217
Learned, H. B., residence	217
Learned, J. F., residence	114
Learned, W. H., portrait	136
Lefebvre, Wm., portrait	51
Léger, C. A., store	267
Lemieux, Nap., store	276
Leonard, Hugh, portrait	51
Lord Erne, L. O. L., hall	200
Macaulay, Lieut.-col., M. B., residence	263
Mackay, Wm., residence	207
Mackenzie, D. G., store	277
Macrae, T., & Co., store	119

	Page
Macrae, Mrs. Wm., residence	124
Manning, G. A., residence	92
Map of Compton county	2
Martin, C., portrait	50
Matheson, Malcolm, portrait	277
May, Jas., residence	85
McClary, Charles, M. L. A., portrait	44
McGovern, Jas., portrait	189
McGovern, Jas., residence	192
McIntosh, Jas., portrait	185
McIntosh, John, ex-M. L. A., portrait	197
McLeod, Allan, portrait	51
McLeod, J. J., store	123
McLeod, K. W., portrait	51
Melrose, Wm., portrait	239
Miller, Capt. Jas., residence	275
Morrison, J. D., portrait	50
Munn, D., residence	225
Noble, C., residence	120
Nutt, W., residence	86
Nutt, W., portrait	136
Osgood, F. E., American House	112
Parker, C. H., residence	265
Pennoyer, H. J., portrait	185
Perryboro Cheese Factory	239
Phillimore, R. H., M. D., residence	122
Phelps, W. J., residence	151
Plaisance, F. L. de P., portrait	128
Pocock, Mrs. Sarah, residence	180
Pomroy, Col. Benj., portrait	172
Pomroy, Selah J., residence	174
Pope, Lieut.-col. F. M., portrait	245
Pope, Lieut.-col. F. M., residence	245
Pope, H. H., residence	126
Pope, Hon. J. H., portrait	157
Pope, Mrs. L., sr., family group	138
Pope, L. C., portrait	136
Pope, R. H., M. P., portrait	43
Pope, R. H., M. P., residence	106
Powers, G. W., M. D., portrait	189
Prevost, P. L. N., portrait	51
Rand, W. S., residence	126
Roberge, E., portrait	50
Rogers, J. W., portrait	50
Rogers, J. W., residence	149
Rosa, P., portrait	50
Ross, A., portrait	50
Ross, Jas., ex-M. L. A., portrait	259
Royal Paper Mills Co., mills	229 and 231
Sawyer, Wm., ex-M. L. A., residence	143
Sawyer, Wm., ex-M. L. A., mills	143
Smith, E. P., residence	100
Smith, H. D., residence	176
Smith, H. D., farm buildings	177
Smith, John, residence	100
Smith, L. A., residence	210
Smith, W. C., residence	101
Stearns, G. M., portrait	50
Stokes, Thos., & Sons, factory	250
Swanson, C. O., portrait	189
Swanson, C. O., residence	191

INDEX—Engravings.

	Page		Page
Taylor, H. B., residence	150	Waterville, councillors for 1895	189
Taylor, J. L., residence	84	Waterville, church of England	194
Terrill, C. D., residence	207	Waterville, Congregational church	195
Thompson, Henry, residence	152	Waterville, Congregational parsonage	196
Tite, Ernest, residence	251	Waterville, model school	188
Todd, Alonzo, residence	90	Wiggett, Wm., portrait	185
Todd, R. L., residence	222	Wilford, F. R., residence	127
Trenholme, G. A., M. D., group	96	Wilford, J. L., portrait	136
		Wilford, R. H., store	220
Wales, B. N., M. D., residence	251	Wilford, W. C., portrait	136
Warner, E. C., residence	85	Wilkinson Bros., studio	118
Warner, Mrs. E. M., residence	91	Willard, R. T., residence	94
Warren, Chas., residence	249	Wilson, J. F., portrait	51 and 232
Waterville, first councillors	185	Wyman, L. W., portrait	185

BIOGRAPHIES.

Adams, Orien A.	211	Buchanan, Robert	226
Agagnier, Joseph	53 and 288	Butler, Edwin	211
Albro, Henry William	278		
Alden, Augustus Heber	226	Cable, Lewis	288
Alger, B. A.	104	Cairns, Herbert	145
Alger, Edwin Diah	104	Cairns, H. A.	53
Anderson, Steen	254	Cairns, Hugh E.	205
Andrews, William	238	Cairns, late Robert	145
Annable, Edward Timothy	219	Cairns, Robert	147
Austin, Hezekiah L.	223	Campean, Remi	53
		Carbee, Alphonso	193
Bailey, A. A.	95	Carr, Guy	179
Bailey, Arthur H. W.	112	Carr, W. T.	183
Bailey, Charles Cleveland	112	Cass, Carlos N.	53 and 210
Bailey, Benj. Cook	212	Caswell, Erastus	117
Bailey, Cyrus Alexander	107	Chaddock, Edgar N.	103
Bailey, George Ozro	99	Chaddock, Robert Henry, sr.	103
Bailey, Horace Henry	110	Chaddock, Robert Henry	104
Bailey, Mrs. Horace Henry	112	Chambers, H. E.	96
Bailey, William D.	180	Channell, L. S.	138
Bailey, William Ward	109	Chase, Edgar	182
Baker, Edward Standish	121	Church, A. H.	93
Ball, Joseph Rice	202	Clark, A. M.	239
Bartholomew, Jas. George	227	Clark, Herbert	139
Bartlett, Stephen	183	Clark, Robert	246
Bean, Edwin	237	Coates, Barlow	91
Beaton, Capt. Donald	289	Coates, George	255
Beaton, Norman	274	Cochrane, Hon. M. H.	45
Bennett, John	254	Colby, William Oscar	103
Bennett, Lewis A.	247	Cook, George W.	115
Bennett, Thomas	251	Cook, Capt. John H.	116
Bernard, Henry Mountague	192	Cookshire council, R. T. of T.	129
Betts, George	181	Cookshire Flour Mill Co.	125
Bibeau, Nap. Joseph	141	Cookshire Mill Co.	131
Birch, Knightly	239	Cooper, James A.	140
Black, John	266	Cooper, Samuel	119
Blossom, Joseph	181	Cork, Simon Peter	98
Bowen, A. F.	88	Court Cariboo, C. O. F.	134
Bowen, Ezekiel Elliott	219	Court Island Brook, I. O. F.	218
Bowker, Lewis L.	225	Court Sawyerville, I. O. F.	151
Bown, William	254	Cowan, Geo. Franklin	261
Boydell, Josiah	247	Cowan, Henry	260
Bridgette, Robert	92	Cowan, R. Y.	53
Brouillette, Charles George	151	Cromwell, Ayton	129
Brown, B. F.	89		
Brown, Isaac	240	Danforth, Lawson	98
Bryant, James	232	Darker, Robert A.	131

INDEX—Biographies.

Name	Page	Name	Page
Delisle, Jean-Baptiste	102	Hodge, Volney F.	52 and 79
Desrochers, Moses T. O.	141	Holbrook, Lysander W.	180
Desruisseaux, Oliver	94	Holbrook, Manlius	226
Desruisseaux, Olivier	87	Hooker, Wallace E.	252
Dinsmore, Sanford	86	Hurd, Edmund Haskell	222
Doe, Liberty Eaton	180	Hurd, George Gibeon	222
Downes, John	255	Hunt, James	52
Downes, John W.	252	Hurd, Samuel Newel	225
		Hurd, Tyler W.	123
Equity Lodge, I. O. O. F.	133	Husbands, A. I.	128
Evans, W. J. Allen	151	Hyatt, Stephen A.	183
Farnsworth, Artemus Stevens	52 and 218	Irwin, Andrew Henry	104
Farnsworth, Charles L.	182	Irwin, William John	104
Farnsworth, D. A.	87	Ives, Hon. W. B.	45
Fish, W. L.	97	Ives, Thaddeus O.	181
Flaws, George	140		
Fournier, Elzéar	289	Johnson, Lars M.	187
Francis, William	248	Johnston, Thomas	95
French, Capt. C. W. B.	264	Jones, Daniel	187
French, Clyde Wolseley	138		
French, Elon R.	149	Kelly, James	275
French, Hiram	76	Kerr, George H.	275
French, John	221	King, Reginald A. D., M. D.	174
French, John Dean	93	Kingsley, Edgar Austin	154
French, John Haines	101	Kingsley, John W.	240
French, Jonas Ludiah	117	Kirby, George E.	98
French, Lieut. G. W. L.	224		
French, Luther	223	Laberee, Benj. R.	82
French, William	103	Laberee, Henry James	154
Friendship Lodge, A. F. & A. M.	135	Laberee, John H.	83
Frizzle, Benj. William	103	Laberee, Joseph	147
Frizzle, Ezra	91	Laberee, Rufus E.	84
		Lake, Samuel	98
Gale, Adelbert H.	201	Lang, Edgar	183
Gale, Francis Gilbert	190	Langmade, E. H.	187
Gale, George, & Sons	197	Lavallier, Robert W.	227
Gallup, Ira	98	Lawton, Amos W.	240
Gates, H. F.	95	Learned, Alden	113
Gauthier, L. J. D.	130	Learned, Ebenezer	216
Gilbert, Jesse Orlin	248	Learned, Hower B.	217
Gillies, Rev. Archibald	143	Learned, John F.	114
Graham, Edward	207	Learned, J. M.	97
Gray, James A.	240	Learned, Wm. Henry	114
Grenier, J. E.	53	Lebourveau, Henry	102
Griffin, Lischer D.	212	Lefebvre, Alfred	53
Groome, George	211	Lefebvre, Archibald	140
Groome, James E.	211	Lefebvre, John	253
		Leger, C. A.	267
Haines, Benj. N.	211	Leggett, Elijah	288
Hall, Daniel B.	233	Lemay, Joseph	212
Halliday, Robert	154	Lemieux, Nap.	276
Hamilton, Matthew	94	Leonard, Edward	252
Hand, Walter	278	Leonard, Hugh	52 and 270
Harkness, James	184	Leonard, James Hugh	253
Harvey, Arthur W.	146	Lindsay, Edward N.	99
Harvey, Charles H.	145	Lord Erne Loyal Orange Lodge	199
Haseltine, Danforth	213	Lothrop, Franklin	234
Haseltine, Edson A.	101		
Heath, John	238	Macaulay, Lieut.-col. M. B.	264
Hitchcock, Nelson D.	213	Mackay, Donald	278
Hodge, Capt. A. T.	81	Mackay, John J.	261
Hodge, George A.	80	Mackay, Malcolm	274
Hodge, Horace Edward	240	Mackay, William	206
Hodge, H. M.	81	Mackenzie, Donald A.	267
Hodge, J. Alton	78	Mackenzie, D. G.	276
Hodge, S. Alonzo	77	Mackenzie, William D.	278

INDEX—Biographies.

Name	Page
Mackey, James	212
Mackie, Joseph I.	141
Macrae, Thomas	119
Macrae, William, L. D. S.	124
Manning, G. A.	92
Marcotte, Joseph de Lancy	183
Martin, Charles	53
Martin, Joshua	212
Martin, Philonas K.	99
Matheson, Donald P.	278
Matheson, Malcolm	277
May, James	84
May, S. J.	85
Mayhew, Wm. James	213
McClary, Charles, M. L. A.	44
McClary, Ozro Baxter	183
McCullough, Robert	153
McGovern, James	191
McIntosh, Alexander	201
McIntosh, James	186
McIntosh, John, ex-M. L. A.	196
McIver, Capt. Alex. Lewis	254
McIver, Capt. John F.	282
McKay, Angus Gordon	261
McKay, Ebenezer Malloy	267
McLennan, Donald B.	270
McLeod, Allan	52 and 282
McLeod, John J.	122
McLeod, Kenneth W.	52 and 274
McLeod, Lieut. Duncan L.	282
McRae, Ken. D.	261
McVetty, James	99
Melrose, William	238
Merrill, Alonzo T.	211
Merrill, George W.	177
Metcalf, David Edward	152
Metcalf, Horace	223
Miller, Capt. James	274
Mills, Samuel	233
Morrison, Donald	261
Morrison, Donald K.	282
Morrison, J. D.	53
Morrow, Henry	226
Munn, Demmon	225
Murray, Norman	260
Nason, William	97
Nish, James	239
Noble, Colin	120
Nutt, Walter	86
Orr, Elias Samuel	123
Ord, Henry	253
Ord, Samuel	253
Osgood, Frederick E.	113
Osgood, Stephen J.	139
Painter, Thomas	225
Paquet, Oliver	227
Parker, Carlos H.	265
Parker, George H.	102
Parry, Horace Weston	181
Parsons, Abner W.	213
Parsons, Josiah J.	212
Parsons, Stephen	181
Parsons, Wesley J.	182
Pennoyer, Alexander R.	140
Pennoyer, Henry J.	186
Pennoyer, James Austin	260
Pennoyer, William F.	140
Phillimore, R. H., M. D.	121
Phelps, Willis J.	150
Pierce, Densmore C.	211
Pierce, Frederick	212
Pierce, Wm. Augustus	211
Plaisance, Frank L. P. de	128
Planche, James	232
Planche, John Harold	140
Planche, John Wm.	220
Pocock, Frederick	179
Pomroy, Col. Benj.	172
Pomroy, Selah J.	173
Pope, Lt.-Col. F. M.	245
Pope, Horace Henry	126
Pope, Hon. J. H.	155
Pope, Lemuel, sr.	137
Pope, Lemuel, jr.	246
Pope, Rufus H., M. P.	43
Powers, G. W., M.D.	192
Prevost, P. L. N.	52 and 288
Rand, G. S. D.	218
Rand, Newell C.	220
Rand, Willard S.	126
Rand, Willard S.	220
Roberge, Elzear	52 and 288
Robertson, Robert	183
Robinson, John W.	141
Rogers, J. W.	53 and 148
Rosa, Pierre	53
Ross, Alexander	53 and 118
Ross, James, ex-M.L.A.	258
Rowe, Henry Spooner	232
Royal Paper Mills Co.	230
Sample, Andrew	226
Sanborn, Hon. John Sewell	41
Saultery, Daniel	181
Saunders, Amos Walter	252
Sawyer, Wm., ex-M.L.A.	142
Sharman, Ebenezer	252
Simpson, James	227
Smith, Charles	261
Smith, Donald	270
Smith, Frederick E.	212
Smith, George Edgar	97
Smith, George W.	101
Smith, Herbert Dudley	175
Smith, Isaac Coit	99
Smith, John	100
Smith, Lyman A.	209
Smith, Warren C.	100
Smith, William H.	99
Stearns, George M.	52
Stevenson, Herman A.	218
Stevenson, Walter R.	238
Stewart, Donald	282
Stokes, Thomas	249
Stone, Samuel H.	99
Sunbury, Heman E.	227
Sunbury, John G.	102
Swanson, Charles O.	191
Taylor, Charles W.	140

INDEX.—Biographies.

Name	Page
Taylor, Henry E.	149
Taylor, Lt.-Col. J. H.	127
Taylor, Joseph L.	84
Terrill, Charles D.	207
Thompson, Henry	151
Tite, Dennis	252
Tite, Ernest	251
Todd, Alonzo	90
Todd, Herbert I.	97
Todd, Ralph L.	222
Trenholme, G. A., M.D.	96
Tubbs, Wm. L.	99
Van Luven, Leonard	202
Vernon, J. Walter M.	182
Villeneuve, Louis P.	278
Waldron, Alfred J.	182
Wales, Benj. N., M.D.	250
Ward, Charles H.	253
Ward, Ephraim A.	102
Ward, William S.	97
Warner, E. C.	85
Warner, Mrs. E. M.	91
Warner, Wellington A.	97
Warren, Charles	249
Weir, James	253
Weston, Elgin R.	278
Wheeler, William W.	101
Whiteman, William J.	102
Wiggett, William	186
Wilford, Frederick R.	127
Wilford, Richard H.	220
Wilkinson, Alfred	118
Wilkinson, John	118
Willard, Lockhart R.	232
Willard, R. T.	94
Williams, Amos W.	97
Williams, William B.	153
Wilson, James F.	52 and 231
Wilson, Jas. S.	278
Woodrow, James	234
Wright, William	254
Wyman, Levi W.	185
Young, Peter	182

www.ingramcontent.com/pod-product-compliance
Lightning Source LLC
Chambersburg PA
CBHW032051230426
43672CB00009B/1559